The emergenc

CW01082038

Manchester University Press

The emergence of footballing cultures

Manchester, 1840–1919

GARY JAMES

Manchester University Press

Published by Manchester University Press
Altrincham Street, Manchester M1 7JA, UK
www.manchesteruniversitypress.co.uk

British Library Cataloguing-in-Publication Data is available

ISBN 978 1 5261 1447 1 hardback
ISBN 978 1 5261 4800 1 paperback

First published by Manchester University Press in hardback 2019

This edition published 2020

The publisher has no responsibility for the persistence or accuracy of URLs for any external or third-party internet websites referred to in this book, and does not guarantee that any content on such websites is, or will remain, accurate or appropriate.

Typeset by Servis Filmsetting Ltd, Stockport, Cheshire

To Mancunians and those with an interest in Manchester around the globe.
Also dedicated to my wife, Heidi,
who has provided constant support throughout our adult lives.

Contents

Figures and tables

Figures

Tables

Acknowledgements

A significant number of people have contributed to this publication, including library staff, archivists and curators at a variety of locations across Europe. These include the British Library, the British Newspaper Library, The National Archives, the North-West Film Archive at Manchester Metropolitan University, Manchester Central Library, the Rylands Library at Manchester University, Heritage Quay, Tameside Libraries, the People's History Museum, the British Film Institute, World of Rugby Museum, Manchester City, Manchester United, Rochdale FC, Oldham Athletic, Bury FC, Stockport County, the Manchester FA, Lancashire, FA, the Football Association, the Professional Footballers' Association and the National Football Museum. In addition, I have explored the private and personal collections of former players, managers, supporters and directors of the Manchester regions football clubs. The support of a considerable number of individuals is appreciated and these include: Eric Alexander, Len Balaam, Phil Brennan, Tony Bugby, Tony Collins, Dave Day, Alan Hardy, Brian Houghton, John Hughson, Mike Pavasovic, Dil Porter, Dave Russell, Gordon Sorfleet, Gordon Taylor, Matthew Taylor, Wray Vamplew and Mark Wylie. I am also grateful to fellow members of the North American Society for Sports History and the British Society of Sports History who offered advice and support and questioned my material and findings. I would also like to thank everyone at De Montfort University for their support and interest, especially Martin Polley, and the delegates and supporters of the International Football History conference, including Chris Bolsmann, Brian Marwood and Stefan Szymanski. The management and staff at Manchester University Press, especially Tom Dark and Rob Byron, have been supportive throughout, demonstrating great patience and helpfulness during several significant delays over the last couple of years. I would also like to thank my family for their continuing support throughout the research and writing of this book, during which their support and enthusiasm has encouraged me.

Finally, thanks to those purchasers and readers of this book who, I hope, will gain a great deal from the material produced and the research performed: without readers, our work means little. I hope you enjoy this journey through Manchester's formative footballing experiences.

Abbreviations

CCC	County Cricket Club
CE	Common Era
FA	Football Association
FC	Football Club
IFAB	International Football Association Board
L&YR	Lancashire and Yorkshire Railway
LFA	Lancashire Football Association
MFA	Manchester Football Association
MSFA	Manchester Schools Football Association

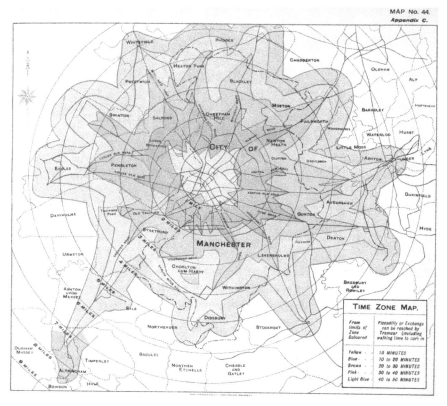

1 Time zone map of tramways in Manchester and surrounding districts, 1916,
   showing the main area of the conurbation covered by this book.

Introduction

Traditionally, association football's history has been told through a range of narratives that have focused either on the national picture or on specific clubs, with some studies focusing on how football was introduced, developed and propagated across a region.[1] There have been notable studies which have added to our knowledge but, as studies into Spanish football have identified, there are also significant gaps both in our knowledge and in the regions covered.[2] This publication fills one of those gaps while also providing an example of a framework for sporting origins research which, it is hoped, will be adopted in other regional studies to ensure consistency. The focus here is on the culture of football before 1919 as experienced in Manchester. Manchester provides an important opportunity to study football within a city-region as a result of its rapid growth, with workers arriving from across the British Isles and mainland Europe. This ensured a regular influx of cultures, ideas and skills, including sporting interests, and helped football to become woven into Manchester's cultural fabric. The role and function of cities as places of innovation, production, distribution and consumption is clear, and studying city-regions is important in understanding how cities impact on wider themes, whether political, economic or social.[3] The successes of Manchester United and Manchester City have given global exposure to the region and this interest continues to expand in the world's fastest-growing economies, with Manchester's football promoted extensively. While many regions struggle for attention, Greater Manchester is mentioned globally on a frequent basis, and at no direct cost to the city.[4] Association football has become central to Mancunian life and the sport establishes perceptions of Manchester, its image and power globally. It is for these reasons that a study of cities, and of Manchester in particular, is important, as it can add a level of detail that will provide an understanding of how the sport became significant to the local population. Research has 'returned to the centrality of cities to innovation, technology diffusion and overall economic growth', and the suggestion that the 'three C's of compact, concentrated and connected cities' are the key to 'fostering cohesion', adds to the significance of studying city-regions and their sporting developments.[5]

Prior to 1919 Manchester was the scene of a series of developments which saw football banned; a professional League established; an international law-making body created; an offshoot of rugby developed; the finest club stadium in England constructed and another major one in the planning stage; participants fighting for rights and establishing their union; scandal rocking the footballing world not once but twice; and the development of an elaborate industry of supporting businesses such as newspaper production. A regional sporting press to challenge that of London was established, which included the *Athletic News*, *Umpire* and *Sporting Chronicle*, while the *Athletic News*' circulation rose from 50,000 to 100,000 between 1891 and 1893. Its proprietor, Edward Hulton, claimed that by using the rail network he could deliver newspapers 'anywhere north of the Midlands' hours earlier than his London-based rivals, and he recognised the significance of the sport when he became a director and chairman of Manchester City Football Club.[6]

Before progressing through Manchester's footballing development, it is essential to outline what is meant by Manchester in this book. By the 1840s it had 'become commonplace to discuss Manchester as the commercial centre of a vast region of towns and villages' which had merged into one city-region, regardless of administrative areas.[7] Using Manchester's city boundaries is inappropriate, especially as this would exclude prominent Manchester sporting institutions such as Manchester Football Club, the city's traditional Rugby Union club. Similarly, using Mancunian postcodes would be inappropriate, as these are artificial boundaries established after the period under consideration and do not bear any relation to the communities and their connections, employment and social sphere. To overcome the dilemma of what constitutes Manchester this research utilises a rule devised by the Manchester Football Association at its formation in 1884, which determined that the Association represented footballing activity within eight miles of the city centre.[8] As communities are not restricted by imaginary boundary lines there is flexibility, of course, but within those eight miles are the cities of Manchester and Salford and a series of satellite towns such as Altrincham, Ashton-under-Lyne, Stockport and Hyde, which were connected to Manchester by transport links and, in some areas, an unbroken chain of housing and urbanisation. Some of these towns were boroughs within Lancashire and some were in Cheshire, while the counties of Derbyshire and Yorkshire were also a mere twelve miles from Manchester city centre, adding a level of complexity that was not apparent when walking the streets or kicking a ball around the neighbourhood.

Manchester's city boundaries were still expanding into the twentieth century, with the last major changes coming in 1931 (Wythenshawe) and 1974 (Ringway), when parts of Cheshire were added. Much of east Manchester was still, politically at least, regarded as separate independent boroughs before 1890, while areas such as Moss Side and Didsbury in the south became part of Manchester only in 1904. Even today, west of the city, Trafford, where

Manchester United has been based since 1910, is not within Manchester's city boundaries, nor was the area of Newton Heath at the time of the club's initial formation, to the east of the city. Towns like Ashton, Stalybridge, Stretford, Gorton and Broughton were still outside of the city of Manchester boundaries in 1884, but they all looked towards Manchester. These towns combined to form a whole with many relationships, both business and social, and connections which have endured and resulted in inhabitants of towns such as Hyde, a Cheshire town in the 1880s, perceiving themselves to be Mancunians.[9] These points can be illustrated, within a sporting context, by the use of the Manchester name. Lancashire County Cricket Club, when first established, utilised the Manchester name, yet it resided outside of the city, as did the rugby team Manchester Football Club. If those clubs considered themselves as Mancunian, then an analysis of Manchester must include them. The ties that bind the conurbation became strong over the nineteenth and twentieth centuries, ensuring that political boundaries never stood in the way of Manchester's footballing communities.

One of the issues in writing a historical analysis of a subject is that we know our current position, and that can cloud our judgement. Within Manchester's footballing histories some have assumed that the modern-day United, for example, is an indicator of what that club has always been, and this has shaped some analysis of the club. For example, during the 1990s, as United found domestic and European success, Harding claimed that the United of 1908 was the most glamourous and popular club of the era, but the facts show that to be an exaggeration.[10] It is vital that contemporary sources are reviewed and understood without prejudice, regardless of the modern-day stature of any organisation.

Establishing a start and an end for this project was necessary, and football has some natural breaks where it is possible to see the conclusion of a transformational period. This book varies from others in taking as its end 1919, rather than the more typical 1915, when football was suspended due to the First World War. The decision to use this later date was reached after detailed investigation into the Manchester United fixed-match scandal of 1915.[11] On the face of it, that game means little, other than that it highlights the greed of some football players; but when a full analysis is made it becomes apparent that this event was the catalyst for a new, transformational period. The scandal could be said to have been the most visible episode in a chain of activities which reached their conclusion in 1919. While 1915 may seem an appropriate point to end a book on football's development, in Manchester's case it was 1919 that brought resolution to the pre-war issues and transformed both the League structure and perceptions of players.

Another necessary decision was to concentrate on soccer, rather than the development of rugby in Manchester. There were sound reasons for both including and excluding the development of rugby, with the main argument for inclusion being that both sports – or all three, if we consider the two variants of rugby – came from the same roots. Where appropriate, this book discusses some of the key moments in rugby's development within Manchester, but the focus throughout is on association football's development. There is already some published material on the origins of rugby in the Manchester region, but an in-depth study would contribute further to our understanding of how both versions of rugby developed, divided and evolved.[12]

Manchester and football

This book considers one sporting region which, it is hoped, will provide evidence of how a footballing culture develops, focusing on the professional male version of soccer.[13] Manchester's footballing activity prior to 1919 progressed through eight developmental phases, starting with traditional mob football, which resulted in a ban in 1608.[14] This was followed by informal and sometimes illegal football being played up to the 1860s. The third phase included the formation of the city's first rugby clubs and the development of an association football club, Hulme Athenaeum. Phase four saw experienced Manchester-based footballers create a club which established regular fixtures with teams in Sheffield, Stoke and Cheshire, followed by another soccer team formed by a well-established rugby club. The fifth phase marked the birth of several clubs across the city, the creation of the Manchester Football Association in 1884 and the establishment of cup competitions. The sixth phase ended with Manchester's first national success and the development of a footballing identity, while phase seven saw football grow across Manchester and reach maturity. Phase eight brought the rights of professional footballers to the fore, while match attendance increased.

Most would accept that it would be an error to assume that association football across the world developed in the same way as it did in Manchester, and it should be argued that the development of the sport varied from region to region. What applies in Preston, within the same county but thirty-one miles distant, may not apply in Manchester, as the circumstances of the conurbation, community links and working patterns differ. Rather than publish a study as if it is the definitive word, we need to consider how to frame all these regional and national studies into one framework that accommodates all cycles and regions. This study of Manchester provides an example of how a city-region's footballing development can be researched based on an all-encompassing methodology. This could be applied to any city-region in any location around the world.

Methodology

A history of football, whether regionally based or not, appears as a progression through time, but in truth it is a collection of multiple histories and experiences which include those of people, society, sport, institutions and so on. Each goes at its own pace, but combined they progress the sport. Throughout the new millennium researchers have been questioning some of sport's long-established 'truths' and this has led to healthy debate and, occasionally, unhelpful criticism.[15] Consider the origins of football debate, which is pertinent to this study of Manchester football and has been raging since the beginning of the twenty-first century.[16] Prior to this, historians and the general public felt that they knew how association football was born, developed and propagated around the country, believing that there had been mob football, followed by a rediscovery of the game via the public schools, whose pupils subsequently travelled around the country promoting the sport to communities. This explanation was chronicled extensively; but then historians researching at a local level started to question the earlier findings. Rather than establishing a common theme, this research led to competing theories, with some historians believing in the orthodox position, keeping faith with the traditional view that the public schools were most influential in developing the game, while revisionists argued that the public schools were not as influential as traditionalists thought and that the lower-middle classes were more relevant in the game's development. Some researchers have published academic articles listing every occurrence of the word football that they have identified in online newspaper archives, in the belief that presenting a wealth of material would lead to the acceptance that their viewpoint is the right one. Of course, researchers on all sides of the debate could apply similar logic and, probably, discover material that implies that their version of the game's development is the right one.

The debate between historians has appeared personal, and occasionally the authors of academic papers have conflicted with and ridiculed others for their mistakes or for conclusions disagreed with.[17] Academic rigour is vital, of course, and we should challenge each other's findings, but when we are arguing over minor mentions of the word football and what they mean this can be damaging. It could lead to a return to the days when the social history of sport was looked upon as 'just another discrete historical ghetto where fans with typewriters practice their esoteric craft with little contact with the historical mainstream'.[18] At a time when academia should engage more than ever with the public, it is vital that we co-operate rather than criticise. We have powerful stories of social change to highlight and with which to inform the wider public, and the story of football's development can be utilised to establish good audiences for academia, proving the worth of our work and discipline.

The analytical challenge for those researching the origins of sport or the centrality of cities is the method of interrogation employed, which is why this book utilises an all-encompassing framework based on the work of French historian Fernand Braudel.[19] In 1958 he published on the *longue durée*, arguing that historians should consider three categories of social time – the *longue durée*, *moyenne durée* and *courte durée*. Although these are not direct translations, the categories can be understood as the long term, cyclical history and the history of events.[20] It should be stressed, however, that cyclical history does not mean a repetitive process; rather, it refers to the fact that activities at that level are cycles within a larger time frame. Each definition is explored further later on, but for the purpose of this section it is important to consider these periods at a high level, with the *longue durée* itself an embracing concept, providing the unifying element of human history.[21] Braudel aimed to show that the historian's focus solely on event-led history was flawed and that only by considering the long term, and indeed the cyclical or middle level, can we establish a true understanding of the manner in which a society was established. He argued that over the long term our collective behaviour is established alongside our enduring societal structures, while the cyclical level includes periods of major change. Some of these cycles may last for several decades or even centuries, while others last just a few years, but each one adds to the overall progression. Braudel believed that his views were marginalised by 'old-fashioned historians who emphasised political events and personalities' and, ironically, short-term history has again dominated since the late twentieth century.[22]

The *longue durée* encompasses the full history of a subject and it is worth considering how the framework is relevant to football and to this book.[23] This history of Manchester football up to 1919 uses a version of Braudel's framework based on three adapted levels of time.

Full-time

No game is complete until the final whistle is blown, and it is only then that points are allocated and winners can celebrate, as they have a complete understanding of the game's life. Contestants, spectators and the game's chroniclers have experienced the full length of the contest, and analysis can be made of the entire match, its twists and turns, teams' periods of dominance and possession, goals scored, corners taken, injuries suffered and so on. Each game has phases of play and specific incidents that shape its direction. It is logical to consider the entire history of Manchester football up to 1919 as one of 'full-time' where every moment leads to its development. Based on Braudel's highest level of time, the *longue durée*, this book uses the term 'full-time' for the full duration of the sport up to 1919. On its own, this macro history level is important, but it is only when it is combined with more detailed time frames at lower levels that we can start to consider the complete picture. At full-time in an ordinary game, scores are known, but only analysis within that game will show how that score was achieved, and the same is true for the full-time history of football. Full-time allows us to contextualise events and their significance over the life of the sport.

Transformational level

This level is characterised by periods where Manchester football has developed or been transformed in some way. Dramatic fluctuations or attention-grabbing events can be better interpreted within cycles, with the trend becoming apparent the more we understand the individual events and the circumstances that surround them.[24] The way these middle-level time periods are organised provides the structure and the 'coherent and fairly fixed series of relationships between realities'.[25] These cycles, with their influences, outputs and inputs, demonstrate the general tendencies of sporting activity over time without being obscured by the attention-grabbing individual events. An individual game may be significant, but in terms of history it is the general pattern demonstrated within cycles that proves whether the individual game is part of a wider development or simply a one-off based on local influences. The aim of this level is to determine links and comparisons with individual episodes acting as rungs in a ladder moving the development of football in Manchester onwards. Transformational cycles vary in length, as there are some periods where little occurred as football trundled on as an activity for centuries, with the occasional ban or high-profile contest, before the pace of its formalisation quickened. Each cycle has its own causal explanations for how it developed, and these can include environmental conditions, for example the opportunity to use a field for sport; legislation, such as the banning of football activity; employment needs, such as longer working hours in a growing industrial city; or a multitude of other factors.

Episodal level

Event-led history is perceived as important to sports enthusiasts, where we often fixate on specific games, goals, trophy successes and so on. Braudel has documented his belief that events are the dust of time, with many events selected either retrospectively, once a pattern is known, or by those who have something to gain from highlighting one event at the expense of another.[26] In the origins debate, significance has been placed on villagers signing up to a Lancastrian football club in 1871, based on a booklet written – some thirty-eight years after the event was alleged to have taken place – by someone with a vested interest.[27] It is plausible that Braudel would have taken issue with judgements made on that individual event, especially as others claim that club's formation as occurring the following year.[28] Braudel would have looked for the event's significance within the overall pattern.[29] It is important to remember that events on their own are not the 'story', and it may be that data, particularly that unearthed during an online search of a digitised newspaper, is abused if it is considered in isolation. The role of the historian as a challenging, interpretive analyst of all that is uncovered remains central, and, with so much data available, all angles must be considered. To interpret sport's development it is important to look at every angle so as to search for that event's true significance, and we must not abuse or misuse the records of the past.[30] Those focusing wholly on data gathering may be unable to appreciate this and may be prone to focus on individual episodes without performing any true critical analysis of intellectual substance.[31] Analysis is vital, and we must consider if events are relevant to a wider theme, Eureka moments or inconsequential occurrences.

It is the investigation of events that adds to transformational cycles which progress the sport, and we need to interrogate these episodes in order to understand how they develop football. Within a *longue durée* framework it is possible to record and integrate short-term human experiences of the moment with long-range developments.[32] Consider Manchester's earliest known club, Hulme Athenaeum, and the suggestion that the club is not significant, as it struggled for opponents and did not progress beyond 1863–72.[33] Looking simply at the individual events for Hulme could indeed suggest little significance; however, this is to overlook that a community was developed via that club which, over thirty years later, had one founding member who was still playing a leading role in developing and promoting regional football. His club may have died, but he remained a leading footballing figure in the region for the rest of his life. The interactions of both the individual and the team tell us a great deal about how football in Manchester developed, and it is that level of detail, analysis and interpretation which is required. Webs of social activity can be identified and their influence on the wider history of soccer can be determined. Social interactions lead to invention and innovation and help to progress the *longue durée* of a topic.[34] Considering three levels of time establishes a true understanding of the way a society was established, and this is important to the soccer origins debate, as Curry and Dunning have argued.[35]

This framework has been used to assess every event/episode identified to date in order to consider how those activities form part of transformational cycles connected with the development of soccer in Manchester. It is essential that a critical reading of the available data is reached, and this enables an increased emphasis on local experiences, rather than a decrease in detail. By researching at three levels of time it becomes clear how football in Manchester developed, and it is apparent how relationships, interdependencies, myths, successes and institutions were formed.

By the time that organised team sports were emerging in the mid-nineteenth century Manchester was a major conurbation with a strong mix of classes and backgrounds. Ultimately, the city would have a strong footballing identity and by the end of the twentieth century would be recognised around the world for that activity more than for any other. Its footballing importance in the twenty-first century, combined with its social and working life in the nineteenth century, means that Manchester provides a good case study to identify the circumstances surrounding the birth of an association football culture. This book adds to the debate concerning the game's growth and demonstrates how football became embedded within Manchester during the formative years of the professional version of the sport. It is hoped that the themes, cycles and events highlighted here provide evidence of the game's transition within a city region. It is inevitably impossible to include every moment and trend witnessed, but it is hoped that enough spread has been included to inform the debate on the origins of football and to engage the reader.

Notes

1 A. Benkwitz and G. Molnar, 'The emergence and development of association football: Influential sociocultural factors in Victorian Birmingham', *Soccer and Society*, 18:7, 1027; A. Gomez-Bantel, 'Football clubs as symbols of regional identities', *Soccer and Society*, 17:5 (2016), 692–702; H. Shobe, 'Place, identity and football: Catalonia, Catalanisme and Football Club Barcelona, 1899–1975', *National Identities*, 10:3 (2008), 329–343; G. Curry, 'Football spectatorship in mid to late Victorian Sheffield', *Soccer and Society*, 8:2–3 (2007), 185–204; M. Cooke and G. James, 'Myths, truths and pioneers: The early development of association football in the Potteries', *Soccer and Society*, 19:1 (2018), 5–23.

2 X. Torrebadella-Flix, J. Olivera-Betran and M. M. Bou, 'The origins of football in Spain: From the first press appearance to the constitution of the first clubs (1858–1903)', *The International Journal of the History of Sport*, 34:7–8 (2017), 471–497.

3 J. Clark, J. Harrison and E. Miguelez, 'Connecting cities, revitalizing regions: The centrality of cities to regional development', *Regional Studies*, 52:8 (2018), 1025–1028.

4 *Analysis of the value of football to Greater Manchester* (Sheffield: Sport Industry Research Centre & Cambridge Economics, 2013), 47.

5 Clark et al., 'Connecting cities', 1025.

6 S. Tate, 'Edward Hulton and sports journalism in late-Victorian Manchester', in D. Russell (ed.), *Sport in Manchester, Manchester Region History Review*, 20 (2009), 57.

7 T. Wyke, 'Rise and Decline of Cottonopolis', in A. Kidd and T. Wyke (eds), *Manchester: Making the modern city* (Liverpool: Liverpool University Press, 2016), 11 and 83.

8 In 1884 the Manchester FA decided to have authority for all football clubs within

an eight-mile radius of St Ann's Square in Manchester, although this was extended in later decades. 'Manchester and District Football Association', *Athletic News*, 17 September 1884, 2.

9 For example, the boxer Ricky Hatton was born in Stockport, Cheshire and has lived his entire life since boyhood in Hyde, Cheshire, but perceives himself to be a Mancunian. Similarly, the author of this book was born and raised in Hyde, but is perceived to be a Mancunian.

10 J. Harding, *For the good of the game: The official history of the Professional Footballers' Association* (London: Robson Books, 1991), 43–44. Manchester United's average attendance in 1906 was 13,950 and they were the eighth-best supported club. This grew to 20,050 in 1907–8, their first title-winning season, when they were the fourth-highest crowd-puller, but had dropped to 16,950 (ninth highest) by 1910, despite further trophy success.

11 F. Braudel, *On history* (Chicago: The University of Chicago Press, 1980).

12 G. Norris, *Rugby League in Manchester* (Stroud: Tempus Publishing, 2003).

13 Braudel, *On history*, 15.

14 'Old Manchester', *Manchester Guardian*, 6 November 1847, 4.

15 Examples include P. Swain, 'Early football and the emergence of modern soccer: A reply to Tony Collins', *The International Journal of the History of Sport*, 33:3 (2016), 257–71; G. Curry and E. Dunning, *Association football: A study in figurational sociology* (Abingdon: Routledge, 2015), 155–174; R. W. Lewis, 'Innovation not invention: A reply to Peter Swain regarding the professionalization of association football in England and its diffusion', *Sport in History*, 30:3 (2010), 475–488; A. Harvey, 'Curate's egg pursued by red herrings: A reply to Eric Dunning and Graham Curry', *The International Journal of the History of Sport*, 21:1 (2004), 127–31.

16 Articles include T. Collins, 'Early football and the emergence of modern soccer, c.1840–1880', *The International Journal of the History of Sport*, 32:9 (2015), 1127–1142; P. Swain and A. Harvey, 'On Bosworth Field or the playing fields of Eton and Rugby? Who really invented modern football?', *The International Journal of the History of Sport*, 29:10 (2012), 1425–1445; G. Kitching, '"Old" football and the "new" codes: Some thoughts on the origins of "football" debate and suggestions for further research', *The International Journal of the History of Sport*, 28:13 (2011), 1733–1749; R. Lewis, 'The genesis of professional football: Bolton–Blackburn–Darwen, the centre of innovation, 1878–85', *The International Journal of the History of Sport*, 14:1 (1997), 21–54.

17 Examples include P. Swain and R. Lewis, 'Manchester and the emergence of an association football culture: An alternative viewpoint', *The International Journal of the History of Sport*, 32:9 (2015), 1160–1180; Lewis, 'Innovation'; and Harvey, 'Curate's egg pursued'.

18 T. Mason, 'Writing the history of sport', unpublished seminar paper, Centre for the Study of Social History, University of Warwick, 10 October 1991, quoted in J. Hill, 'British sports history: A post-modern future?', *Journal of Sport History*, 23:1 (1996), 2.

19 Clark et al., 'Connecting cities', 1025; F. Braudel, 'Histoire et science sociale: La longue durée', *Annales*, 13:4 (1958), 725–753.

20 I. Wallerstein, *Unthinking social science* (Philadelphia: Temple University Press, 2001), 136.

21 D. Tomich, 'The order of historical time: The longue durée and micro-history', *The longue durée and world-systems analysis* (Binghamton: Binghamton University, 2008), 2.

22 W. H. McNeill, 'Fernand Braudel, historian', *The Journal of Modern History*, 73:1 (2001), 133; J. Guldi and D. Armitage, *The history manifesto* (Cambridge: Cambridge University Press, 2014), 63.

23 F. Braudel, 'History and the social sciences: the longue durée', in R. E. Lee (ed.) *The Longue durée and world systems analysis* (Albany: State University of New York, 2012), 241–276.

24 P. Stanfield, '"Pix biz spurts with war fever": Film and the public sphere – cycles and topicality', *Film History: An International Journal*, 25:1–2 (2013): 222.

25 Braudel, *On history*, 30–31.

26 M. Ermarth, 'On history. By Fernand Braudel', *The Business History Review*, 56:1 (1982): 90; Wallerstein, *Unthinking social science*, 137.

27 W. T. Dixon, *History of Turton Football Club and souvenir of carnival and sports* (Bolton: Unknown publisher, 1909), 5.

28 C. E. Sutcliffe and F. Hargreaves, *The history of the Lancashire Football Association* (Blackburn: Geo. Toulmin and Sons, 1928), 32.

29 Fernand Braudel, *The Mediterranean and the Mediterranean World in the Age of Philip II* (London: Harper and Row, 1972), Volume II, 901.

30 R. Aldrich, 'The three duties of the historian of education', *History of Education: Journal of the History of Education Society*, 32:2 (2010), 136.

31 G. M. Hodgson, 'Darwin, Veblen and the problem of causality in economics', *History and Philosophy of the Life Sciences*, 23 (2001), 385–423.

32 R. A. Gould, 'Ethnoarchaeology and the past: Our search for the "real thing"', *Fennoscandia archaeologica*, 6 (1989), 7.

33 Swain and Lewis, 'An alternative viewpoint'.

34 A. P. Molella, 'The longue durée of Abbott Payson Usher: A. P. Usher, A history of mechanical inventions', *Technology and Culture*, 46:4 (2005), 796.

35 G. Curry and E. Dunning, 'The power game: Continued reflections on the early development of modern football', *The International Journal of the History of Sport*, 33:3 (2016), 239–250.

1

Folk football and early activity

Manchester

To understand the role that football plays in Mancunian life it is first important to appreciate how the city and its surrounding area evolved, and how sport took a hold of the region. Today Manchester is known throughout the world primarily for its football. This recognition of Manchester's footballing culture has developed in the wake of the conurbation's footballing successes since the beginning of the television era in the 1950s, but the city's roots go back much further. As the eagle on Manchester City's former badge (1997–2016) and on United's 1958 FA Cup final shirt signifies, the city of Manchester began as a Roman outpost.[1] Mamucium, a Latinised version of a Celtic word meaning 'breast-shaped hill', was established in the year 79 CE, close to the junction of the rivers Medlock and Irwell. Over the course of the following three hundred years a small town became established around the original Roman fort. The Roman presence lasted until the year 410, following which the Saxons renamed the area Manigceastre before, in 870, the Danes seized control. During the tenth century the church of St Mary was established a mile north of the old fort, where a town had started to develop in what became the present-day cathedral area of the city. In 923 a Mercian force sent by Edward the Elder is understood to have expelled the Danes and then went on to repair and garrison Manchester's old Roman fort. The whole district between the Mersey and the Ribble was wrested from Danish Northumbria and the diocese of York and was reorganised as a royal frontier domain within the Mercian diocese of Lichfield. Salford became a great royal manor and the centre of the civil administration of the south-eastern part of the district, but Manchester remained the ecclesiastical centre.[2]

After the 1066 Norman invasion the manor of Manchester, or Mamecestre as it was recorded in the Domesday book, was valued at £1,000 and was given to Roger de Poitou, who had helped William the Conqueror to victory. Roger kept the manor of Salford for himself but divided the rest of his newly acquired lands among other Norman knights. In 1129 he passed the barony of Manchester to Albert de Gresley and it remained in his family for several generations.[3] In 1223 Manchester gained the right to hold an annual fair, which was staged at the site of the present-day St Ann's Square, and in 1301 the town became a free borough. A survey of the land by Thomas de Gresley, the lord of the manor, noted several important areas, including what became central Manchester and neighbouring hamlets, such as Ardwick: 'There is a mill at Manchester, running by the water of the Irk, value ten pounds, at which the burgesses and all the tenants of Manchester, with the hamlets, and Ardwick, Pensham, Crummeshall, Moston, Notchurst, Getheswych, and Ancotes ought to grind.'[4] At this time Gresley granted a charter establishing a system of local government for Manchester and this was to last for the following five centuries.[5] Later in the fourteenth century Manchester's link to the clothing trade became established following the arrival of a community of Flemish weavers, and the industry developed, making Manchester a leading centre for the textile industry. During the sixteenth century local prosperity ensured that the people suffered fewer hardships than were experienced in many other English towns, and the demand for Manchester cottons continued to grow, but the trade did not dominate until after the middle of the seventeenth century.[6] By the 1500s Manchester had developed, with the collegiate church of St Mary, the present-day cathedral, being established, and within a century a Free Grammar School was founded. This was followed in 1653 by Humphrey Chetham's hospital and library, often considered the first free public library in Europe, close by. However the town's growth was not accompanied by any adequate provision for sanitation and on several occasions the town suffered with the plague, notably in 1605, when about 1,000 people died from it.

By this time the Mosley family owned the rights of the lord of the manor. Under their control during the seventeenth and eighteenth centuries there was major change, with the erection of a second church, St Ann's, in 1709. Between 1719 and 1739 no fewer than 2,000 new houses were built. In July 1761 the opening of the Bridgewater canal, which reached Castlefield, close to the site of the old Roman fort, allowed coal to be easily transported into the heart of Manchester, while cotton was transferred via the Mersey and Irwell rivers, which had been made navigable from the 1720s onwards. The Bridgewater canal opened in stages, with the section between Worsley and Manchester established in 1763. Over the following decades it was extended to Runcorn and linked to other canals such as the Trent and Mersey and the Leeds and Liverpool. The eighteenth and nineteenth centuries saw Manchester continue to grow at a phenomenal rate, and prominent civic buildings were opened, including the first infirmary (1752), a subscription library (1756), the Theatre Royal (1775), the Concert Hall (1777) and the Assembly Rooms (1792), with the Portico Library following in 1805.[7] During the 1770s Manchester was said to have 'extended on every side, and such was the influx of inhabitants that though a great number of houses were built, they were occupied even before they were finished'.[8] The city had strong trading links across Europe, prompting historian John Aikin to comment in 1795 that 'the town has now in every respect assumed the style and manners of one of the commercial capitals of Europe'.[9] Manchester was one of the fastest-growing towns in late Hanoverian England and between 1775 and 1830 the population 'increased at least three fold' and its wealth was growing as a result of its development.[10]

By the first decade of the nineteenth century the population had reached approximately 80,000 and Manchester was considered 'the icon of a new age: industrial, urban, and ferociously modern'.[11] It was never solely a mill town in the way some of its neighbours were, and in 1815, when employment in the cotton industry was at its height, the estimated number of cotton workers was less than 12 per cent of the population.[12] Nevertheless, cotton was important to the city and by 1816 there were eighty-six steam-powered spinning factories in Manchester and Salford, with the number increasing over the following decades, so that by 1841 there were almost 20,000 people employed in cotton manufacture.[13] The importance of the cotton industry to Manchester's economy was illustrated in a survey of the workforce carried out in 1839 which revealed a range of supporting businesses, such as warehouses, offices and packaging companies, and their presence helped to shape Manchester's physical appearance.[14] Between 1820 and 1830 the number of warehouses in the city had grown from 126 to over 1,000 as the city moved away from production and into distribution. This growth continued, and between 1841 and 1861 the number of warehouse workers increased from 5,000 to 12,000; the number of clerks rose by 2,000 to over 5,000; and the numbers engaged in the transport industry, including porters, carters, and railway workers, quadrupled to almost 8,000.[15]

Both the cotton industry and the subsequent period of industrialisation saw a significant influx, swelling the population from 142,026 in 1831 to over 400,000 by 1871. This growth in population 'breached existing administrative boundaries', meaning that analysis of census figures can be misleading and the age-old question of what is Manchester rears its head once more.[16] Manchester was allowed its first Members of Parliament under the Great Reform Act of 1832 and it became a borough in 1838, obtaining city status in 1853. The Industrial Revolution and subsequent growth of both industry and population had prompted an expansion of the suburbs around Manchester, with the south of the city seeing middle-class developments and east Manchester becoming characterised by working-class districts.[17] The disadvantage for Manchester in being the birthplace of the Industrial Revolution was the decline in the quality of life of the city's poor. The Reverend Richard Parkinson, canon of Manchester, had recognised this as early as 1841 when he commented that 'there is no town in the world where the distance between the rich and the poor is so great or the barrier between them so difficult to cross'.[18] By 1861 approximately 20,000 were employed in engineering and this number continued to increase, making metals and engineering the leading industries in Manchester, employing twice as many as cotton, by the beginning of the twentieth century. Textile work continued in the form of clothing manufacture in workshops spread across the city and the wider area.[19]

Demonstrating how much land now formed part of Manchester's conurbation, it should be noted that while the population increased four-fold in the first half of the nineteenth century, the urban area grew seven-fold.[20] Manchester's expansion in the early nineteenth century was viewed positively by some, Joseph Aston commenting: 'during the last fifty years, perhaps no town in the United Kingdom, has made such rapid improvements as Manchester. Every year has witnessed an increase of buildings. Churches, Chapels, places of amusement and streets, have started into existence.'[21] This growth came partly because Manchester was almost entirely devoid of a resident aristocracy by 1825, allowing a 'relatively unencumbered urban development' without the constraints of a landowning class, differentiating Manchester from other cities such as Birmingham.[22] Their place was filled with 'hard-headed shopkeepers' and businessmen who, via the local council, had taken the power, prestige and patronage relinquished by the aristocracy by the middle of the nineteenth century.[23] This power was based on consensus and negotiation rather than on inheritance and social standing and the commercial class appeared to be more focused on social progress than the aristocracy were. However, this rapid urban development was highly beneficial for some Mancunians who were 'rewarded for speculative ventures, but catastrophic for others, as bad luck, poor judgement and external economic factors produced financial ruin'.[24]

In 1819 one of the most important moments in Manchester's history occurred when the reform meeting held in St Peter's fields, close to present-day St Peter's Square, ended with the infamous Peterloo Massacre. The meeting was planned to be a visible but peaceful demonstration against the Corn Laws and was also campaigning for parliamentary reform, but it became much more than that, with an estimated eighteen deaths and almost 700 people suffering serious injury. The authorities tried to put an end to the meeting shortly after it started and, as a result, conflict arose.[25]

The injustice of Peterloo was a pivotal moment in Manchester's history and gave inhabitants their strong belief in fairness, equality and justice. It is no coincidence that enterprises like the co-operative movement became established in the region and that Manchester became recognised as a radical city. Regardless of the growth of radicalism and the Mancunian spirit, Manchester developed quickly during the nineteenth century, due to its location and the opportunities that this presented. By the early nineteenth century the people of Manchester were considered to live in a city 'dominated by factories, workshops and the pursuit of money and their characters were shaped accordingly'.[26] This may seem a little harsh, but what it signified was that Mancunians were keen to work and, like the worker bee that came to symbolise the Manchester of the nineteenth century, its inhabitants were not afraid of labour.

Manchester developed a proud reputation of firsts, such as the first industrial canals and the passenger railway service. The world's first steam-powered passenger railway opened in 1830, connecting Liverpool and Manchester and aiding the import of raw materials, especially cotton. The railway's arrival precipitated and encouraged the development of 'dormitory suburbs along the major routes' around the city.[27] It also encouraged sports teams to travel along its routes and brought further industry to the region. At the opening of the railway the people of Manchester demonstrated their free spirit when they pelted the passenger carriages with stones. The reason was that they wanted the duke of Wellington, one of the chief guests, to suffer for his part in the Peterloo Massacre, as many Mancunians blamed him for the heavy-handed military presence. Within eleven years of the railway's opening Manchester was connected to Hull, Birmingham and London, as well as Liverpool, and therefore little could stop the industrialisation of the region. The transport links allowed others to settle and, while working conditions were often difficult, the region could to some extent guarantee employment, including opportunities for women. Manchester's factories provided stable and predictable incomes which in many cases were higher than those in other regions, and the textile industry allowed young women to earn an income which gave them more freedom than their mothers had experienced. By this time Manchester was about delivery, 'displaying a "can do" attitude that went beyond the usual civic pride that could be witnessed in other cities'.[28] Farming was always at the mercy of the weather, but in Manchester the new mills seemed able to guarantee employment. And Manchester's existence as an industrial city was linked to its climate.[29]

The region welcomed new residents from Ireland, particularly after the suffering they endured in the Potato Famine, and Germans, Italians and Polish, together with members of the Jewish community. Neighbouring boroughs began to grow and industrialise, with towns such as Ardwick and West Gorton beginning to appear as extended areas of the city, although they remained independent boroughs until late in the century. As the population of the city grew, new arrivals encountered many social issues, including the emergence of a gang culture, political issues, religious divides and conflicts between different nationalities. There were also the usual class divisions experienced in cities of this type, although Gatrell has observed that Manchester in the early 1800s was 'innocent … of all forms of inherited influence … it lacked even a resident gentry'.[30] Rose cited the Reverend Richard Parkinson's views of 1841, arguing that the general population in Victorian Manchester knew little about each other and that there was little or no affinity between the classes and this disparate society was developing at pace, with the city changing and evolving as industries grew and new inhabitants arrived.[31]

Early Victorian perceptions of what the city was continued into the twentieth century, with 'Cottonopolis and Coketown' established as Manchester's identity regardless of the city's actual state as the capital city of the North by the mid-nineteenth century, becoming the most significant northern city in terms of politics and economics by 1900.[32] Manchester was more than merely a northern city: it was the most important industrial centre in the world, with a rapid pace of change. The conurbation prided itself on being at the cutting edge of industry, thinking and achievement, and the saying 'What Manchester thinks today, the world does tomorrow' became known around the world.[33]

The expansion of Manchester continued, and the population rose to over 400,000 by 1871. However, conditions for new arrivals were often poor: 'the town at the lower end of Oxford-road has the appearance of one dense volume of smoke, more forbidding than the entrance to Dante's inferno'.[34] The rural landscape changed to one with factory chimneys dominating the skyline, and the city was hidden amid a cloud of smog.[35] As the city's population and its industries grew, the need for leisure activities and a release from the drudgery of everyday life increased.

Sport

For centuries, forms of football existed within Manchester. They were dominated by the availability of a ball or suitable spherical object, space to play, willing participants and those who saw the activity as a problem, such as the region's law-makers and community leaders. The activity continued, despite local bans, in the same approximate form for generation after generation, and may well have continued into the twenty-first century in that manner if a series of events had not helped to develop, shape and divert it into a form of organised sport. Recognising how this occurred is important in determining how the conurbation and society evolved, too. Football did not emerge one day as a fully thought-out, rounded sport, but developed through time in a series of transformational cycles comprising a multitude of events, some important in developing the cycle, others not so. By the mid-seventeenth century, a form of football had not only been practised in Manchester, but had also been outlawed. In 1608 Manchester followed the examples of London, Shrewsbury and Chester in banning the activity:

Whereas there hath been heretofore great disorder in our town of Manchester, and the inhabitants thereof greatly wronged ... by a company of lewd and disordered persons using that unlawful exercise of playing with the footeball in ye streets of the said town, breaking many men's glass windows at their pleasures, and other great enormities. Therefore, we of this jury do order that no manner of persons hereafter shall play or use the footeball in the said town of Manchester, sub pena to every one that shall so use the same, for every time, twelve pence.[36]

Football was considered socially unacceptable and did little to improve skills from a military perspective. Activities such as archery helped to develop military skills, but football was perceived as a futile activity, and the determination to suppress it existed for at least three centuries. There were also occasions when the term 'football' was utilised in connection with problematic or criminal activities, such as at Darnhall, near Winsford in Cheshire, when a couple of brothers called Oldington cut off the head of a monk, John Budworth, and then 'played at football with it' in 1321.[37] Edward II had already banned the game in April 1314, and thirty-five years later Edward III issued a royal proclamation deploring the fall in popularity of archery, commanding that all able-bodied men should pass their leisure time practising with bows and arrows in the event of war.[38] Similar bans were introduced in 1388 by Richard II, and in various regions such as Halifax (1450) and the City of London (1572).[39] In 1618 two 'offic'rs for ye footeball' were employed in Manchester, George Richardson and Robarte Boardman, although it is unclear exactly what their duties were and the hours they worked. It is known that they were expected to keep the streets safe from the distractions of the game. As the seventeenth century also saw the major conflict of the English Civil War it is possible that there was great concern that young men could be distracted by a futile pastime. In July 1642, the first action of the Civil War took place in the Manchester region, between Charles I's troops and the Manchester Parliamentarians, being reported in London as the beginning of a civil war.[40]

The 1608 football ban was succeeded with further bans in 1609, 1656, 1657, 1666 and 1667 as the popularity of the pastime was again considered to be problematic. However, whether football could be classed as true sporting activity is open to debate, with academics such as Graham Curry and Eric Dunning being of the opinion that these contests were more akin to 'real' fighting than to sport.[41] Richard Carew provided a contemporary view: 'I cannot well resolve, whether I should more commend this game, for the manhood and exercise, or condemn it for the boisterousness and harms which it begetteth.'[42]

The debate on whether these pastimes progressed on to the modern-day version of football has been raging for some time and seems no nearer to being resolved now than it was at the start of the twenty-first century. It seems natural that games involving some form of invasion, such as football of every variety, evolved out of the mob football activities of earlier centuries. These invasion-style combat games utilising a ball existed in many locations and were popular enough for others to feel disrupted by them, but it could be argued that similar activities involving smaller numbers may also have occurred without causing any issue for the local civic leaders. It is possible that small groups of men may have played an invasion-style game with a ball in the fields, away from any potential negative impact on wider society, on a frequent basis. Such activities may never have been mentioned in newspapers, law reports or at a civic level simply because they were not perceived as a threat to daily life or military activity. When considering the concept of the *longue durée* or full-time framework as discussed in the Introduction, it should be recognised that a sport evolves through several transformational cycles where social interactions lead to invention and help the sport to develop. As discussed above, in early seventeenth-century Manchester a combat-style form of football was so popular that it was banned, and in later years men were appointed to suppress the sport, demonstrating that, regardless of the law, people were so keen to participate in the activity that it continued. This suggests that, prior to 1608, Manchester had experienced a transformational cycle during which the pastime had evolved from a few people participating in a field to one where enough people were involved, and damage was caused to property, resulting in the town's law-makers attempting to clamp down on the activity. This is typical of many towns and cities during this period and provides a good example of how the conurbation was, on the one hand, becoming increasingly controlled, while on the other its citizens were keen to perform acts that they wanted to, not what they were told to do. This anti-establishment position was not unique to Manchester, but it did develop during the seventeenth to nineteenth centuries as the population found its voice.

It has been argued that this form of football evolved into a rule-based game over the following centuries; however, the traditional conclusion is that mob football was unruly, disorganised and dangerous and that it was ultimately prohibited in most regions. In Manchester's case it seems evident that the law-makers saw the activity as a form of football whether it was an inconvenient pastime or not, and that enough people participated for it to be known by the wider population of the town, but this does not identify whether the sport led to footballing activity in later years. Following the full-time theory through, it should be recognised that these primitive football games did involve some basic rules. We may never know exactly what they were, as no written records appear to survive; however, it should be recognised that for people to have participated in a form of mob football there had to have been some discussion on the basic idea. For example, these games tended to need two goals, – often buildings, trees, gateposts or stones at either end of the town, street or field – and opposing groups would need to capture the ball and take it to their opponents' post or goal in order to score. Teams would both defend and attack, with wild scrummages occurring often. Other rules may have set a time for the activity, or a simple 'first goal wins' style of game. Without detailed documentary evidence, it is impossible to know precisely what rules were in force in Manchester, but it is evident that people knew it was played with a football, suggesting that it was not a form of hurling, knappan or football-like game involving a bottle or other object as was the case in some other regions.[43] To suggest that these activities led to modern versions of the game requires identifying enough footballing activity in the years following each ban to determine continuity or not. In Manchester, football survived into the eighteenth century, albeit in a primitive form, despite bans appearing over a sixty-year period.

Approximately a century after Manchester's last reported ban a football match is alleged to have been played that was regarded by later chroniclers as the earliest recorded football match in Lancashire. The *Athletic News* included brief details of a game from 11 February 1776 that occurred in Manchester: 'when Assheton Lever, Esq., gave a dinner to eighty of the Manchester Royal volunteers, at Middleton; at same time a great football match'.[44] Although this does not provide enough information to identify how the game was organised, the number of participants, the rules and so on, it does provide an indication that the game was known and played in Manchester a century after it had been banned in the region. This fits with Cunningham's assertion that 'there is no "vacuum" in the history of popular recreations, where many "traditional" sports and customs survived much longer than one might suppose, sometimes after their demise had been celebrated.'[45] Much of the football activity would have been inconsequential, with little impact on anyone but the participants, but some would have been part of a transformational cycle during which knowledge of the game, or at least the basic idea of carrying, throwing and kicking a ball towards a target or goal would have become embedded within communities. The suppression of football in Manchester, no matter how rudimentary it was, demonstrates that the activity lasted throughout the seventeenth century, despite the bans, and the appointment of officers to quell the game indicates that this was not merely an annual event but something that was perceived as a more frequent pastime. The idea that the game was completely killed off during this period seems weak and hard to accept, but it is also clear that this was not a well-controlled sporting spectacle that could be directly compared to today's games. Rather, the period prior to 1840 is one of several transformational cycles where football activity first grew, then was legislated against and then somehow survived in a more subdued form than had gone before.

While football had been banned often, other activities were considered legitimate pastimes, such as cock-fighting, which staged inter-county tournaments, and Simon Inglis has documented the details of a Lancashire–Cheshire match at the Royal Exchange in Manchester in 1786.[46] There were cockpits established across the region, including at Market Street (1650), Cross Street (1730), the top of Deansgate (1760), Kersal Moor (also the site of Manchester's racecourse from 1681 to 1847) and Chorlton. The 'sport' was eventually banned in 1849, although reports of its activity continued into modern times. Another activity popular in Manchester was bear-baiting, and illustrations survive of bear-baiting being performed during the eighteenth century at a site close to the modern-day National Football Museum, while the baiting of bulls and bears and other blood sports such as hunting were common across the region.[47]

Sports participation continued; however, increased industrial activity and availability of land limited opportunities by 1839, prompting the Chartist Peter M'Douall to lecture on his observations of Manchester and its neighbouring town of Hyde: 'The young people have no football matches, there is no time for field rambling – nay, that is now counted to be a sin.'[48] Specifically, M'Douall was challenging a Hyde factory owner over the conditions for his workforce, and while M'Douall's own political views will have influenced the statement, the fact that football was mentioned at all demonstrates that the game was known and, if conditions permitted, was being played. Similarly, an article on the Cotton Famine in 1863 looked back on the industry some sixty years earlier and talked of workers participating in 'foot racing or football' on Saint Monday.[49] When football was being played it was often reported as a nuisance or due to criminal activity, such as when, a year before M'Douall's speech, a thirteen-year-old boy in Rochdale had his leg amputated after he had broken it in three places while playing at football.[50]

The demand for leisure activities increased with the city's growth. Despite being officially banned, bear-baiting and cock-fighting continued, while horse racing, pugilism, pedestrianism and other sports suitable for gambling increased, generating a thriving sporting culture across the city and laying the foundations for the subsequent enthusiasm for organised team games, including football.[51] One team sport that developed locally around this time was cricket, which gained some prominence with the establishment of Aurora Cricket Club and clubs at Broughton and Denton prior to 1824.[52] The first recorded Manchester game had occurred around 1823 at the Adelphi ground in Salford and the Aurora club developed, becoming Manchester Cricket Club based at Old Trafford from 1857, before reforming as Lancashire County Cricket Club in 1864. By that time the club had engaged professional players.[53] The formalising of cricketing activity may have aided those with a footballing interest, for, despite several centuries of football-like events, the state of football in the Manchester region by the end of the 1830s was one where ball-playing was known but there was not a widespread community of football participants. Reports of casual footballing activity continued to appear in the press, often with negative connotations, but evidence of organised clubs or games is limited, although it has been recorded that soldiers billeted at the Bull's Head Inn at Reddish in 1835 'amused themselves by sliding and kicking the football'.[54] This is interesting, because it is known that the Bull's Head staged sporting events over the decades, such as rabbit coursing, pigeon shooting and quoits, and between 1885 and 1887 was the home venue of Manchester City's predecessor, Gorton Association Football Club.[55] By that time, football was a recognisable activity across Manchester.

Notes

1 People often assume that the emblem on Manchester United's 1958 shirt is a phoenix; however, it is the same style of eagle as that utilised by Manchester City in later decades and came from an emblem which the city of Manchester established in 1957 for the use of sports and leisure organisations instead of the Manchester coat of arms.

2 H. M. McKechnie, *Manchester in 1915; being the handbook for the eighty-fifth meeting of the British Association for the Advancement of Science held in Manchester, Sept. seven to ten, 1915, with an appendix containing the programme of the meeting* (Manchester: Manchester University Press, 1915), 2.

3 There are several competing versions of the family name, including De Grelley and de Gresle.

4 John Heywood, *The Manchester Historical Recorder* (Manchester: John Heywood, 1875), 11.

5 A. Kidd and T. Wyke, 'Introduction', in A. Kidd and T. Wyke (eds), *Manchester: Making the modern city* (Liverpool: Liverpool University Press, 2016), 22.

6 McKechnie, *Manchester in 1915*, 4–5.

7 H. Barker, '"Smoke cities": Northern industrial towns in late Georgian England', *Urban History*, 31:2 (2004), 178–9.

8 T. Henry, cited in W. H. Chaloner, 'Manchester in the latter half of the eighteenth century', *Bulletin of the John Rylands Library*, 42:1 (1959), 41.

9 J. Aikin, *A Description of the country from thirty to forty miles round Manchester* (London, 1795), 184.

10 Barker, 'Smoke cities', 177.

11 H. Barker, 'Soul, purse and family: Middling and lower-class masculinity in eighteenth-century Manchester', *Social History*, 33:1 (February 2008), 15; T. Hunt, 'Manufacturing culture: The 1857 art treasures exhibition in historical context', in T. Hunt and V. Whitfield (eds), *Art treasures in Manchester: 150 years on* (London: Philips Wilson Publishers, 2007), 41.

12 Barker, 'Smoke cities', 180.

13 A. Kidd, *Manchester* (Keele: Ryburn Publishing, 1993), 24–25.

14 H. Clay and K. Brady (eds), *Manchester at work: A survey* (Manchester, 1929), 29.

15 M. Hewitt, *The emergence of stability in the industrial city: Manchester 1832–67* (Cambridge: Cambridge University Press 1996), 30.

16 Hewitt, *The emergence*, 21; T. Wyke, 'Rise and decline of Cottonopolis', in A. Kidd and T. Wyke (eds), *Manchester: Making the modern city* (Liverpool: Liverpool University Press, 2016), 86.

17 C. O'Reilly, 'Re-ordering the landscape', *Urban History Review*, 40:1 (2011), 31.

18 Ibid., 34; Revd R. Parkinson, *On the present condition of the labouring poor in Manchester* (1841), reprinted in *Focal aspects of the Industrial Revolution 1825–1842* (Shannon: Irish University Press, 1971), 114.

19 D. McHugh, 'A "mass" party frustrated? The development of the Labour Party in Manchester, 1918–31' (PhD dissertation, University of Salford, 2001), 29.

20 F. MacKillop, 'Climatic city: Two centuries of urban planning and climate science in Manchester (UK) and its region', *Cities*, 29 (2012), 245.

21 J. Aston, *Picture of Manchester* (Manchester, 1816), 19.

22 C. O'Reilly, 'From "the people" to "the citizen": The emergence of the Edwardian municipal park in Manchester, 1902–1912', *Urban History*, 40:1 (2013), 137.

23 Kidd, *Manchester*, 59–60; O'Reilly, 'Re-ordering the landscape', 32.

24 O'Reilly, 'Re-ordering the landscape', 32; Barker, 'Soul, purse and family', 15.

25 J. Tyas, 'Editorial', *The Times*, 19 August 1819, 1.

26 Barker, 'Smoke cities', 188.

27 O'Reilly, 'Re-ordering the landscape', 31.

28 J. K. Walton, 'The origins of working class spectator sport: Lancashire, England 1870–1914', *Historia y Comunicacion Social*, 17 (2012), 127; MacKillop, 'Climatic city', 247.

29 MacKillop, 'Climatic city', 245.

30 V. A. C. Gatrell, 'Incorporation and the pursuit of liberal hegemony in Manchester 1790–1839', in D. Fraser (ed.), *Patricians, power and politics in nineteenth century towns* (Leicester: Leicester University Press, 1982).

31 M. E. Rose, 'Culture, philanthropy and the Manchester middle classes', in A. J. Kidd and K. W. Roberts (eds), *City, class and culture* (Manchester: Manchester University Press, 1985), 105.

32 D. Russell, *Looking north: Northern England and the national imagination* (Manchester: Manchester University Press, 2004), 21.

33 It has often been reported that Robert Peel is alleged to have been the first to use the phrase during the 1840s, for example 'The secret negotiations to return Manchester to greatness', *Guardian*, 12 February 2015, https://www.theguardian.com/uk-news/2015/feb/12/secret-negotiations-restore-manchester-greatness.

34 Hewitt, *The emergence*, 21; J. K. Walton, *Lancashire: A social history 1558–1939* (Manchester: Manchester University Press, 1987); *The Reasoner, Mr Holyoake's provincial records*, 5:10 (1884), 92.

35 A. de Tocqueville, *Journeys to England and Ireland* (New Jersey: Transaction Publishers, 2003), 106.

36 John Heywood, *The Court Leet Records of the Manor of Manchester* (Manchester: Henry Blacklock, 1888), entry dated 12 October 1608.

37 A commission was set up on 20 October 1321 to investigate the attack. C. G. Smith, *Rural rambles in Cheshire; or walks, rides and drives for Manchester and other people* (Manchester: John Heywood, 1862), 71–72.

38 https://www.historychannel.com.au/articles/edward-iii-bans-football-promotes-archery/ (accessed 8 January 2019).

39 Curry and Dunning, *Association football*, 15.

40 J. Barratt, *The siege of Manchester 1642* (Stuart Press, 1993).

41 Curry and Dunning, *Association football*, 16–17.

42 R. Carew, *The survey of Cornwall* (London: John Jaggard, 1602), 199 [Reprinted in 1811 by C. Bensley, London].

43 Knappan utilised a wooden disc, while hurling-like games were popular in Cornwall.

In Leicestershire, a version of football using a wooden keg known as the 'bottle' still exists as an Easter Monday tradition.

44 'En passant', *Athletic News*, 17 March 1877, 1.

45 H. Cunningham, *Leisure in the Industrial Revolution* (London: Croom Helm, 1980), 22.

46 S. Inglis, *Played in Manchester: the architectural heritage of a city at play* (London: English Heritage, 2004), 15–18.

47 Ibid.

48 'The cotton famine', *Manchester Guardian*, 23 January 1863, 3; 'British Association and the factory system', *The Times*, 2 February 1839, 6.

49 'The cotton famine', *Manchester Guardian*, 23 January 1863, 3.

50 'Local & provincial Intelligence', *Manchester Guardian*, 6 January 1838, 3.

51 Cunningham, *Leisure*, 22.

52 B. Bearshaw, *From the Stretford End: Official history of the Lancashire County Cricket Club* (London: Partridge Press), 1–3.

53 Old Trafford cricket ground is outside the city boundary. By the mid-nineteenth century 'Manchester' was viewed as a conurbation that stretched beyond the city boundary; P. Swain, 'Cultural continuity and football in nineteenth-century Lancashire', *Sport in History*, 28:4 (2008), 573.

54 'Local and provincial Intelligence', *Manchester Guardian*, 6 January 1838, 3; 'Reddish', *Ashton Reporter*, 21 January 1871, 7.

55 Manchester City went through several incarnations before becoming established as City in 1894. These were: pre-1883 St Mark's (West Gorton); 1883–84 West Gorton; 1884 Gorton AFC; and 1887 Ardwick AFC.

2

Origins

Recreational activities

As noted in the previous chapter, the *Athletic News* claimed that the earliest recorded football match played in Manchester was on 11 February 1776, indicating that football had survived the 1608 ban and supporting Cunningham's assertion that traditional sports and customs survived for longer than had previously been supposed.[1] Football references appear frequently between 1840 and 1860 within the Manchester region, suggesting that there were enough people playing some form of football to enable the game to be passed on through successive generations. Reports often relate to individuals being injured while playing football, and matches being played during excursions and festivities.[2] Reports include the term 'football' used to help visualise the size of an object, and a football-shaped flower arrangement; and while Kitching notes that it is important not to overstate the significance of phrases such as 'playing at football' these reports do emphasise the fact that 'football' of some description was known, reported and played in Manchester.[3] The term 'football' was embedded into the local vernacular, possibly from the time of the seventeenth-century bans. In fact, the 1840s saw the *Manchester Guardian* remind its readers of the 1608 ban in a an article about old Manchester. Its inclusion, alongside obsolete laws about sanitary conditions and taxes raised to combat the plague, indicates that the football ban was already viewed with a certain amount of incredulity.[4]

While football may have been known, or at least residents had knowledge of what a football was, Manchester did not have many facilities for recreation and the 1833 Select Committee on Public Walks singled out the conurbation, saying it needed leisure facilities, including walkways lined with plants to facilitate strolling. It was recognised that the local population had issues with drinking and gambling, and it was felt that by the establishment of strolling space residents would be encouraged to behave in an orderly manner. It was hoped that the values of a new, urban middle class which considered itself both culturally and morally superior would prevail. Victorian parks were approved of by both the police and the church as a source of good moral influence and social control, having a civilising effect on visitors.[5] Whether this inspired the local authorities is not evident, but from the 1840s Manchester became one of the most active local authorities in providing municipal parks and in 1893 the council established an Open Spaces Committee, followed a year later by a Special Committee to consider the need for public leisure spaces.[6]

In parks, physical activity was sometimes frowned upon; but in Manchester in 1844 plans for a new public park in Harpurhey included facilities for team sports including grounds for cricket, knur and spell, foot-races and football.[7] The park became known as Queens Park and, along with Philips Park and Peel Park (Salford), was opened in 1846. That same year newspapers carried reports of football-related thefts in the area, indicating that the game was an activity which the poorer members of society wished to participate in and that footballs of some description were available to buy in the city.[8] In 1866, a time when football is thought to have been more prevalent, an article concerning Peel Park suggested that football had been a regular activity for decades: 'whilst "children of a larger growth", may be seen in groups competing in the active exercise of foot-ball, the elders, whose prime has long since passed, meantime looking on approvingly at games that remind them of their own youthful career'.[9] Facilities at the region's parks improved over time, with some providing 'segregated sports facilities, reflecting the differing appeal of certain sports to men and women'.[10] By the early twentieth century these included football and cricket for men and cycling and tennis for women, while Philips Park, close to the present-day Etihad Stadium and widely acknowledged as the world's first municipal park, had the first free municipal open-air swimming baths in the country by 1891. The site guaranteed an area of green among a rapidly developing industrial landscape and this area became crucial to the development of sport in the city. Ultimately, the park became recognised for a variety of leisure activities and United's second ground (Bank Street) and City's modern-day venue (Etihad Stadium) would later become its neighbours. After the development of Philips Park, the sporting life of Manchester grew rapidly.

The formalised development of sports such as association football, rugby and lacrosse did not occur until the second half of the nineteenth century, when Acts of Parliament such as the 1847 and 1850 Factory Acts, which reduced the working week, combined with the increase in public park provision.[11] It is accepted that Manchester was the first major British city in which all trades obtained a 2pm finish on Saturdays, although Hewitt believes that the 1847 Ten Hours Act was 'reneged on as soon as the act was passed', and claims that the 1850 Act was for 'cotton operatives as much a symbol of middle-class perfidy as it was of a new humanitarian state'.[12] Nevertheless, these provided some with the opportunity for leisure and the opportunity for football to be played.[13] *Bell's Life in London and Sporting Chronicle* reported that Manchester was a 'notoriously sporting city', and evidence exists of football activity in the Manchester region during the 1830s to 1860s.[14] There were regular football sessions at the Manchester Athenaeum between 1847 and 1850, following the establishment of Manchester Athenaeum's gymnastic club in 1839 with a 'cricket, quoiting and archery' ground developed in Great Clowes Street, Lower Broughton, in 1845.[15] By 1847 football and other field sports were played there on Saturdays, but no record has been identified of games played with other clubs, suggesting that all footballing activity consisted of internal games between members.[16] The form of football played has not been identified either, and it is therefore unwise to consider this as a fully functioning football club of any specific code. Instead, football was a relatively informal activity played on a weekly basis over a three-year period, 1847–50. Nevertheless, it adds to the general belief that football of some description was known and understood within the Manchester region at this time.

There is evidence to show that both street football and a form of organised game were known to some extent locally, and before the influence from those well versed in the game at public schools.[17] It has already been identified that Manchester was without a resident aristocracy, and while the wealthier members of society may well have sent their children to public schools there is little obvious connection to Manchester's footballing development at this time. As well as football, there were cricket and quoiting at the Manchester Athenaeum and at other locations in the region, and there was a thriving pedestrianism community, this latter being described as 'the recreation of the hard-working artisans of the cotton metropolis'.[18] This could attract crowds of 10,000 to the same districts of Manchester as soccer would later on, namely but not exclusively Hulme, Bradford, Newton Heath and eastwards to areas now within the Tameside Metropolitan Borough. Pedestrianism was promoted by entrepreneurial publicans, who enclosed their grounds to collect entrance fees and control drink and food sales, and by the gambling trade. Many pedestrian events moved into 'purpose-built stadiums where publicans had control over the sport and athletes could be monitored'.[19] Other entertainments were offered at these grounds, such as wrestling, rabbit coursing, pigeon shooting, quoits and pony trotting, which guaranteed attendance from the working-class community. Colours were often worn, helping to establish a spectacle that, to the twenty-first century football aficionado, would seem reminiscent of their sport.

Manchester became recognised as the leading centre for competition at mile distances, while the Newton Heath district is known to have housed popular venues and meets which were reported on extensively.[20] Betting was a prominent feature of pedestrian meets, while events at the City Grounds on Ashton New Road often attracted crowds of over a thousand.[21] The role of pedestrianism has to be considered when analysing how soccer developed in Manchester, as this thriving professional business provided a model of how a sport could be promoted, developed and participated in by the working classes. Several of the region's pedestrians would later take their techniques into football, with Fred

Bacon and Jimmy Broad contributing to the first major trophy successes of United and City, respectively, where they became renowned trainers.[22]

Pedestrianism had formal organisation and popularity and was profitable, attracting a predominantly working-class crowd, making it difficult for other working-class sports to break through. This began to change during the 1860s as reformists objected to the rowdy behaviour often associated with pedestrian meets, while allegations of fixed races further tainted the sport. As early as 1870 some local newspapers were proclaiming that pedestrianism had lost its attraction, although Manchester did remain the home of the mile until the 1880s, but by that time soccer was making progress.[23] Often the growth and success of one city, organisation or sport means the eclipse of another, and this appears to be what happened with soccer replacing pedestrianism as the Mancunian working-class spectator sport of choice between 1875 and 1885. Pedestrian events tended to attract the working class and, typically, there was minimal interaction between the classes.[24] However, the nature of Manchester's growth created a multi-layered society with many factors impacting on the relationships between classes. The city's social structure was complex, and Hewitt warns against interpreting 'its social and political history simply in terms of broad socio-economic classifications: even within layers, class positions based on economic position were far from clear cut'.[25] Like pedestrianism, the opportunity for gambling ensured that horse racing, which appealed to a higher class of spectator, could draw large crowds to Castle Irwell and New Barns.[26]

While pedestrianism flourished, Manchester's working class had little need for any other sporting spectacle, and the attractions of football were not apparent to the wider population prior to the 1870s, possibly later. However, there was footballing activity in Manchester during the 1840s to 1860s. In terms of organised football, Goulstone has identified games or challenges taking place at Openshaw, Pendlebury and Rochdale, in the Manchester area, between 1841 and 1844.[27] There was also a game organised at Ashton-under-Lyne between teams consisting of eight players each in 1846. An actual report of the match has not been discovered; however, there was a pre-game notice published in *Bell's Life in London and Sporting Chronicle*:

> FOOT BALL – A foot ball match will take place at Charlestown, near Ashton-under-Lyne, on Friday, the 25th inst. Between eight of the Charlestown heroes, with John Greenwood from the United States of America, as backgroundsman, and eight of the Boston players, with Samuel o'the Georges and Long Tom Kershaw of Waterhouses, Lancashire as backgroundsmen. The ball to be turned down at eleven o'clock, a.m. and taken up precisely at three o'clock, p.m.; the party getting the most goals to be declared the winners. The parties will then adjourn to the Old Ship public-house, Charlestown, to partake of a substantial dinner. The losing parties pay the piper. Mr Samuel Leech of Boston House has consented to officiate as umpire.[28]

It is possible that this match had been organised more as a form of entertainment, in a similar way to some pedestrian challenges, than as a competitive fixture. The report gives details of the duration of the game and other organisational information such as refereeing and positional play. Research into the names and locations has revealed some detail, including the knowledge that the area where the game occurred was at the northern edge of Ashton-under-Lyne, Waterhouses being situated north-west of the town. The area has been transformed somewhat since 1846, with Charlestown becoming subsumed into the modern Ashton townscape while Waterhouses forms part of the Daisy Nook country park, close to the former Hollinwood Canal. Long Tom Kershaw was the son of the landlord of the Old Ship Inn.[29] It is worth noting at this point that Charlestown was part of the railway line that connected Manchester with Sheffield and that Charlestown railway station, present-day Ashton-under-Lyne station, had opened earlier that year. This may well have been significant, in that it meant that travel and communication between the two cities allowed ideas, goods and newspapers to travel with ease across the Pennines.

It has been argued that the Pennines created a barrier preventing a cross-fertilisation of sporting cultures from Yorkshire to Lancashire and vice versa, but this was not the case. Pendleton talks of a trans-Pennine pedestrianism network, and challenges those who stress the barriers and 'overlook the parallel developments' occurring on both sides of the hills, while Huggins, Tolson and Vamplew have documented the significance of railways to the growth of sport.[30] It is possible that this route allowed the earliest forms of association football to flow westwards, and there are clues in local newspapers. For example, the *Manchester Courier* published a letter complaining about boys connected with the Roman Catholic Chapel in Glossop – the first significant town on the Manchester side of the Pennines – playing football. The letter writer claimed that the football was 'not an unusual custom, and therefore must have the sanction of the priest'.[31] Although Glossop is fourteen miles from Manchester's St Ann's Square and therefore falls outside the Manchester region under consideration here by six miles, it is fair to say that this report in a Manchester newspaper adds to the argument that Mancunians knew about football during this period, and that the direct railway link with both Sheffield and Manchester is of significance. Broadbottom, a village slightly closer to Manchester on the same line, had an association football team playing home games against Manchester sides in 1880.[32] At Mottram, the neighbouring village to Broadbottom, the boys of the local school defeated Glossop Grammar School 2–0 in a game in March 1870; the report of the game implies that participants had an understanding of the rules and ends with a suggestion that football knowledge was growing: 'As the district was once famous for this bracing sport, we are glad to see the rising generation have inherited the old spirit.'[33] Today, Mottram forms part of Tameside, as does Broadbottom, a metropolitan borough stretching from

Denton, Manchester to the edge of the Pennines. Many of the city's association football clubs created in the late 1870s/early 1880s were situated along this route and within the Tameside area.[34] Bale has speculated that football spread outwards from neighbouring areas and that the direct line from Manchester to Sheffield established a conduit for its possible diffusion between these two major industrial cities.[35]

The announcement of the Charlestown game may be the most detailed mention of football within the Manchester area during this period. However, it should be stressed that while individual match announcements, reports and other documents are important, in isolation they add little. We know what is written and we can assume that because it has been recorded it was perceived as being of some significance, but we should not read too much into these individual items until we can identify a trend. Investigations into the game are inconclusive, and it may or may not have occurred, leading to differing interpretations by modern-day historians, some suggesting that the advertisement means little, while others use it as evidence that a footballing culture was in existence.[36] On its own, the advertisement can indeed be interpreted either way, but what it actually demonstrates is that our knowledge of the circumstances peculiar to that event is not yet sufficient to provide a definitive answer. Investigation into the environment around Ashton-under-Lyne at that time, along with analysis of the named individuals, groups and locations, has yet to prove conclusively whether the pattern within that locality adds to evidence that can then be interpreted as part of a transformational period of activity. The Ashton area had multiple teams in existence by the end of the 1870s, with other footballing activity reported between 1846 and the 1870s, in addition to school trips and the like, indicating that the 1846 advertised game may well have been a key episode in the development of the sport locally.[37] However, at present we cannot say whether it is an outlier, statistical evidence of activity that was not part of an overall pattern, or whether it represents a much stronger community of activity than was previously understood. If it could be proved that subsequent footballing activity in the Ashton area involved some of the people mentioned in the advertisement, then that would be significant. Utilising the full-time framework allows historians to question what an event or period meant to long-term development; it encourages historians to ask whether it was 'epiphenomenal? Was it momentary? Was it a kind of flash? Or did it really make a difference?'[38] It enables us to take a more considered approach when analysing an event's significance. An event on its own means little unless it has context and we can determine its impact.[39] One event, such as the formation of a football club, is significant to the overall story only if that club's establishment tells us something that influences our understanding at the transformational level and, indeed, within the full-time history. It is important to recognise that newspaper mentions of the word football, for example, were published for a reason, and not necessarily for the same reason that modern historians are interested in the report. It is important to separate ourselves from the uncritical use of data and theories that were collected by another generation for other purposes.[40]

Footballing mentions

Other forms of footballing activity were being reported around this time in the region, usually connected with festivals, excursions or nuisance activity. For example, in May 1850 the United Presbyterian Church Sunday School on Lower King Street travelled to Bramall Hall for an outing. Servants from the hall were sent to help the children play games in the gardens. According to one report, 'swings were erected – wickets were pitched for cricket – runs for football were marked out – and other spaces set aside for the gentler exercise of battledore and shuttlecock'.[41]

In June 1848, the Manchester *Guardian* referred to a game played in Bowdon between school children on a specially prepared field: 'The boys were then conducted to a meadow prepared for the occasion, where they amused themselves for a short time with a game at football.'[42] Approximately 140 boys attended the day's activities, suggesting that this game may have been similar to the traditional form of mob football rather than the 1846 Ashton match. The following Easter the *Manchester Guardian* mentioned the popularity of football:

> It was formerly a custom in some churches, for even bishops and archbishops themselves to play with the inferior clergy at handball, and on Easter Sunday; and this game, or football, is still the favourite sport of Easter … In some counties, the custom is still to play at handball for a tansy cake. The winning at this game depends chiefly on swiftness of foot.[43]

The mob aspect of football was referred to in a letter to the *Manchester Guardian* about a cricket match between a team of eleven representing 'All England' and another of twenty-two representing Manchester. Focusing on the number of players, the author explained: 'It is cumbrous to manage, difficult to handle, and looks as much like football as cricket.' It is worth noting that the author also raised the question of whether people in Manchester had enough opportunity to focus on sport:

> Take the ordinary occupation of a Manchester merchant or tradesman. Do you expect him to attend his warehouse, day by day, snatching a few hours once or twice in the week to hurry down to Old Trafford, take a few balls and return; do you expect him with this driblet of practice to compete with the champions of England … with men who have no other occupation, and who to extraordinary natural endowments, unite constant practice, and habitual training?[44]

There were frequent mentions of football in the columns of Manchester's newspapers, such as in 1849 in an article on a British Arctic expedition in which games of football were played between the crews of two ships.[45] There were also references to football in day-to-day activity, such as the public display of Thomas Webster's painting *The Football Game* at Mr Grundy's, Exchange Street, Manchester.[46] It should be noted that exhibitions like Grundy's pre-dated Manchester's public art gallery by three decades, although Salford did have a picture gallery at Peel Park from 1850.[47] In 1854 Grundy's exhibited Webster again, prompting the *Manchester Guardian* to comment on its vitality: 'full of life and animation, in strong contrast to the staid and thoughtful char-acter of these busts; a school let loose, and alive with boyish excitement in the games of pegtop and football'.[48]

An article on the Lloyd Street United Presbyterian Church in 1852 talked of a Whitsuntide excursion to Bromley Cross, where 'the usual exercises of football, cricket, running, and singing, were prosecuted with great avidity and enjoyment'.[49] Bromley Cross was a village in the township of Bradshaw, about thirteen miles north-west of Manchester city centre, and this trip saw the elder members of the party walk two miles to the church at Chapeltown, next to which Turton Football Club would play some twenty years later. It must be noted that this football activity, like others from the 1840s–1850s, was reported in connection with holiday excursions and activities. Another such outing in 1852 concerned workers from the John Whittaker and Sons mill in Hurst, Ashton-under-Lyne, their friends, a local band and children from the Higher Hurst New Connexion Methodist Sunday School. John Whittaker paid for the trip, which took 1,800 people to Lincoln. During the excursion the children 'commenced their sports. Rings, football, and other favourite out-door games diverted them for several hours.'[50] Hurst is today the home of Ashton United Football Club and was an early developer of the game within the region. Other trips included 'tens of thousands' of Sunday school attend-ees travelling at Whitsuntide up to thirty miles from central Manchester to participate in 'football and cricket' and other activities.[51] Similarly, in 1854 the Peter Street Methodist New Connexion Sunday School enjoyed 'the sports of cricket, skipping rope, football' on a trip to Ramsbottom.[52] Whitsuntide provided an opportunity to travel, and outings like these demonstrate that the participants were taking footballs and other equipment for the purpose of participation in a large group activity. These are different to kickabouts on an ad hoc basis in the streets and fields of Manchester, and form part of a cultural activity developed over the decades. The examples provided here are not comprehensive, but they demonstrate that there were enough individual events or episodes to ensure that football of some description was known. They form part of a transformational cycle whereby football became estab-lished as one of society's cultural pastimes; however, it must be conceded that the activity was not recognised as a sport in the manner that it would be a decade or so later. It was an activity, nothing more, that occupied some people on days of celebration or in community festivals and on an ad hoc basis.

It was not simply schools or excursionists who played these types of football games. In the West Gorton area of Manchester, later famed as the birthplace of Manchester City Football Club, workers celebrated the opening of the new Beyer Peacock engineering works with an organised game. The founder of the works, Richard Peacock, became an early member of and subscriber to Gorton Association Football Club, a predecessor of City. The number of players in the Beyer Peacock game was unlimited and the report fails to provide details of participants: 'As the amusements were in connection with a private firm, we abstain from publishing the names of the competitors'. However, by using terminology such as 'football match' it indicates that this internal game played by Beyer Peacock workers at the Belle Vue Pleasure Gardens, had rules attached to it.[53] The same venue organised its own footballing games in 1856 and subsequent years, sometimes as part of holiday festivals or as added attractions to its annual band contest.[54] As far as individual events are concerned, football mentions like these demonstrate little in terms of the development of the sport and should not be perceived as an example of the activity's growth into a major sport. However, the frequency of these mentions demonstrates that football was not an alien activity and that perhaps all that communities required in order to develop the game was someone with the will to formalise activity. In twentieth-century Britain football became recognised in every town and village, but it is important to remember that the sport had not always existed in an organised form. It came via several processes and influences stretching over several decades and it is still evolving, although its 'prior history ... creates the framework within [which] any particular action occurs'.[55]

Due to the frequency of mentions of the sport, even though 'this kind of football, precisely because it was so casual, was unlikely to leave behind many records', it is evident that children and young men in the Manchester area knew about football.[56] They may not have played it through organised rules or clubs, but they did participate in the sport whenever the opportunity came. Cunningham recorded that 'much of the history of leisure has been written on the assumption that what is new starts from high up the social scale and is diffused downwards', and argued that this was not accurate. He thought that the flow of leisure development happened in both directions.[57] He also challenged football's traditionally held development by middle-class 'missionaries, using football as, amongst other things, a forum for class conciliation' and remarked that 'this history is inadequate'. He explained: 'seeing things through public school spectacles, it ignores the continuous history of football as a popular sport ... it seems highly likely that the more casual practice of kicking a ball around, a practice much closer to the modern game of football, survived'.[58] This is logical for the development of football within Manchester.

In Manchester, formal sports clubs, such as the Manchester Athenaeum, were essentially middle- and upper-middle-class in social composition until at least the 1850s. According to Adrian Harvey, a Manchester Garrison officers' football club was in operation in 1859, but this is based on a single reference to footballing activity by the men. However, their interest supports the view of exclusivity at this time within organised footballing activities.[59] Informal activity does not appear to have been class exclusive and it did occur, such as in 1860 at Stockport, where young men met at the 'Bongs' each evening: '"Bongs" they are called, and will be in all probability, as long as they endure for the boys and young men to assemble on in evenings, for cricket and football. They are simply masses of irregular rocks.'[60] While the Stockport youths were playing on the 'Bongs', others from that town were taking the first steps towards organising competitive footballing activity. Richard Sykes was born in Stockport and was a captain at Rugby School, being credited with taking rugby balls to Liverpool for a game on 19 December 1857. Three years later he founded Manchester Football Club, regarded as one of the first rugby clubs, while another club, Sale Football Club, followed in 1861.[61] The Manchester club claimed to have played association football by Harrow rules and the rules utilised by Hallam on occasion a decade or so after its formation.[62] Football was still developing as a sport and the differences between rugby, association and other forms of the game were not clearly defined, making it difficult to identify exactly what form of football was being played unless it was specifically stated – and even then the rules could vary, game by game, within the same team, subject to the opposition.

Sykes' former school at Rugby was one of many educational establishments to establish a version of football and we can track that sport's evolution through to both Rugby League and Rugby Union. It is widely acknowledged that the first institution to develop rules that are more in keeping with our modern game of association football was Cambridge University in 1848. These became the first formulated rules of association football and had been established by representatives of the leading public schools before being publicised on posters at Parker's Piece, Cambridge. The university became influential in the creation of the Football Association (FA) rules of 1863, but it was not the only institution whose rules were influential. From a local perspective, the rules of Harrow School were adopted by Bolton side Turton in 1872. More significantly, there is evidence that a team from Manchester utilised what they perceived as association rules during the 1860s. Their story is documented in the following chapter.

Notes

1 'En passant', *Athletic News*, 17 March 1877, 1; Cunningham, *Leisure*, 22.
2 'Easter customs', *Manchester Guardian*, 7 April 1849, 9; 'Whitsuntide festivities', *Manchester Guardian*, 25 May 1850, 5; 'Bowdon National and Sunday School treat', *Manchester Guardian*, 28 June 1848, 5; 'Methodist New Connexion Sunday School Union', *Manchester Guardian*, 10 June 1854, 5; 'Sunday Scholars Excursion to Lincoln', *Manchester Guardian*, 9 June 1852, 6; *Bell's Life in London and Sporting Chronicle*, 6 January 1856, 6; 'Belle Vue wakes', *Bell's Life in London and Sporting Chronicle*, 31 August 1856, 7; 'Band contest at Belle Vue Gardens', *Manchester Times*, 7 September 1861.
3 Examples include 'Find of eight hundred ancient coins at Hooley Bridge', *Manchester Guardian*, 22 February 1856, 2; 'Pictures and other works of art at the Peel Park Museum', *Manchester Guardian*, 2 June 1860, 6; 'The Arctic expedition', *Manchester Guardian*, 14 November 1849, 3; 'Choice pictures', *Manchester Guardian*, 15 August 1849, 5; 'Mr Park's busts of the Emperor Louis Napoleon, Mark Phillips, Esq. and Mrs Henry Houldsworth', *Manchester Guardian*, 16 August 1854, 7; 'Whitsuntide festivities', *Manchester Times*, 5 June 1852. Kitching, '"Old" football', 1733–1749.
4 'Old Manchester', *Manchester Guardian*, 6 November 1847, 4.
5 O'Reilly, 'From "the people"', 140.
6 Ibid., 138.
7 'The Harpurhey park', *Manchester Courier*, , 6 December 1844, 10. Improvements to the park in 1865 led to further football fields being opened up: 'Two small plantations have been removed, affording an improved view from the adjoining walks, and opening up a capital ground for football and other games.' 'Queens Park', *Manchester Guardian*, 2 June 1865, 3. The game of knur and spell is played in a similar style to golf, with players hitting the knur (ball-like object) with the spell (a stick-like object). The aim is to send the knur the greatest distance, rather than to aim for a hole or target.
8 Examples include 'Felony', *Manchester Courier*, 6 January 1844, 4: 'Michael Brady and Isaac Whittle, were committed for trial, charged with stealing several football cases from the shop door of Mr. John Clegg, shoemaker, in Deansgate', and 'Juvenile offenders', *Manchester Guardian*, 18 December 1844, 7 of a 12-year-old and two 9-year-olds found guilty of stealing £10 which they used to travel into Manchester and purchase 'a pair of new clogs each, a football, a quantity of oranges, &c.'
9 'Whitsuntide Festivities', *Manchester Courier*, 19 May 1866, 6.
10 O'Reilly, 'From "the people"', 145.
11 G. James, *Manchester, a football history* (Halifax: James Ward, 2008), 15–24.
12 T. Mason, *Association football and English society 1863–1915* (Brighton: The Harvester Press Ltd., 1981), 2, quoting M. A. Bienefeld, *Working hours in British industry* (1972), 79–94; P. Bailey, *Leisure and class in Victorian England* (London: Methuen & Co., 1987), 27; Hewitt, *The emergence*, 6; 'A Manchester cardroom operative', *Ashton Standard*, 1 May 1858, news cutting.

13 Mason, *Association football*, 2 quoting Bienefeld, *Working hours*, 79–94; Bailey, *Leisure and class*, 27; Hewitt, *The emergence*, 6; 'A Manchester cardroom operative', *Ashton Standard*, 1 May 1858, news cutting.

14 Examples include 'Local & provincial intelligence', *Manchester Guardian*, 6 January 1838, 3; 'Easter customs', *Manchester Guardian*, 7 April 1849, 9; 'Whitsuntide festivities', *Manchester Guardian*, 25 May 1850, 5. J. Goulstone, *Football's secret history* (Upminster: 3-2 Books, 2001), 23–26.

15 See *Athenaeum Gazette*, 10 November 1847 to 17 November 1851 for reports of activity.

16 *Athenaeum Gazette*, 22 September 1848, 2.

17 J. Goulstone, 'The working class origins of modern football', *The International Journal of the History of Sport*, 17:1 (2008), 135–143; 'The nuisance at the new burying ground', *Manchester Courier*, 9 October 1866, 3 (a report of children playing football with skulls at a city-centre graveyard); 'Football', *Bell's Life in London and Sporting Chronicle*, 20 December 1846, 7 (an article on an eight-a-side game to be played on Christmas Day in Ashton-under-Lyne with a named umpire (referee)).

18 'Wednesday', *Bell's Life in London and Sporting Chronicle*, 6 January 1856, 6.

19 S. J. Oldfield, 'Running pedestrianism in Victorian Manchester', *Sport in History*, 34:2 (2014), 229.

20 For example, 'Pedestrianism at Newton Heath', *Ashton Reporter*, 20 January 1866, 4; S. J. Oldfield, 'Narratives of Manchester pedestrianism: using biographical methods to explore the development of athletics during the nineteenth century' (PhD dissertation, Manchester Metropolitan University, 2014), 79.

21 'Pedestrianism', *Ashton Reporter*, 31 March 1866, 5; 'Pedestrianism', *Ashton Reporter*, 8 September 1866, 5; 'Pedestrianism', *Gorton Reporter*, 16 April 1870, 3.

22 G. James, 'The sporting Broads', in D. Day (ed.), *Pedestrianism* (Crewe: MMU Sport and Leisure History, 2014), 195–212.

23 'Modern pedestrianism', *Gorton Reporter*, 12 March 1870, 5.

24 H. B. Rodgers, 'The suburban growth of Victorian Manchester', *Journal of Manchester Geographical Society* 58 (1962), 4–5; J. Seed and J. Wolff, 'Class and culture in nineteenth-century Manchester', *Theory, Culture and Society*, 2:2 (1984), 48–49.

25 Hewitt, *The emergence*, 64–65.

26 M. Huggins, 'Betting capital of the provinces: Manchester, 1800–1900', in D. Russell (ed.) *Sport in Manchester, Manchester Region History Review*, 20 (2009), 24–45; Manchester's race meetings were held at Castle Irwell from 1847 to 1867 and from 1902, and at New Barns from 1876 to 1901. Neither course was within the city of Manchester boundary but both were perceived as the Manchester Racecourse during their periods of operation, adding to the view that by the mid-nineteenth century Manchester was perceived as a conurbation stretching beyond its city boundary.

27 Goulstone, *Football's secret history*, 23–26.

28 'Foot ball', *Bell's Life in London and Sporting Chronicle*, 20 December 1846, 7.

29 'Transfer of license', *Ashton Reporter*, 21 January 1860, 3.

30 D. Pendleton, 'Sport and the Victorian city: The development of commercialised

spectator sport, Bradford 1836–1908' (PhD dissertation, De Montfort University, 2015), 414; M. Huggins and J. Tolson, 'Victorian sport and the railways: a reconsideration', *Journal of Transport Studies*, 23, January 2001, 23–45; W. Vamplew, *Pay up and play the game* (Cambridge: Cambridge University Press, 1988), 47–48.

31 'Sunday desecration', *Manchester Courier*, 14 December 1850, 11.

32 'Clarence v Broadbottom', *Gorton Reporter*, 20 November 1880, n.p.

33 'Football match', *Ashton Reporter*, 19 March 1870, 5.

34 James, *Manchester, a football history*, 31–54.

35 *Bell's Life in London and Sporting Chronicle*, 20 December 1846, 7; J. Bale, *Sport and place: A geography of sport in England, Scotland and Wales* (London: C. Hurst, 1982), 23.

36 Goulstone, *Football's secret history*; A. Harvey, *Football: The first hundred years the untold story* (Abingdon: Routledge, 2005), 76; Curry and Dunning, *Association football*, 158–159.

37 G. James and D. Day, 'The emergence of an association football culture in Manchester, 1840–1884', *Sport in History*, 23:1 (2014), 54–56.

38 I. Wallerstein et al., 'Discussion', *Review*, 1 (1978), 98.

39 Wallerstein, *Unthinking social science*, 259.

40 Guldi and Armitage, *The history manifesto*, 111.

41 'Whitsuntide festivities', *Manchester Guardian*, 25 May 1850, 5.

42 'Bowdon National and Sunday School treat', *Manchester Guardian*, 28 June 1848, 5.

43 'Easter customs', *Manchester Guardian*, 7 April 1849, 9.

44 'Letter from "A country cricketer"', *Manchester Guardian*, 15 September 1849, 10.

45 'The Arctic expedition', *Manchester Guardian*, 14 November 1849, 3.

46 'Choice pictures', *Manchester Guardian*, 15 August 1849, 5.

47 'Salford park memorial', *Manchester Examiner and Times*, 10 August 1850, 4.

48 'Mr Park's busts of the emperor Louis Napoleon, Mark Phillips, Esq. and Mrs Henry Houldsworth', *Manchester Guardian*, 16 August 1854, 7.

49 'Whitsuntide festivities', *Manchester Times*, 5 June 1852, 6.

50 'Sunday scholars excursion to Lincoln', *Manchester Guardian*, 9 June 1852, 6.

51 'Whitsuntide', *Manchester Times*, 21 May 1853, 4.

52 'Methodist New Connexion Sunday School Union', *Manchester Guardian*, 10 June 1854, 5.

53 'Wednesday', *Bell's Life in London and Sporting Chronicle*, 6 January 1856, 6.

54 For example, 'Bellevue Wakes', *Bell's Life in London and Sporting Chronicle*, 31 August 1856, 7 and 'Band contest at Belle Vue Gardens', *Manchester Times*, 7 September 1861, 6.

55 I. Wallerstein (ed.), *The modern world system in the longue durée* (Abingdon: Routledge, 2016), 1.

56 Cunningham, *Leisure*, 128.

57 Ibid., 10.

58 Ibid., 127.

59 A. Harvey, 'The public schools and organized football in Britain: Fresh perspectives on old paradigms', *International Journal of the History of Sport*, 33:3 (2016), 276.

60 D. Russell, 'Sporting Manchester, from c1800 to the present: an introduction', in D. Russell (ed.) *Sport in Manchester, Manchester Region History Review*, 20 (2009), 4; 'Sketch of Stockport', *Manchester Courier*, 7 April 1860, 7.

61 L. Allison and R. Maclean, 'There's a deathless myth on the close tonight: Re-assessing rugby's place in the history of sport', *International Journal of the History of Sport*, 29:13 (2012), 1880; C. W. Alcock (ed.), *John Lillywhite's football annual* (London: Lillywhite, 1868), 83; L. Balaam, *Centenary of the Manchester Football Club – Souvenir brochure* (Manchester: Manchester Football Club, 1959), 1–5.

62 James, *Manchester, a football history*, 25–30.

3

The earliest club

The development of football clubs

The growth of football in Manchester saw clubs such as Manchester Football Club, the 'absolute pioneers' of rugby in the region, being established in 1860, with several other clubs founded mostly in the then wealthier residential areas such as Broughton, Didsbury, Sale, Whalley Range and Old Trafford.[1] The prominent members of these clubs appear to have been from the upper-, or from respected middle-class occupations, many of them former public school-boys.[2] Manchester Football Club regarded themselves as the guardians of the sport and, in effect, the organising members of their committee positioned themselves as the Lancastrian rugby elite, playing the leading role in all areas of the game's management locally. Another early football club was Sale, which, according to some reports, can trace its formation back to 1859 and was for several years perceived as an association football club.[3] Reports and discussion of association-style games in the 1860s do exist for several occasions, suggesting that Sale alternated their style of play at times, with their preference changing to rugby.[4] Some of these games involved up to forty players, which could at first glance imply that this was a form of rugby; however, the 1860s was still a period when the number of participants was not fixed, nor were there a consistent set of rules, and therefore it is impossible to state with certainty what form of foot-ball was being played.[5]

Regardless of the numbers, the view exists that Sale rugby club began life as a soccer club circa 1859, and that other rugby teams played soccer games from time to time; however, it is debatable whether those mentions represent fully fledged association football clubs.[6] Similarly, the Manchester Athenaeum football sessions of the 1840s may represent an actual football club, but we do not know what style of game they played. It is known that by 1854 reports of the Manchester Athenaeum's activities discuss gymnastics and also talk of reviving its cricketing interests, alongside purchases of new equipment; but to date no mentions of football-related activity, even within detailed sporting features, have been identified.[7] Data can be abused if it is examined as a single facet of historical experience, and that means that one or two mentions of football activity, such as in Manchester Athenaeum's case, do not imply that this was a fully functioning football club.[8] 'Researchers concerned wholly with data-gathering ... often seem unable to appreciate the underlying problems' of this type of research, and this is the case with Manchester Athenaeum.[9]

Understandably, there is much debate on the style and type of football being played throughout the 1860s at a variety of clubs across the United Kingdom and, without sight of the specific rules for each game, it would be foolish to make claims that any of the matches regarded as association, or indeed rugby, were played to the recognisable basic rules of the game as understood in the twenty-first century. On occasion those involved classified their games as association in later decades when they reflected on their experiences, but this does not mean that they played FA rules. It means that they thought they were playing a soccer-style game, as opposed to a rugby format. What they considered was the difference is debatable. It could be argued that prior to 1863 and the formation of the FA no football activity could be described as truly association football, but that would be a mistake, as contemporary authors talked of soccer-based rules being developed and promoted prior to the FA's birth. Significantly, rightly or wrongly the FA was perceived more as a London association of clubs than as a national governing body by those in the north. It has been widely written that Sheffield had a developed soccer community and it has been argued that this was more influential than is traditionally thought. There were also association communities in Stoke and Nottingham in the 1860s that were progressive.[10] Activity in those regions was perceived as independent of the FA but was still, unmistakably, considered association-like rather than comparable to rugby rules of the period. If those clubs later considered themselves to be playing a form of association football at their foundation, then clearly they recognised differences between their version of the sport and the version of those participating in rugby, some of whom would have been participants of both sports.

In Sheffield on 29 December 1862 association football was used, perhaps for the first time, to aid the people of the Manchester conurbation when a charity match was staged between Sheffield and Hallam to raise funds for the Central Relief Committee, an organisation set up in Manchester to help those suffering because of the Cotton Famine. This soccer link is important and suggests that the people of Sheffield had connections with Manchester that are not clear but that may have influenced activities in later years. This game may have had little bearing on playing activities in Manchester, but it did occur at a time when some were beginning to see that football could be of value in developing communities, and within a year the earliest known association club in the Manchester area, Hulme Athenaeum, was founded, in 1863.[11] Despite mentions in *A History of British Football*, the club had not been referred to in footballing or Manchester-focused publications until the twenty-first century, while the simple mentions in Young's book, such as 'Hulme Athenaeum had their ground at Moss Side, Manchester', hardly did the club justice.[12] The assumption that could be drawn from the lack of coverage is that the side was to some extent an irrelevance; however, ongoing research has identified that Hulme Athenaeum's role in the birth of Manchester's association football history is significant. The growth of football in Lancashire has been considered and revisited by academics over the years and, although Manchester at this time was recognised as a key part of the county, the growth and development of the city often led to different issues, and potentially alternative approaches to leisure activities.[13] It has been accepted that association football was late to arrive in Manchester as compared with other areas of Lancashire because rugby was the dominant local sport; yet evidence suggests that this is not accurate, as Manchester did possess an association football club in the 1860s. That club was formed at least eight years earlier than Turton Football Club, often perceived as the earliest club in Lancashire. The conurbation was on a par with, if not ahead of, the rest of Lancashire through to the early 1870s.[14] The Hulme Athenaeum Football Club was formed in November 1863, although the roots of the organisation stretched back to 1859, and it consisted entirely of working men living within the Hulme district of Manchester.[15] It is significant that this side, which did play fixtures against teams from Sheffield and was recognised in sporting publications as an association side for several years in the 1860s and 1870s, existed in a predominantly working-class area for almost a decade.[16]

Vamplew states that football clubs have 'a special place in sports history' and 'deserve categorization as a long residual', becoming stable elements in our society over numerous decades or even centuries. Their continual presence means that they can shape history.[17] Some clubs may last only a few years, or even months, but these short-lived clubs can still shape the history of the sport by providing us with examples of how society acted or by generating interest in the game, such as with Hulme Athenaeum. Their successes and failures are important to understanding how and why sports developed, and while historical focus within the origins debate has often been on individual games and on the establishment of successful clubs, less attention has been paid to failing clubs and the people involved. It is therefore important to record the steps that led to the formation of the Hulme Athenaeum side. The parent organisation, Hulme Athenaeum, was founded as a working men's club by Sir William Thackeray Marriott in 1859, in an area that knew great hardship.[18] Hewitt writes of the poverty experienced in Manchester, with specific reference to the studies by John Layhe and James Harrop into the conditions in Hulme during the period 1848–67, and a picture has been painted of extreme poverty, sickness and little opportunity for improvement.[19] Whether the Athenaeum was aimed directly at those who were struggling the most is unlikely, as it was described as 'one of the first working-men's clubs established in England, whose members were all working men'.[20]

At a time when poverty, ignorance, criminality and morality were constant issues in Manchester, organisations like the Hulme Athenaeum were established by individuals from the middle classes as a means to develop minds and appropriate interests, as well as to engender a community spirit.[21] Its target demographics indicate that members were recruited from the lower-middle class and skilled artisans, but contemporary Mancunians appear to have held a different opinion as to what constituted a working man; it was suggested that a working man 'was a machine for burning tobacco and swallowing beer, and devouring such literature as *Bell's Life*'.[22] Regardless of specific classification, if that is possible in nineteenth-century Hulme, it is true that Marriott wanted to improve conditions for all, and in 1860 he issued a pamphlet, *Some Real Wants and some Legitimate Claims of the Working Classes*, advocating parks, gymnasiums and 'clubs for working people'.[23] It is worth noting that the area around St George's Church and other areas of Hulme were regarded as slums by some, and 'covered in a mosaic of workshops and factories and the densely packed houses of those who worked in them'.[24]

Contemporary reports identify that the organisation was founded as the St George's Mutual Improvement Society some time prior to 1858, being initially based at St George's school. That year, as the organisation struggled, its leaders introduced cricket and other outdoor games, resulting in a larger membership, and 'the exclusion of the society was broken down by the admission of persons of any creed'.[25] The introduction of sports enabled the organisation to grow, and in 1860 a new club house was opened in Hargreaves Street, Hulme and the new name of Hulme Athenaeum was selected after some debate.[26] The premises consisted of: 'Reading and coffee rooms on the ground floor, with draughts and other games, large room for fencing, lectures &c., upstairs, and a small room that may be used for smoking. The terms are 4s per quarter, and 2s entrance, and the club is intended for warehousemen, clerks, and skilled mechanics.' The chief objectives of the organisation were 'physical and mental culture'.[27]

The cost of four shillings per quarter and two shillings entrance fee suggests that the club was not aimed at all working-class members of the local population, and it is accepted that many of the Athenaeum clubs established around the country to provide cultural advancement were 'beyond the means of working people'.[28] This raises a question mark over the success of the organisation in relation to involvement of the working classes, although photographic evidence shows that the residences of some of the club's members were, at best, lower middle-class homes in terraced streets in a densely packed area of Hulme. Engels was extremely negative in his judgement of these streets when he published in 1845: 'Farther down, on the left side of the Medlock, lies Hulme, which, properly speaking, is one great working-people's district, the condition of which coincides almost exactly with that of Ancoats; the more thickly built-up regions chiefly bad and approaching ruin, the less populous of more modern structure, but generally sunk in filth.'[29] Despite the 'filth' 'thousands of dignified lives were lived in Ancoats and Hulme, lives of self-improvement'.[30] References to Hulme during the period 1848–67 painted a picture of extreme poverty, sickness and little opportunity for improvement.[31] Hulme had become transformed from a relatively peaceful, rural setting close to a growing town into an inner-city district of a major metropolis within a space of forty years.

At the annual meeting of the Hulme Athenaeum in 1861 Thomas Bazley, MP highlighted that he would 'do all he could to forward the views of the meeting, in the way of extending the means of recreation to the young men of large towns', and added that he hoped to bring the Manchester Botanical Gardens into ownership of the city of Manchester for 'the use and benefit of every class and their children, so that it might become a place where all classes could meet on common ground and cultivate an intercourse with each other, which was at present too much restricted in a great manufacturing community like Manchester'.[32] The Gardens were struggling financially, despite only four years earlier having staged a major art and treasures exhibition visited by Queen Victoria, demonstrating that even when leisure facilities were provided they could not be guaranteed to succeed. The Gardens did survive for a time and in 1887 staged another major exhibition, which included association football activities, and later still became home to Manchester's White City stadium.

The Gardens were not the only strugglers, as the Athenaeum also had financial issues during the early 1860s, recording a deficit of £14 7s 2d in its annual report for 1862–63. However, the members vowed to carry on: 'this institution, offering the means of education and social recreation, is much required in the neighbourhood'.[33] In the months that followed the financial situation improved when the Athenaeum merged with the St Michael's Institute, with Hugh Birley becoming the merged organisation's president. Birley, who would in 1868 become a Conservative MP for Manchester, was educated at Winchester School, known for its football activities, as was his nephew Francis Hornby Birley, who later played for FA Cup-winning sides The Wanderers (in 1876 and 1877) and Oxford University (1874). Under Birley the Athenaeum's focus on sporting activity increased, with 'cricket and other field sports' promoted, a gymnasium planned and physical science classes created.[34] Cricket reports and details of participation in athletic festivals exist for the early 1860s.[35] The influence of the Birley family on Hulme Athenaeum's association football development is not clear and not enough connections have been made to prove that any Birley had a direct impact on the club's decision to establish a soccer club. However, the fact that members of the family attended Winchester School, held prominent positions at Hulme and played in FA Cup finals demonstrates that association football knowledge was there and could be consulted. In addition, some members of the Birley family were councillors for Rossall School at Fleetwood, which possessed excellent 'cricket and football grounds for all ages' within forty acres by 1869. Regrettably, Rossall's role in the development of association football has largely been ignored by those researching Lancashire's soccer history. When their Rossall link is combined with all their Hulme and other footballing connections, it suggests that association football was recognised, and it may well be that the Birleys themselves instigated the association football team at Hulme.[36]

Regardless of whether the Birleys played a role in the establishment of soccer at the Athenaeum, their involvement was important as it provided credibility to the parent organisation. It was at the Athenaeum that the earliest known Manchester club to style itself as an association football club was founded. For a couple of seasons Hulme Athenaeum, established only three years after the founding of the rugby-playing Manchester Football Club, was recognised as the only association football club in the area, and during this time games were played between the Athenaeum and a combined team from Sale and Bowdon.[37] It is of course possible that organised football of one form or another was occurring in the Hulme area earlier than 1863, and evidence exists linking the sport with the mill of J. Pooley and Sons at Hulme. Correspondence discusses Pooley's mill as being in 'excellent order', adding that they 'employ fifty children' whom they sent to the nearby National School, before commenting that some boys had 'time for their education ... and have a game at football in the green fields besides'.[38] The Pooley family were established members of the community and some were directly involved with the Hulme Athenaeum too, while the club's earliest known home ground was referred to locally as Pooley's Park, close to the Athenaeum's club house. This open field was utilised for cricket and football and its owners, the Pooley family, engaged in sporting activities from time to time.[39] Mill owner John Pooley had a close relationship with several institutions in the area, including the local cavalry barracks and St George's Church, while Fred Pooley was treasurer of the Athenaeum in 1863.[40]

The question of why football clubs are created is a fascinating one and may well vary from club to club, but there is a simple explanation. Groups establish football clubs because they want to play more football, and by establishing a structure they can then create opportunities to enable games and improve their experience. The same basic idea exists for leagues and footballing bodies, each being established to enable more footballing activity to take place. Initiatives like these require prominent and committed individuals to progress and establish their sporting community and the dominant figure behind Hulme was John Nall, who was born and raised in Hulme, an area characterised by casual labour.[41] Nall was particularly active with the Athenaeum's sporting pursuits and it seems that his influences came from within the local community, either through his family or through contacts made during his adult life.[42] Nall was self-motivated and a product of an increasingly urbanised community where the influence of societal groups shaped lives. His male family members were also active within the Hulme Athenaeum and he would have encountered members of the Birley family. Hugh Birley attended enough club events throughout the 1860s, a time when Nall's name was recorded as secretary for the entire club, for the two men to have discussed sporting initiatives and performances.[43]

The specifics of what happened in 1863 can only be surmised, based on evidence gathered, archival research and triangulation. It is an interpretation of what occurred, and much more would be gained if it were possible to spend an hour in the company of Nall or one of his contemporaries. Nall would be able to explain how football was viewed; what the differences were between the version of the game his team played and that of later years; how frequently the game was played; what was unreported; why the game truly took hold; whether it helped to bind society or create divisions; whether participants treated each other differently based on their class or their nationality of birth; and what the views of ordinary Mancunians were. Being able to walk in 1860s Manchester and to observe society would provide so many answers and we would immediately notice differences which to our modern eye may prove unfathomable, but which to Nall and his contemporaries may have been perfectly normal. Society often speculates on what a Victorian might think of modern-day technology or of the game of football today, and we talk about the differences, but our perception of their incredulity might well apply if roles and times were switched. Our modern selves may eagerly anticipate the latest piece of technology, or rush to our local mobile phone stockist for the newest version, and our Victorian selves may have been similarly intrigued when the local cobbler made his first leather football, or when we saw our first spherical or oval ball. It is this level of understanding which we should all strive to reach if we hope to explain fully how football, or any other activity for that matter, became an everyday part of life. Sadly, so much evidence is lost and the specifics of how pioneering figures like Nall felt at the time were never captured.

John Nall

To gain a greater understanding of how Hulme Athenaeum became established and recognised as an association football club it is important to consider the life of John Nall. He was born in Manchester in 1840 and his parents were Matthew Nall, a commercial clerk, and Maria Platford, the daughter of James Platford, the owner of public houses in the area. By 1851 Platford was the owner of the White House Gardens public house off Stretford Road, where sporting activities such as cricket and wrestling, organised by the Manchester Wrestling Society, occurred. Platford's entrepreneurial approach was typical of landlords across Lancashire. Swain has documented the scenario in the Bolton area of Lancashire, where he highlights publicans involved with promoting sporting activities and challenges, including football matches, during the 1830s.[44]

In 1852 James Platford funded the building of a new public house, which he subsequently named the Platford Hotel, later the site of meetings establishing Manchester Association Football Club. While his parents-in-law were involved with the brewing trade, John Nall's father was a town councillor involved with several organisations in the Hulme area, and was recognised for his eighteen years' service to the township of Hulme at a presentation dinner in his honour at which over 170 attended.[45] It has been identified that at this time Manchester City Council members came from occupational groups such as wholesale and retail merchants and professionals, such as journalists, estate agents and civil engineers, and this elite was more socially diverse than the old landowning aristocratic elite.[46] Matthew Nall would have been recognised as a dedicated servant of the people of Hulme, where he was a Liberal and supported Thomas Bazley, an active member of the Anti-Corn Law League and president of the Manchester Chamber of Trade, when he stood for re-election to Parliament during the 1860s.[47] Matthew Nall was also treasurer for the Christ Church Building Society Trust and a respected member of the community, while the Platford family would have been equally known for their involvement with the sporting landscape of the area.[48] Lawson noted that 'there were only two places to go in spending spare time away from one's own house – church, chapel or alehouse; the former were seldom open, while the latter was seldom closed. The first was not attractive, the second was made attractive.'[49] This is particularly relevant to the Nall/Platford family, with the Nalls focusing on church activities and the Platfords on the brewing trade, leading to an interesting coming together via the life of John Nall. Platford's sporting entrepreneurial skills and Nall's civic responsibilities provided a mechanism whereby John was able to see the possibilities of combining the two. At a time when public houses played a major part in the social life of a large proportion of the working classes and competed for customers by providing entertainment such as music, sport, art and theatre, Nall was able to see how the successes of the Platford Hotel and similar could be used to increase participation in more sober environments.[50]

Nall's formative years were spent at 45 Percy Street, Hulme.[51] At the time of his marriage at Manchester Cathedral in 1865 he was living in Tamworth Street. He then spent his early married life in Mytton Street, before moving to Yarburgh Street, Moss Side.[52] Each of these properties appears to have been a terraced house, with Mytton Street understood to have been a standard two-up two-down house of the period. The property in Yarburgh Street was more substantial and was to become the family home for the rest of Nall's life; indeed his son Arthur was still living in the property at the time of his death in 1948.[53] In 1876 a similar property on the opposite side of Yarburgh Road could be rented for £36 per annum, while a five-bedroomed house closer to Nall's could be rented for £26 in 1888.[54] Nall lived his entire life in the densely populated Hulme and Moss Side areas of Manchester and, as his own status within

Mancunian life improved, he followed the actions suggested by Rose, who claimed that the middle classes, having 'pulled themselves up by their own boot straps, … got out of the city'. It should be noted that Moss Side was considered a middle-class suburb at the time of Nall's move.[55]

By the age of twenty-three Nall was active with the Hulme Athenaeum and, together with his father, was a committee member at a time when the organisation was needed to provide education and social recreation to the local population.[56] He became Hulme Athenaeum's secretary, and in the years that followed he was the leading figure behind the development of the Athenaeum's sporting activities. In November 1865 the first contemporary reference identified so far that mentions football activity appeared, in an article outlining some of the activities of the organisation and including the simple statement that football and cricket clubs had been established.[57] No results of cricket or football games appeared in that report, although the results of a successful chess competition against a neighbouring institution were given, implying that either the cricket and football clubs had played in-house competitions or they had been less successful than the chess games. If the Hulme Athenaeum's only footballing activity during this time was in-house games, then that would be typical of the earliest clubs, such as Sheffield Football Club (FC). If that was the case, then the mission for Nall would be to find opposition players or to encourage others to participate. Nall dedicated his time at the Athenaeum to helping the organisation's sporting activities develop, and even after the club's collapse in the 1870s he remained interested in association football and the development of sporting activities within Hulme and at his maternal family's Platford Hotel.[58] By the summer of 1887, Nall was the Manchester FA vice-president, suggesting that he had retained involvement with the sport.[59]

Whether there is any significance behind the date of 1863 in terms of Hulme Athenaeum's footballing formation is not clear. The FA was established in that year, but this was such a minor story as far as those in the north were concerned at the time that it may be pure coincidence, and for the next decade or so the FA was often described incorrectly in the north as the London Association.[60] One of the main issues when researching history is that successes and survivors tend to dominate our thinking, and while nationally the FA is perhaps the most significant success story, its modern-day status can cloud our thinking. It is important to consider whether an embryonic association in London had any bearing on daily footballing life in a city like Manchester. We may never know for certain. As with Manchester's two leading successes, City and United, the FA's existence allows us to consider what success and survival look like, but to truly understand sport's development we need to recognise that those clubs and communities that failed are also important and have contributed along the way. It is important to review all known events during the period covered, not merely those that have been successful, and to place them within the framework. We

2 Hulme Athenaeum's listing in the first edition of *John Lillywhite's Football Annual* (1868).

must study not only progress but also the 'opposite, that harvest of contrary experiences which fought hard before they went down'.[61] Hulme Athenaeum is one such organisation, but its history is important in Manchester's footballing development.

In 1868 John Nall placed an advertisement requesting 'challenges from any club in the district within a radius of 20 miles', and he ensured that Hulme was recorded that year in the first *John Lillywhite's Football Annual* (Figure 2).[62] This is significant, as it shows that within five years of its inauguration the club was well established and formally organised. Nall went on to perform the role of Hulme Athenaeum football secretary into the 1870s, and played the game, establishing club nights on Mondays, Wednesdays and Fridays. He was the leading organiser of football activity throughout the 1860s and into the early 1870s.[63] Dunning and Sheard write of football clubs created during this period as being formed by 'members of the upper and middle-classes', and that is true in Hulme's case; however, that does not mean they were exclusively for those classes, nor does it mean that members of those classes were the ones who suggested playing the game.[64] In 2013 Dunning and Curry proposed the existence of local footballing elites who 'employed sources such as the major public schools, their own local grammar schools and diverse varieties of mob football to reach agreement on codes which enabled them to participate in their favourite pastime'.[65] Others have argued that embryonic forms of football existed outside of these environments.[66]

Thinking specifically of 1860s Manchester, it is possible that a regular working man with knowledge of the game on the streets, or at venues such as Belle Vue, may have heard about the formalisation of football via newspapers such as *Bell's Life in London and Sporting Chronicle*, and proposed something similar. Unless contemporary evidence is identified specifically stating who came up with the idea of forming teams like Hulme Athenaeum, this is an area that can never be proved. Dunning and Sheard do outline some of the key members of Manchester's leading rugby sides of this period, including Manchester Rangers, formed in Hulme in 1870 by members of St Michael's Church. It should be remembered St Michael's was one of the ingredients that led to Hulme Athenaeum's development at the start of the 1860s. As demonstrated at Sale, soccer and rugby often lived side by side, sometimes within the same club, and the St Michael's connection adds to the theory that in Manchester soccer and rugby developed together before rugby gained the upper hand later in the decade.[67] It seems feasible that members of the St Michael's congregation would have been committee men at the Athenaeum, and potentially members of Manchester Rangers. Even if there were no direct connections, it is possible that church attendees would have been aware of the activities of fellow members of the congregation and their neighbours. Without exception, Dunning and Sheard identified Manchester Rangers men as being from the upper-class or middle-class occupations.[68] However, focusing on national class structures may not provide the right approach because, in Manchester for example, the nature of the city's growth created a society that was multi-layered, with many factors impacting on the relationships between classes.[69]

Comments in 1878 on the formation of rugby teams in Manchester recognised that there were initially several soccer clubs in the area in the 1860s, with one article naming four such teams.[70] Birch, established in 1869, was one such club and had played an association game during its formative period.[71] As with many of the clubs established as 'Manchester' clubs during this time, Birch played outside of the city boundaries but was perceived as a Mancunian team, as was another prominent team, Free Wanderers.[72] Free Wanderers was based in Didsbury, adding to the complex nature of Mancunian identity and the need to focus on the region rather than specific city boundaries, and was typical of the majority of rugby clubs established in the area during this time as it was formed by 'old boys' from a prominent local school.[73] The different variations of football were known within the Manchester area in the 1860s. Handbooks were available, and reviews appeared in publications that would have been available to members of the Hulme Athenaeum. *The Athenaeum* review of one such book talked of the key versions of the game, including Eton, Harrow and FA rules, although it did imply that the Rugby form of the game was the best.[74] Another book described a version of the game that was more association-like than rugby and, in its introduction, described how traditional football had been dying out while a more formal version had grown up.[75] Football of some description was an activity that was becoming established through educational establishments in the region and several Manchester schools possessed footballing facilities during the 1860s and early 1870s, with Holly Bank, in Cheetham Hill, established 1864, containing 'a large field for cricket and football, a good playground provided with gymnastic apparatus, and a spacious drillroom'.[76]

Excluding Manchester Athenaeum, there were eight football clubs established in the Manchester–Salford area by 1870 – ten if neighbouring Sale and Bowdon are included.[77] These were mainly playing a version of football more in keeping with rugby than with association football, but contemporary newspapers do carry mention of soccer-like activity participated in by groups on an ad hoc basis, much as modern-day street football occurs. As discussed earlier, some local rugby-playing sides either began life as association clubs or utilised that form of football as a training technique. This makes it exceptionally difficult to state with confidence that a mention of association football was part of a wider pattern of activity even within a recognisable club. The only Manchester-area clubs recorded in an 1868 annual were the rugby clubs Sale, with a recorded establishment date of 1859, Rochdale (no formation date recorded) and Manchester Athletic (1866); plus, of course, the association club Hulme Athenaeum, which claimed to have forty-eight members, play home games at Hullard Hall, Old Trafford, have a membership fee of 1s pro rata and wear a kit of 'white and blue trimmings' (see Figure 2). Hulme continued to be listed in *Lillywhite's Annual*, with continual updating of details such as membership, ground and secretary, for the following four seasons, so it was a relatively stable organisation. Its membership increased to fifty-nine (1869), but was recorded as forty-five in subsequent annuals. The home ground changed to Moss Side, and more specifically games were played at Alexandra Park.[78] During 1866 and 1867 the side played Sale in what appear to be soccer games, the second of which ended in a 2–1 victory for Hulme.[79] Reports and discussion of soccer games between those clubs exist for several years in the 1860s, and this suggests that Sale alternated their style of play at times, with their preference changing to rugby.[80] Some of these games involved thirty to forty players, during a period when the number of participants was not fixed, nor was there a consistent set of rules, and therefore it is impossible to state with clarity what form of football was being played.[81] Hulme thought they were playing a form of association football by 1868, and that they knew how to differentiate between their form of the game and that of rugby, with records in football annuals, articles focusing on former Hulme players and letters by early players making it abundantly clear that they were playing a form of association football, even if the term at formation was not recognised.

Wood's rules

The formation of the FA in 1863 is inevitably considered by some as the point when association football became recognised; however, the establishment of the association was merely one attempt at agreeing a standard set of rules. Regionally, other bodies, such as those in Sheffield, may have been of equal or greater significance, while publications may also have contributed to the growth of formalised versions of the sport.[82] Frederick Wood, who documented rules which he claimed to have established at several clubs across the country over a ten-year period, may have been of significance.[83] He went into considerable detail, explaining how he had refined his rules season after season until they became relatively simple, producing what was in effect

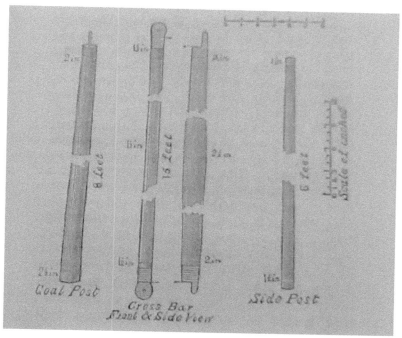

3 How to construct goal posts, as documented in F. Wood, *Beeton's football.*

a handbook for setting up clubs and playing the sport. He even described how to make goal posts with a wooden crossbar (Figure 3) and, unlike the FA rules, he was clear that a bar was needed to ensure that only goals scored beneath the bar would count, and he explained why games without crossbars led to disputed goals and ill-feeling. His preferred size for the goals was '8 feet in height, and 15 feet in width'. This was in 1865, ten years before crossbars are recognised to have been introduced, and around the time that goal tape was set at eight feet.[84] Wood's rules were clearly association based and he stated that he was on the side of the 'abolitionists' who wanted to move away from the use of hands. His intent was to establish one set of rules which, he felt, were superior, though similar, to those of the newly formed FA and the Cambridge rules, but with differences, including Wood opposing the use of scoring through touchdowns or rouges.[85] His view on the use of hands was that players could make a fair catch but they must not 'carry the ball, hold it, throw it, pass it to another with his hands, under any pretence whatever'. The only method of scoring was to kick the ball 'between the uprights and beneath the cross-bar'.[86] Wood's rules were more association-like than even the FA's original rules, and he went to great lengths to explain all aspects of what was, in effect, association football. He even discussed the price of footballs, how to

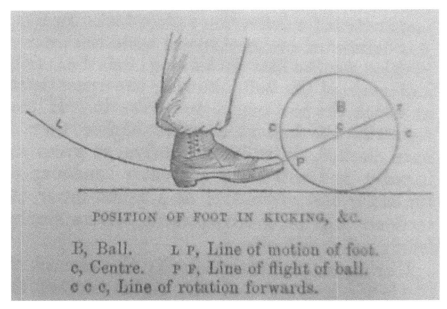

4 How to take a kick, as documented in F. Wood, *Beeton's football*.

repair them and where to buy them from, along with specific details on how to kick the ball (Figure 4).

From a Manchester perspective, Wood's rules are important, as it is known that they were aimed at a populist market and on general sale at railway stationers and at bookstores. The librarian of the Manchester Literature and Philosophical Society had his own personal copy.[87] It is impossible to state with certainty how many copies of this one-shilling book were sold in Manchester, or whether those copies played any part in the establishment of clubs or rules in the region, but what can be stated is that some Mancunians knew of the book and that differences between association and rugby versions of the game were clear, regardless of whether the FA rules were formally adopted by clubs. Manchester newspapers frequently carried news of games staged outside the region, while the availability of Wood's work cannot be understated.[88] It was part of a series which included Isabella Beeton's *The Englishwoman's Cookery Book* and other informative editions. These were not books aimed only at the richest members of society.

Wood felt that his soccer-like version of the game was gaining in popularity as a consequence of the waning popularity of the traditional game, stating that football had 'risen considerably in public estimation, and has spread over much new ground'.[89] However, the greatest issue affecting the growth of the sport was the great diversity of rules and, in contrast to the modern-day views of orthodox theorists, the author blamed the public schools for stunting the sport's growth. He claimed that football rules needed to be devised and agreed outside of the schools, as they would not relinquish control of their preferred rules. He also felt that they had to be devised for adults to follow, as they were less willing to engage in the rough versions of the games in force at public schools. It is recognised that Mancunians in 1866 were aware of football's differing rules, as that year the *Manchester Courier* printed a lengthy article, originally appearing in the *Pall Mall Gazette*, explaining about the game and its variations. This variety of rules limited the sport's growth: 'A great drawback to a more popular appreciation of football is that it is not regulated by any uniform code of laws.' The article included details on the size and shape of the balls, the method of scoring and positioning of goals and the number of players, as well as giving an indication on the length of time needed to play the different versions. It outlined the similarities of the prominent versions of the game, including public school versions of association football and rugby football, before concluding: 'We cannot attempt to strike a balance in favour of any one system. There are advantages and imperfections in all. The absolute condemnation of "hands", even to the extent of a "fair catch", as in the Etonian game, seems, for instance, rather an extreme measure, though the principle of invariably keeping the ball down is in the spirit of true sport.'[90] The *Manchester Courier* often claimed to be one of the most-circulated newspapers in the country, and it could be purchased across Lancashire, North Wales, West Yorkshire and in the districts surrounding Manchester, which suggests that the editor selected the article because he knew that readers were in a position to be able to debate the merits of the various codes – or, at the very least, he felt that they should be made aware that differing codes existed.[91]

In May 1867 a letter writer to the *Manchester Courier* did not stress a preference when he proposed establishing a football club, arguing that cricket was dangerous, while football was 'a harmless game; it is equally exciting and requires far less expensive "fixings"'. He suggested forming a club in the Cheetham or Broughton area, where Broughton School had established a football team earlier that year which is recorded as being rugby-like but did not include hacking, emphasising how both forms of football were still evolving at this time.[92] During the mid-1860s football was discussed in a positive manner across the city and in the media, with the mayor of Manchester encouraging people to 'take part in cricket, football and other manly exercises'. He went on to talk of the growth in participation in 'manly' sporting activity in Manchester: 'I am proud to think that Manchester is not behind in this respect – although much remains to be done.' He added that he wanted 'to create a growing taste among young men for these manly exercises'.[93] He was mostly referring to gymnastics and athletics; however, his mention of football gave a strong indication that the sport was viewed positively in Manchester.

The number of participants is often considered relevant in determining whether a game was more soccer-like or rugby based, but Wood's book recommended teams of twenty, stating that it was possible to use the rules documented for teams consisting of ten through to twenty-five, with the size of pitch varying to suit the number of players, and a proposed '150 yards long by fifty-five yards in breadth'.[94] From a Mancunian perspective, as late as 1880 some soccer games were composed of twelve players each side, including the first known game of St Mark's, the club that evolved into Manchester City.

Regardless of the possible influence of Wood and/or the FA's rules, Hulme Athenaeum progressed and references to football continued throughout the 1860s in Manchester, including mentions of youngsters enjoying the activity in Stockport, Peel Park and elsewhere and the mayor of Manchester encouraging participation.[95] The frequency of mentions makes it clear that Mancunians knew about football. They may not all have played it through organised rules or clubs, but they did participate whenever the opportunity arose and, as Kitching points out, the development of football is more than the establishment of rules, it's about 'learning through playing'.[96]

Despite attempts at spreading soccer, the game could only prosper if there were enough people participating in it, and with only one recognised soccer club, Hulme Athenaeum, it was tough. At least one other organisation based in Hulme rented a field for football in 1863, although whether they played a version of football closely aligned with soccer or rugby is unclear.[97] It is known that unemployed men were encouraged to participate in these activities, and that, if nothing else, indicates a more open policy than the rugby clubs were perceived to have at this time. A couple of years earlier that organisation's secretary described the literacy of its membership: 'Some cannot read ... there are many who cannot write.'[98] Attempts were made to improve literacy, while at Hulme Athenaeum a well-established reading room provided members with the latest publications. It addition to the reading room it is recorded that the Athenaeum consisted of a large exercise room with a plentiful supply of Indian clubs, boxing gloves, dumb bells and other equipment, dressing rooms and a well-equipped gymnasium.[99] On the ground floor there were a lounge and a smoking room where chess, draughts and dominoes were played, and there was also a newsroom where the latest newspapers were available.[100] The club's boxing instructor, Phil Clare, was a well-known former prize fighter and several members became established boxers on the regional circuit, while others became 'famous gymnasts'.[101]

Hulme Athenaeum ventured outside of the Manchester area, playing against Sheffield's Garrick club, with the direct train from city centre Manchester to Sheffield aiding travel.[102] Interestingly, the notice for a game in 1870 shows that Sheffield-rules playing Garrick had to organise a series of practice matches every day over the Christmas period in the build-up to the game, as their

form of football had different rules to Hulme's.[103] Detailed match reports listing players are rare for these games, but one exists for a meeting between
Garrick and Hulme – although the club is incorrectly recorded as Manchester
Athenaeum – that took place in February 1871.[104] This provides an interesting
insight into the form of football being played. Sheffield rules were used, which
surprised the journalist, who commented: 'Why these rules were played by two
clubs belonging to the "London Association" is difficult to conjecture.' This
was an uneven match, with twelve players for the away team and fifteen for
Garrick, but it suggests that Hulme's form of football was closer to FA rules
than Garrick's was.

The report went on to discuss post-match commemorations for both clubs
at the Garrick Hotel and mentioned that the previous meeting in Manchester a
few weeks earlier had ended in a draw, despite Hulme's having an extra player.
That game was played to FA rules, which adds to the belief that Hulme utilised FA rules, or FA-like rules, and Garrick utilised Sheffield rules.[105] Hulme
and Garrick met home and away for at least three seasons, with the last known
report coming in 1872.[106] Records of Hulme matches appear for every year
from 1866 through to 1872, and the Athenaeum's home ground for many of
these games is known with the team playing at Withington Road in 1870 and at
Alexandra Park, Moss Side in 1872, close to John Nall's home.[107] The games
with Sheffield clubs raise the question of how the team travelled. Did they
organise train travel or coach and horses, as Manchester FC did for some of
their early games?[108] How did they fund this travel? Did members contribute?
In addition, how would working men afford to take time off work for these
excursions? It has often been determined that income levels and occupations
limited the opportunity for sports participation, with Russell commenting that
'the greater the degree of individual wealth, the greater the opportunity for the
fullest participation across the sporting world'. He added that 'divisions within
classes also come into play here'.[109] Hulme were not the only Manchester side
playing against Sheffield-based teams during this period, and it is known that
when Sheffield Garrick and Manchester Free Wanderers met in 1872 the decision was taken to play each club's rules on their opponent's ground, with the
Sheffield game proclaimed as the first time that the rugby rules had been played
there.[110] Sheffield, due to its strong footballing community, was the obvious
choice for those involved in soccer in Manchester.

Recognising that Hulme considered itself an association club is important,
but it is also important to identify how they played. Research shows that Hulme
at formation played an 'elementary association game, but soon introduced dribbling and passing', and that they played teams comprising of players from Sale
and Bowdon within their first two years.[111] Triangulation of sources ensures that
both the adoption of dribbling and the games with teams from Sale and Bowdon
occurred prior to 1866. Hulme Athenaeum's first ground, Pooley's Park, helps

to date the organisation's footballing activities, and its development can be measured through a series of maps which, when compared, show the development of housing and roads across the park throughout the 1860s and 1870s. These maps have provided some confirmation of when the Athenaeum was able to utilise the park and the years that they played there.[112] Reminiscences several years later discuss how 'the building of the Wesleyan Chapel considerably curtailed our field of play, and the further building of shops and houses caused our removal to a field on the opposite side of City Road'.[113] Based on maps, newspaper reports and information on building work in the area, together with the known activities of members, it is possible to date the Pooley Park association activity to the early to mid-1860s.[114] In addition to the geographical changes, the reminiscences of the former members and football players cannot be ignored, and Jim Warrington, a prominent member of the football club during the 1860s, documented with clarity when his own involvement ceased. Naturally, it is possible that memories can become confused over time, but triangulation has demonstrated that his memories of playing a form of football that included dribbling and passing at a specific location and against recognisable opponents by the mid-1860s appears to be correct. Further, the testimony of other Athenaeum members, who discuss many of the same people engaged in activities at the organisation, correspond with Warrington's accounts, as do their ages. It is also known that Hulme Athenaeum commenced the 1867–68 season playing home games at a different venue, Hullard Hall.[115]

Regardless of accounts written decades later on the origins of association football in the Lancashire region, it is evident there was an association football club operating out of the Hulme Athenaeum from the early 1860s until the 1870s and that this club participated in the sport before Turton, often proclaimed as the trailblazer but whose earliest known game did not occur until after Hulme had become defunct. Some events are recorded at the time; some may never be recorded at all; while some are 'discerned later by historians as events and others are not'.[116] In Hulme's case a lack of records in accessible regional newspapers meant that those chronicling Lancashire's early soccer activities simply did not identify or grasp what had occurred in Manchester. Accessing newspaper records beyond the date range of Hulme Athenaeum's existence provided material on the club's life in the 1860s, and this type of deep trawling of traditional records and collections is important. The abundance of data allows *longue durée* research to be performed and provides opportunities to identify trends and transformational cycles and, in Hulme's case, articles in newspapers published as much as fifty years after the club was formed have helped to identify its significance, structure and position within the full-time framework of Manchester football.

Where the specific football influence came from is not clear, but it is quite likely that the adoption of dribbling occurred after a discussion with members of the Birley family or, indeed, a close study of one of the articles or football books in existence. Peter Bailey concluded that many members of the working class used institutions like Hulme Athenaeum as a 'socially neutral locus for the formation of their clubs and teams' and, clearly, the working classes may well have used the Hulme Athenaeum primarily as a means of enabling them to play football.[117] W. H. Williams admitted that he had joined 'for the sake of the gymnasium', and the majority of members were local working men who saw the Athenaeum as a local gathering point where they could, for relatively low subscriptions, enjoy access to facilities for sport, leisure and educational purposes.[118]

Analysis of known members of the Athenaeum during the football club's existence provides recognition that the Athenaeum did appeal to a variety of working men. More than eighty men have been identified and, of these, the known occupations of those involved in footballing activities include printers, carters, warehousemen, boiler makers and clerks, while the residential status of these men also varies, with some living in lodgings, some with parents and some in rented accommodation with their own families.[119] The membership also had a wide variety of sporting interests, including athletics, fencing, rugby, cricket, wrestling and boxing, with several gaining fame as a result of their sporting endeavours. Charles Pickering was one such person who, in 1875, had the entire front page of the *Athletic News* dedicated to his sporting endeavours (Figure 5).[120] Another, gas rental collector Jim Warrington, was a noted boxer and competed in the heavyweight category at the first Manchester Athletics Festival in 1864.[121] Pickering, like the Hulme Athenaeum itself, was predominantly known for his athletic achievements, but he was also a soccer player with both the Athenaeum and Manchester's second prominent soccer club, Manchester Association Football Club in the mid-1870s. It is appropriate to note that Pickering frequently encountered the Cleggs of Sheffield, who were not only noted athletes but also important figures behind the development of soccer in that region. While it is impossible to prove how connected the men were, it is apparent that Clegg and Pickering were frequently bracketed together as combatants and it seems likely that they may have discussed soccer contests. Potentially they facilitated Hulme's games against Sheffield clubs, in which Pickering participated. Pickering's background is somewhat different to those of many other members of Hulme, as he enjoyed an upper-middle-class upbringing in contrast to the working men and lower-middle-class members. This suggests that the organisation did cross some societal boundaries in a manner that Wood proposed when he stated that football and other social games could bring 'together upon a common footing men of all classes and conditions, united for the time being by the tie of community of interest and similarity of pursuit ... clearing away the cobwebs of class prejudices, and substituting in their stead sentiments of mutual consideration and respect'.[122] In contrast,

5 Portrait of Charles Pickering, Hulme Athenaeum.

rugby tended to be played among the wealthier members of Manchester society, with clubs established in areas of relative prosperity such as Broughton, Sale, Whalley Range and Old Trafford.[123]

How often Hulme played and trained during the 1860s and early 1870s is not entirely clear. In correspondence published in *Athletic News* in 1875 concerning the formation of a new club the author discussed how he played every Saturday, and occasionally twice a week, for five consecutive seasons, indicating that games organised between members were a regular feature.[124] The names of the club and the author are not revealed; however, it is fair to assume that this was Hulme's John Nall, as he did help to organise formation meetings for the new club in 1875 and, with another former Hulme player, was appointed secretary at formation.[125]

Sometime after the 1872 Garrick match Hulme gave up competitive association football, being listed for the last time in *The Football Annual* for 1873 under secretary Charles Barton.[126] Barton had replaced John Nall as secretary in 1871 and it seems that association football was not an activity that he was as interested in as regular player Nall. Barton's name does not appear on any team list for the sport at the Athenaeum, although he appears to have been prominent with Manchester Athenaeum in subsequent years, suggesting that at a time when association football was growing across the nation the driving force required to maintain a club was not in evidence at Hulme.[127] This followed a period when Nall's address had changed to his maternal family's Platford

Hotel, indicating that his domestic circumstances may have impacted on his final period as secretary.[128] In 1871 Nall had a four-year-old son, a two-year-old daughter and a baby, having married in 1865. To ensure that sports clubs grew and developed usually required a key driving force, and often during the 1860s and 1870s, when soccer was in its infancy, that would come from the club secretary and/or the club captain. Contemporary sources suggested that for embryonic football clubs these roles were best filled by experienced cricket officials who knew how to promote and encourage others to get involved, and Nall was certainly a cricketer at the Hulme Athenaeum, whereas Barton does not appear to have been.[129]

Within a few years there were only occasional mentions or reminiscences concerning Hulme Athenaeum, which adds to the view that the entire operation had ceased around 1873. This may explain Barton's appearance as a member of the Manchester Athenaeum committee and leading to the fading of the Hulme Athenaeum name, particularly within a footballing context. A club is 'a dynamic institution; one that can grow or fail, cope or not cope with internal and external change', and in Hulme Athenaeum's case the reasons for its existence or the dedication of committee men had changed in some way.[130] There are conflicting reports of what happened to the Athenaeum, some suggesting that it had moved to premises in Drake Street and others saying that it moved to Blake Street and became the South Manchester Conservative Club, which opened at premises in Blake Street in approximately 1872.[131] The Athenaeum had certainly ceased before Turton Football Club had played their earliest known association games in the mid-1870s.[132] Had Hulme survived to this point it may well have played a prominent role in the formalising of a regionalised structure and competition. Despite this, the significance of Hulme cannot be overlooked and it is evident from their recorded games and their 1868 appeal for fixtures that there was a desire to establish a regular pattern of matches. There may not have been enough active clubs within easy travelling distance of team members' homes in south and central Manchester to sustain a strong fixture list, but there was enough activity to generate a lifetime's interest in the sport for several members. Those men in turn helped to develop and establish the game in the region in subsequent years and their interest at a time when formal association football – if later chroniclers of the game are to be believed – did not exist in Lancashire may well have sown the seeds for the sport in the region.

The active involvement of Hulme Athenaeum players in later years ensured that Manchester would become established as a prominent soccer city by the time of Hulme secretary John Nall's death. Significantly, Hulme Athenaeum deliberately engaged with lower middle-class and working men within a densely populated area of the city and it had 'just cause to be proud of the good men it has sent into the athletic world', who went on to play association football for

Manchester's next significant club from December 1875 onwards.[133] When considering the role of Hulme as part of a 'full-time' framework for the sport, rather than each game or mention of the club being an unimportant one-off event, they are actually linked and form part of a transitional phase during which the game developed and individuals were enthused and encouraged to participate, generating a lifetime involvement in some cases of the game's development.

Hulme Athenaeum was of course not the only organisation playing football during this period, as the Manchester region saw several rugby clubs come to prominence. While Hulme struggled to find competition, there were enough rugby clubs and enthusiasts to ensure that that version of football became established as the preferred form in the region. Nevertheless, football regardless of codification continued to be known and played in the parks and schools, on the streets and wherever the opportunity presented across the city. Organisations offering a field for football included Mr Templar's School at Tetlow Fold in 1864, the Athenaeum Cricket Club in Salford in 1869 and Longsight Cricket Club, which told cricketers that 'Members of the Football Club will meet every Saturday afternoon at three o'clock, weather permitting' in November 1864.[134] As with other such mentions, not enough evidence exists to determine whether Longsight Football Club was rugby or soccer based, whether it competed against other clubs, how long it lasted or whether it was merely for training purposes. As in earlier decades, football games continued to occur at fetes, festivals and excursions.[135] Larger streets, such as Oldham Road heading out of the city towards Newton Heath and Hyde Road towards Gorton, were often the leisure areas for families living in small houses in densely packed streets, and all sorts of activities were performed on these streets, including various sports; but other urbanised locations were also utilised when fields and open spaces were not available.[136] It is known that football was played in graveyards by children who used skulls as balls in the impoverished district of Angel Meadow, until the supply of skulls had been exhausted.[137] Although the practice received much criticism and is particularly abhorrent, it demonstrates that, no matter what their class, facilities or venue, young people in Manchester did know about a form of the game. Had these young graveyard participants had the right equipment and a better place to play, they might have helped the formal versions of football to develop further. As it is, it might be suggested that these young people would ultimately participate in the sport, either as spectators or players, when the formal game became more widespread.

Even the strongest and most well-known rugby clubs, such as Manchester, played a form of soccer on occasion, usually against Sheffield.[138] After one game in 1866 the reporter implied that Manchester did not understand the Sheffield rules.[139] Two years later the two sides played a game at Newhall Gardens to Sheffield rules, which the home side won by two rouges to nil, and followed this with a thirty-minute game of rugby which Manchester won by one touchdown to nothing.[140] Apparently, this time it was the Sheffield side that were in the dark about rules. Those watching were 'much amused by the difference of those from the Sheffield rules', and this was followed by a plea: 'it would conduce much to the comfort of the game if a general code of rules could be established similar to those of cricket, as towns playing matches would play with much more spirit'.[141] An eleven-a-side game between Manchester Athenaeum and Sale played near Old Trafford was reported in December 1867, while Sale also played a team from Ashton-under-Lyne that month in a game that ended with two goals each side.[142] During 1873 a call was made for Manchester Football Club to stage a showpiece game in Sheffield to promote rugby there, as 'association rules have taken firm root.'[143] By this point rugby was undoubtedly the dominant form of football in Manchester, with many significant sides and a regular fixture list: 'At Liverpool, Manchester, Hull, Rochdale, Doncaster, and Leeds, the number of rugby clubs is very large; and so much is the game in favour in the neighbourhood of Manchester that a Manchester District Association has been formed, binding all the clubs belonging to it to join the Union, and to play by its code of rules.'[144] The rugby game continued to grow, while formal association football stuttered in the region, causing the *Manchester Courier* to become strict in its publishing of football reports after receiving conflicting notes of incidents and scores.[145] The newspaper published a letter questioning the report of Weaste v Moss Side Wanderers, an alleged disputed goal and the incorrect reporting of the number of players appearing for Weaste.[146] Such disputes appeared in local newspapers throughout the mid-1870s as football of both codes remained in a developing state.

Rugby dominated the footballing coverage in the Manchester press, but local newspapers did carry association football reports for clubs and games outside of the Manchester conurbation. Major games, such as FA Cup finals, internationals and Sheffield v London contests, were reported, but so were matches played in neighbouring towns such as Macclesfield.[147] There was certainly an appetite for information on the game, or at the least a desire by the press to provide column space to the sport, but it seems likely that soccer activity was taking place in the Manchester region without coverage. In October 1874 a match report for Stockport Wellington v Fairfield Academy, which ended in a 1–1 draw played to association rules, appeared in the *Manchester Courier* and was one of only two football reports in that edition, the other being for a rugby game.[148] To date, other match reports involving Fairfield Academy have not been identified; however, it seems unlikely that this was the one and only soccer game played by the organisation. Fairfield Academy was a school for 'Young Gentlemen' within the Moravian settlement in the Droylsden area of east Manchester.[149] Sport played a key part of its offering, with reports of cricket games existing in the 1860s, while school ledgers record expenditure related to a football.[150] It seems that Fairfield had no intention of competing beyond the Manchester region, nor did they have any ambition to represent the entire city.

Hulme Athenaeum's legacy

As early as 1906 the key individuals who had originally influenced the city's football activity were being neglected by historians of the game.[151] This meant that material on Manchester's formative years was limited, while historians of the game promoted the role played in football's development by their own clubs and, as Taylor commented when considering the same individuals' analysis of the history of the Football League, their approach was to write 'uncritically and with no analytical perspective'.[152] Taylor's words are appropriate, as it was, primarily, the same men writing the history of Lancashire football as were writing about League football, and they established uncritical analyses of their clubs, committees and social networks at the expense of those from outside of their sphere.[153] These accounts set the tone for the accepted history of football within the North-West. Hulme Athenaeum pre-dated the earliest formal association clubs in the rest of Lancashire. Hulme's formative experiences of the game appear to have been connected to Sheffield and not Lancashire, while the influence of the Birley family cannot be overlooked. John Nall knew members of that family and he was the driving force seeking to establish a viable footballing community, promoting the club nationally.[154] It should be recognised that at this point there was no national competition within the sport, and Hulme Athenaeum was one of the few association clubs that existed outside of Sheffield, the public schools and the Midlands, adding to the view that the more innovative societal groups generally exist within industrialised, urban landscapes.[155]

Hulme did not survive long enough to claim their place as a founder of the game in Lancashire, and they were not influential in the formation of regional football associations, although Nall was; but they did help to create an association football culture in Manchester. Without reducing Turton's position as a pioneer in Lancashire, it has to be stressed that Hulme's organisational structures pre-dated Turton's by several years and that the team was regarded, by both its own members and leading football annuals of the era, as an association football club.[156] The lack of references to Hulme in early histories, even though it appeared in the leading football annual from 1868 to 1873, suggests that there may be similar organisations in other regions that have largely been forgotten.

The story of Hulme Athenaeum provides an example of how early association clubs may have been under-represented in discussion of the sport's progress both at a regional level and as a national game. Had Lancashire possessed an association footballing culture, Hulme Athenaeum might well have prospered, but the fact that the soccer club continued for almost a decade and played clubs in Sheffield, Sale, Bowdon and internally shows that a determination was there and, from comments appearing in the years after its demise, it is clear that it was of some significance and well respected. Hulme's greatest achievement was that it survived for so long and allowed several prominent figures, such as John Nall, Charles Pickering and Tom Barlow, to develop an interest in soccer that was to see them involved for many years, Nall playing a prominent role until his death in 1897.[157] When considering *longue durée* or the full-time concept, Hulme Athenaeum's influence was felt from 1863 through to the establishment of the Manchester County Football Association in the mid-1880s, and on to the professional game. Manchester's first trophy successes came at a time when John Nall was still an active member of the conurbation's footballing community.

Notes

1 Balaam, *Centenary* 1–5; 'Introduction of rugby football into Manchester', *Athletic News*, 24 December 1878, 2; Hewitt, *The emergence*, 58; 'Football in the north', *Athletic News*, 18 March 1876; 'Football in the north', *Athletic News*, 26 February 1876, 2.

2 E. Dunning and K. Sheard, *Barbarians, gentlemen and players* (London: Routledge, 2005), 116–117; T. Collins, *Rugby's great split: Class, culture and the origins of rugby league* (Abingdon: Routledge, 2006), 9.

3 Although match reports in the late 1860s suggest that Sale played a rugby-style version of the game, references to Sale as a soccer club continue into the 1870s. See 'Sale Football Club: resident v non-resident', *Manchester Courier*, 15 December 1868, 8; Alcock (ed.), *John Lillywhite's football annual*, 83; 'Football notes', *Athletic News*, 4 March 1876, 5.

4 See 'Letter from J. Warrington', *Manchester City News*, 14 February 1914, 6; 'Football', *Manchester Courier*, 11 December 1866, 8; M. Barak, *A century of rugby at Sale* (Manchester: Percy Brothers Limited, for Sale Football Club, 1962), 10.

5 Barak, *A century of rugby*, 10; 'Football – Garrick v Hulme Athenaeum', *Sheffield Daily Telegraph*, 4 January 1872, 3.

6 'Football notes', *Athletic News*, 4 March 1876, 5; and see note 3 above.

7 'Manchester Athenaeum', *Manchester Guardian*, 13 January 1849 1; 'Athenaeum Annual Meeting', *Manchester Guardian*, 28 January 1854, 8; 'Athenaeum Annual Meeting', *Manchester Guardian*, 3 February 1855, 8.

8 Guldi and Armitage, *The history manifesto*, 59.

9 Hodgson, 'Darwin, Veblen', 385–423.

10 Cooke and James, 'Myths, truths and pioneers'; G. Curry and E. Dunning, 'The "origins of football debate" and the early development of the game in Nottinghamshire', *Soccer and Society*, 18:7 (2017), 866–879.

11 Alcock (ed.), *John Lillywhite's football annual*, 82–83; C. W. Alcock (ed.), *The football annual* (London: Lillywhite, 1869), 66.

12 P. M. Young, *A history of British football* (London: Stanley Paul & Co Ltd., 1968), 98–99; James, *Manchester, a football history* , 26; Harvey, *Football: The first hundred*, 193.

13 For example: Swain, 'Cultural continuity', 566–582; and Lewis, 'The genesis of professional football', 21.

14 Turton Football Club's formation date is usually recorded as 1871 and this year forms part of their badge – see http://www.pitchero.com/clubs/turtonfc/. In Sutcliffe and Hargreaves, *The history of the Lancashire*, 32 the formation date is recorded as 1872.

15 'The Right Hon Sir W. T. Marriott B.A.', *The Eagle* (Cambridge: W. Metcalf & Son, 1904), Vol. 25, 73.

16 Hulme Athenaeum was recorded in every *Lillywhite's football annual* from 1868 (the first edition) through to 1873.

17 W. Vamplew, 'Playing together: Towards a theory of the British sports club in history', *Sport in Society*, 19:3 (2016), 456.

18 'The Right Hon Sir W. T. Marriott B.A.', *The Eagle*, Vol. 25, 73.

19 Hewitt, *The emergence*, 52–54.

20 'The Right Hon Sir W. T. Marriott B.A.', *The Eagle*, Vol. 25, 73..

21 Rose, 'Culture, philanthropy', 48–67.

22 *Manchester City News*, 27 January 1866, n.p.

23 'The Right Hon Sir W. T. Marriott B.A.', *The Eagle*, Vol. 25, 73..

24 Hewitt, *The emergence*, 58.

25 'Annual meeting of the Hulme Athenaeum', *Manchester Courier*, 26 January 1861, 9.

26 It was reported in ibid. that the 'St. George's Club' name was 'not sufficiently Catholic to please members, other titles were suggested, and at last the name of the "Hulme Athenaeum" met with general concurrence'.

27 'St. George's Club, Hulme', *Manchester Courier*, 17 November 1860, 7.

28 Cunningham, *Leisure*, 83.

29 F. Engels *The condition of the working class in England*, ed. D. McLellan (Oxford: Oxford University Press, 2009), 73. The book was originally published in German in 1845, with English editions published New York (1887) and London (1891).

30 M. Kennedy, *Portrait of Manchester* (London: Robert Hale, 1970), 57.

31 Hewitt, *The emergence*, 52–54.

32 'Annual meeting of the Hulme Athenaeum', *Manchester Courier*, 26 January 1861, 9.

33 'Hulme Athenaeum', *Manchester Courier*, 7 February 1863, 9.

34 'Hulme Athenaeum', *Manchester Courier*, 24 October 1863, 9.

35 Examples include 'Manchester grand athletic festival', *Manchester Courier*, 29 August 1864, 3; 'Cricket', *Manchester Courier*, 15 August 1863, 11; and 'St Michael's Institute and Hulme Athenaeum Gymnastic Club', *Manchester Courier*, 7 October 1865, 6.

36 *Rossall School 1869* (Fleetwood: W. Porter, 1869), 11.

37 Alcock (ed.), *John Lillywhite's football annual*, 82; *Manchester City News*, 14 February 1914, 6.

38 *Letters on the Factory Act, as it affects the cotton manufacture, addressed to the Right Honourable the President of the Board of Trade by Nassau W Senior Esq* (London: B. Fellows, 1837), 36–37.

39 Cricket reports exist for games from the 1850s, such as 'Cricket', *Manchester Times*, 26 April 1856, 7 and 'Sporting intelligence', *Manchester Weekly Times*, 11 August 1866, 7.

40 'I remember', *Manchester City News*, 21 March 1914, 5. No family relationship between John Pooley and Fred Pooley has, as yet, been established.

41 A. J. Kidd, 'Charity organization and the unemployed in Manchester c.1870–1914', *Social History*, 9:1 (1984), 52.

42 *Manchester City News*, 14 February 1914, 6.

43 For example, Hugh Birley attended the annual soirée in 1866. 'St Michael's Institute and Hulme Athenaeum – Annual soiree', *Manchester Courier*, 6 November 1866, 1.

44 'A Freehold Plot of Land', *Manchester Guardian*, 13 November 1855, 1; P. Swain, 'Benjamin Bradley Hart, the all-England sprint champion of the 1820s and 30s', in D. Day (ed.), *Pedestrianism* (Crewe: MMU Sport and Leisure History 2014), 35–36.

45 'Testimonial to Mr Matthew Nall', *Manchester Guardian*, 31 December 1856, 3.

46 G. S. Law, 'Manchester politics 1885–1906' (PhD dissertation, University of Pennsylvania, 1975), 295–296.

47 'Representation of Manchester', *Manchester Guardian*, 8 July 1865, 7.

48 *Manchester Courier*, 30 June 1860, 1.

49 Lawson, *Letters to the young*, 58.

50 S. J. Oldfield, 'The Manchester Milers 1850–1870', in D. Day (ed.), *Pedestrianism* (Crewe: MMU Sport and Leisure History, 2014), 81; B. Harrison, *Drink and the Victorians: The temperance question in England 1815–1872* (London: Faber and Faber, 1971).

51 Census returns, John Nall 1861, https//:www.findmypast.co.uk (RG 9/2894).

52 'Married', *Manchester Guardian*, 27 September 1865, 4;, Marriage records, 23 September 1865, https//:www.findmypast.co.uk; 'Hulme Athenaeum Football Club', *Manchester Guardian*, 28 November 1868, 1; Alcock (ed.), *John Lillywhite's football annual*, 83.

53 'Deaths', *Manchester Guardian*, 6 November 1948, 3.

54 'No. 91, Yarburgh Street', *Manchester Guardian*, 1 November 1876, 3; 'Alexandra Park', *Manchester Guardian*, 27 June 1888, 2.

55 Rose, 'Culture, philanthropy', 103.

56 'Hulme Athenaeum', *Manchester Courier*, 7 February 1863, 9.

57 'Hulme Athenaeum', *Manchester Guardian*, 4 November 1865, 4; Alcock (ed.), *John Lillywhite's football annual*, 83.

58 For example, both Manchester Association and Hulme Athenaeum utilised the venue on occasion. 'Football', *Athletic News*, 23 October 1875, 5.

59 *The Rules of the Manchester District Football Association* (Ashton-under-Lyne: William Brown and Son, 1887), 3; *The Sportsman's year book for 1880* (London: Cassell, Petter, Galpin & Co.), 166.

60 For example, 'Commencement of the football season', *Sheffield Independent*, 10 October 1874, 10; 'Proposed changes in London Association rules', *Sheffield Independent*, 6 February 1875, 7; 'Football: Turton v Egerton', *Bolton Evening News*, 17 November 1874, 3.

61 Braudel, *On history*, 84.

62 'Hulme Athenaeum', *Manchester Guardian*, 4 November 1865, 4; Alcock (ed.), *John Lillywhite's football annual*, 83.

63 'St Michael's Institute and Hulme Athenaeum Gymnastic Club', *Manchester Guardian*, 1 October 1864, 1.

64 Dunning and Sheard, *Barbarians*, 91.

65 G. Curry and E. Dunning, 'The problem with revisionism: How new data on the origins of modern football have led to hasty conclusions', *Soccer and Society*, 14:4 (2013), 13–14.

66 Harvey, *Football: The first hundred*, 52–54.

67 'Football in the north', *Athletic News*, 26 February 1876, 2.

68 Dunning and Sheard, *Barbarians*, 116–117.

69 Hewitt, *The emergence*, 64–65.

70 'Introduction of rugby football into Manchester', *Athletic News*, 24 December 1878, 2.

71 'Stoke v Birch (Manchester)', *Staffordshire Sentinel*, 29 April 1878, 3.

72 Ibid.

73 'Football in the north', *Athletic News*, 18 March 1876, 2.

74 'Our library table: Routledge's handbook of football', *The Athenaeum*, 23 November 1867, 683.

75 F. Wood, *Beeton's football* (London: Frederick Warne & Co, 1865), 6.

76 B. Templar, *Questions for school boards: a pamphlet upon the important questions of compulsory education, the establishment of free schools, the use of the bible, moral and religious instruction, etc.* (London: Simpkin, Marshall & Co, 1871), 8–9.

77 P. Swain, 'Football club formation and the leisure class, 1857–1870', *International Journal of the History of Sport*, 34:7–8 (2017), 498–516.

78 'Football – Garrick v Hulme Athenaeum', *Sheffield Daily Telegraph*, 4 January 1872, 3.

79 Alcock, *John Lillywhite's football annual* (1869), 49 reports a game played on 7 November 1867; and 'Football', *Manchester Courier*, 11 December 1866, 8 lists a Sale victory but not the score.

80 Games with Hulme Athenaeum took place within two years of Hulme being established in 1863. See 'Letter from J. Warrington', *Manchester City News*, 14 February 1914, 6; 'Football', *Manchester Courier*, 11 December 1866, 8; Barak, *A century of rugby*, 10.

81 Barak, *A century of rugby*, 10; 'Football – Garrick v Hulme Athenaeum', *Sheffield Daily Telegraph*, 4 January 1872, 3.

82 Harvey, *Football: The first hundred*.

83 Wood, *Beeton's football*, 6–8. This book suggested a series of rules for adoption nationwide and was available in Manchester during the 1860s.

84 Ibid., 24; the string crossbar used on the original goals was replaced by tape for the

first-ever FA cup final in 1872. The crossbar was finally made compulsory in the FA rules of 1882, which specified that it should be at a height of eight feet above the ground. According to *News of the World Football Annual 1966–67* (London: News of the World, 1966), 175 and all subsequent editions, crossbars were introduced in 1875.

85 For a review of football styles played during these years see G. Kitching, 'Modern sport: Society and competition', *History Workshop Journal*, 79:1 (2015), 127–153.
86 Wood, *Beeton's football*, 38.
87 Thomas Windsor's copy survives, and research is ongoing into his sporting activities. He was living in central Manchester in 1861 and newspaper reports confirm his role as librarian to the Literature and Philosophical Society.
88 'Football', *Manchester Courier*, 20 November 1866, 3.
89 Wood, *Beeton's football*, 6.
90 'Football', *Manchester Courier*, 20 November 1866, 3
91 'The Manchester Courier: published daily', *Manchester Courier*, 29 May 1866, 2.
92 C. W. Alcock (ed.), *John Lillywhite's football annual* (London: Lillywhite, 1870), 56–8; 'Football v Cricket', *Manchester Courier*, 21 May 1867, 7.
93 'Manchester Athletic Festival', *Manchester Courier*, 21 September 1864, 3.
94 Wood, *Beeton's football*, 24–26.
95 'Sketch of Stockport', *Manchester Courier*, 7 April 1860, 7; 'Manchester Athletic Festival', *Manchester Courier*, 21September 1864, 3; 'Whitsuntide festivities', *Manchester Courier*, 19 May 1866, 6.
96 Kitching, '"Old" football', 1738.
97 Articles for a working men's institute in Hulme appeared in the same week as Hulme Athenaeum held a significant meeting. These were two separate organisations, with the Athenaeum aiming for a membership comprising young warehousemen, as opposed to older working men of all types at the institute. See 'Hulme Working Men's Institution', *Manchester Guardian*, 23 October 1863, 2; 'Hulme Athenaeum', *Manchester Courier*, 24 October 1863, 9; and 'Hulme Athenaeum', *Manchester Courier*, 1 February 1863, 9.
98 'Working men's institute', *Manchester Guardian*, 25 November 1861, 2.
99 *Manchester City News*, 31 January 1914, 2.
100 *Manchester City News*, 14 February 1914, 6.
101 *Manchester City News*, 31 January 1914, 2.
102 'This day: Garrick Football Club', *Sheffield Independent*, 27 December 1869, 1; 'This day: Garrick Football Club', *Sheffield Independent*, 19 February 1870, 1; 'Fixtures', *Bell's Life in London and Sporting Chronicle*, 10 December 1870, 4; 'Football – Garrick v Hulme Athenaeum', *Sheffield Daily Telegraph*, 4 January 1872, 3.
103 'This day: Garrick Football Club', *Sheffield Independent*, 27 December 1869, 1.
104 'Football: Manchester Athenaeum v Sheffield Garrick', *Sheffield Daily Telegraph*, 20 February 1871, 3.
105 'Football notes', *Sporting Gazette*, 4 February 1871, 71.
106 'Football – Garrick v Hulme Athenaeum', *Sheffield Daily Telegraph*, 4 January 1872, 3.

107 For example, 'Football: Manchester Athenaeum v Sheffield Garrick', *Sheffield Daily Telegraph*, 20 February 1871, 3; 'Football notes', *Sporting Gazette*, 4 February 1871, 71; 'Football – Garrick v Hulme Athenaeum', *Sheffield Daily Telegraph*, 4 January 1872, 3; 'Football – Garrick (Sheffield) v Hulme Athenaeum (Manchester)', *Sheffield Independent*, 8 January 1870, 10.

108 'This day: Garrick Football Club', *Sheffield Independent*, 27 December 1869, 1; 'This day: Garrick Football Club', *Sheffield Independent*, 19 February 1870, 1; and 'Fixtures', *Bell's Life in London and Sporting Chronicle*, 10 December 1870, 4.

109 Russell, 'Sporting Manchester', 7.

110 'Football', *Sheffield and Rotherham Independent*, 11 March 1872, 4.

111 'Letter from J. Warrington', *Manchester City News*, 14 February 1914, 6.

112 The local studies street map collection at Manchester University has been explored extensively and compared with contemporary reports and later reminiscences by players to ensure triangulation of material.

113 *Manchester City News*, 14 February 1914, 6.

114 For example, Jim Warrington focused his energies on rowing from approximately 1864, and began to drift away from the club.

115 'The Hulme Athenaeum Football Club', *Manchester Guardian*, 10 October 1867, 1.

116 Wallerstein, *Unthinking social science*, 137.

117 Bailey, *Leisure and class*, 139.

118 *Manchester City News*, 31 January 1914, 2; in excess of eighty active members of the Hulme Athenaeum from 1863 to 1873 have been identified from contemporary newspaper reports, with the majority of these participating in multiple sports.

119 A database of Hulme Athenaeum players and members has been established based on census records, advertisements and council poor rate records. These show, for example, that Alan Grattan was renting a property for 5 shillings per week in 1876.

120 'Eminent athletes No. IV – CF Pickering, Manchester', *Athletic News*, 26 June 1875, 1.

121 Census returns, James Warrington 1871, https//:www.findmypast.co.uk (RG 10/4012); *Manchester City News*, 14 February 1914, 6.

122 Wood, *Beeton's football*, 15–16.

123 Dunning and Sheard, *Barbarians*, 116–117; Collins, *Rugby's great split*, 9; Hewitt, *The emergence*, 58.

124 'To the editor of the Athletic News', *Athletic News*, 23 October 1875, 4; 'Association football', *Athletic News*, 30 October 1875, 4.

125 'Association football', *Athletic News*, 30 October 1875, 4.

126 C. W. Alcock (ed.), *The football annual* (London: Lillywhite, 1873), 78.

127 'Manchester Athenaeum Gymnastic Club', *Athletic News*, 12 October 1881, 7.

128 Alcock (ed.), *The football annual* (1873), 57.

129 Wood, *Beeton's football*, 27–28.

130 Vamplew, 'Playing together', 464.

131 The Athenaeum did move to Drake Street by February 1865, and the Conservative Club did become established at Blake Street circa 1872, which could fit with the disappearance of the name Hulme Athenaeum from contemporary records around

that time. Some of the facilities were similar to those offered at the Athenaeum and some of the Conservative officials were also Athenaeum members, although the leading figures within Hulme's community at this time tended to be involved with multiple organisations. 'Lecture by JT Slugg', *Manchester Courier*, 14 February 1865, 1; *Manchester City News*, 31 January 1914, 2; *Manchester City News*, 7 February 1914, 12; *Manchester City News*, 14 February 1914, 6.

132 A report of Turton playing to 'London Association rules', assumed to be FA rules, appears in 1874: 'Football: Turton v Egerton', *Bolton Evening News*, 17 November 1874, 3. By the summer of 1875 it was reported that Turton had played ten games to London Association rules that season, presumably meaning FA rules, with a game with Egerton being the first. See 'Turton Football Club', *Bolton Evening News*, 19 March 1875, 3.

133 'Association football', *Athletic News*, 30 October 1875, 5; 'Association football for Manchester', *Athletic News*, 6 November 1875, 3.

134 'Holly Bank, Tetlow Fold', *Manchester Guardian*, 9 July 1864, 8; 'Longsight Cricket Club – notice', *Manchester Guardian*, 12 November 1864, 1; and 'A cricket club in the county court', *Manchester Guardian*, 9 June 1869, 6.

135 'Third Manchester Regiment', *Manchester Courier*, 14 October 1865, 11; and 'Church of England – St. Philip's, Hulme', *Manchester Courier*, 23 May 1866, 3.

136 'Our public footpaths', *Manchester Guardian*, 26 October 1859, 3.

137 'A disgrace to Manchester', *Manchester Guardian*, 20 April 1865, 4; 'The nuisance at the new burying ground', *Manchester Courier*, 9 October 1866, 3; and 'St. Michael's burying ground, Angel Meadow', *Manchester Times*, 24 November 1866, 5.

138 'Football in the north, Second Series', *Athletic News*, 23 December 1876, 2.

139 'Football – Sheffield v Manchester', *Sheffield Daily Telegraph*, 11 December 1866, 8.

140 'Manchester v Sheffield', *Bell's Life in London and Sporting Chronicle*, 4 April 1868, 7.

141 'Football – Sheffield v Manchester', *Sheffield Daily Telegraph*, 4 April 1868, 10.

142 *Sportsman*, 12 December 1867; 'Football – Sale v Ashton-under-Lyne', *Manchester Courier*, 31 December 1867, 7.

143 'Manchester club v combined team', *Bell's Life in London and Sporting Chronicle*, 12 April 1873, 9.

144 'Football – The past season', *Bell's Life in London and Sporting Chronicle*, 5 April 1873, 4.

145 'Football', *Manchester Courier*, 4 March 1874, 7.

146 'To the editor of the Manchester Courier', *Manchester Courier*, 4 March 1874, 7.

147 'Eighth Cheshire Rifles v Stoke-upon-Trent (Association rules, thirteen a side)', *Manchester Courier*, 10 November 1874, 7; and 'Sheffield v London', *Manchester Courier*, 6 April 1874, 6.

148 'Football', *Manchester Courier*, 19 October 1874, 7.

149 'Fairfield Academy (Moravian)', *Manchester Guardian*, 6 January 1869, 1.

150 'Fairfield v Fairfield Academy', *Manchester Courier*, 15 September 1868, 7.

151 W. MacGregor, *The book of football* (London: Amalgamated Press, 1906); Sutcliffe and Hargreaves, *The history of the Lancashire*, 17–18.
152 M. Taylor, *The leaguers: The making of professional football in England, 1900–1939* (Liverpool: Liverpool University Press, 2005), 21.
153 Ibid., 21; MacGregor, *The book of football*; Sutcliffe and Hargreaves, *The history of the Lancashire*.
154 Alcock (ed.), *John Lillywhite's football annual*, 83.
155 Lewis, 'Innovation not invention', 481.
156 Sutcliffe and Hargreaves, *The history of the Lancashire*, 17.
157 Lancashire Archives, DDX2708, Minutes of the Lancashire Football Association, 29 June 1889–15 April 1897.

4

Footballing communities

During the decade of Hulme Athenaeum's existence the population of Manchester continued to grow, reaching over 400,000 by 1871. This exacerbated existing problems such as overcrowding in the slum areas, and although most cellar dwellings had gone by 1874, it would be another forty years until the majority of the back-to-back houses had been demolished.[1] The problems were those of a big commercial city, and polluted Manchester epitomised all that was socially bad in the effects of the Industrial Revolution.[2] The nature of the city's growth created a multi-layered society in which many factors impacted on the relationships between classes. Mancunians with a desire for self-improvement and to make life more tolerable established new social groups,[3] although whether this was evident within the sporting context is debatable. Hulme Athenaeum appeared to support that suggestion, but the organisation had collapsed by 1873 and Manchester's main team sport, rugby football, appeared to be controlled by an elite consisting mainly of middle-class enthusiasts and former public schoolboys. Nonetheless, the rugby community did engage across class boundaries and continued to grow. While rugby remained the conurbation's most prominent team sport, association football struggled for attention, being kept alive by a small band of soccer enthusiasts. Assisted by John Nall's driving force, Hulme Athenaeum had ignited an interest, but in the two years following its demise Manchester seems to have been bereft of a club. There was also criticism from high-ranking community leaders, and the bishop of Manchester commented that in general sport was given too much attention and significance: 'the development of athletic habits' had negatively affected the youth and 'people would say that the thing was lamentably over done'.[4] He was also critical of the role of gambling, which was becoming a 'growing evil' in football – although the reporting made no distinction between the association and rugby formats.[5] In later weeks the bishop added that 'he had known parents, and those not the wisest, who felt more pleasure in a boy coming home from the University with a silver scull or prize for football than if he had gained the Arnold scholarship at Balliol and he thought sport was being pushed "to too great an extreme".'[6] His criticism, published in *Athletic News*, Manchester's leading sports newspaper, supports Bailey's view that sporting churchmen remained a rarity at this time.[7]

Gambling had helped to generate a thriving sporting culture – pedestrianism was particularly strong in Manchester – laying the foundation for the later enthusiasm for organised team games. But issues caused by gambling would inevitably be considered a threat by the bishop.[8]

The bishop's comments came at a time when association football was increasing in popularity across Lancashire, and two years after a writer for *Athletic News* expressed that 'It is somewhat singular that the Eton football game, which used to have half a dozen teams playing it five years ago, should have lost such favour that eighteen months since Manchester was entirely without a club under Association rules.'[9] That report, in itself an exaggeration, can be used to illustrate that there was a significant difference between the two forms of football. Despite the greater frequency of match reports and advertisements, by 1875 almost all association football in Manchester had ceased, if the *Athletic News'* comments are accepted.[10] The newspaper was inaccurate; nonetheless, the sport was not as prevalent as it had been. The *Athletic News* was a boost to all forms of football and actively encouraged rugby clubs to participate in the association game during 1875; and, significantly, it was a Manchester-produced publication, providing Mancunian residents with the opportunity to understand the variety of sports being played in the region and beyond.[11] The newspaper carried significant information about sporting organisations across the country, although it tended to be biased towards the North and Scotland in its formative years. Also, via its editorials and letters columns it often proposed rule changes and encouraged participation in developing sports, allowing its readers to promote new sports clubs.[12] At the start of October 1875, under the pseudonym 'An Old Wanderer', *Athletic News* published a letter from a former Nottingham Forest footballer, Fitzroy Norris, calling for a meeting to be held to discuss the formation of a Manchester-based soccer club: 'so that I may see how many admirers of the Association game there are in Manchester, and how many will play the rules, and if I have sufficient encouragement to establish a good club'.[13]

Norris did not aim his letter at a specific class of people, nor place any restrictions on membership. His suggestion was simply to form a football club, and was aimed at those who participated in athletics, which in 1870s Manchester was a very popular activity, particularly with the working and middle classes.[14] Pedestrianism, with its associated gambling, wagers and prize money, was not a sport which the upper classes would have approved of, and Norris would have been aware of this. In Manchester the links between athletics and association football were strong, and Fitzroy Norris, Jonathan Nall and Charles Pickering all involved in athletics, Norris later competing under the club name of Manchester Association Football Club.[15] If Norris wanted to create a football team for athletes to keep fit during the winter, it was inevitable that his target audience would cross class divisions – but also be of interest to the former Hulme Athenaeum men.

Fitzroy Norris

Developing a framework for Manchester's footballing development inevitably focuses on structures, the regional governing body and the clubs established, but it is also important to consider individuals, particularly during the region's formative footballing years. Individuals cross time periods, just as clubs do (in some cases more so), and they also traverse clubs, communities and organisations. Fitzroy Norris, like John Nall before him, is critical in aiding our understanding of football's growth in Manchester.

Thomas Valentine Fitzroy Norris, generally known as Fitzroy, was born in Ledbury, Herefordshire, in 1847. His parents were married in Holborn in 1845 and his father was a commercial traveller who, by 1863, is recorded as being employed by the brewer Ind Coope & Co.[16] His two grandfathers were recorded as a cooper and a gardener. Census records show that by 1851 Fitzroy was living with his uncle and aunt in Ledbury, where his uncle was the inn-keeper of the Talbot Inn. The brewing industry had been central to the family's livelihood for a number of years and Fitzroy's grandfather had been landlord at the Talbot in the early 1840s. Fitzroy's time there was to ensure stability in his family life while his father travelled as a brewery salesman. If stability is what the family wanted for the young Fitzroy, it was not to be. In 1851 his uncle Thomas died suddenly of typhus fever, forcing the family to put the Talbot Inn out to rent.[17] The next census, in 1861, records Fitzroy as living with his parents in the St Clements area of Worcester, the family now comprised of a daughter and four sons aged between five and fourteen.[18] It is not known what schooling Fitzroy received, but in 1863 his younger brother John was attending a school in St Clements managed by 'a person named Brewer'.[19] The family were also known to attend church, presumably St Clements, close to their residence, and that church held a number of events each year which would end with the children of the parish playing various sports, 'cricket, ball, racing' etc., in a field nearby.[20]

In 1871 Fitzroy Norris was recorded as an accountant lodging in a house on Moor Street, Burton-on-Trent. How he came to be in Burton it is not known, but the location implies a connection with his father's employer, Ind Coope, as their Burton brewery was a short walk from Norris's home. It can be surmised that Fitzroy began working for Ind Coope through his family connections and moved to Burton as his career developed.[21] His signature 'An Old Wanderer' in the *Athletic News* may have been because of the travelling nature of his work. Alternatively, he may have played football for the Wanderers or Burton Wanderers (founded in 1871) association football teams, although no evidence for this has been found to date.[22] However, Norris may have been an active sportsman while in Burton, as a cricket match report exists detailing a game between office staff of Ind Coope and the staff of Worthington's. A person by the name of T. Norris – potentially standing for Thomas Norris, a name under which Fitzroy occasionally appeared – played in that match.[23] Ind Coope was known to have an active sports committee, and games of football – typically a form of rugby, but descriptions indicate some games may have been association based – were played during the 1860s and early 1870s.[24] Whether Norris participated in football activity in Burton is not clear but, as Possing comments, 'it must be stressed that a human individual is not conceivable without the surrounding society', and it is likely that Norris would have been influenced by what he saw and experienced throughout his life, especially in this period when he was living away from his family and establishing his own life.[25]

The wandering nature of Norris's life came to the fore again as the 1870s progressed. From Burton, approximately twenty-eight miles from Nottingham, Norris became involved with Nottingham Forest. At Forest he played in at least thirteen games, his first being on 18 January 1873 against Burton-on-Trent at the Burton Cricket Ground. Whether Norris was living in Burton at the time is not known, but the location of this match raises some questions.[26] Forest was a progressive club and included Sam Widdowson, who later played for England. Norris would have enjoyed a positive experience of how the game could be played and would have seen the benefits which the sport could bring, especially when he was a member of the side that faced 1872 FA Cup finalists the Royal Engineers.[27] Forest lost that game 2–1 but the Engineers' captain, Major Francis Marindin, claimed that it was the best game his team had ever been involved with in the North.[28] Norris's own style of play was not particularly commented on in the few match reports that exist, but he was commended for his skills in a game with Sheffield's Norfolk club in 1874.[29] Norris's last known game for Forest was against Mansfield in February 1874. Employment opportunities caused him to move further north, and while his specific employment is not recorded his address in 1875, possibly his business address, was 6 Short Street, Tib Street, Manchester.[30] This street survives today and has the appearance of a back entry between the once-popular commercial thoroughfares of Oldham Street and Tib Street in the northern quarter area of the city centre.

When Norris arrived in Manchester he discovered that whereas Nottingham had a thriving association football community with multiple clubs, Manchester's soccer culture was still some way behind those of Nottingham, Sheffield and Stoke, despite the efforts of John Nall. Norris's October 1875 letter suggesting a new association club signified his belief that the sport should be popularised and that it was superior to rugby. He made disparaging comments about the rival code, such as: 'as the Unionists play it is not football at all, brute force and wrestling being the chief characteristics'.[31] The animosity between those promoting the rival codes continued for a number of years and was not helpful to the development of association football, and Norris, by his actions and comments, may have unwittingly damaged the growth of his preferred version of the game. Norris was determined to see association football develop in the city and he spoke 'in eulogistic terms' about the sport and the good that 'it afforded running men during the slack season'.[32]

Norris's appeal produced interest from Mancunians, but a review of newspaper reports from this period identifies that John Nall was also keen to develop a new club, and it may well be that it was Nall who organised the actual meeting that was staged to discuss establishing a club. Whereas Hulme Athenaeum had attempted to adopt a game that was still, in many respects, in its infancy, the situation in 1875 was somewhat different. Significantly, as Norris's letter had indicated, the FA Cup was now in operation and beginning to prove popular. In addition, he had had the experience of playing alongside some of the pioneering figures of the game during his time at Nottingham and he knew what an association football team could look like, believing passionately in the association game. It should be noted that the fixture list for 23 October 1875 listed thirteen football games locally, all of which were a version of rugby. These were spread across the Manchester region and included teams from Broughton, Sale, Moss Side, Birch, Bury, Chorlton, Levenshulme, Ordsall, Greenheys, Cheetham Hill, Stretford, Altrincham and Stalybridge.[33] This was a typical day's fixtures.

Nall's role as football secretary at the Hulme Athenaeum had ended around 1871–72 and it is unclear what involvement he had enjoyed with the sport in the immediate aftermath. However, it seems likely that he would have been involved with other sports organisations during the period 1872–75; or he may have been active with some of the sporting activities pursued at the Platford Hotel, which had for a time been recorded as the secretarial address of the Hulme Athenaeum. The Platford was at the centre of leisure activities from the 1850s through to the twentieth century, with a variety of sporting organisations and community clubs holding meetings there, including the Manchester Clifford Cricket Club, of which John Nall's brother James was the secretary.[34] Clifford also established an association football club at the Platford in 1884, with which the Nalls may have been involved.[35] The Platford family connection with sport pre-dated their time at the Platford Hotel; indeed, the public house took the family's name so as to ensure that locals recognised that the venue would continue the sporting and leisure activities that had existed at their earlier venue, the White House Gardens, where a cricket ground was established in 1833 and wrestling occurred.[36] In 1852 James Platford built the Platford Hotel in front of the White House Gardens, which was later demolished and built over. By 1871 a professional billiards player was renting a room at the hotel, and John Nall had listed it as his home address.[37] When the renowned Lancashire county cricketer Richard Barlow advertised his sports shop he referred to its proximity to the Platford Hotel, which suggests that its reputation was well known to sports enthusiasts.

Nall's strengths came to the fore during the formative weeks for Manchester Association and he may have been the author of a letter to the *Athletic News* in which the writer offered to provide goalposts and other equipment (presumably from his time at Hulme Athenaeum and possibly stored at the Platford Hotel).[38] That letter appeared three weeks after Norris's initial letter and the author explained his interest in the game and offered to provide assistance: 'I shall only be too glad to assist 'Old Wanderer' in his proposals. I will go so far as to say that if he can provide a field for practice, I will find the ball, goal posts, flags &c., and then we can invite the athletes at large; in fact, invite all eligible persons to come and participate in the opening game free of charge.'[39] The writer added that he hoped 'the young blood of Manchester, who have an aversion to the rough "horse play of Rugby" will soon learn to love the Association rules'. Although the author did not reveal his name, the letter appears to have been from Nall, as he mentioned that he had had five years' active involvement with the game. It seems unlikely that the writer could have been anyone but an Athenaeum player, unless, of course, they were a new arrival to Manchester with experience of the game from outside the region who also happened to have all the necessary equipment to hand. Further evidence suggests it was Nall because he chaired the first meeting of the new club at the Prince of Wales Hotel in Moss Side and organised for the second meeting to occur at the Platford Hotel.[40] Both meetings had been advertised beforehand in the *Manchester Guardian*.[41] On 23 October the advertisement stated: 'Football – Association Rules. Gentlemen wishful to join a club to play according to the above rules are invited to attend a meeting at the Prince of Wales Hotel, Moss Side, on Wednesday next, October 27, at 8.30p.m.' That first meeting elected Nall and former Hulme Athenaeum team mate Charles Pickering as honorary secretaries, with the *Athletic News* clearly mentioning they were former Hulme Athenaeum players, indicating an awareness of the sport's history.[42] The following month *Bell's Life in London and Sporting Chronicle* focused on the involvement, during this period of the club's formation, of Pickering 'of hurdle-racing fame, who, we believe, has years ago been celebrated as an Association player'.[43] From the brief report in the *Athletic News* it is unclear whether Fitzroy Norris attended the meeting. His second letter on the subject, which revealed his name and address, was dated 27 October, the same date as the inaugural meeting of the new club, and was published in the 30 October edition of the newspaper.[44] The editor commented at the foot of Norris's letter: 'Our correspondent will see from another portion of our paper that an Association Club for Manchester has been already initiated.' Whether it was Nall or Norris who organised the first meeting is immaterial; however, it is significant that they shared a desire to resurrect the sport in the city at this time, and they ultimately worked together.

Manchester Association

During the formative weeks of Manchester Association Football Club 35-year-old John Nall worked closely with 29-year-old Fitzroy Norris on establishing the club. Whether the two men knew each other already is not known, and no evidence has been found suggesting they did meet prior to October 1875. However, both men had an interest in other sports and were involved with athletics, and they both lived in Hulme for a period.[45]

After the second meeting the *Athletic News* included positive coverage of the events and commented that 'many men attended, amongst them being noticed the old blood of the "Hulme Athenaeum Club"'. Over thirty people attended the meeting, and although reports did not quantify how many were former Hulme members, the *Athletic News*'s tone suggested that there were quite a few.[46] A committee of six was set up and included at least four former Athenaeum players (Sanderson, Pickering, Nall and former captain Barlow). The other two committee men, Haigh and Railton, have so far not been identified on the existing detailed Hulme match reports, but it may be that they had also been members, although 18-year-old Railton was perhaps too young to have been a member of the Athenaeum team. He did, however, have links with Manchester FC and appears on rugby reports.[47] Pickering was known as a good footballer, while Nall's administrative and organisational skills would have been of benefit.

Nall, Pickering and others knew each other via the Hulme Athenaeum and these connections allowed the new organisation, supplemented by Fitzroy Norris and others experienced in the sport from other regions, to make progress. The *Athletic News* coverage of the soccer meeting described it as an organised affair, adding: 'The subscription to the club – which will be called the "Manchester Association Football Club" – will be 5s per season, payable in advance.' It also stated that the club had already arranged for a field close to Alexandra Park, where Hulme had played, that Stuart G. Smith had been appointed secretary and that a practice match had been organised for 13 November 1875. The article outlined the colours to be worn – 'scarlet and black hoops' – and mentioned that the football kit would be obtained from Charles Pickering's hosier business in Deansgate.[48] However the facts are reviewed, at the birth of Manchester Association Football Club the influence of Hulme Athenaeum was strong – including the use of Nall's maternal family's Platford Hotel – further demonstrating a continuity that early chroniclers of the game did not understand.[49] The importance of community and place in the establishment of football and of clubs should be recognised; and, in the case of Manchester's footballing development, the involvement of former Athenaeum members Nall and Pickering, together with the others, demonstrates how Manchester's soccer development is a continuum from the early 1860s through to the birth of teams in the 1870s. As will be documented in later chapters, those connections and influences continued into the twentieth century. Manchester may not have been prominent at the beginning of professional football and the Football League in the 1880s, but it did have individuals who were instrumental in developing clubs locally a decade before teams like Turton played their earliest known games and, more importantly, they remained active as the sport became transformed into a professional one. They worked with others arriving in the region to develop new clubs. Across the country football relied on dedicated enthusiasts to keep the sport progressing and, while clubs may have died along the way, enthusiasm for the sport grew. The specific formation dates of clubs are important, as are written accounts of the game's history; however, what matter most are the individuals who worked hard to generate interest and enthusiasm within communities.

It has been said that 'Turton F.C. were the pioneers who introduced FA rules to the seminal clubs, many of them not transitory but still in existence today' and that they adopted the rules of the 'London Football Association', meaning the FA, in August 1874, having previously utilised Harrow rules.[50] It appears that the first game utilising FA rules was staged against Egerton; however, the club's own history documents that it was not until a meeting on 6 October 1876, a year after Manchester Association first played to FA rules, that a resolution was passed that the Darwen v Turton match would be played 'according to the Association rules as interpreted by the London Association' and that the game would be called off if Darwen did not agree.[51] From that point on Turton claimed to be 'not only the pioneers but the jealous guardians of the right interpretation of the rules. As new clubs sprang up in Bolton, Darwen, and Blackburn, they were anxious to put themselves under the guidance of the Turton Football Club.'[52] This may be true for an area of Lancashire including Blackburn, Bolton and Darwen, but it has to be stressed that Manchester Association, which included Hulme Athenaeum men who had claimed to use FA rules a few years earlier, was playing football to FA rules without direct influence from Turton in 1875. According to Swain, much of the Turton area was 'virtually inaccessible' at this time and 'Football games, initially, would have been few and far between and even when played who would report them to the press – which existed in Bolton, Darwen and Blackburn and not in Turton'.[53] The *Bolton Evening News* had been covering Turton games since 1874 and it seems logical that any earlier activity would also have been reported. It must be reiterated that Manchester's influences during the mid-1870s did not come from Turton, and that it was the influence of experienced football participants from Nottingham Forest and Hulme Athenaeum, where members of the Birley family attended meetings, that was important. No one should under-estimate the role of Turton, the Lancashire FA and men like 'W.T. Dixon from Turton F.C., Thomas Hindle from Darwen F.C. and John

Lewis from Blackburn Rovers' in football's growth and professionalism in later years; however, nor should the role of the men who established Manchester's earliest association clubs in the 1860s and 1870s be overlooked. Those clubs may not have survived, but their existence and influence were significant. It is obvious we know which football clubs were to prevail, and this can shape our thinking; but we must avoid focusing on what has survived and instead dig deeper to uncover what shaped our history. Turton, which still claims to be the oldest association club in Lancashire, has itself been reformed over the years and, as Swain points out, had 'fallen by the wayside' by 1928.[54] Of the survivors locally, Bolton Wanderers were the first of the Greater Manchester sides to be formed when, in 1874, a teacher at Christ Church called a meeting of teachers and other young men. From that meeting Christ Church Football Club was formed, and in 1877 it changed its name to Bolton Wanderers. However, in 1894 the Bolton newspaper *The Football Field* claimed that Christ Church had played rugby for its first two years of existence, while other sources claim that the club alternated codes depending on the wishes of their opponents. It should be noted that Turton claim to have provided Christ Church with their FA-based rules.[55]

It is apparent from the scant reporting of Turton in the sporting and regional press prior to the formation of Manchester Association that their situation was not known or understood in Manchester at this time and, as Swain has discussed, the geography of the area limited opportunities for participation. A growing city like Manchester had every opportunity to hear about initiatives elsewhere, particularly sporting activities, due to its many media outlets; and it is illogical to think that a community in the city which included men experienced in association football – including at least one player who had appeared in a game against the renowned FA Cup side Royal Engineers – did not exist when the evidence demonstrates otherwise. It has been suggested that Turton is important because a continuum developed of institutions that have lasted to the present day and that there does not seem to be a 'continuum' evident in Manchester established by these people; but that is incorrect because, via the deep interrogation of evidence and the identification of events and transformational periods, we can see a continuum from 1863 through to the present, via Nall, Norris and others.[56]

The addition of Fitzroy Norris helped to develop Manchester's community and he brought practical experience from his time at Burton and with Nottingham Forest. Norris felt that association football had helped to shape his own sporting life, and it may have helped him to find stability. His early life had been transient in nature, but he had enjoyed a positive association with a progressive football club, Nottingham Forest, where he had added to his network of connections.[57] The occupations and education of Norris, Pickering and Nall suggest that at the formation of the Manchester Association they were part of the city's growing lower-middle class, their ideas shaped by experience that crossed class boundaries. Within Manchester's sporting community the connections were varied and were added to and often influenced by new arrivals to the city. The class background of sportsmen during this period highlights how sports developed and whether they were promoted across societal boundaries. Class was not an issue to those who played football, which contrasts with the way the early game is portrayed today.

The opening game of the new club saw membership and potential members divided into two teams, with one selected by John Nall.[58] The game occurred at Mr Flint's Farm, Moss Side, close to Pepper Hill cottage, a short distance north of the eventual home of Manchester City, Maine Road. It was also close to Alexandra Park, where Hulme Athenaeum had played, and the Manchester players utilised the Alexandra Hotel, Moss Side, as changing rooms. The game ended in a 1–0 defeat for Nall's team.[59] Conditions on the day were poor, and caused the *Athletic News* to comment that 'the downpour was such as to make the pursuit of the game a mockery to all but the most ardent spirits', adding that 'the players would have done much better to have gone in for the new and fashionable pastime of water-polo, which consists in splashing your opponent with all the vigour at your command'.[60] The newspaper tended to be supportive and in its previous editions had given fair assessments of the club: 'The club has been started on a sound basis, is governed by practical men, and it is therefore fair to presume that among so many athletes as there are in Manchester and district, the Association rules will in time become more popular.'[61] On 6 November it was reported that the sport was becoming 'an institution in Manchester', but it was recognised that 'the popularity of the Rugby game indicates a decided preference for it amongst the votaries of football. Those, however, who prefer the Association rules have now a chance of satisfying their predilections.'[62]

The second Manchester Association game was played between sides captained by Stuart G. Smith and Fitzroy Norris, with Jonathan Nall appearing in Norris's line-up, and ended 2–0 to Smith's team.[63] Further games occurred at Flint's Farm, with the most significant being a First Eleven against a Next Sixteen match in December. This is significant, as it shows how the club was developing and gives an indication of where the actual soccer expertise lay. The sixteen was captained by Norris, while the eleven included former Athenaeum players Charles Pickering, J. G. Sanderson, Tom Barlow, E. Powell and Jonathan Nall, alongside Stuart Smith, John Railton, R. A. Thorp, S. Starey, F. Haigh and J. Haigh, some of whom may have previously played for Hulme.[64] The First Eleven won the match 3–0 despite being two men short for the opening fifteen minutes. By 27 November Manchester Association had announced that it was to play games with teams from 'Sheffield, Nottingham, Stoke, Northwich, &c', with specific dates documented for meetings in Northwich and Stoke.[65] The club played practice games between its members, with a special challenge match arranged for 4 December, when 'the first twelve' would play against a 'selected twenty' who would be made up of friends of players and other members.[66] The first twelve was to be: Pickering, the brothers Haigh, Railton, Sanderson, Barlow, Nall, Norris, Thorp, Starey, Powell, with Smith as captain. Of these, five are known to have been prominent Hulme Athenaeum members, and after the match a first eleven was established which included those five former Athenaeum players.[67] The club had decided to find a base for meetings in the city centre, rather than in Hulme, and the Falstaff Hotel, Market Place became their headquarters.[68]

In 1875 Manchester Association included a mix of former Hulme Athenaeum players, lower-middle-class personnel, local businessmen and those experienced in the game from other regions, including, as time progressed, former public schoolboys, and the club appeared to have a strong base. At this time the northern middle classes were more closely aligned with the working classes than were their equivalents in the south, adding to the complex nature of the game's growth in the city and indicating that Norris and Nall's achievement in Manchester Association was either of great significance or, more likely, simply representative of the mix of backgrounds and personalities in Mancunian society at this time.[69] This adds credence to the argument that the game in Manchester was the product of many different class influences, with the major role being played by individuals from the lower-middle classes, although neither Norris nor Nall was specifically named when the *Athletic News* provided a mini-history of Manchester Association in 1882. Nevertheless, their contribution and that of others like them in the city was recognised, as the newspaper commented that there had 'always been a certain number of admirers of the dribbling game who have stuck manfully together, and by this means the Manchester organisation has succeeded in filling a niche in the temple erected to the perpetuation of Association worship'.[70]

While the Manchester Association first eleven continued to be selected as part of trial games and training sessions the club searched for fixtures. As there were no other recognisable soccer teams in Manchester (although it should be mentioned that a match report exists for the First Manchester Rifle Volunteers defeating the Eighth Cheshire Rifle Volunteers 5–0 in December 1875) the club needed to look further afield.[71] In January 1876 a game was organised at Liverpool against a team calling itself The Casuals: 'men of football fame from both the universities'.[72] This game brought a realisation that the club was still some way off genuine competition, as Manchester was defeated 3–0; but worse, only six Manchester men took part, with three substitutes being added in Liverpool, meaning that the side was still two men short of the Casuals' line-up. The six Manchester men who did play were Smith (captain), Railton, Norris, F. J. Haigh, J. W. Haigh and Sanderson, a known Hulme

Athenaeum player. Of these, Norris and Railton were regarded as putting in the best performances.[73] This disappointing start was followed with a 1–0 victory at Northwich Victoria and then a 5–2 home win over a combined team of Manchester-based association and rugby players, before the return match was played with Northwich on 12 February 1876, which appears to be the first home game with another organised club.[74]

By this time the antagonism between the leading rugby club, Manchester Football Club, and the new association side had grown, with public arguments raging between the two forms of football. As the more junior club, the soccer side was in a difficult position, and Norris's initial comments about soccer being scientific whereas rugby was all about brute force may have riled those with rugby at their heart, leading to criticism of association in a tit-for-tat manner. A serious incident led to the strongest criticisms of each sport when 15-year-old Joseph Ison died after being charged in a game of rugby at Moss Side.[75] Much debate followed on whether it was the circumstances of that individual game that led to the player's death, or a misunderstanding of the rules, or whether the game of rugby itself was unsafe.[76] The reporting of the death, and those commenting on it, created a clash between the codes that rumbled on for several years. On 23 February 1876 correspondence was published from an unnamed member of Manchester Association in which he commented: 'Rugby Union has gradually receded farther and farther from any likeness to the Association game, and has now nothing in common except the name. The Association game, everybody will admit, best deserves the name of football, if it is a question of best claim to the name.' He continued:

> In the Association game the feet are all in all. The rules forbid the use of the hands entirely; handling the ball being punished by a free kick to the opposite side. In Rugby Union, on the contrary, the hands are everything, handling and carrying being a distinctive feature of the play … Let the public calmly and dispassionately compare the rival merits of the two styles of play, and award their verdict accordingly. For my own part I feel confident that the Association game is slowly but surely winning its way into the public favour, and will soon become deservedly popular.[77]

Letters on the rival codes appeared in national, sporting and regional newspapers, but the *Athletic News* tried to calm the situation with a full-page editorial, although it had initially seemed to support the rugby view by quoting the views of the Manchester Football Club's secretary who, it said, 'very pertinently points out that the few accidents which do occur in the game arise from charging, an essential feature of the sport as played by the Association'. The article continued: 'The rivalry between the two organisations need not necessarily go to the length of saddling all manner of enormities upon each other, which we regret to find some letter writers on the Association side inclined to do with regard to the Rugby Union game.'[78] In March the newspaper added:

The daily papers continue to publish letters on the 'brutality' &c. of the Rugby Union game. We think, however, that some of those letter writers protest too much, and are disposed to exaggerate the number of accidents that happen at each game. In our opinion, these misfortunes are about equally divided between Rugby and Association, but Mr. Maclaren rather throws the balance against the Eton game, as, in a letter written to a contemporary, he states that the Manchester Club has played four Association and above 100 Rugby Union games since it was started, and has only had four serious accidents that he can remember – two against each way of playing the game. No less than three serious accidents happened to Association players last week in London.'[79]

Two years later the *Athletic News* used the death of a soccer player to 'dispose of the fallacy that Rugby Union is necessarily the more "brutal" of the two'.[80]

While these debates were raging in 1876 Manchester Association played the renowned rugby side Broughton Wasps in an association game at Broughton, admission sixpence, which the rugby side won 1–0, and followed this with a similar challenge and matching result against rugby side Levenshulme.[81] Interestingly, the Levenshulme game was played with crossbars that were at least three feet too high according to one observer.[82] Manchester Association also played a thirteen-a-side association game against Wellington, which they won 1–0.[83] These matches imply that animosity between the codes was not apparent at every level or club, but the tone of the letters and criticisms may have discouraged some potential participants. At the start of April 1876, following another death, the *Athletic News* included a full-page editorial on the safety or otherwise of the sports, but seemed to support rugby over soccer: 'we certainly will uphold the Rugby Union game as being undeserving the opprobrium that has been so liberally bestowed upon it'.[84] Occasionally the newspaper encouraged rugby clubs to play association matches from time to time: 'We hope next year to hear of every good Union club in and around the district playing the Association game now and then.'[85] The newspaper promoted both sports and felt that each had 'a fair right to endeavour to popularise its own peculiar sport, but the means ought not to be by trying to hurt the reputation of the other'.[86]

An article on the inaugural campaign of the association club highlighted 'a series of difficulties which, had they not existed, may well have allowed the sport to develop in a way that it had in the south, Sheffield and Scotland'.[87] Note that there was no mention of Turton or other areas of Lancashire at this time, and the article continued to document that the club had suffered many defeats but suggested that this was because of luck working in favour of their opponents rather than due to any inferiority in quality or play on the part of the club. It added that, had these results been slightly different, then the club might have entered its second season with a large membership list. Records show that the first season ended with Manchester Association playing nine games, other than sides matches, with a record of three victories (against Northwich Victoria, Vipers and Broughton Wasps), one draw (Macclesfield) and five defeats (Liverpool Casuals, Stoke, Northwich Victoria, Broughton Wasps and Levenshulme). All games appear to have been played to FA rules apart from Stoke, which was played to Sheffield rules, which – if the comments in Turton's own history are correct – suggests that this recognisable series of games occurred earlier than that experienced by Turton, the so-called pioneers of FA rules in Lancashire.[88]

For their second season Manchester moved headquarters to the Waterloo Hotel, an imposing building close to Piccadilly where Masonic lodges and other prominent middle-class societies met, and their committee was announced as F. J. Haigh, T. A. C. Hampson, H. R. Lewis, A. Mason, A. B. Potter, S. G. Smith and R. A. Thorp, with J. A. Railton now taking on the role of secretary and treasurer. The subscription had been raised to ten shillings and sixpence, which indicates that the intended membership was more closely aligned to the middle class than the working class, this being a significant proportion of income within the Manchester region.[89] It was also double the membership cost at the club's formation only a year earlier. Had the wealthier members of the club decided to price others out and make this a more exclusive club? This could explain the disappearance of some of the Hulme Athenaeum names from team lists and committee positions, and may have led to Nall, and potentially Norris, distancing themselves a little from the organisation. A decade or so later Norris is known to have arranged fixtures specifically to 'suit the working-class', while throughout Hulme Athenaeum's sporting existence Nall had held key positions at the club which had been established for all working men, regardless of class.[90] It is apparent that Nall encouraged all to participate in sport. Any attempt at making sport elitist was unlikely to have been supported by Nall, and it may well be that he withdrew from the Manchester committee for a reason such as this. He did remain an active participant in the association community and was well respected within Manchester's sporting circles, and it may be that he remained a member but was no longer a driving force. Alternatively, he could have become more involved with sporting teams established at the Platford Hotel, including Manchester Clifford Cricket Club, where a football club later became established.

With or without Nall's presence, Manchester Association appeared to make progress, with a fixture list that included a few high-profile games, although the club suffered four defeats in the opening six matches, one of which was played under Sheffield rules and one against Rossall public school in Fleetwood using the Eton-inspired Rossall rules.[91] It should be noted that the Rossall fixture may have come via Nall's connections, as members of the Birley family were councillors for the school and George Bowers, the dean of Manchester, was its chair. These games were followed by what was perceived as a landmark moment for the game in Manchester: the visit of a side representing the Sheffield Association.[92] While Manchester was still considered the home of rugby in the North, Sheffield was perceived as the leading association football city, certainly in the North, which meant that the meeting was expected to provide an impetus to the sport. It was moved to Longsight from Moss Side to accommodate a larger attendance, with the club setting a minimum admission fee of sixpence.[93] The venue was the original Longsight Cricket ground on Albert Grove, Longsight, approximately 100 yards from the St Mark's rectory, where the Reverend Arthur Connell lived and performed parish duties. Connell had an interest in all the activities of his parish and the staging of this game may have been significant, as two years later the earliest known match report for a game of association football organised by Connell's St Mark's exists. That team ultimately evolved into Manchester City, and it seems plausible that at least one of the young St Mark's parishioners who played for the church's cricket club at this time would have watched this match, although rain limited the attendance to less than 500.[94] The *Sheffield Daily Telegraph* remained positive, observing that 'with fine weather and good matches, there is no reason why association football should not in time be as popular and well supported in Manchester as it is now in Glasgow and Sheffield'.[95]

Whether or not Manchester Association deliberately tried to stress their members' sporting credentials is unclear, but for the first time the line-up of the Manchester side included details of the public schools/universities attended by four of their eleven players and the former association clubs of two of the others. The line-up listed S. G. Smith, Notts (captain), J. J. Richardson (goal), A. B. Potter (Eton) and J. Jones (half-backs); F. J. Haigh (back); A. Mason (Shropshire Wanderers), J. A. C. Hampton (Oxford), J. A. Railton, junior (Forest School), S. Starey, H. Ellis (Forest School), and R. A. Thorp.[96] This indicates that the team was composed of a mix of players from varying backgrounds, although with a membership of ten shillings and sixpence they would predominantly have been from the middle classes. Despite the team suffering a 4–0 defeat, reporters noted that 'We were astonished at the skill shown by the Manchester men ... there are the elements of a really good club in the Manchester Association.'[97] These comments were important because the *Athletic News* had been urging the club to import outside players such as Elba Markendale, a prominent rugby player, Albert Neilson Hornby, the well-known rugby and cricket player and former Harrow pupil and Francis Birley from the Wanderers, the nephew of former Hulme Athenaeum president Hugh Birley.[98] The decision to select players already involved with the club was justified, although it did not stop the *Athletic News* from arguing for the selection of Hornby for the return fixture the following February.[99] Hornby and Birley were both well-regarded footballers and they had also played cricket for Lancashire County Cricket Club (CCC). Hornby was one of the county's most influential men, and Birley was a player at the start of the 1870s. There were family ties between the men and, demonstrating the close relationship between Manchester sports at this time, Hornby went on to become the president of Manchester Association in 1882.[100]

One set of rules

Manchester resumed fixtures with association sides in Cheshire and rugby clubs from the Manchester area, before further high-profile games with Stoke, Nottingham and the return match with Sheffield.[101] The Sheffield game proved to be an embarrassment and one that prompted a debate on the differing rules of association football. Sheffield won 14–0 but, most significantly, reports commented on Manchester Association's lack of understanding of Sheffield's main rules, most notably their version of the offside law and their '"kick in any direction" clause when the ball goes into touch', as the *Athletic News* described it.[102] At one point the Sheffield goalkeeper was so bored that he obtained another ball and had a kickabout with another player while play was taking place at the other end. Manchester's captain, Stuart G. Smith, thought unfamiliarity with the rules was the issue but, rather than focus on developing knowledge of the Sheffield game, Smith took a more pro-active approach as far as the national game was concerned when he wrote to the *Field* urging that one set of football laws should be produced. His letter was published on 10 March 1877, around two weeks after the Sheffield debacle, and is recognised as accelerating the process of merging the rules of the two main footballing associations.[103] It should be highlighted once again that at this stage in association football's development the city's soccer influences were not from Lancashire. Manchester's leading figures included men such as Fitzroy Norris and Stuart G. Smith, who had both gained their footballing experience in Nottingham. Smith was a former pupil at Uppingham School.[104] Thanks to Smith, the new clarity of rules curtailed some of the barriers that had prevented association football from growing in the Lancashire region.

Manchester possessed a small community of soccer enthusiasts in comparison with the regions south and east of the city, particularly Cheshire, Staffordshire and Sheffield, but for much of the period prior to 1875 there was enough soccer activity to place it on a par with, or possibly ahead of, the rest of Lancashire. In fact, as early as 1876 there were attempts to establish a football association consisting of the Manchester region, Staffordshire and all areas in between, pre-dating the Lancashire FA and demonstrating that Manchester's soccer community existed and was perceived as having more in common with the areas south of the city than north of it. This was evidenced by the fixture list of Manchester Association Football Club (AFC), who tended to face association sides from Cheshire, Stoke, Nottingham and Sheffield, or Mancunian rugby clubs.[105] The proposed development of the Manchester–Staffordshire FA did not progress. Had the regional FA proposal been pursued, then it is likely that Manchester's soccer community would have developed at a relatively fast pace, with competitions following and an increase in the number of clubs.

In October 1877 Manchester played an away match with Broughton Wasps in the first reported game under the new combined rules in the area. One journalist claimed that these new rules 'are almost universally considered a great improvement on the old ones'.[106] It was the establishment of one set of rules that enabled the sport to grow, and association football certainly developed, although Lancashire remained 'the headquarters of the "handling" style of play, but there are … indications that the "dribbling" sport is making an unmistakable headway down in this district'.[107] Those indications were predominantly in east Lancashire rather than in Manchester, and the sport's popularity was growing rapidly in the area around Bolton and Blackburn. Several clubs were engaging in activity with each other, while Manchester Association continued to struggle to find organised association participation locally and looked towards Sheffield, Cheshire, Derbyshire and Nottinghamshire for its rivals.[108] It is logical to suggest that rugby, with several giants of the game in Manchester and Salford, simply had too great a stronghold and support for soccer to compete. Over twenty established rugby sides are known to have existed within the Manchester region, with many more in the rest of Lancashire.[109] Arthur Andrews, a prominent association footballer who spent much of his career with Manchester Association, explained in the 1920s that both the city's rugby and association footballing cultures were evident, however:

> Manchester on a Saturday night was pandemonium with Rugby and Association players and supporters going from pub to pub to pick up football news. Alton House, in Mount Street (where the Midland Hotel now stands) and the Café Royal in Peter Street, were the first to pin up results. Later we got the manager of the Crown Hotel, Booth Street, to provide a baize covered board for the same object, and this house was the recognised rendezvous for players and was in later years the first headquarters of the Manchester Football Council. Its telegraphic address was registered as "Football".[110]

Andrews endeavoured to get coverage for the team's soccer exploits but found that newspapers were often unwilling to include association reports. In an attempt to ensure that some focus on the game occurred he would 'set off for Stoke, Blackburn, Sheffield etc., with a prepaid press telegraph form to send the result of the match to the papers', thereby making life easier for the media. At this time most football match reports were sent in by either one of the committee or an observer appointed by clubs; the ability to get your team featured all depended on your own determination and the willingness of the editorial team at the newspaper. If the newspaper was sympathetic to your sport or team, then the report might make it, but newspapers were a business and needed every space to add value, so that some reports never appeared in the press. This is a point worth considering when trying to establish what the footballing community consisted of.

Regardless of the ifs and maybes surrounding the amount of unreported soccer activity, it is correct to state that rugby was the undisputed leader over soccer in terms of participation, number of clubs and general activity across most of Lancashire county prior to 1877, but between then and 1900 it lost its place to soccer. Apart from a few strongholds, such as Wigan, association football colonised Lancashire, town by town, city by city, throughout the period. The popularity of rugby in Lancashire was often remarked upon, and Manchester was viewed as the flag bearer for the region; but in soccer the city was now falling behind other areas of the county.[111] Association activity north of Manchester was making progress, particularly around Bolton and Blackburn. Manchester, despite the initial efforts of Hulme Athenaeum and those of Manchester Association, continued to grow at a relative slow pace in comparison.

One reason why Manchester's association football stagnated is that another rival team sport was introduced into the city. A high-profile series of lacrosse matches between Canadians and members of the Iroquois tribe were staged, and Manchester became (and remains) a major centre for the sport.[112] Analysis shows that the efforts of the visitors from North America inspired the Manchester public. The game was viewed positively and considered more attractive than soccer.[113] It rapidly became established in the region and leading sporting figures, such as rugby international Elba Markendale, established their own clubs within weeks of the promotional game.[114] Markendale was an interesting figure and his sporting career and residency demonstrate a mix of influences and cross-conurbation activities that add to the concept of a Manchester region rather than a Lancashire county focus. He was born in Salford, and by the time he was actively involved in lacrosse he was a resident of Hyde, a Cheshire town less than eight miles east of Manchester. His sporting connections included an early career in association football, experience of athletics, promotion of rowing contests and some acclaim at rugby.[115] With a growing lacrosse community and dominant rugby culture, soccer's opportunities in Manchester were limited and the city lagged behind east Lancashire, where clubs such as Darwen demonstrated their superiority, such as when they defeated Manchester AFC in the county's first FA Cup tie.[116]

In terms of association experience, the Darwen club was of similar age to Manchester and came from a much smaller conurbation; however, in terms of development they were typical of many growing Lancastrian sides of the era. Maybe this was because those sides had more opportunity for football, with several clubs being formed nearby, while Manchester seemed to struggle for properly organised association activity. Soccer enthusiasts in the area still needed to travel to find opponents, and when they did the game often ended in defeat, such as the 7–0 defeat at Derby Grammar School in October 1877 and the 6–0 loss against Nottinghamshire in December.[117]

Other clubs continued to try the game on occasion, most notably rugby clubs, but often this was to aid with their skills at rugby.[118] In terms of actual soccer competition the *Athletic News* pointed out that 'An Association game is somewhat of a rarity in the neighbourhood of Manchester', before commenting on the performance of Manchester players: 'all worked hard for the credit of Cottonopolis in a style of play which, to say the least of it, has never been popular in this immediate district'.[119] That seemed a little harsh, but by this time the newspaper was carrying a large number of association football reports from across the country, and it was clear the association game was increasing in popularity elsewhere. Perhaps because it was not perceived as much of a threat, in February 1878 Manchester Association met Manchester FC in an association game for the first time. The match ended in a 1–0 victory to the 'strongest, if not absolutely the best club in England playing the Rugby Union's rules'.[120]

Those behind Manchester Association continued to promote the sport in the city, and in January 1878 they organised a high-profile match with Stoke, captained by Thomas Slaney. Slaney was one of the game's early influencers, certainly in the Staffordshire area, and he frequently supported Manchester during its developmental phase. He is thought to have been the person who proposed a Manchester–Staffordshire FA in 1876. Like the 1876 Sheffield game, the Stoke match was staged at the original Longsight Cricket ground on Albert Grove, Longsight. Home games against larger opposition tended to be played there, where a 'large assembly of spectators' would attend on days when the weather was not a deterrent or if the opposition was particularly attractive.[121]

Manchester's soccer community was developing, even if the speed of progress was not as great at that now occurring further north in Lancashire. Despite the dominance of rugby and the counter attraction of lacrosse, Manchester did have multiple clubs by the end of 1877. Birch rugby club, established in 1869, had created its own association side in November 1877 and its members did much to promote the game. The club had previously played the game on occasion; why they formally moved into the sport is unclear, although two factors appear to have been influential. First, their home venue during 1877–78 was the Longsight Cricket Ground, where Manchester Association had played their significant matches, and second, an ex-Queens Park player, James Strang, had moved to the area and joined the club, later becoming Birch's first association captain.[122] The creation of the club fits with the view that 'football as developed by the amateurs required a defined space and some capital investment, and that access to land and money was beyond the working-class'.[123] Even though Hulme Athenaeum and Manchester Association had generated a degree of interest in the sport and provided examples of what could be achieved, the creation of their own sustainable football clubs had proved difficult for poorer members of the community and the increase in Manchester Association's membership fee suggested that some working-class members had been priced out. After playing practice games and local fixtures under association rules, the club arranged fixtures with Stoke, through Slaney, and Scottish pioneers Queens Park, through James Strang, in Manchester.[124]

While Manchester Association had been encouraged and promoted but often criticised in the media for its delivery, Birch was viewed as a success, even after its first few tentative steps, mainly because it had emerged from an already established administrative base.[125] In preparation for the Queens Park meeting Birch trained at least twice a week, and then nightly in the build-up to the match.[126] For this high-profile association game, Birch decided to use Manchester FC's rugby ground instead of the Longsight Cricket Club ground, perhaps demonstrating the height of the club's ambition. They also provided a guarantee to Queens Park to cover all expenses, although the latter returned a proportion, nine pounds, to Birch in a grand gesture because they 'needed it more'.[127] The game, with a reported attendance of 2,000 and which Queens Park won 6–0, was regarded as a great success, causing the press to note the association side's rapid development and leading to Birch being described as 'the strongest in the cotton' district.[128] On occasion, Stoke's Slaney played for Birch, suggesting that the club's development was viewed positively within association football circles.[129] Perhaps with an eye on establishing themselves as Manchester's main team, Birch relaunched themselves as Manchester Wanderers by the end of October 1878 and had separated from their parent organisation by moving to a ground at Brooks' Bar for their second season, in 1878.[130] In the middle of this transformation Birch had entered the FA Cup, but had withdrawn prior to their scheduled match with Darwen. These were the only two Lancashire clubs who had entered the competition, an indication that Birch was perceived as a prominent club in the region.[131]

Separating from Birch was a gamble, but perhaps a necessary one if the association club was to develop its own identity and improve its standing. It was during this formative period for the club that it attracted one of the city's newest residents, Scotsman Lachie Sinclair. He came to Manchester as a young man and was unaware of any association team, instead playing shinty at a club based at Old Trafford.[132] One day while walking from Old Trafford to his home in Ardwick he was delighted to find some goalposts and a game of association football.[133] He sought out the club secretary, explained confidently that he was a good player from his time in Scotland, and went on to become a regular with the team, Manchester Wanderers, and also a prominent official in the region and leading figure behind the Manchester FA, joining John Nall as one of the area's football influencers. Manchester may not possess nationally renowned names as footballing pioneers, such as those men from further north in Lancashire who played key roles in the development of the Football League, but the conurbation did possess a community of similarly interested individuals who were able to shape and promote the sport at a local level. Sinclair often told a story to demonstrate the lengths to which he and others went to develop the soccer community. He was responsible for the Wanderers' football, and while he was using it to practise one day it was captured by a group of youths who threw the ball from one to another before one of them was 'collared' by Sinclair. He said that they could keep the ball so long as they played association football with their feet and not rugby with their hands.[134] Under pressure, the boys agreed and, according to Sinclair, they created a football team and developed it into a good club. Sinclair encouraged many to take up the sport, and in later years he played for West Manchester, which became the leading Mancunian side for a time in the 1880s.

The *Athletic News* commented that by that time Manchester Wanderers had been strengthened by the arrival of James McIntyre from Queens Park, J. Turner (former Nottingham Forest player) and C. N. Wilson from Sheffield FC, demonstrating that Manchester's soccer growth matched that of its wider development, inasmuch as the city relied on an influx of specialists, workers, enthusiasts and entrepreneurs.[135] Manchester became prominent due to the exploits of many arrivals in the city, and this is certainly true for its footballing growth as it is for its industrial life. Without the arrival of experienced men like Norris, Smith and others, Manchester might never have become recognised as a footballing city. Norris engaged in a wide social and sporting landscape within the region and was often mentioned in the leading sports newspapers. Occasionally humorous, sometimes critical, he would frequently be referred to as Fitzroy or Fitz, suggesting that his popularity was such that the wider sporting population knew exactly who he was.[136] He was known for rigidly applying rules in whatever sport he officiated over, and he was recognised as a man who utilised his skills for sport's benefit, participating however and wherever he could, as when he offered to represent England in the United States as part of a grand amateur athletic challenge.[137] Newspaper reports imply that Norris was a well-loved and well-meaning individual who, despite whatever limitations presented themselves, would do his utmost to aid the sports clubs he was connected to. After moving to Bolton he became more involved with refereeing and football administration than with playing, and was recognised as a zealous official who lived by the rules at a time when there was increasing regulation in the sport.[138] After a period on the committee at Eagley Football Club, close to his Bolton home, in the early 1880s, Norris joined the higher-profile Bolton Wanderers, and by February 1887 he was the club's secretary.[139] He resigned after a brief and at times controversial time in the role, but remained a member of the footballing community for the rest of his life and was recognised for his contribution to refereeing.[140] The achievements of Norris and the others deserve to be remembered, yet their names have in general slipped from our collective memory.

Notes

1 MacKillop, 'Climatic city', 245; Hewitt, *The emergence*, 21; Walton, *Lancashire*; A. J. Kidd, 'Introduction: The middle-class', in A. J. Kidd and K. W. Roberts (eds), *City, class and culture* (Manchester: Manchester University Press, 1985), 15.

2 Kidd, 'Introduction', 15; Rose, 'Culture, philanthropy', 103; Tocqueville, *Journeys to England*, 106.

3 Hewitt, *The emergence*, 64–65; B. Williams, 'The antisemitism of tolerance', in A. J. Kidd and K. W. Roberts (eds), *City, class and culture* (Manchester: Manchester University Press, 1985), 77.

4 'The bishop of Manchester on athletics', *Athletic News*, 15 December 1877, 4.

5 'Abuse of football', *Athletic News*, 1 December 1877, 8.

6 'The bishop of Manchester and the "Athletic News"', *Athletic News*, 29 December 1877, 4.

7 Bailey, *Leisure and class*, 145–146.

8 Cunningham, *Leisure*, 22.

9 'Football in the north, second series', *Athletic News*, 23 December 1876, 1.

10 The oldest surviving issue at the British Newspaper Library is from 12 June 1875. This was recorded as volume 1 number 2 on its masthead.

11 'Last year it will be recollected, we strongly counselled rugby union clubs to cultivate the association game in this immediate neighbourhood.' 'Football notes', *Athletic News*, 30 September 1876, 6.

12 Examples are a letter to *Athletic News* from Manchester FC's secretary, Ernest E. Marriott, explaining that 'rouges' are no longer valid in any form of rugby, and an editorial in the same issue suggesting that: 'the game as played in this district, which is in accordance with the Rugby Union Rules (for we understand that Association football is not practised by any local club), might be much improved by the adoption of certain alterations. For instance, if none of the forwards was allowed to pick up a ball and run with it the scrimmages would be neither so long nor so severe. There would be more dribbling, the game would assume a more open and interesting character and offer greater variety to the spectators; hacking would be diminished.' 'Incorrect terms in football', *Athletic News*, 23 October 1875, 5.

13 'Football', *Athletic News*, 2 October 1875, 7.

14 Hewitt, *The emergence*, 64–65; Williams, 'The antisemitism of tolerance', 77.

15 'Football', *Athletic News*, 2 October 1875, 7; 'Moseley Football Club', *Bell's Life in London and Sporting Chronicle*, 19 August 1876, 5.

16 'Action for false Imprisonment', *Worcestershire Chronicle*, 15 April 1863, 2.

17 'Deaths', *Hereford Times*, 21 June 1851, 5; 'To be let', *Hereford Times*, 28 June 1851, 4.

18 Census returns, Richard Norris 1871, https//:www.findmypast.co.uk (RG 9/2089).
19 'Action for false imprisonment', *Worcestershire Chronicle*, 15 April 1863, 2.
20 'St. Clement's', *Worcester Journal*, 30 May 1863, 6.
21 Census returns, Thomas F. Norris 1871, https//:www.findmypast.co.uk (RG 10/2905).
22 'Football', *Athletic News*, 2 October 1875, 7.
23 'Ind Coope & Co.'s Office v Worthington and Co.'s Cricket Club', *Derbyshire Times*, 31 August 1872, 8.
24 'Football', *Derbyshire Times*, 28 December 1872, 5; 'Ind Coope and Co. (Burton) v Sneiton (Notts)', *Derbyshire Times*, 26 February 1873, 2.
25 B. Possing, 'The historical biography: Genre, history and methodology', in J. Bale, M. K. Christensen and G. Pfister (eds), *Writing lives in sports: Biographies, life-histories and methods* (Aarhus: Aarhus University Press, 2004), 22.
26 Norris's total match appearances have been provided by Nottingham Forest historian Rob Jovanovic. 'Nottingham Forest club v Burton-on-Trent', *Bell's Life in London and Sporting Chronicle*, 25 January 1873, 8.
27 Norris produced and presented an illuminated address to Walter Lymbery in 1874 to mark this period; 'It just blew my mind – as an artefact from Forest's history, it is the best we have found', *Nottingham Post*, 7 April 2014, n.p.; 'Nottingham Forest v Royal Engineers', *Sheffield Daily Telegraph*, 24 December 1873, 6.
28 'Nottingham Forest v Royal Engineers', *Sheffield Daily Telegraph*, 24 December 1873, 6. Note: Marindin had played in the 1862 fundraising game for the Central Relief Committee discussed in the previous chapter.
29 'Sheffield (Norfolk club) v Notts (Forest club)', *Sheffield Daily Telegraph*, 19 January 1874, 4.
30 'Football', *Athletic News*, 30 October 1875, 5.
31 'Football', *Athletic News*, 2 October 1875, 7.
32 'To the editor of the Athletic News', *Athletic News*, 23 October 1875, 5; 'Football – to the editor of the *Manchester Courier*', *Manchester Courier*, 23 February 1876, 7; 'Football in the north, second series', *Athletic News*, 23 December 1876, 1.
33 'Football fixtures – this day, October 23', *Athletic News*, 23 October 1875, 5.
34 Organisations such as the Trafford Benefit Building Society were established at the Platford, see *Rules of the Trafford Benefit Building Society*, 12 April 1858. 'Clifford Cricket Club', *Manchester Times*, 29 November 1856, 5; 'Correspondence', *Athletic News*, 6 July 1881, 1.
35 For example, 'Cricketers' depot', *Athletic News*, 22 February 1882, 1.
36 B. Potts, *The old pubs of Hulme Manchester (1) 1770–1930* (Manchester: Neil Richardson, 1983); 'Wrestling at Manchester', *Kendal Mercury*, 3 April 1841, 3.
37 Potts, *The old pubs*; C. W. Alcock (ed.), *The football annual* (London: Lillywhite, 1870), 57.
38 'To the Editor of the Athletic News', *Athletic News*, 23 October 1875, 5.
39 'To the editor of the *Athletic News*', *Athletic News*, 23 October 1875, 5.
40 'Football Association rules', *Athletic News*, 30 October 1875, 5 and Alcock (ed.), *The football annual*, 57.

41 'Football – Association rules', *Manchester Guardian*, 23 October 1875, 8; 'Football – Association rules', *Manchester Guardian*, 30 October 1875, 8.

42 'Football Association rules', *Athletic News*, 30 October 1875, 5; 'Editorial', *Athletic News*, 23 October 1875, 4; 'Football – Association rules', *Athletic News*, 30 October 1875, 8; 'Manchester Association Football Club', *Bell's Life in London and Sporting Chronicle*, 20 November 1875, 8.

43 'Manchester Association Football Club', *Bell's Life in London and Sporting Chronicle*, 20 November 1875, 8.

44 'Football Association rules', *Athletic News*, 30 October 1875, 5.

45 'Moseley Football Club', *Bell's Life in London and Sporting Chronicle* 19 August 1876, 5.

46 'Football notes', *Athletic News*, 6 November 1875, 5; 'Manchester Association Football Club', *Bell's Life in London and Sporting Chronicle* 20 November 1875, 8; 'Football', *Manchester Guardian*, 17 November 1875, 6; 'Football notes', *Athletic News*, 20 November 1875, 5; 'The Association Football Club', *Athletic News*, 13 November 1875, 7.

47 'Football – Garrick v Hulme Athenaeum', *Sheffield Daily Telegraph*, 4 January 1872, 3; 'Manchester Football Club – past v present', *Athletic News*, 12 October 1881, 2 and 1911 Census records for Joseph Arthur Railton, https//:www.find mypast.co.uk, RG14, PN23665, registration district Chorlton.

48 Isaac Slater, *Slater's royal national commercial directory of Manchester and Salford with their vicinities, 1877–8* (Manchester: Isaac Slater, 1877), 104.

49 'Football', *Manchester Guardian*, 17 November 1875, 6; 'Football notes', *Athletic News*, 20 November 1875, 5; 'The Association Football Club', *Athletic News*, 13 November 1875, 7.

50 Swain and Lewis, 'An alternative viewpoint', 1162; *History of Turton Football Club and carnival and sports handbook* (Turton: Turton Football Club, 1909), 5–8.

51 By the summer of 1875 it was reported that Turton had played ten games to London Association rules that season, presumably meaning Football Association rules, with a game with Egerton being the first. See 'Turton Football Club', *Bolton Evening News*, 19 March 1875, 3; 'Football: Turton v Egerton', *Bolton Evening News*, 17 November 1874, 3; *History of Turton Football Club*, 7–9.

52 *History of Turton Football Club*, 5–8.

53 Email correspondence with Peter Swain, 7 May 2016.

54 Swain and Lewis, 'An alternative viewpoint', 1163.

55 *History of Turton Football Club*, 5–8.

56 Swain and Lewis, 'An alternative viewpoint', 1163.

57 M. Johnes, 'Pigeon racing and working-class culture in Britain, c.1870–1950', *Cultural and Social History*, 4:3 (2007), 361; 'Nottingham Forest Club v Burton-on-Trent', *Bell's Life in London and Sporting Chronicle*, 25 January 1873, 8.

58 'Football', *Manchester Guardian*, 17 November 1875, 6.

59 'The association football club', *Athletic News*, 13 November 1875, 7 and 'Football', *Manchester Guardian*, 17 November 1875, 6.

60 'Football notes', *Athletic News*, 20 November 1875, 5.

61 'The association football club', *Athletic News*, 13 November 1875, 7.

62 'Football notes', *Athletic News*, 6 November 1875, 5.
63 'Manchester Association Football Club', *Athletic News*, 27 November 1875, 7.
64 'Manchester Association Club (1st eleven) v Next 16', *Athletic News*, 11 December 1875, 5.
65 'Manchester Association Football Club', *Athletic News*, 27 November 1875, 7.
66 Ibid.
67 Ibid.; 'Manchester Association Club (1st eleven) v Next 16', *Athletic News*, 11 December 1875, 5.
68 'Manchester Association Football Club', *Athletic News*, 27 November 1875, 7.
69 R. McKibbin, *Classes and cultures, England 1918–1951* (Oxford: Oxford University Press 2000), 86 and 101.
70 'Manchester Association FC, late Manchester Wanderers', *Athletic News*, 30 October 1882, 2.
71 'Football notes', *The Sporting Gazette*, 25 December 1875, 1267.
72 'Manchester Association Football Club', *Athletic News*, 15 January 1876, 5.
73 'Manchester Association v Liverpool Casuals', *Athletic News*, 22 January 1876, 5 and 'Manchester Association v Liverpool Casuals', *The Sporting Gazette*, 22 January 1876, 81.
74 'Manchester Association club v Mr. Piper's team', *Athletic News*, 12 February 1876, 6.
75 'Death in the football field', *Athletic News*, 12 February 1876, 1.
76 'The late football fatality – to the editor of the Athletic News', *Athletic News*, 12 February 1876, 4.
77 'Football – To the editor of the Manchester Courier', *Manchester Courier*, 23 February 1876, 7.
78 'Football notes', *Athletic News*, 26 February 1876, 4.
79 'Football notes', *Athletic News*, 4 March 1876, 5.
80 'The late football fatality', *Athletic News*,16 March 1878, 4.
81 'Broughton Wasps Football Club – match', *Manchester Courier*, 11 March 1876, 1 and 'Football', *Manchester Courier*, 14 March 1876, 7.
82 'Levenshulme v Manchester Association', *Athletic News*, 8 April 1876, 2.
83 'Manchester Association v Wellington', *Athletic News*, 22 April 1876, 5.
84 'Football and its detractors', *Athletic News*, 1 April 1876, 4.
85 'Levenshulme v Manchester Association Football Club', *Athletic News*, 8 April 1876, 2.
86 'Football in the north, second series', *Athletic News*, 23 December 1876, 1.
87 Ibid.
88 Ibid.; *History of Turton Football Club*, 8.
89 'Football', *Athletic News*, 2 September 1876, 3; advertisements in 1876 show a range of working-class wages including moulders at 36 shillings, corn delivery person 27 shillings, iron dresser 22 shillings, warehouse workers from 10 shillings, office boys 6 shillings. For example, see *Manchester Courier*, 13 March 1876, 2; *Manchester Courier*, 3 June 1876, 2.
90 'Bolton Wanderers' Football Club', *Cricket and Football Field*, 9 April 1887, 8.
91 'Football in the north, second series', *Athletic News*, 23 December 1876, 1.

92 'Stoke-on-Trent v Manchester Association', *Bell's Life in London and Sporting Chronicle* 11 November 1876, 9; 'Football – Sheffield v Manchester', *Rotherham Independent*, 12 December 1876, 7.

93 'Football notes', *Athletic News*, 30 September 1876, 6; 'Grand Football Match', *Manchester Courier*, 14 December 1876, 1; 'Grand football match – Manchester AFC v Sheffield', *Manchester Guardian*, 16 December 1876, 8.

94 St Mark's had been playing cricket since the 1860s and it was the young men of the cricket team who established the football offshoot, adding to the theory that the sport was of more appeal to the younger generation than those that had preceded them.

95 'Sheffield v Manchester', *Sheffield Daily Telegraph*, December 18, 1876, 4.

96 Ibid.

97 'Football notes and gossip', *Athletic News*, 23 December 1876, 2.

98 'Football in the north', *Athletic News*, 23 December 1876, 1; 'Football Notes and Gossip', *Athletic News*, 18 November 1876, 3.

99 'Sheffield v Manchester', *Athletic News*, 24 February 1877, 2.

100 'En passant', *Athletic News*, 27 September 1882, 1.

101 'Football', *Manchester Guardian*, 15 January 1877, 3, 'Football', *Athletic News*, 6 January 1876, 1; 'Manchester Association v Northwich Victoria', *Athletic News*, 27 January 1877, 2; 'Football Notes and Gossip', *Athletic News*, 3 March 1877, 2; 'Sheffield v Manchester', *Athletic News*, 24 February 1877, 2; 'Fixtures for today', *Athletic News*, 10 February 1877, 1.

102 'Football Notes and Gossip', *Athletic News*, 3 March 1877, 1.

103 P. M. Young, *Football in Sheffield* (London: Stanley Paul & Co Ltd., 1962), 29.

104 Census returns, S. G. Smith 1871, https//:www.findmypast.co.uk (RG 10/3301); 'Football Notes and Gossip', *Athletic News*, 3 March 1877, 1.

105 Cooke and James, 'Myths, truths and pioneers'; 'Manchester Association v Liverpool Public Schools', *Athletic News*, 14 October 1876, 5; 'Football', *Manchester Guardian*, 15 January 1877, 3, 'Football', *Athletic News*, 6 January 1876, 1; 'Manchester Association v Northwich Victoria', *Athletic News*, 27 January 1877, 2; 'Football Notes and Gossip', *Athletic News*, 3 March 1877, 2; 'Sheffield v Manchester', *Athletic News*, 24 February 1877, 2; 'Fixtures for today', *Athletic News*, 10 February 1877, 1; 'Manchester Association v Derby Grammar School', *Athletic News*, 3 November 1877, 3; 'Nottinghamshire club v Manchester', *Bell's Life in London and Sporting Chronicle*, 22 December 1877, 9.

106 'Manchester Association v Broughton Wasps', *Manchester Courier*, 22 October 1877, 3.

107 'Football notes', *Athletic News*, 22 September 1877, 2.

108 'Manchester Association v Derby Grammar School', *Athletic News*, 3 November 1877, 3; 'Nottinghamshire club v Manchester', *Bell's Life in London and Sporting Chronicle*, 22 December 1877, 9.

109 'County organisation', *Athletic News*, 9 February 1878, 3.

110 'Familiar faces', *Manchester Football Chronicle*, 7 October 1922, 3.

111 'Football notes', *Athletic News*, 22 September 1877, 2; 'The new season', *Athletic News*, 6 October 1877, 4.

112 'La crosse', *Athletic News*, 1 July 1876, 1.
113 Russell, 'Sporting Manchester', 7; 'North of England Lacrosse Association', *Athletic News*, 21 April 1880, 6; 'Football notes and gossip', *Athletic News*, 28 April 1880, 5.
114 Elba Markendale was a committee member at the launch of the Manchester Rangers Lacrosse club. 'Manchester Rangers La Crosse Club', *Athletic News*, 15 July 1876, 7.
115 'Football notes', *Athletic News*, 26 February 1876, 4; Ibid., 24 June 1876, 2; Ibid., 12 August 1876, 1; Ibid., 18 November 1876, 3.
116 'The Association challenge cup', *Bell's Life in London and Sporting Chronicle*, 17 November 1877, 9.
117 'Manchester Association v Derby Grammar School', *Athletic News*, 3 November 1877, 3 and 'Nottinghamshire club v Manchester', *Bell's Life in London and Sporting Chronicle*, 22 December 1877, 9.
118 'Football Notes and Gossip', *Athletic News*, 16 March 1878, 1.
119 'Football notes', *Athletic News*, 2 February 1878, 1.
120 'Football', *Manchester Guardian*, 28 February 1878, 7; 'Manchester Football Club', *Manchester Guardian*, 23 February 1878, 1 and 'Football notes and gossip', *Athletic News*, 3 November 1877, 2.
121 'Manchester v Stoke', *Sheffield Telegraph*, 28 January 1878, 4 and 'Nottinghamshire v Manchester Association', *Manchester Times*, 16 February 1878, 7.
122 'Stoke-on-Trent v Birch Association (Manchester)', *Sheffield Daily Telegraph*, 29 April 1878, 3; 'Football notes', *Athletic News*, 2 February 1878, 2.
123 Cunningham, *Leisure*, 128.
124 'Football', *Manchester Guardian*, 17 December 1877, 6.
125 'Football notes and gossip', *Athletic News*, 16 March 1878, 1.
126 'Queen's Park (Glasgow) v Birch (Manchester')', *Sheffield Independent*, 28 March 1878, 7; 'Football notes and gossip', *Athletic News*, 16 March 1878, 1; 'Football Notes and Gossip', *Athletic News*, 30 March 1878, 1.
127 R. Robinson, *History of the Queen's Park Football Club 1867–1917* (Glasgow: Hay Nisbet, 1920), chapter 26.
128 'Queen's Park, Glasgow v Birch', *Athletic News*, 13 April 1878, 2; 'Football', *Manchester Guardian*, 8 April 1878, 7; 'Football notes', *Athletic News*, 2 February 1878, 2; 'Birch (Manchester) v Stoke-on-Trent', *Athletic News*, 1 May 1878, 3.
129 Cooke and James, 'Myths, truths and pioneers'; 'Queen's Park, Glasgow v Birch, Manchester', unknown newspaper cutting dated 8 April 1878.
130 'Football Notes and Gossip', *Athletic News*, 23 October 1878, 2.
131 'Football', *Morning Post*, 30 September 1878, 2.
132 Shinty is a hockey-like game during which the ball is allowed to travel and be struck in the air as well as on the ground. It remains popular in Scotland and some areas of Northern England.
133 'Mr LM Sinclair', *Manchester Football Chronicle*, 28 January 1922, 3.
134 Ibid.
135 'Manchester Association FC, late Manchester Wanderers', *Athletic News*, 30 October 1882, 2.

136 'En passant', *Athletic News*, 11 June 1879, 1.
137 'En passant', *Athletic News*, 3 September 1879, 1.
138 *Bolton Football Field*, 20 September 1884, 8.
139 Lancashire Archives, DDX2708, Minutes of the Lancashire Football Association, 24 February 1887.
140 For example, *Bolton Football Field*, 3 September 1887.

5

Formation of clubs

Innovation

By 1878 Manchester had emerged as a modern, essentially metropolitan city – a relatively compact city borough surrounded by a ring, stretching some twelve miles from the centre, containing a complex polycentric mix of districts and towns.[1] The city's influence stretched some distance beyond its boundaries and the council had been known to invest in projects outside of the city when, for example, it built the Thirlmere aqueduct in 1877.[2] There was also the city's investment in the Manchester Ship Canal, which had been ongoing for several decades. The canal opened in 1894, by which time the city was recognised as an enterprising body and beginning to be perceived as an association football-ing city. Manchester's footballing community had grown by 1878 but was still somewhat smaller than its rugby equivalent. Association clubs were beginning to develop across Manchester, although many of their earliest games either were ignored by the local media or club secretaries neglected to send in reports. Sporting newspapers such as the *Athletic News* provided coverage and became the organs for club promotion, but local newspapers tended to mention club activity infrequently.

The year 1878 is important in the north-west of England as that was the year when formal football governance occurred locally, with the founding of the Lancashire FA, which aided the formalisation of rules at a local level and a variety of competitions in areas such as Blackburn and Turton became established.[3] The inauguration of the Lancashire Cup came in 1879–80, with Darwen as the first winners after beating Blackburn Rovers 3–0 in the final. Although a significant number of teams from Bolton, to the north of the city, took part the only club from the immediate Manchester region was Manchester Wanderers. Had other Manchester sides been involved in the organisation or contributed to the inaugural meetings of the Lancashire FA, then football might well have been recognised as a prominent local activity. While the Bolton–Blackburn area of Lancashire was in the main switching to soccer rather than rugby, if the earlier plan to have a Manchester–Staffordshire football association had come to fruition it is highly plausible that Manchester would have been regarded as a soccer city earlier than 1878.[4] The *Athletic News* rightly believed that the formation of the Lancashire FA would encourage the creation of sides in Lancashire, and the same would surely have been true for Manchester.[5] Instead, Manchester Association arranged ambitious individual fixtures, often against renowned clubs where the Mancunian side stood little chance of success. It is unclear why Manchester Association did not join the Lancashire FA at its formation, although the club appeared to be experiencing some difficulties at this time and may have seen little value in adding to their expenses membership in an association and cup competition which would have necessitated travel costs.

Manchester Wanderers, the relaunched former Birch club, moved to a ground at Brooks' Bar, and defeated Blackburn Rovers – seen as a major coup – in a high-profile game during 1878. They possessed a bright future according to the *Athletic News*: 'They have got some first-class members' and their ground was considered 'the most accessible' in Manchester.[6] Wanderers also competed in one of the first floodlit soccer games when they faced Stoke at Cauldon Place, Stoke in November 1878, less than four weeks after the first-ever game played under lights at Sheffield, and two weeks after the first floodlit rugby game in Manchester.[7] There were other experimental floodlit football matches involving Manchester sides in November 1878, including an exhibition match between the best players in the district, assumed to be rugby, at Pomona Palace; and what would have been the earliest-recorded Manchester-related floodlit game when Swinton travelled to Chorley in October, excepting that the lights failed to work.[8]

Manchester Wanderers' local rival, the four-year-old Manchester Association, were struggling, causing them to merge with Wanderers in 1879. The newly merged club created a four-a-side club tournament which was aimed at promoting the sport to rugby clubs. This was staged at the Manchester (rugby) Football Club but received negative press in Sheffield, which claimed that the event was 'the last struggle of the association enthusiasts' due to the relatively small attendance.[9] That year the merged club was described as the 'only association club in the Cottonopolis', even though other teams were certainly already playing the game. The merged club did compete in the Lancashire Cup, reaching the fourth round in its first season, and travelled to Glasgow to face Queens Park and Glasgow University in friendly matches, demonstrating that, if nothing else, there was a dedicated band of enthusiasts prepared to back their sport.[10] The famous Lancashire CCC cricketer Richard Barlow kept goal for the club during this period and later became a shareholder in another club, West Manchester, when it became a company in 1892, adding to the view that Manchester's sporting community was one which crossed sports.[11]

Despite high-profile activities such as the floodlit games and the Scottish friendlies, Manchester's footballing development at this time consisted of several Braudelian events, most of which did not progress the game in the region. A transformation required a chain of events during which progress could be achieved, but this process was not apparent among the prominent clubs. Rather than linked chains of events coming from Manchester's clubs, they came through individuals. John Nall, Fitzroy Norris and some of the original Hulme Athenaeum men had provided them so far, but the period around 1878 saw others join Manchester's soccer community and become dependable figures in the development of the sport, such as Arthur Andrews who participated in the floodlit match at Stoke. He often talked of the financial difficulties experienced by Manchester Wanderers at this time, such as paying a gate operator two shillings and sixpence for collecting 'three sixpences'.[12] Wanderers experienced a number of financial and organisational difficulties, although they were helped by clubs such as Queens Park, who came to Manchester for a second time and again returned expenses to help the Manchester club.[13] A match programme produced for that game contained drawings that contrasted the two sides, Queens Park being represented by a smart military officer while Wanderers appeared as a seedy tramp 'making the best of his way to Withington Workhouse'.[14] The difference in status was clear, reinforcing the view that Manchester was still a long way behind, although the club had established a strong fixture list against local rugby sides, including Birch, their original parent, and the best association teams in the Midlands and northern England.[15] Wanderers set up a second team during 1878–79.[16]

Andrews remained a prominent Manchester-based football official for the rest of his life and others, such as Jack Prowse who later became a Manchester City committee member and referee, also joined the community during the late 1870s. These people brought influences from a variety of places, such as when Mancunian Prowse studied at Chester College in the early 1870s.[17] While he was at Chester College Prowse began playing association football within a team environment, at first representing the college against clubs in Wrexham as a right-winger but soon moving to the left when it became clear that he had a strong left foot. Although Prowse's love of the game and his first experience of playing in an organised team came at Chester, it is recorded that the majority of association players in that team were from Manchester. Prowse, from the Harpurhey district, demonstrated that while the region lagged behind rugby in terms of volume of clubs, it did have communities of association players. On his return to Manchester in the late 1870s Prowse became a teacher and later a head teacher at a variety of schools in the region; at each one he established football teams and competitions, and he spent much of his life promoting football at a junior level. He was credited with being largely instrumental in the establishment of the Manchester Schoolboys football association.[18] By developing interest within schools, Prowse helped to ensure that the sport had a future, and it is through men like him that sports such as football became community activities.

Hurst

Another influencer during this period was Jim Ingham from Hurst, who was regarded by many of the leading figures in Manchester's footballing development of the late 1870s and 1880s as one of the architects of the game locally. Ingham was so well known for his commitment to association football that when a reporter was trying to track him down for an interview he was told to 'ask the first man you meet in Ashton or Hurst and he will tell you'.[19] The reporter asked the porter at Ashton train station and, sure enough, he gave directions to Ingham's home almost two miles away. As a boy, Ingham had played football in the fields at Hurst: 'far away over fences and ditch – often by moonlight', and as he developed he became 'a centre half-back, standing over six feet, teetotal for thirteen years because he wanted to keep fit, walking two miles to his work, walking at night with the Hurst team for training purposes, playing fifteen seasons without missing a single Saturday match'.[20] Ingham was instrumental in the development of Hurst Association Football Club, which was formed in 1878, although some sources claim 1877, and he was Hurst secretary and a player from 1878 until 1886. He held a responsible position as checkweighman in a local colliery, a role that was often voted for by the workforce or given to a respected, experienced member of staff. Checkweighmen were responsible for determining how much coal each worker had mined and, therefore, how much pay was owed. Men who held these positions were perceived as trustworthy by their fellow workers and often became trade union officials. Ingham, both at work and within footballing circles, was perceived as a positive, honest man contributing to his community. After his playing career ended he continued to watch Hurst home and away and remained an active committeeman. The Hurst region of Ashton-under-Lyne was perhaps the strongest area for association football in the entire conurbation at this time. Earlier chapters have discussed ad hoc activities in both Hurst and Ashton; and that activity in the 1840s and 1850s helped to encourage men like Ingham to perceive association football as a natural sporting activity. Multiple clubs were developed in Hurst during the 1870s and 1880s. Utilising a long-range framework it is evident that individual footballing events during earlier decades did lead to a more rapid transition to soccer than was experienced in central Manchester. Hurst contained several mills and factories, but despite the industry it retained a village-like existence and was surrounded by fields. The combination of potential spaces for recreation, a dedicated working-class community and the idea of sporting competition created an appropriate environment for team sport to develop.

Ingham was at Hurst from the time of its formation in 1878, when the differences between the codes were still being established locally, and he remembered that the game was much more physical at that time than it was in the 1900s: 'We used our shoulders, and there was no ankle-tapping. Referees let you charge a man in those days.'[21] One of Ingham's favourite games was against Blackburn Rovers when Fergie Suter played: 'I never saw a finer back than Fergie Suter, but we beat the Blackburn men that day, much to their surprise. Herby Arthur, the famous Blackburn goalkeeper, went in goal with his raincoat on, but when we put two past him he took that coat off. We won 2–1 and they didn't like it!'[22] Hurst was recognised as a working-class community and in terms of contribution to Manchester's soccer history it was a pioneering club, helping the sport to transition from an inconsequential pastime performed on an ad hoc basis to a thriving community.

Historians and supporters often refer to the formation of another club, Newton Heath, occurring in 1878, but no evidence has been discovered of the club's playing football fixtures prior to 1880.[23] It is widely accepted that United began life as a club established by workers from the Newton Heath base of the Lancashire and Yorkshire Railway in 1878; however, there are many unknowns surrounding the club's birth and evidence on the formative years of the club is limited, with numerous myths continuing up to the present.

Newton Heath

Myths about the past have proliferated since the 1970s, and this is certainly true for football in Manchester, as both United and City have developed stories based on rumour, myth and inaccurate assumptions.[24] At Manchester City the daughter of the Reverend Arthur Connell has been credited with forming the club, based on supposition and an inaccurate analysis of the facts. Similar supposition exists for United. It has been assumed that United, as Newton Heath, played a fully formed version of association football from 1878, but this does not square with the contemporary evidence and later interviews with founding members. In 1922 Herbert Dale, a railway worker at the time of the club's formation who played at centre-forward on occasion and continued to play during the club's Alliance days over a decade later, provided his version of the club's transformation into a soccer club. In the 1920s Dale was respected for his contribution to the game and was remembered as a prominent figure at Newton Heath. If anyone knew the truth of the club's formation, then it was Dale, who became a well-known and respected Football League referee and a significant influence on the development of football in Manchester, dedicating his time to the Manchester Wednesday League during its first two decades and being presented with a medal to mark his connection in 1911.[25]

Dale has explained that the club when first formed had a cricket team, pre-sumably established in 1878, and that after some time a member of the committee bought a football from a shop on Market Street in the city centre. This appears to have been in 1880. According to Dale, the instigator of the club was Sam Black (Figure 6) and the original colours were red-and-white quartered

6 Sam Black, considered to be the man who introduced soccer to Newton Heath.

shirts.[26] Although he has also been named by others as a potential founder, this has been disputed based on his age in 1878.[27] However, as no game has been identified prior to November 1880, when he would have been seventeen, it is possible that Black did propose and establish a soccer club, or an offshoot of the cricket club, during 1880. His age would be consistent with those of other 'founders', secretaries and captains of clubs in nineteenth-century Manchester, such as Stuart G. Smith, a leading figure at Manchester Association, and those responsible for the development of St Mark's in West Gorton. Black was a prominent early player at Newton Heath and later became a referee. The question of shirt colours has been debated by historians for some time. Both United and their fans accept that green and gold were the initial colours of the club, based on two sources: first, green and gold were two colours used by the Lancashire and Yorkshire Railway, and second, a Bolton newspaper report of the club's earliest known game is supposed to have stated the colours worn as green and gold.[28] This appears to be a foundation myth, developed at some point after the club had become Manchester United. In 1887 the club's colours were recorded as red and white, and no contemporary mentions of green and gold have been found. This suggests that the club's first choice of kit was red and white quarters as stated by Dale, who claimed to have been there at the time. Souvenirs of the period, such as cards bearing the club's name, are often red and white and sometimes the colours are quartered, implying that green and gold was not utilised as the club's first choice of kit.

The matter is further complicated by references to the club in the *Sportsman's Yearbook* for 1880 and 1881 which state that the club's colours were 'white with blue cord'; however, further analysis demonstrates that the club was also listed as a cricket club, whose colours were 'white with blue cord'.[29] It seems that the details for the football club simply repeated those in the cricket section. Perhaps the secretary had requested an entry in both sections but completed only one submission form, and if that is indeed the case it is possible that the kit described was the cricket one, as the clothing was consistent with cricket clubs of that period. A review of the other clubs listed shows a variety of kits, but the majority are white with some form of coloured identification, such as a cap or handkerchief.[30] As these yearbooks were the publications closest in date to the first reported games of the club and the details would have been sent in by the secretary, Francis H. Dunn, or with his support, then they have to be considered accurate – certainly for the cricket team. The question remains whether green and gold was utilised at all at this time. Of course, it may well have been worn as an away kit, although this has not yet been seen in any contemporary reports. Similarly, despite extensive research, no evidence of a Newton Heath game during the 1870s has been identified, even though much detail exists on other sporting activity from the Newton Heath area. For example, on 12 October 1878 there is coverage of rugby in the area, including a report of another Newton Heath beating Fairfield by two touchdowns to one.[31] The local newspapers, most notably the *Gorton Reporter*, based in Ashton-under-Lyne and with local issues across east Manchester and neighbouring towns, covered sport in detail during the 1870s and 1880s and considerable local activity connected with the game is documented. As there is no mention of association football being played by Newton Heath it is unlikely that the Heathens played competitive games prior to 1880. On 20 November 1880 Newton Heath staged their first reported game when they were defeated 6–0 by Bolton Wanderers' second team. United's museum holds a fixture list from 1882 which states 'Established 1878', while a brochure for the 1901 fund-raising bazaar at St James's Hall in the city centre includes what seems to be the first officially produced acknowledgement of 1878 as the foundation year.[32] Details contained in the brochure indicate that at its formation the team played 'side games', meaning competition between teams from different sections of the railway company. Games played between sides within the same organisation are unlikely to have been reported.

According to the 1882 fixture list the club was known as 'Newton Heath (LYR) Cricket and Football Club', and it is possible that cricket was the only

7 The earliest known newspaper report of a Newton Heath game.

game played by the Heathens in 1878 and 1879. It is widely accepted that the club was established by the Dining Room committee of the railway works with the aim of developing team spirit and social skills and generally to improve employees' social well-being. East Manchester's railways, heavy industry and the region's canals meant an influx of people during the nineteenth century. The Newton Heath Lancashire and Yorkshire Railway (L&YR) depot grew rapidly and employed a workforce that arrived from a variety of locations around the British Isles, including many from Ireland. The east of Manchester, where both Newton Heath and the predecessor of City were established, was home to heavy industry. The most common form of occupation was in metals and engineering, where boilers, motors and textile machinery were produced in plants such as the enormous Beyer-Peacock works in Gorton. The works were supplied with coal from the Bradford district, which later (from 2003) became the site of City's Etihad campus. Two Bradford mines produced around a quarter of a million tons of coal each year, while the Moston colliery at Newton Heath employed 850 workers above and below ground.[33] While these areas were similar in terms of the type of residents, industry and housing, the individual identities of each district or town were strong, and during the 1880s football clubs developed that represented the various localities. Even towns such as Gorton were divided into different communities, and clubs such as Gorton Villa grew at a similar rate to Manchester City's West Gorton predecessors, and were still in existence around seventy years later.[34] Newton Heath Loco was another long-standing club, established by another department within the Lancashire and Yorkshire Railway L&YR works.

A Newton Heath Loco committee member, quoted in the 1970s, explained that in 1859 a series of Improvement Classes had been instigated by the Dining Room Committee, and these ultimately led to the formation of various sports clubs at the railway works. The Carriage and Wagon department formed Newton Heath L&YR, while the Motive Power section formed Newton Heath Loco and played at Ceylon Street. In the beginning, games were played on an inter-departmental basis, the Carriage and Wagon department ultimately pulling out of internal competition in order to compete solely against other sides in the region. This change of direction occurred during the 1880s, and Newton Heath's game against Bolton Wanderers' second team was potentially their first actual match. However, confusion remains regarding the club's formation.[35] As Dale claimed to have been present at the time and other information that he provided is generally accepted, then it needs to be recognised that Sam Black instigated the football club in 1880 as part of the parent organisation established in 1878, and that they played in red and white as described above. Newton Heath L&YR ultimately evolved into Manchester United, but its early existence was somewhat challenging: its first ground was at North Road (present day Northampton Road) and was 'little better than a clay pit'.[36]

The Heathens are known to have played several friendlies by 1882, against teams such as Hurst, Manchester Arcadians, Blackburn Olympic's second team, Bootle reserves and the forerunners of Manchester City, St Mark's. The first meeting with St Mark's ended in a 3–0 win at North Road, with the return resulting in a 2–1 defeat at Kirkmanshulme CC.[37] The club were developing, however, and when they produced their fixture card for the 1882–83 season they announced twenty-six fixtures, including games against fellow railway team Southport LYR and the reserve side of 1883 FA Cup winners Blackburn Olympic.

The Newton Heath president was recorded as Frederick (sometimes Fredrick) Attock, who was a thirty-six-year-old Carriage and Wagon works superintendent in 1882. The 1881 census records that he shared a house with his two young sons, Frederick William, aged six, and George Henry, aged eight. The children had been born in Essex, so the Attocks must have arrived in Newton Heath at some time between 1876 and 1881. In addition to Frederick and his sons, Frederick's mother, Hephzibah Attock, aged seventy in 1882, and servants Mary Forturn (fifty-two) and Jane Smith (thirty-six) lived in the family home, Sommerseat House. None of the residents had been born in Manchester – Jane came from Chester, Mary from Ireland, Hephzibah from Lincoln and Frederick himself was born in Liverpool. Both Hephzibah and Frederick were widowed, and the children had experienced hardship in their young lives and the move from Essex to Manchester was significant. Like so many Manchester residents of the period, Attock had moved to the city through his work and not by choice. In later life he was recorded as a retired engineer and lived in Westmoreland, while his sons were both lived in Lancashire – Frederick junior in Horwich and George close to Lancaster. As well as Attock, the 1882 fixture card lists of vice-presidents, committeemen, the club captain, secretary and vice-captain.[38] Under Attock's presidency the club entered the Lancashire Cup for the first time in 1883–84 but were defeated 7–2 in the first round by Blackburn Olympic, the 1883 FA Cup winners.

St Mark's (West Gorton)

Newton Heath's initial interest in soccer came at a time when there were signs that a preference for the association version of football was developing among young working-class residents. Arthur Connell's St Mark's Church (West Gorton) developed its sporting activities by adding both soccer and rugby teams to its existing community offerings in 1880.[39] Both Newton Heath and St Mark's developed in growing, densely populated areas where housing and factories were being built at a rapid rate. The construction work caused some problems, such as on Clowes Street, West Gorton in 1866, which was 'notorious for its jerry buildings, few, if any, properly drained; streets without any light, where people have to grope their way through mud and dirt, at the risk of life and limb'.[40] These problems continued for years, but there were other issues which made life difficult in east Manchester. Male inhabitants were spending too much time in the area's public houses and beer houses, while most children seemed to focus their energies on unsavoury activities. When pursuits for men and boys were shared, the activities tended to be ones that the wider public would frown upon, such as bare-knuckle fighting, which was popular on waste land in West Gorton, close to St Mark's Church, and in Ardwick. Fights would be staged between men of varying ages and watched by large crowds. There was also scuttling, a form of gang warfare: 'The weapons were belts, slings, sticks and stones.'[41]

Despite the negative aspects and obvious concerns about violence, the scuttlers developed a community spirit of their own at a time when the community at large seemed to care little for their well-being. Some schools, churches and local initiatives hoped to give the scuttlers some positive experiences and focus. In West Gorton William Beastow, a church warden at St Mark's and a senior figure at the Brooks and Doxey's engineering works as well as a prominent member of the local Masonic lodge, tried to establish a working men's club during the mid-1870s. It struggled for support and eventually folded, causing Beastow to speak with local employers in the hope that they would engage more and encourage their workers to demonstrate some community spirit. He became frustrated with the response, as employers claimed that working men in the district were not interested in self-improvement.[42]

Beastow focused his attentions on his Masonic links and became more involved with St Mark's Church, where by the end of the 1870s he became, in effect, the chairman of the St Mark's Cricket Club. Some cricket activity occurred during the 1860s, with brief match reports existing for games in 1867 and 1868. Cricket was known to have occurred in the southernmost part of St Mark's parish many years earlier, where Longsight Cricket Club was established in 1848, being based for its first few decades at Albert Grove, Longsight. It is possible that a St Mark's cricket team was established by summer 1866, as soon as the church was officially active, as it is known that the Reverend Arthur Connell had experienced successful cricket clubs during his time at Harrogate, before coming to West Gorton. The cricket club grew, and frequent match reports appeared in the local newspapers for both a first team and a junior team during the 1860s and 1870s.[43] Beastow, together with another member of the Ashbury's Masonic Lodge, James Moores, presided over the cricket meetings. Moores was also a St Mark's Church sidesman and his brother played for the church's cricket team, as did Beastow's son and stepson, who appeared in the junior cricket team by the summer of 1879. The cricket team prospered, particularly once the junior side became established, and Beastow must have been pleased that progress was finally being made in establishing a positive spirit among some of the young men of the parish.

Problems with youth-related activities continued to be a blight on the district, and visits by Connell and his family to households in the parish uncovered other issues including domestic violence, poverty, alcoholism and hunger. Crime was also an issue. In January 1874 a West Gorton man named James Clarke was sentenced to three months in prison with hard labour for stealing a shirt from a clothes line, while in October of that year a nine-year-old boy stabbed thirteen-year-old telegraph messenger and Clowes Street resident, Arthur Robbins. Local newspapers carried many stories of violence, crime and domestic issues in east Manchester during this period.[44] The Connells, together with Beastow and some of the other senior parishioners, tried to improve all aspects of West Gorton life and the St Mark's Mutual Improvement Society made significant progress during the 1870s. By the end of 1877 a women's group had been established by Georgina Connell, Arthur's youngest daughter, with much success. A few months later St Mark's opened a new church hall, and in 1879 Arthur set up a soup kitchen and a relief fund. On the kitchen's first day of operation in January 300 people queued for soup, bread and other food, and within a week over 1,500 gallons of soup, 1,000 loaves of bread and ten tons of coal had been distributed from the church.

Despite multiple initiatives, the young men and boys continued to engage in scuttling. In May 1879 it was claimed that more than 500 young men had been involved in a battle a short distance from West Gorton in an area reported as Bradford-cum-Beswick, which was between West Gorton and the present-day Etihad Stadium. Another report of scuttling from this period appeared in the *Ashton Reporter* under the title 'Openshaw v. Gorton'.[45] Scuttling had plagued the east Manchester districts of West Gorton, Openshaw and Bradford throughout the 1870s and 1880s and was a menace throughout the developing years of the area. Almost two decades after scuttling first plagued West Gorton, the journalist Alexander Devine defined those involved and their activities: 'A scuttler is a lad, usually between the ages of 14 and 18, or even 19, and scuttling consists of the fighting of two opposed bands of youths, who are armed with various weapons.'[46]

Four years before making those comments, Devine had founded a Lads' Club in Hulme, and this was followed by similar organisations, including the Adelphi Club in Salford in 1888 and the Ardwick Lads' Club in 1889, close to West Gorton.[47] Devine himself was a social pioneer and performed voluntary work with disaffected youths across Manchester throughout the 1880s. He explained that the scuttlers were suffering from a society that cared little about these young men who, at the age of twelve, were in employment but had little by way of role models or family support. West Gorton resident Sam Kirkman held similar views: 'there was nothing for the lads but the streets'.[48] Scuttlers tended all to dress in a similar manner, wearing metal-tipped clogs, brass-studded belts and bell-bottomed trousers, and some people suggested that they were not only keen to fight with rival gangs but would also attack 'any harmless pedestrian who happened to be passing. The lack of opportunity for recreation was the cause of all this misdirected energy, for in those days there were no playing fields.'[49] In the 1880s and 1890s as scuttling became an issue across Manchester and Salford, Devine brought it to the attention of the wider population, helping to improve the situation. The West Gorton scuttles were an issue in the 1870s before widespread efforts to tackle the problem through the formation of lads' clubs and related initiatives. Scuttlers fought for their turf, and although the locals would rather that they did not fight in their name, it is fair to say that some form of identity was established. The aim for community leaders had to be to focus the scuttlers' attention on more worthwhile activities, and to develop a positive identity for the young men of the area to rally around.

In 1879 the Reverend Arthur Connell's eldest daughter, Anna, established a working men's club with Beastow's support. She had been employed as a governess in Coppull during the early 1870s, and maybe in the late 1860s, and little mention of her appears in contemporary West Gorton or Manchester-based publications. From 1879 she is frequently mentioned in the local press. This suggests that, had she been resident in the parish earlier in the decade, she would have been as active as she was to be later on. From the late 1870s she is often mentioned in relation to St Mark's School, where her earlier governess experience proved its worth. For Anna, the establishment of a working men's club was something that she was determined to make happen. The formation of the Working Men's Meetings and related activities helped to focus minds, but their influence on the sporting direction of the parish is not apparent. The cricket club pre-dated these meetings by over a decade, but through William Beastow both organisations received a consistent message and direction. Ever since the mid-1980s the myth has developed of Anna Connell's role as 'founder' of the football club, based on research in the 1970s by Tony Heap which claimed that the cricket team was formed in 1879 directly from the Working Men's Meetings.[50] Heap did not have access to material which has since made it clear that the cricket team pre-dated the Men's Meetings by many years.

By the late 1870s the cricket club had proved relatively successful. Its junior players were the same age as many of the people engaged in scuttling and is it possible that some may have also engaged in that activity. Church activities were unlikely to give the young men what they craved, nor would a drawn-out game of cricket produce the kind of excitement that they derived from scuttling. At some point during the late 1870s or early in 1880 someone promoted footballing activities within the church and both rugby and association football teams were created. Whether this was as a counter attraction to scuttling is not clear, but by autumn 1880 both sports had been so well received by the boys and young men of the parish that games were arranged. The first reported games for both sports occurred in November 1880. The soccer team followed the conurbation's traditional association route by playing a Cheshire-based club, while the rugby opponents were from the Manchester region. However, it was the soccer team that developed, not the rugby side, and several players, most notably Walter Chew and a later arrival, Lawrence Furniss, remained active soccer administrators into the 1940s.[51] Hulme-born Chew, who was interviewed about the formation of the club for BBC Forces Radio in 1944, has been regarded as the father of Manchester City in numerous books, tributes and records over the years and has been viewed by some as the founder of the club, or at least the founder of its first incarnation, St Mark's (West Gorton). Chew himself claimed that it was his older brother William, along with some of his friends, who founded the club.[52] In 1922 he explained that the older boys founded the St Mark's team and that they played at Farmer's Field in West Gorton. One of the older boys, William Sumner, has been credited as the club's first captain, and his arrival in West Gorton around 1879 at the age of eighteen coincides with St Mark's move into both forms of football. He was an engineering student lodging in Gorton and was also a member of the St Mark's cricket club. In later years Sumner also played for Manchester FC, appearing for them in a FA Cup tie against Stoke in November 1883, and that same season he was possibly in the squad that travelled to Queens Park for the first FA Cup tie ever held in Scotland.

Chew outlined that St Mark's first pitch was Farmer's Field, close to Thomas Street, a few hundred yards north of St Mark's Church. This site formed part of Brooks and Doxey's Union Ironworks, where William Beastow was employed: 'Brooks & Doxey's covers a lot more ground than it did when I was serving my time. On the left or Hyde Road side there was what we called "Farmer's Field".'[53] The land around the ironworks had been utilised at times for boxing and wrestling.

The fledgling club played its first reported game at Farmer's Field on 13 November 1880 against the Baptist church from Macclesfield. A tape was stretched across the goal posts to form the goal, suggesting that either William Chew and his friends were unaware of Wood's suggestion from fifteen years earlier that a cross bar be used, or they simply could not afford or find one. The game was played between sides of twelve players each, which may have been to accommodate all those who had arrived with Macclesfield or may have been agreed some time in advance. Reports appeared in the *Gorton Reporter*, *Cheshire County News*, *Macclesfield Courier* and the *Athletic News*. The person who submitted the report was clearly keen for the game to be highlighted. At no point do the reports state that this was the club's first game, but it is interesting to note that it was the only association football match to appear in that week's *Gorton Reporter*, as all the other games featuring local clubs were rugby based, including games involving Reddish, Failsworth Rangers, Newton Heath Rovers, Newton Heath, Blackley, Sandfield Hornets and St Mary's

Played on the ground of the latter, the Rovers achieving a pretty easy victory by four goals to one.

HURST v. GREAT LEVER (2nd).—This game was played on the ground of the former at Hurst, near Ashton-under-Lyne, the home team winning by three goals to one. Great Lever had to face the wind during the first half, and their opponents scored their three goals before ends were changed. It was not until near the end of the game that Great Lever were able to score their first and only goal. M'Quirk played splendidly for Hurst.

MACCLESFIELD BAPTISTS v. ST. MARK'S, WEST GORTON.—This Association football match was played on the ground of the latter, on Saturday, with the following result: Baptists, two goals; St. Mark's, one goal.

ST. PETER'S ATHLETIC (2nd) v. ST. PETER'S (Everton).—Played on Saturday last on the ground of the

8 Report of St Mark's earliest known game.

CRUMPSALL v. WITHINGTON (2nd Teams).—Played at Withington. Score:—Withington: One try, one touchdown. Crumpsall: One try, five touchdowns, and three dead balls.

CAVENDISH RANGERS v. ST. MARK'S (West Gorton).—The Rangers, after a good game, managed to win this contest by two tries and five touchdowns to one try and two touchdowns.

DEWSBURY FRIENDS v. DODWORTH.—Played at Dewsbury, and, after forty minutes' play, the Friends were declared winners by one goal, one try, and three smaller points, to nothing. Pearcy dropped the goal in

9 Report of St Mark's earliest known rugby game.

(Failsworth). St Mark's first reported (and first known) game was a 2–1 defeat, staged at 3.15pm (Figure 8).

Historians of football writing about the Manchester clubs have assumed that Walter Chew was the more enthusiastic footballer in the Chew household, and it seems he has often been credited with appearances for the team when his own brother may actually have played. Reports of the earliest known game include W. Chew as a player and, if Walter's later comments on the club's formation are accurate, then this was William Chew, Walter's older brother. William was eighteen at the time of the club's first reported activity, while Walter was fifteen, and contemporary reports do not provide the players' full names, only their initials; even then, they do not consistently include initials. The first known match report showing both Chews in the line-up is from October 1881.[54] That may well have been Walter's first appearance for St Mark's, as he admitted that his own role in City's history came with the later founding of another club, Belle Vue Rangers in 1881–82. Walter claimed that, together with his cousin H. Leach, he had founded the Belle Vue club and bought the first ball.[55] Rangers progressed, although Chew spoke of an embarrassing match at Hurst when his side were being defeated quite heavily and were saved only when Chew's purchased ball burst, avoiding a major embarrassment.[56] Rangers' match reports exist from January 1882 through to 1883 when the club merged with members of West Gorton AFC (the successor to St Mark's) to establish a stronger West Gorton club. Chew had played for both clubs and took a prominent role in the merger, and in the years that followed he became the driving force behind the merged organisation. The growth of regular footballing activity in Gorton appears to have diverted attention from scuttling for some of the local population, demonstrating, perhaps for the first time in the region, how association football could be a positive influence on the city's youths.

Widespread participation

After their first reported games in 1880 both St Mark's and Newton Heath progressed, although St Mark's development stuttered and the club went through several incarnations before Walter Chew became the driving force. Other clubs developed, but none of the local football action could compare with the city's role in national soccer activities. A home FA Cup tie was played in the conurbation when Hurst faced Turton in October 1882, but it was not the first FA Cup tie in the city, as two FA Cup semi-finals had been played at Manchester's Whalley Range ground in the early 1880s. On 15 March 1882 Blackburn Rovers defeated Sheffield Wednesday 5–1 in a replay played in front of a crowd reported to be 10,000, the largest recorded for a semi-final at that time.[57] The following year another Blackburn club, Olympic, defeated Old Carthusians 4–0 on their way to becoming the North's first FA Cup winners. These games were important, as they demonstrated the attention which football could generate in the area, and for any neutral fixture to attract a crowd of around 10,000 was a great achievement. The games would have inspired the local association footballing community and the competitive nature of the FA Cup may have encouraged some to establish the Manchester Cup in 1884.[58] The staging of showpiece games raised soccer's status and demonstrated that it could be popular. The 1882 semi-final made the wider public aware of how soccer was progressing within Manchester, and brought positive coverage nationally. Some reporters highlighted comparisons with rugby's support, which tended to work positively for soccer.[59] The 1883 semi-final was moved from Birmingham to Manchester on the Tuesday prior to the game and had an attendance of around 3,000, which was considered impressive in view of the short notice.[60]

By 1882 the former Manchester Wanderers–Manchester Association merged club had renamed itself Manchester Association after a period in which various combinations of Wanderers, Association and Manchester had been utilised. The club appointed Hornby as president and was established at a ground on Dog Kennel Lane, Moss, Side, later renamed Maine Road and the home of Manchester City between 1923 and 2003.[61] Unlike West Gorton, Bradford and Newton Heath, Moss Side 'was a socially mixed suburb, popular not only with the wealthy, but also one accessible to clerks, shopkeepers, foremen and better off workers'.[62] At that time it was an almost exclusively residential area where population density was low and professionals, managers and the commercial middle class made up more than 25 per cent of the residents. Shopkeepers and small tradesmen made up around 30 per cent and clerks were around 15 per cent, and it was a wealthier area than east Manchester's districts. In effect, Moss Side and neighbouring Rusholme were suburbs of the city, while east Manchester was its industrial heart. Clubs established in east Manchester tended to be working-class and those south of the city were usually middle-class. During the opening years of the 1880s teams from across Manchester began to meet and play each other, meaning that social cohesion came through teams from working-class areas facing those from middle-class districts, highlighting the interdependencies created by sporting activities. This mix developed the Manchester region's football culture.

Manchester Association was heralded as the most significant association club in the area: 'If the Association game fails to make headway in our good city fault cannot in any way be charged to the account of the Manchester Association Football Club.'[63] The club's development was being noticed, and *Athletic News* commented in 1883 that the organisation 'is slowly coming into prominence again'.[64] At this time football was noticeably gaining more focus in local newspapers, with FA Cup games being documented extensively. The *Manchester Courier* even had a regular journalist called 'Dribbler' focusing on the association game.[65] In November 1883 Manchester Association defeated old foes Stoke 2–1 in the FA Cup and this was seen by participants as a proud moment.[66] Manchester's tie with Stoke was viewed by neutrals, including Dribbler, as a significant point in the development of the game in the city, particularly because prior to the tie only Nottingham Forest had managed to defeat Stoke that season.[67] The attendance, estimated as 700, was considered significant, even though it was lower than the crowds Manchester had attracted in previous years. Interest in association football increased as a result of this victory, and intensified when it became clear that Manchester would face the great Scottish side Queens Park in the next round. This was to be a British first for Manchester, as the tie, played at Queens Park's temporary home of Titwood, the home of Clydesdale cricket club, was the first FA Cup tie played in Scotland and thus Manchester Association were the first English side to play a competitive English fixture north of the border.[68] Queens Park had entered the FA Cup in its inaugural season, but this was the first time they had competed in a home fixture. They were Scotland's dominant club and were in the process of building Hampden Park, hence the temporary use of the cricket ground. Unfortunately, the game ended in a 15–0 Mancunian defeat by the eventual FA Cup finalists. The first season to see widespread Mancunian interest in the FA Cup was 1887–88, in which six local clubs competed, although the predecessors of Manchester City and United did not enter. In fact, Newton Heath, present-day United, chose to enter the national competition only once prior to 1889.

Despite its apparent lack of significance as an association football district (if modern interpretations of contemporary sources are to be accepted), the city was viewed as a significant gathering place and of strategic importance in the game's development. On 6 December 1882 a grand footballing conference was held in Manchester whereby representatives from each of the four home nations' football associations came together with the idea to produce a uniform code of laws and that this body would become the new guardians of the game. The Manchester Conference led to the creation of the International Football Association Board (IFAB), which was established in the summer of 1885 and became the only body able to change the laws of the game. After the establishment of FIFA in 1904 the game was structured with FIFA sitting below IFAB, which remains the highest governing body for the game's laws.

Manchester regards itself as a city of firsts in scientific and industrial development but, as the establishment of the IFAB and Stuart G. Smith's letter on rule development demonstrate, it was also important in the transition of association football into a major sport unified by a single set of rules and possessing a rule-based hierarchical structure and process. Up to 1877 the city had housed a community of footballers who initially, in several cases, attempted versions of the game which sometimes were more closely aligned with soccer than rugby, but predominantly were more characteristic of rugby.[69] The students of Owens College, which later became the University of Manchester, were typical: they established a team playing along rugby lines in 1872, but it soon folded. Another attempt at establishing a college rugby team came in 1875 before a more permanent club was established in 1881, with an association football club coming in 1883.[70] The sport was growing, and it is known that the teams listed in Table 1 were in existence by 1884.

The precise details of some of these clubs' formation, are not known; however, the list provides a general view of the game as it was from a local perspective. The profusion of sides in the east Manchester area aided the establishment of viable fixture lists for multiple clubs, but the exact conditions of competition were not well defined. A typical example was the 3 January 1885 meeting between Levenshulme and West Gorton. The away team, West Gorton, was recorded as winning the match but the game was never actually finished, as Levenshulme disputed the only goal and walked off the field, refusing to accept either the goal or the result.[71] Situations such as this were repeated around the region and frustrated those hoping to establish regular association activity. Across Manchester, discussions took place on how the situation could be improved for the growing network of clubs, players and enthusiasts.

Table 1 Manchester-region association football clubs known to be in existence by 1884

Club	Date	Other information
Arcadians	1880	Ground: Moston Lane, Harpurhey
		Founding members of the Manchester FA
Astley Bridge	1881	
Bardsley		
Belle Vue Rangers	1882	Ground: Belle Vue
		Split in 1884 to become Gorton AFC and West Gorton AFC
Bentfield	1881	Ground: Greenfield
Birch	1869	Originally founded as a soccer club but officially established association activities in November 1877 at the Longsight Cricket Ground.
Broadbottom	1881	Ground: Broadbottom cricket pitch
Broughton Wasps (rugby)	1876	Played soccer on occasion
Cheetham	1879	Ground: Tetlow Fold, Cheetham Hill
Dalton Hall	1884	Ground: Dog Kennel Lane, Moss Side
		Founding members of the Manchester FA
Darnton Road		
Denton	1882	Ground: Ashton Road, 1/4 mile from Denton Station
		Colours: Red and white
Earlstown	1883	
Eccles	1884	Ground: Ellesmere Park
		Colours: Light and dark blue
		Founding members of the Manchester FA
Farnworth Parish church	1884	Ground: Lord Street, Kearsley
		Colours: Blue and white
Furness Vale	1883	
Gorton AFC	1884	Ground: Pink Bank Lane
		Colours: Black shirts with white cross pattee
Gorton Tank Rovers	1882	
Gorton Villa	1883	Ground: Bulls Head Hotel, Reddish Lane
		Colours: Red and blue (known to be wearing green shirts with red sleeves in 1949)
Greenheys	1882	Ground: Alexandra Park (1887)
		Colours: Navy blue and white
		Founding members of the Manchester FA
Haughton Dale	1882	Founding members of the Manchester FA
Heaton Norris Rovers	1883	
Heywood	1884	
Heywood Central		Ground: Phoenix Pleasure Ground
Heywood Rovers	1883	
Heywood St James	1884	
Hooley Hill	1884	Ground: Canning Street, 1/2 mile from the Pack Horse Inn, Guide Bridge
		Colours: Red, white and Blue

Table 1 (*cont.*)

Club	Date	Other information
Hooley Hill Rovers	1882	
Hulme Athenaeum	1863	Ground: Pooley's Park and Hullard Hall, near Old Trafford, 1/4 mile from Old Trafford Station Colours: White and blue trimmings
Hurdsfield	1883	
Hurst	1878	Ground: Church Inn Colours: Red and white Founding members of the Manchester FA
Hurst Brook Olympic	1884	Founding members of the Manchester FA
Hurst Brook Rovers		
Hurst Clarence	1881	Founding members of the Manchester FA
Hurst Knowl Light Foots		
Hurst Lees Street Rangers	1883	
Hurst Park Road	1884	Founding members of the Manchester FA
Hurst Ramblers		
Hurst Star		
Hyde	1884	Ground: Opposite the Bankfield Hotel Colours: Oxford/Cambridge blue halves
Levenshulme	1876	Unclear what style of football was played at Levenshulme
Levenshulme	1884	Founding members of the Manchester FA
Lower Hurst	1884	Ground: Park Road, near infirmary Colours: Blue and white
Manchester Association	1875	Ground: Flint's Farm (Moss Side) in 1875; Greenheys in 1882; Hullard Hall Lane in 1887 Colours: Scarlet and black hoops (1875); blue and French grey (1877); blue and white quarters, white shorts (1887) Merged with Manchester Wanderers and renamed Manchester Association in 1882 Founding members of the Manchester FA
Manchester Clifford	1884	Ground: Trafford Hotel, Old Trafford, 1/2 mile from Old Trafford station Colours: Maroon and blue
Manchester Wanderers	1878	Ground: Upper Chorlton Road, Brooks Bar (1878) Renamed Manchester Association in 1882
Marple	1882	
Middleton	1882	
Miles Platting		
Newton Heath L&YR	1878	Ground: North Road, 1/2 mile from Newton Heath station Colours: Red and white (1880) Founding members of the Manchester FA
Oldham Olympic	1887	Became members of the Manchester FA by 1887

Table 1 (*cont.*)

Club	Date	Other information
Oughtrington Park	1884	
Pendleton Olympic	1883	Ground: Whit Lane, Pendleton
		Founding members of the Manchester FA
Royton	1887	Became members of the Manchester FA by 1887
Rusholme Gymnastic Club	1870	
Stalybridge Clarence	1880	Ground: Tame Valley, Stalybridge
Stalybridge St Georges	1883	Ground: Bulls Head Inn and Crookbottom
		Colours: Blue and white
Stretford	1887	Became members of the Manchester FA by 1887
Tame Valley Rangers	1883	
Ten Acres	1884	Ground: Three Crowns Hotel and Ten Acres Lane
Thornham	1883	Founding members of the Manchester FA
Uppermill Congregational	1883	
Wellington (Stockport)	1876	
West Gorton	1884	Ground: Queen's Road, West Gorton
		De-merged to establish West Gorton AFC and Gorton AFC
		Founding members of the Manchester FA
West Manchester	1884	Ground: Brooks Bar and Northumberland Hotel
		Colours: White
		Defunct 1897
		Founding members of the Manchester FA

Note: Date signifies date when the club was established or its earliest mention identified to date in contemporary sources. Ground and colour information are provided where they have been identified.

Notes

1 MacKillop, 'Climatic city', 245.
2 C. O'Reilly, 'Re-ordering the landscape', 35.
3 'Our National Winter Game', *Athletic News*, 25 September 1878, 7.
4 'Proposed Lancashire Football Association', *Manchester Guardian*, 30 September 1878, 7; 'Lancashire Football Association', *Athletic News*, 25 September 1878, 7; 'Lancashire Football Association', *Athletic News*, 2 October 1878, 6.
5 'Football', *Athletic News*, 2 October 1878, 6.
6 'Football Notes and Gossip', *Athletic News*, 23 October 1878, 2.
7 'Grand football match by electric light at Sheffield', *Athletic News*, 16 October 1878, 8; 'Football by the electric light', *Staffordshire Sentinel*, 14 November 1878, 3; 'Football by the electric light', *Athletic News*, 30 October 1878, 8; 'Football by the electric light', *Staffordshire Sentinel*, 12 November 1878, 3.
8 'En passant', *Athletic News*, 30 October 1878, 1; 'Evening amusement by electric light', *Athletic News* 30 October 1878, 8.
9 'En passant', *Athletic News*, 19 February 1879, 1; 'En passant', *Athletic News*,

23 April 1879, 1; 'A four a side tournament', *Athletic News*, 30 April 1879, 2; 'Football tournament in Manchester', *Sheffield Daily Telegraph*, 28 April 1879, 4.

10 'Football', *Sheffield Daily Telegraph*, 5 May 1879, 4; 'Lancashire Football Association', *Blackburn Standard,* 23 August 1879, 8; 'Manchester Wanderers v Darwen', *Athletic News*, 25 February 1880, 6; 'Manchester Wanderers v Queen's Park', *Athletic News*, 31 March 1880, 2.

11 R. G. Barlow, *Forty seasons of first-class cricket: being the autobiography and reminiscences of Richard Gorton Barlow* (Manchester: John Heywood Ltd., 1908), 45–46.

12 'Familiar faces', *Manchester Football Chronicle*, 7 October 1922.

13 Queens Park were not happy that Manchester Wanderers did not express enough gratitude after the second visit and believed that their 'benevolence was wasted' and that they 'were done with the Wanderers'. Queens Park's games in Manchester are detailed in Robinson, *History of the Queen's Park*, chapter 16.

14 'Football', *Athletic News*, 16 April 1879, 1.

15 'Manchester Wanderers Association', *Athletic News*, 8 January 1879, 6.

16 'Manchester Wanderers (2nd) v Bollington', *Athletic News*, 19 March 1879, 3.

17 'Well-known figure in City circles', *Manchester Football Chronicle*, 28 April 1923, 3; 'Man who made United', *Manchester Football Chronicle*, 20 January 1923, 3.

18 'Well-known figure in City circles', *Manchester Football Chronicle*, 28 April 1923, 3.

19 'Man who made Hurst club famous', *Manchester Football Chronicle*, 21 October 1922, 3.

20 Ibid.

21 Ibid.

22 Suter played for Blackburn between 1880 and 1888 and was recognised as a professional player. 'Man who made Hurst club famous', *Manchester Football Chronicle*, 21 October 1922, 3.

23 James, *Manchester, a football history*.

24 Guldi and Armitage, *The history manifesto*, 54.

25 'Forty years of the football field: experience as a referee', *Manchester Football Chronicle*, 14 October 1922, 3.

26 'Familiar faces', *Manchester Football Chronicle*, 14 October 1922, 3.

27 C. Boujaoude, *The story of the green and gold* (Manchester: Empire Publications, 2010), 12.

28 It has been repeated often that a newspaper report in the *Bolton Evening News* mentioned the colours of green and gold were worn for Newton Heath's first reported match. The origin of this is unclear but the *Manchester United pictorial history and club record* (Charles Zahra, Joseph Muscat, Iain McCartney and Keith Mellor; Nottingham: Temple Press, 1986) specifically refers to the match report on page 11 as being published on 24 November 1880 and implies that it stated the team colours. It also suggests that Bolton wore scarlet shirts. Research for this book has included a review of every Bolton newspaper for that period and a match report was discovered in the *Bolton Evening News* on the date mentioned but this did not include any reference to the colours worn. 'Bolton Wanderers (a team) v Newton Heath (Lancashire and Yorkshire Railway)', *Bolton Evening News*, 24 November 1880, 4.

29 J. K. Angus, *The sportsman's year-book for 1880* (London: Cassell, Petter, Galpin &

Co., 1880), 165 and 182; J. K. Angus, *The sportsman's year-book for 1881* (London: Cassell, Petter, Galpin & Co., 1881), 155 and 182.

30 Angus, *The sportsman's year-book for 1881*, 152–156.

31 *The Gorton Reporter*, 12 October 1878.

32 *Newton Heath Football Club: grand bazaar* (Manchester: Newton Heath Football Club, 1901).

33 Clay and Brady (eds), *Manchester at work*, 119.

34 *Rusholme Football League handbook 1949–50* (Manchester: Rusholme Football League, 1949), 25.

35 G. Green, *There's only one United* (London: Hodder and Stoughton, 1978), 252–255.

36 MacGregor, *The book of football*, 242.

37 S. Cawley and G. James, *The pride of Manchester: a history of the Manchester derby matches* (Leicester: ACL & Polar Publishing, 1991).

38 The full names of some of these have now been identified and they include vice-president Thomas Gorst, born in 1830 in Liverpool, who lived at 5 Church Terrace and was employed as a railway clerk; and vice-captain John Cramphorn, who was 23 in 1882 and lodged at 31 Ten Acres Lane. He was born in Shalford, Essex. At both Cramphorn's and Gorst's addresses lodged other railway workers from other parts of the British Isles.

39 'Baptist (Macclesfield) v St Mark's (West Gorton)', *Gorton Reporter*, 20 November 1880, n.p.; 'Cavendish Rangers v St Mark's (West Gorton)', *Athletic News*, 17 November 1880, 3.

40 'Mud in Gorton', *Manchester Courier*, 6 February 1866, 7.

41 In 1931 Sam Kirkman wrote his memories in the *Gorton Reporter* as documented in G. James, *Manchester, the City years* (Halifax: James Ward, 2012), 24–32.

42 James, *Manchester, the City years*, 26.

43 For example, 'St Mark's West Gorton v Hyde-road Britannia', *Gorton Reporter*, 4 June 1870, 6; 'St Mark's, West Gorton (second eleven) v. Longsight Juniors', *Gorton Reporter*, 23 July 1870, 6.

44 A review of the *Gorton Reporter* for January to April 1879 carries details of a variety of incidents including several stabbings, including, in April, an attack on a fourteen-year-old who was playing cricket at a site that would become St Mark's' first pitch.

45 See G. James, *Manchester the greatest city* (Leicester: Polar Publishing, 1997), 9–14 for further details on the scuttling in West Gorton and its possible connections to footballing development.

46 'Scuttlers and scuttling', *Manchester Guardian*, 5 September 1890, 8.

47 McKechnie, *Manchester in 1915*, 107–109.

48 James, *Manchester, the City years*, 24–32.

49 McKechnie, *Manchester in 1915*, 107–109.

50 Tony Heap produced a four-volume unpublished history of Manchester City's origins, focusing on the years 1880 to 1894. His research focused solely on material included in the *Gorton Reporter*. He had limited access to other sources and elaborated on the material he had found. He assumed that the efforts of Miss G. Connell created a working men's club at St Mark's church and that this led on to the

establishment of a cricket club in 1879, which in turn led to the establishment of a football club. Heap's material was deposited at Manchester City following his death and writers since the 1980s have elaborated further on Heap's work, and the story of the 'vicar's daughter' and her role in establishing a football club has developed further. Later research, most notably by Paul Toovey and Gary James, has highlighted a number of incorrect assumptions in Heap's work and that of researchers in later years. The key facts uncovered since 2008 are that the cricket club was in existence from the mid-1860s; that there were two Connell sisters, with Georgina concentrating on female activities and Anna being absent from the region for much of the 1870s, although she did establish a working men's group in 1878.

51 Furniss was ever present during Manchester City's development, fulfilling roles such as player, secretary-manager, director, chair and life president, until his death in 1941, while Chew focused his attention on the Manchester Football Association, where he spent many years as treasurer, becoming the first recipient of its long service award and remaining active until his death in 1948. Both men worked with the development of football in Manchester alongside John Nall and Nall's son, who was a Manchester Football Association committee member for most of his life, becoming the first person to receive a long service award from the organisation. *Manchester County Football Association souvenir brochure 1884–1984* (Manchester: Manchester County Football Association), 14.

52 'General forces', *Manchester Evening News*, 26 July 1944, 4; 'The discoverer of Hyde Road', *Manchester Football Chronicle*, 23 March 1922, 3.

53 James, *Manchester, the City years*, 31–32.

54 Most reports show W. Chew playing for the club, but when the two brothers appear together William is recorded as W. H. Chew. When Walter is not in the team the middle initial to differentiate the brothers is not required.

55 Walter Chew was the captain of Belle Vue Rangers and some of their games occur at the same time as W. Chew appeared for the St Mark's club in their own fixtures, suggesting that this could not be the same person and adding to Chew's memories of this period. This leads to the inevitable conclusion that mentions of W. Chew playing for St Mark's during its formative seasons and prior to its merger with Belle Vue referred to William H. Chew and not Walter Chew. 'The discoverer of Hyde Road', *Manchester Football Chronicle*, 23 March 1922, 3.

56 Ibid.

57 M. Collett, *The complete record of the FA Cup* (Cheltenham: Sportsbooks, 2003), 834.

58 'English Association Challenge Cup', *Athletic News*, 22 March 1882, 3.

59 'English Association Challenge Cup', *Athletic News*, 22 March 1882, 1–5.

60 'Football', *Bell's Life in London and Sporting Chronicle*, 17 March 1883, 3; *Athletic News*, 21 March 1883, 1–3.

61 'En passant', *Athletic News*, 27 September 1882, 1.

62 Moore, 'Liberalism', 240. [full reference]

63 'Manchester Association F.C., late Manchester Wanderers', *Manchester Courier*, 30 October 1882, 2.

64 'En passant', *Athletic News*, 3 January 1883, 1.

65 'West Gorton Association Football Club', *Manchester Courier*, 30 October 1883, 7; James, *Manchester, a football history*, 38.

66 'Familiar faces', *Manchester Football Chronicle*, 7 October 1922, 3.

67 'Sporting intelligence', *Manchester Courier*, 12 November 1883, 3.

68 James, *Manchester, a football history,* 37.

69 As an example of a soccer school see: 'Stockport Wellington v Fairfield Academy', *Manchester Courier*, 19 October 1874, 7.

70 Email correspondence with the University of Manchester archivist James Peters, 19 July 2013. The sports clubs at Owens College tended to be established by students, with some clubs founded at the college and some at the Dalton Hall student accommodation.

71 *Gorton Reporter*, 10 January 1885.

6

Organisation and competition

The Manchester Football Association

Following the aborted attempt to establish a Manchester–Staffordshire Football Association in 1876 and the establishment of the Lancashire Football Association (Lancashire FA) in 1878, the requirement to establish regular competition and localised rules was recognised in numerous locations around the country. The growth of soccer in Lancashire following the establishment of the county FA demonstrated that formalised competition aided Lancashire's soccer development, and this was replicated across the regions.[1] Whenever a regional association was established the sport developed at a faster rate than in comparable districts, and by 1880 regional associations existed in Birmingham (1875), Staffordshire (1877), Surrey (1877), Berkshire and Buckinghamshire (1878), Cheshire (1878) and Shropshire (1878). In the north-west of England the Lancashire FA was viewed as the local governing body; but with its power base and the majority of clubs north of Manchester, and with its aim to focus solely on the clubs within the county boundary, this meant that Manchester's entire conurbation was not served. The Manchester clubs established during the 1870s and 1880s played across the conurbation, which by 1884 included areas of Lancashire, north-east Cheshire, north-west Derbyshire and part of the West Riding of Yorkshire. No county-specific football association could be fully representative of the community of footballing enthusiasts and connections within the expanding Manchester conurbation, whose connections were often based on railway routes, allowing central Manchester clubs to engage frequently in competition with teams at the extremes of the region. This was demonstrated by the activities of the Gorton club, which, by 1884, had frequent fixtures with Broadbottom, a village straddling the border between Cheshire and Derbyshire, eleven miles east of Gorton; Stretford, six miles west of Gorton; Bentfield, based in Greenfield, West Riding of Yorkshire, ten miles north-east of Gorton; and Marple, Cheshire, eight miles south-east of Gorton. There were also regular fixtures beyond these relatively simple train routes, with Manchester clubs penetrating further south into Macclesfield, Cheshire (eighteen miles from Gorton) and to Earlstown (sic), based in Earlestown, Newton-le-Willows (twenty-one miles west of Gorton). Of the fourteen teams played by Gorton during 1883–84 seven were from Lancashire (all within the Manchester region), four from Cheshire, two from Derbyshire and one from Yorkshire. While none of these teams was further north than Middleton, seven miles north of Gorton, it should be remembered that some areas of the Manchester conurbation were in Cheshire, such as Sale, Altrincham, Hyde and Stalybridge.

Manchester clubs needed to establish a formal body to represent them all and their connections, but in 1883 the Manchester soccer community's only opportunity for competition and structure was to form part of the Lancashire FA. Some Manchester clubs did this, but fixtures would have to be played across Lancashire, and for some in the Manchester region this was inconvenient because it was considerably easier to travel south, towards Crewe and Stoke, or east, towards Sheffield. Manchester was right at the edge of southeast Lancashire. Hurst Park Road from Ashton-under-Lyne, a Lancashire town within Manchester's conurbation, was one of the local teams to enter the Lancashire Cup, but – perhaps showing the difference in the appeal of the competition – it was commented that Park Road players were more interested in ensuring that they got their share of the gate receipts than in winning the tie.[2] While the Lancashire Cup may have brought some financial benefits to those teams that were in Lancashire and could travel, it did little for the rest. It is notable that when the men who established Manchester's FA were interviewed during the twentieth century and asked to consider the developmental moments in the conurbation's football growth they invariably talked of friendlies with prominent sides, such as an 1883 meeting between Manchester and Blackburn, as being significant, but not of Lancashire Cup matches.[3] By 1883 discussions had been held on the formation of Manchester's own football association, but they rarely progressed beyond the agreement that an association and related cup competitions were needed. Arthur Andrews, a prominent member of Manchester's soccer community since the mid-1870s, decided that someone had to take ownership of the idea and he sent a letter to several clubs proposing a meeting at the City Hotel, Cooper Street. Other meetings were held at the Crown Hotel, Booth Street, Manchester as Andrews and other attendees established the Manchester and District Football Association.[4] It initially comprised sixteen clubs: Arcadians, Dalton Hall, Eccles, Hurst, Greenheys, Haughton Dale, Hurst Brook Olympic, Hurst Clarence, Hurst Park Road, Levenshulme, Manchester, Newton Heath (United), Pendleton Olympic, Thornham, West Gorton (City) and West Manchester.[5]

A quarter of all the teams were from the Hurst district of Ashton-under-Lyne, while students at Manchester University were represented by Dalton Hall and Manchester's more historic clubs, West Manchester and Manchester Association, were also founding members.[6] In December 1884 the Manchester FA played its inaugural representative match against Hallamshire at Hurst, winning 4–1 before a crowd of 1,500, and games against Blackburn Rovers and Preston North End followed.[7] At its formation the Manchester FA decided to represent clubs within eight miles of Manchester's Royal Exchange in St Ann's Square. The Royal Exchange was erected between 1867 and 1874 and was Manchester's third exchange. It was often viewed as the most important building in the city and handled Manchester's trade, helping to establish the city as the commercial centre of the North.[8] By the 1920s it had become the largest commodity market in the world, boasting 11,000 members, and in 1929 it was commented that while 'it may be inaccurate to call the English a nation of shopkeepers ... one is on safer ground in calling Manchester a city of middle men ... commerce rather than industry is Manchester's most prominent feature'.[9] Maybe symbolically, the Manchester FA felt that this was the heart of Mancunian life. Reports of the formation of the Manchester FA in 1884 mention how many clubs were represented but do not carry the names of those who attended, which is a shame, as the organisation of sport relied heavily on the activities of individuals. It is known that Jim Ingham of the Hurst club received the first nomination to serve on the committee, but he was unable to commit to this and asked for his name to be withdrawn.[10] His nomination was in recognition of his achievements in developing football in Ashton. Another popular presence within Manchester's footballing community was John Nall, the former Hulme Athenaeum secretary and Manchester Association FC co-founder, and he was an early Manchester FA committeeman. By the summer of 1887, less than three years after the founding of the Manchester FA, Nall was its vice-president,[11] an indication that his interest and involvement in the sport had continued.[12] In 1891 his position within Manchester's footballing community was clear when he was selected as the Manchester FA's second president, a role in which he remained until his death, thus demonstrating his centrality and significance to Manchester's footballing community.[13] Nall's presidency established sustained growth for the Manchester FA, and aided the predecessors of Manchester City and United to begin their evolution into leading clubs.[14] In fact, when Nall presented Ardwick (City) with their first trophy, the Manchester Cup, in 1891, he praised Ardwick on their success and Newton Heath (United) on their rise to prominence. It has been suggested that he attended the meeting in 1894 that established Manchester City, thus acting as a link between Manchester's first club, Hulme Athenaeum, and its present-day representatives.[15]

Another prominent footballing figure, Arthur Andrews, acted as the Manchester FA treasurer for several years and in January 1888 the Association recognised his role by presenting him with a gold watch. A decade later they awarded him a medal, like the one received by the Manchester Cup winners, and in the 1920s they marked his entire contribution with a long service medal.[16] As with John Nall and Fitzroy Norris, Andrews' contribution in these formative years was known and understood at the time but, regrettably, faded as football progressed through the twentieth century.

One of the main activities of the new Manchester FA was to set up a cup competition, and within three months of the first meeting of the new Association ties were being staged in the Manchester Cup. The final occurred at the end of 1884–85 season, with some clubs charging 8d and 4d for attendance at ties.[17] Manchester needed the new competition, open to all within the region, to allow the sport to progress in a consistent manner across the region. The inevitable inter-town or district games stimulated interest in the sport but, because the Lancashire FA still insisted on its authority over all the county, the opportunity for Manchester, with its networks linking it to towns officially outside the county, continued to be hampered. Teams in east Manchester were closer, in terms of distance and travelling time, to clubs from Uppermill and Greenfield (both in Yorkshire), Stalybridge or Altrincham (Cheshire), whom they played frequently, than they were to those in the Blackburn area. For this reason the Manchester FA campaigned for direct affiliation to the FA because, inappropriately, it had been approved on the basis that it was a subdivision of the Lancashire FA. It did not see itself as subservient to Lancashire, nor should it have been, and those leading football in Manchester campaigned for greater autonomy throughout the decade following its formation.[18]

Within Manchester the east of the city and the neighbouring towns proved to be the more interested in association football by the mid-1880s. East Manchester was a densely populated, heavily industrialised area and football was a great release from daily life. Due to their rapid development and industrialisation the communities of east Manchester consisted of a mix of locally born citizens, new arrivals and the Manchester-born children of residents who had arrived in the city looking for work some years before. Some had arrived after experiencing soccer elsewhere and contributed their knowledge and expertise, while others were keen to use football as a relatively cheap and simple leisure activity. Perhaps because of the individual identities of each of the districts or towns, football clubs developed to represent the various localities, but it was the formation of the Manchester FA with its own Manchester Cup competition that brought the most visibility to the game locally. The significance of this should not be under-estimated and, in terms of the long-term development of football, the establishment of the Manchester FA was a prominent event during a transformational period. Once Manchester had its own FA, clubs appeared within almost every community of the conurbation, as did other competitions and leagues.[19]

Manchester FC and Hurst had both competed in the FA Cup by this stage and understood the importance of competition. In fact, Hurst were Manchester's only undefeated entrant in the FA Cup at this point. They entered the competition in 1883–84 and defeated Turton 3–0, then defeated Irwell Springs from

Bacup 3–2; however, Irwell protested about the result and the FA ordered a replay. Hurst decided to withdraw from the competition but, despite setbacks like these, recognised the excitement that could be generated by competition. Hurst had joined the Lancashire FA in July 1881, widening their own sphere of connections. For the teams north of Manchester, the Lancashire Cup was significant, but Manchester clubs still felt that travel costs and time inhibited their opportunities, hence the reason why Hurst had withdrawn from the FA Cup tie at Irwell. The concept of local competition ensured that the Manchester Cup became important and, in terms of status, it was regarded in Manchester as of more significance than the Lancashire Cup or even the FA Cup for the following decade. Newton Heath had chosen to enter the FA Cup only once pre-1889, and even then had endured a poor experience when a tie at Fleetwood Rangers in October 1886 ended 2–2, with the referee trying to persuade the Heathens to play extra time. The Heathens, concerned about rail travel back to Manchester, had refused and the tie was awarded to Fleetwood. The first season of the Manchester Cup proved to be exciting, with the games involving Hurst and Newton Heath receiving most attention; although as far as young railway worker Herbert Dale was concerned, the first exciting moment came when he attended the initial cup draw and then rushed across Manchester to the Newton Heath railway works to advise the railwaymen of the draw.[20]

The Manchester Cup raised the profile of the region's existing clubs and gave others the opportunity to become established, Newton Heath becoming one of the first to benefit from the competition. Newton Heath performed well, defeating Dalton Hall in an extraordinary semi-final. The collegians were a side comprised of university students based at Dalton Hall, which was recognised as the country's first purpose-built university hall of residence when it opened in 1882, and this was one of the first occasions when the university demonstrated an interest in association football. This is a surprising aspect to the development of football within Manchester, as universities often played a leading role in the development of football; however, this was not the case in Manchester. Sources from the early 1880s imply that the university was not too active in the sport and in 1883 Dribbler, writing in the *Manchester Courier*, claimed that the university was lagging behind clubs such as Manchester Association and the other developing sides. An Owens College side was in existence, but after one game against Cheadle in Fallowfield the Dribbler suggested that simply using the name Owens College meant that the university was not supportive of the game in the way that it should be. He called for the side to be named after the university itself and argued that the change would help the university become a leading player in the development of the association game.[21] These comments add weight to the view that Manchester's football development owed less to the university and public schools than it did to the working and lower-middle classes. Most of Manchester's earliest sides came from the working classes rather than the educated elite, but the inclusion within Manchester's predominantly working-class footballing community of Dalton Hall and the clubs based in the southern suburbs demonstrates that class boundaries were less important in Mancunian society and to those playing the sport than to those who later chronicled it. The tie between Dalton Hall and Newton Heath ended 3–3 after normal time, and so the clubs decided to play two periods of extra time, each lasting fifteen minutes. This is accepted as the first occasion on which the Heathens played extra time, which was not common practice at the time. Newton Heath won the tie 4–3 and faced Hurst in the first final of the competition. Hurst and Newton Heath were both working-class teams, consisting of men of varied backgrounds who had been attracted to the region by work prospects and the hope of a bright, secure future. Jim Ingham, Hurst's captain, recognised that reaching the final was important and brought some welcome gifts: 'On the Monday before the final each of our players was presented with a bottle of the best port and two score eggs. You see, someone means us to win! Two of our players and their families did their four score of eggs in on the Monday night, and the port as well!'[22] For the struggling families of those players the provision of food and alcohol was a tremendous bonus, while the game's status was such that a potential victory was perceived as enough of an opportunity for the gifts to be distributed as a means of encouragement.

The first Manchester Cup final was played at Manchester FC's Whalley Range ground, watched by approximately 3,500. This was a pivotal moment in Jim Ingham's life: 'I was teetotal for 13 years and I said I would break it if we (Hurst) won the first Manchester Cup. It came off all right. We beat Newton Heath L and Y Railway 3–0 and they had already got cards printed in honour of Newton Heath's victory. We were offering shillings for a card after the match.'[23] At the end of the final Hurst's players were lifted shoulder high by members of the crowd and there was tremendous excitement on the pitch. Significantly, sporting newspapers carried positive coverage of the final: 'I have rarely seen such enthusiasm at a football match in the Manchester district, and certainly never before at an Association game. The most demonstrative portion of the spectators were those who had accompanied the Hurst team. These included a goodly few of the gentler sex … Most of those present wore some token of their partisanship … the Hurst contingent [were] distinguished by mammoth placards placed in their head-gear.'[24] The Manchester Cup gave existing clubs focus, and also provided an impetus to other teams. After the conclusion of the match the president of the Manchester FA, Mr W. Colbert, presented the cup to Jim Ingham before the club embarked on a visible and noisy parade to Ashton, where they had a reception at the Pitt and Nelson public house.

The significance of the night was such that Jim Ingham remembered and frequently discussed the celebrations for the rest of his life: 'What a night it was afterwards! We filled the cup first with champagne, then with whisky, and then with Port.'[25] Hurst were worthy recipients of the praise. After promoting the sport and competition, they were the first prominent ambassadors for football in Manchester after the teams from the 1860s and 1870s, and on occasions they had travelled beyond the region to play the sport. For example, in March 1885 they had welcomed Welsh side Rhyl to Ashton, where the Hurst won 8–1 before 3,000 fans; then on Good Friday they played their return match and over 750 fans travelled from Ashton for the game, which Hurst won 4–0. Considering the nature of travel, working conditions and the state of the game at the time, this was significant.

With the Manchester Cup now providing a focus, Manchester's clubs had something to aim for and the competition's second season included a mix of twenty-four working-class, middle-class, church and student teams.[26] Newton Heath won the trophy that year by defeating Manchester FC. In 1887 another significant side, West Manchester, was successful. Hurst, Newton Heath and West Manchester, based at Whalley Range, were perhaps the three most prominent clubs of the period and all three gained prestige in the mid-to-late-1880s following their exploits in the Manchester Cup and their ability to attract a growing audience. Their interest in Lancashire FA-organised tournaments also grew and West Manchester supporters were known to travel in great numbers to support their side in the Lancashire Junior Cup.[27]

One West Manchester match, played next to the Manchester FC ground at Whalley Range where a county rugby game was being staged, highlighted the changing status of the two sports and reports focused on the difference in size between the crowd watching soccer and the smaller number at the rugby.[28] Soccer crowds are difficult to prove, but contemporary figures refer to multiple attendances of 8,000 to 10,000.[29] West Manchester, due to its proximity to Manchester FC, provided an easy comparison, and with their opponents being Newton Heath, viewed as another leading working-class club, it was becoming obvious that Manchester was no longer reliant on one or two key officials for the sport's promotion.[30] Manchester now possessed multiple clubs with growing support and a thriving, extensive community of soccer enthusiasts, and there were multiple local competitions too.[31] The city might still, officially, have been a rugby stronghold, but that did not mean that its soccer community was not itself a strong and popular presence across the region.[32] High-profile fixtures with renowned clubs such as Aston Villa, Bolton Wanderers and Derby Midland aided the sport's development, although support from some of Lancashire's leading clubs was difficult to achieve. Preston North End, for example, made too-high demands for fees when Newton Heath asked for their support. In contrast, Bolton Wanderers helped Hyde to attract 3,000 spectators to a promotional match.[33]

In subsequent seasons clubs from Denton, Hooley Hill and Royton reached the Manchester Cup final, but Newton Heath managed to lift the trophy on each occasion. Then, in 1891, Ardwick, a predecessor of Manchester City, defeated the Heathens in the final. For the following twenty years or so the competition would be dominated by sides that became well-established Football League clubs, including Bury (first success 1894), Stockport County (1898) and Oldham Athletic (1914). It is interesting to note that Bolton Wanderers won the competition for the first time in 1895, after choosing to join the Manchester FA despite being prominent within the Lancashire FA. This suggests recognition of a strong but distinct soccer community within the Manchester region. Fitzroy Norris, the former Manchester Association committee member, was a prominent figure at Bolton by this time and may have encouraged the Wanderers to engage more in the conurbation's activities, but it seems that his former team mate John Nall was instrumental in bringing Wanderers into the Manchester FA. This ensured the support of Bolton's John Bentley, an accountant, journalist and League official recognised as a driving force in the game. It also demonstrated the willingness of Nall and his contemporaries to supplement Manchester's footballing community with national figures based on interdependencies, supporting Laine's view that 'personal lives and the structures are intertwined with each other in history'.[34] Manchester might not have possessed its own national figures, but with the addition of the Bolton club and individuals such as Joshua Parlby, a Stoke committee member who joined Ardwick in 1892, the conurbation gained leading footballing men.

A mark of the impact of the Manchester FA and its cup competition can be gauged by its own growth. The organisation created a secondary competition, its Junior Cup for newer clubs or those of a lower standard, and within three years of the Manchester FA's formation it had forty clubs competing in its two main competitions.[35] This activity was beginning to be noticed, and it even caused one Manchester-based football enthusiast to urge the FA to move the FA Cup final to the city, stating that 'Association football is not well understood in London', and claiming that within Manchester 'almost every man … is an admirer of football. If the final was played in Cottonopolis we should have a crowd which would break the biggest record.'[36]

John Nall's influence

This period of growth for the Manchester FA came during John Nall's term as president, but his involvement with the administrative side of football did not end with the Manchester FA, for he went on to become a member of the Lancashire FA's committee. As with the Manchester FA, an election process existed for Lancashire's committee, but it was not until the organisation was restructured during the 1888–89 football season that Nall stood for election – one year after Manchester Clifford, a club with connections to both his brother and his family's Platford Hotel, had become members of the Lancashire FA.[37]

It had been determined that as a result of increased participation in the sport the Manchester area would have two representatives from 1889, and Nall was elected in June 1889. There is no record of which club nominated him.[38] The following season he was nominated by West Manchester, and in subsequent years by Ardwick (City) and Newton Heath (United) and other clubs.[39] He was rarely opposed, and when he was, candidates tended to withdraw or the Manchester FA would officially nominate him; at other times multiple clubs would show their support through nominations. It is clear that Nall was a well-respected Manchester official; he had been present at the game's birth and was on both the Manchester FA and Lancashire FA at a time when football was established as a national professional sport.[40] His credibility was based on around forty years of achievements with Hulme Athenaeum, Manchester Association, the Manchester FA and the Lancashire FA, and as he aged his supporters knew that he could be trusted to act positively, in their interests. While on the Lancashire committee Nall demonstrated an interest in the affairs of Lancashire's amateur football clubs, and also appeared on disciplinary committees and at regular meetings, and he continually tried to increase the influence of the Manchester FA.

The Manchester FA remained subservient to the Lancashire FA and was perceived as a subdivision by the national FA. Manchester's clubs and representatives wanted autonomy, and in 1891 Nall presided over Manchester FA's bid to increase their area of authority to twenty miles (it had been eight miles at formation, and then increased to twelve). During his presidency the organisation became affiliated directly with the FA, indicating that Nall's social connections continued to evolve and change as and when required.[41] This was a significant development in the growth of Mancunian football, and it meant that Nall had to steer his way through a potential conflict of interest between his roles in the two regional associations.[42] Joshua Parlby, an experienced official at Stoke but also part of the Ardwick–City set-up and an active member of the League Management committee until 1899, represented Manchester FA during its bid for direct affiliation to the FA, as part of a two-man deputation that successfully lobbied for the improved status in August 1896.[43] In September 1896 Nall attended the Lancashire FA meeting where it was formally announced that this aim had been met and, although this may appear a minor footnote. Manchester's affiliation was a significant development in the growth of Mancunian football, and it occurred seemingly against the Lancashire authority's wishes while Nall was presiding over Manchester FA affairs and a committee member at Lancashire FA.[44] Nall was in a difficult position, but minutes of the Lancashire FA suggest that he handled the dual role well and, ultimately, he retained his position with both organisations. He died in 1897 at the age of fifty-six, while still in office at both the Manchester and the Lancashire associations, but the Nall influence remained until 1948

through the activities of his son, Arthur Nall, who served on the Manchester
FA committee for most of his adult life and was a committee member on the
day that John Nall was elected president in 1891.[45] In 1920 Arthur Nall became
the first person to be awarded life membership of the Manchester FA, as a mark
of his contribution to the organisation.[46]

It should be recorded that Joshua Parlby has been recognised by some historians for his contribution to City's early development, but his role in raising
the status of Manchester football has never been given the focus it deserves.
Parlby was more business minded than John Nall, and his approach was needed
to raise Manchester football to the highest levels, demonstrating how different
types of leader are needed at different stages of a sport's – and indeed society's
– development.

The Manchester FA, particularly under Nall's presidency, and the
Manchester Cup helped to establish Manchester's clubs. However, Manchester
was still perceived as a rugby city, especially as association clubs from northern
Lancashire and the Midlands had become recognised as powers within the
game. By 1890 the FA Cup had already seen winners from Blackburn (Rovers
and Olympic) and Preston, but no credible challenge from Manchester, and
Manchester's growing interest in soccer during the 1880s was not noticed by
all reporters. When Manchester staged its first international soccer match,
England v Ireland, in February 1885 the *Athletic News* claimed that the atmosphere was 'nothing like' that generated by a rugby crowd in the city.[47] Its report
was at odds with others, particularly those by other Manchester-produced
newspapers and those in Ireland, which talked of the crowd's enthusiasm and
the growing interest in soccer and commented on the selection of the ground
as a wise one.[48] The *Belfast Newsletter* estimated the attendance at approximately 7,000 and stated that the Irish team had the greater support – perhaps
an indication that Manchester's Irish community had attended the game. The
international game allowed the growth of soccer to be considered; and some
commentary remarked that the national FA was so delighted with the attendance and organisation that it had decided that another FA Cup semi-final
would be staged in Manchester.[49] It was evident that soccer in Manchester was
developing rapidly after several years of torpor; newspapers commented on the
increasing number of clubs and public houses catering for association players
by housing fixture lists, results and related information.[50] Rugby remained
dominant, but new clubs tended to favour the association version of the game,
and with 'the increasing number of clubs in the district, the leaning towards
the dribbling game is decidedly becoming greater.'[51] Admission fees for the
international soccer match were sixpence and upwards for the stands, and the
most expensive tickets were two shillings and sixpence, although women were
allowed free entry. By way of comparison, according to the official wage census
average female earnings were twelve shillings and eight pence per week, with

cotton operatives earning a little over fifteen shillings.[52] Of course, women had free admission, but even if they had had to pay the most expensive ticket would have been only be about one fifth of the average female worker's weekly pay.

British Football Association

During the formative years of the Manchester FA the debate on professionalism was often central to football's governing bodies and by 1884 several northern clubs were determined to challenge the authority of the FA by creating their own national organisation. The British Football Association (British FA) was established in October 1884, with William Fairhurst, the editor of the *Cricket and Football Field* and *Bolton Evening News*, recognised as its instigator.[53] In November 1884 the strength of the new organisation was clear when thirty-seven clubs or associations met at the Dog and Partridge in Manchester, including Hurst, Newton Heath and the Manchester FA. Several letters were received from supporting clubs who were unable to attend, although one letter was also received from Darwen, whose committee was against the creation of the organisation.[54] The British FA was established because of dissatisfaction with the FA, who had disqualified Preston from the FA Cup after finding them guilty of importing players from other towns and providing them with what were alleged to be excessively well-paid jobs. The professionalism debate had been developing for some time as northern, predominantly working-class clubs began to meet with success in the FA Cup. As its punishment of Preston demonstrated, the FA was determined to change its rules so as to ensure that players were amateurs. Any club attracting players from outside their own region was viewed with suspicion and it was suggested that they had been approached and guaranteed an income. Most northern association clubs saw no issue with professionalism and thought that it should be allowed and performed openly, not via underhand activities. They determined to work collectively to change the FA – and if that could not be achieved, then the new organisation would seek to become the governing body of a professional version of the sport.

The British FA often met behind closed doors, leading to some criticism in the media, and was considered by some as simply an alternative FA with fewer members.[55] It tried to encourage clubs and regional football associations to recognise that professionalism existed and to accept it as an everyday part of the game. Some regional associations reluctantly accepted professionalism, especially when the British FA highlighted situations within their regions, which led to some 'purists' being 'educated'.[56] Other clubs joined or supported the new organisation after the FA had appeared to be somewhat out of touch with their members. At a FA meeting in January 1885 a motion to establish a committee to investigate legalising professionalism received 113 votes in favour and 108 against. However, the FA had required a two-thirds majority and the motion was lost. The FA's authority had been challenged. But some wanted the British FA to make a greater stand and to 'take up the cudgels with more vigour' to challenge the 'sham amateurs' of the FA, including those clubs from the Midlands who had voted against professionalism but appeared to be adopting professional practices when dealing with their own players.[57] Pressure continued to be applied. The British FA's main role was a lobbying one, supporting some of the northern clubs, such as Burnley, when they were faced with punishments by the FA, and pressuring the FA to accept professionalism. The professionalism debate rumbled on for several years, but by September 1885 those behind the British FA were recorded as having achieved all their aims.[58] That was not entirely accurate, but the process had begun, and the British FA gradually faded.

During the twentieth century, analysis of the British FA's actions suggested that it was a short-lived venture that achieved little, but the truth is somewhat different.[59] Had it not been for the British FA, the FA would have steadfastly refused to allow professionalism, and that could have created a similar situation to rugby during the 1890s, when the sport was split in two – a northern professional game and a predominantly southern amateur sport. It is also possible that the FA itself could have crumbled because, according to some journalists, the British FA would 'undoubtedly have taken the control of professional football', which in effect would have been the dominant version of the sport once the Football League became established in 1888.[60]

The FA Cup

Although Manchester did not have a team capable of challenging for the FA Cup, the development of the Manchester FA and the increase in the number of clubs had an effect, and the 1887–88 season saw widespread Mancunian interest in the FA Cup for the first time. Denton, who played at a field dubbed Chapel Green, were drawn away to South Shore (Blackpool), but for some unknown reason pulled out. Possibly the financial or time costs of travelling were a problem for the Dentonians. Although they did travel to the ground, Bury pulled out of their tie at Blackburn Rovers, on account of player ineligibility. Another local side, Central, who played at the Phoenix Pleasure Ground, were defeated 8–1 at Higher Walton and subsequently entered the competition every season until 1895. Hurst defeated Astley Bridge 5–3 but were later disqualified after a protest from Astley. At Fleetwood Rangers, West Manchester were defeated 4–1. The most significant FA Cup story of the period occurred at Preston and featured Hyde FC, who had formed in 1885 at a meeting attended by approximately forty men in the White Lion public house. At the start of the 1886–87 season one of the giants of the period, Blackburn Rovers, were invited to Hyde for a friendly, which Hyde lost 8–0. Afterwards, members of the Blackburn side stressed that they felt Hyde had potential. The comments encouraged Hyde to enter the FA Cup the following season. As in the previous year, they opened the 1887–88 season with a friendly against significant opposition, with Bolton winning 8–1. In the FA Cup Hyde were drawn away to Preston North End, who had reached the semi-finals the previous season and were recognised as a leading club. The game was anticipated to be difficult for Hyde, but Preston, demonstrating that they did not consider the cup game to be an attraction, had arranged a fixture with West Bromwich Albion for the same day. Preston wanted to play the FA Cup tie midweek, but Hyde rightly refused. Preston vowed that they would do all they could to win the match.

Within five minutes of the game's start Dewhurst headed Preston's first goal and the score reached 4–0 after approximately twenty minutes. According to reports the Preston goalkeeper didn't touch the ball until the twenty-fifth minute, when he took a goal kick, but by this point Hyde was already struggling and almost immediately after the goal kick Preston challenged Hyde's goal again, with Hyde conceding three goals in five minutes. By half-time Preston had scored twelve goals.

Hyde commenced the second half determined to demonstrate an attacking spirit and briefly put Preston under some pressure, but Preston soon regained the initiative and the goals flooded in. Match reports simply list the scorers from this point on. Presumably the pace was so frenetic that it was impossible for the reporters to record the general action. The final score was 26–0, but there was controversy and confusion because Hyde's centre-back Bowers had left the pitch with a sprained arm at 3–0. Preston allowed the Hydonians to bring on another player for the second half, even though substitutions were not allowed at this time in football history. Presumably Preston felt that a half-time twelve-goal lead was enough of a cushion. The famous Lancashire cricketer and footballer Richard Barlow played his part in the overwhelming victory, as he was the referee.[61] Barlow had played an additional five minutes, during which time Preston's last goal was scored. The reason for this additional time remains unclear, but this should not detract from Preston's remarkable victory. Despite the scoreline, Hyde's goalkeeper, Bunyan, was regarded as one of the best players on the pitch. The referee, himself a former goalkeeper with Manchester Association, praised Bunyan when reflecting on the game in 1908: 'I may say that had the Hyde goalkeeper not been in good form, North End would have materially increased their score. I have never seen such splendid passing and shooting in my life.'[62]

After the game Hyde and Preston regularly played each other in friendlies, and the two sides also met to raise money for the victims of the Hyde Coal mining disaster of 1889. Newton Heath L&YR and Ardwick also met, under floodlights at Belle Vue in February 1889, to raise money for the families of the twenty-three killed in the disaster. Walter Chew, the Ardwick secretary, was responsible for organising the match, which raised £240.[63] This is thought to be the first floodlit association match played in the area, although there is anecdotal evidence to suggest that Preston played against Ardwick at Hyde Road under artificial light around the same time. There was also a floodlit meeting between Everton and Ardwick on 10 March 1890. In 1987 Preston and Hyde United met to remember the 1887 FA Cup tie in game that ended in a 4–1 Preston victory on Hyde's artificial surface.

The Jubilee tournament

By 1887 Fitzroy Norris, the former Manchester Association committeeman, moved to the Bolton area due to work commitments and became involved first with Eagley and then with Bolton Wanderers, where his experience was appreciated, although his time as secretary-manager proved to be somewhat controversial. Regardless of his position in Bolton, he remained keen to promote association football in Manchester, and in 1887 he arranged for soccer to be included in the Royal Jubilee Exhibition at Manchester's White City.[64] Whether it was the showman in him or a genuine desire to see association football promoted cannot be proved, but he arranged for Bolton Wanderers to play Mancunian teams by enticing them with prizes, forbidden under FA rules at a time when professionalism was still viewed as an issue within the game.[65] Newton Heath accepted the challenge and, believing that they were to receive medals after going two goals in front, were dismayed to be told by Norris 'Oh, this does not count. It's only an exhibition match!'[66] Norris eventually found the winners £6 in prize money. This precipitated further issues with the FA and the suggestion that Norris's club, Bolton Wanderers, should be suspended from all football activity.[67] Norris contributed significantly to the formative years of Manchester's association football, and by organising the Jubilee exhibition football activity had brought Manchester football to a wider audience, which, in turn, added to the prestige of Newton Heath and Bolton Wanderers. However, both clubs were dissatisfied with his organisational skills, and the affair also resulted in professional problems for Norris. Newspapers questioned: 'How will Fitzroy get out of the exhibition tangle?' The following week the answer became clear when it was succinctly recorded: 'Exit Fitzroy, enter JJ'.[68] Norris had been replaced as Bolton secretary by JJ Bentley, the club's former secretary and a journalist. It was recorded that Norris had left by mutual consent, but whether that was on account of the exhibition debacle or because Bolton had also been defeated at Derby is not clear.

After Bolton, Norris continued to referee, often at games in the Manchester area, as well as in FA Cup games and in League matches once the Football League was formed in 1888, and his views were occasionally sought by the media of the day.[69] He also became a key figure in the Lancashire Referees'

Association and remained involved with the game following his move to Liverpool.[70] As with John Nall, Norris had encouraged an interest in association football in his son, Harry Fitzroy Norris, who played for Elton FC, on the Wirral, in the Lancashire Amateur League, Tranmere in the Combination and Everton, although he never appeared in Everton's first team. During the First World War Harry was killed in action at Ypres in 1915.[71] The family posted memorial notices in subsequent years. Fitzroy Norris himself died on 15 May 1921 at the age of seventy-five, leaving effects totalling a little over £54.[72] His sporting life had mirrored his non-sporting existence. From an early age he had needed to adapt, living with family members while his parents were absent, and then moving from town to town through family necessity and for employment. In a sporting context, he tried his hand at football and athletics before becoming a football administrator and a renowned referee.

Ardwick Association Football Club

The status of soccer in Manchester was increasing and the number of clubs also grew, with new clubs often being guided by individuals who became part of a local sporting elite. At Hurst, Jim Ingham demonstrated the tenacity and spirit that John Nall had shown almost two decades earlier, and others were doing similar work at clubs across the region. A new transformational phase began in the aftermath of the formation of Manchester FA as teams like Newton Heath and Gorton – a club that could trace its roots back to St Mark's Church in West Gorton started to develop a more ambitious approach. In 1886 the Gorton Association FC balance sheet included details of the management committee of the club, with Richard Peacock, one of the founders of the engineering firm Beyer-Peacock, as president, Walter Chew club secretary and Lawrence Furniss a committeeman. The balance sheet for the year ending April 1885 recorded that the ground rental was £4 17s 6d, gate money was £2 5s 8d and the balance in hand was £3 4s 9d.[73] The support of businessmen like Peacock was important, but more significant was the commitment of committeemen like Chew and Furniss, and by the summer of 1887 they recognised that Gorton's development stood at the precipice. The club needed a new ground. The decision forced the committee to consider what they wanted from their club. Would their new ground be similar to previous ones, i.e. a park or public house pitch, or would it be a home that would allow the club to grow and, in effect, oversee its own destiny? They chose the latter, and held a meeting in August 1887 to establish a new club called Ardwick Association Football Club.[74] Furniss went on to become the Ardwick secretary, and a profile of him during the 1920s claimed that he was one of the most influential football administrators Manchester had possessed and that he had contributed much to the development of the sport in the city. Furniss threw everything he had into the club, and went on many scouting missions during Ardwick's formative years, including frequent trips to Scotland.[75]

Football's growth relied on individuals constantly looking to improve the situation, as was demonstrated by the discovery of the site for Ardwick's new ground by captain Ken McKenzie, who was a moulder at Bennett's yard. The site was not a particularly inspiring one, but it did allow the club to develop its own ground for the first time and it also had a history as a sporting centre: during the previous decade or so it had frequently been a venue for bare-knuckle fighting. Like many Manchester residents, McKenzie was a newcomer, having come to the city in search of work from his home in East Stirlingshire. It was claimed that he found the site on a convenient short cut from his home to his place of work.[76] Ardwick's opening game at their new ground was scheduled against Salford in August 1887. The Ardwick committee received confirmation from Salford's secretary that his team would play, but he neglected to tell them he was emigrating to America; as a result, his team never appeared at Ardwick. Ardwick Association FC had organised a band and various other celebratory activities for their inaugural match, but due to the non-arrival of Salford the club had no choice but to refund entry money. As most fans had paid on the day and many supporters had sneaked into the newly erected ground by climbing walls and hoardings, the club lost a considerable amount, because they refunded everyone as they left the ground. The season ended with the club reporting a financial loss of £13 5s 1d on account of the expense of developing the new ground and the refunding of entrance fees, but gate receipts had been a healthy £47 9s 9d, while the ground rental was £10.

Ardwick's ground was in a good location, with an extensive tram network at its gates. This was important, and in 1887 horse-drawn trams could bring supporters directly from the suburbs to the ground's entrances with relative ease. Fares were reasonable and were set by the Manchester Corporation Tramways Act of 1899, which established that fares were not to exceed one penny per mile. By the 1890s there were 515 trams and 5,300 horses working eighty-nine miles of route from twenty depots. Electrification of routes followed in the early twentieth century and these transport opportunities, like the railways, aided soccer's development locally. Ardwick, like their east Manchester neighbours Newton Heath, were keen to attract players from outside the area, and if employment was a barrier Ardwick players were often given a job at the neighbouring Galloway's Boilerworks, whose manager, E. Fortune, was encouraged by Walter Chew to attend the club's games. According to Chew, at Fortune's first Ardwick game he shouted; at the second he kicked Chew in his excitement; from that point on he was obsessed with the club.[77] In 1888 Ardwick increased their membership subscription to five shillings, payable in two equal amounts during the season, as they sought to establish the club on a stronger financial basis. Furniss often recalled the support that the fledgling club received from

John Bentley, who helped him with advice and influence and supplied several key players for the club. Once again this supports the view that the development of clubs and footballing communities relies on a variety of individuals and the support of those who may be deemed as rivals on the pitch. The ability of men such as Bentley to help the growth of the sport in Manchester demonstrates that during this period it was the sport itself that mattered most to these men, not the success of their own clubs at the expense of others. Furniss became the driving force as the 1880s moved into the 1890s. Like John Nall and Fitzroy Norris before him, he was 'as well-known on the running path – on track and on road – as he was on the cricket or football field'.[78] He was a familiar competitor in the Midlands and in Derbyshire, where he competed at one-hundred-yards, half-mile and one-mile events. Furniss was born at Cromford, near Matlock, and played soccer for Derby Midland and Derby County where his last game was against Oldham Olympic. He had moved to America at the age of sixteen and worked on the Pennsylvania Railroad, playing cricket in his spare time.[79]

Ardwick developed and became established as an important side locally under Furniss, and he remained involved with the club until his death in 1941. Ardwick's reputation grew, and they also selected colours that remained synonymous with Mancunian football throughout the years that followed – blue and white. Their recorded colours were a different shade to those worn in later years, being royal blue and white stripes in 1887, before a switch to Cambridge blue and white by 1890. Within weeks of the relaunch, Ardwick AFC established a first team, reserve and third team, with a full programme of footballing activity, emphasising the growth of the sport. There were signs that the developing interest in soccer was impacting on other team sports – such as lacrosse, where some clubs were struggling for fixtures.[80] Lacrosse had hampered soccer's progression in the 1870s because potential participants were able to choose between rugby, soccer and lacrosse for their preferred team activity. As soccer had few clubs and a relatively weak hold on the conurbation's affections, lacrosse had gained support and interest, but by the late 1870s the improved status of soccer, the growth of cup competitions and establishment of the Manchester FA had made soccer more appealing.

Newton Heath

The L&YR club Newton Heath developed significantly during the 1880s, especially after the restriction on playing only Newton Heath-based employees was lifted. According to committee member Herbert Dale, this change came about due to monetary problems. He claimed that the Heathens had run into financial difficulties after being sued for an outstanding printing debt. This led to the works superintendent and president of the sports club, Frederick Attock, insisting that the Lancashire and Yorkshire title must be dropped from the club's name and that players from outside the railway company could become members.[81] This ultimately allowed Newton Heath to select from a wider pool of players and, inevitably, led to the further development of the club. Their successes in the Manchester Cup, where they appeared in the first six finals, winning the trophy on four occasions, was a demonstration of their growth and rising status; yet their reputation was not sufficient for the club to be invited to attend the meetings which established the Football League in 1888, despite the first official League meeting being held in Manchester.

William McGregor of Aston Villa founded the Football League as a means of establishing regular competition for clubs. On 2 March 1888 he wrote to several leading clubs stating: 'Every year it is becoming more and more difficult for clubs of any standing to meet their friendly engagements and even arrange friendly matches. The consequence is that at the last moment ... clubs are compelled to take on teams who will not attract the public.'[82] The idea to play a schedule of home and away fixtures is thought to have been based on North American baseball, but McGregor claimed that he had been inspired by cricket's County Championship, while James Catton of the *Athletic News* later claimed that the 'League had more modest antecedents in local football competitions such as the Scarborough Wednesday League (1881) and the Glossop and District Amateur League (1887)', as did the author of a piece published in 1906.[83] By 1903 the Glossop and District Amateur League was aiming to attract clubs from within a fourteen-mile radius of Glossop, which was a vast region stretching from Manchester's St Ann's Square to Holmfirth in Yorkshire and including those areas of Manchester where the majority of the members of the Manchester FA were based.[84] Whatever its inspiration, the Football League proved successful and a multitude of other leagues followed, including the Manchester League in 1893.[85] Charles Sutcliffe, a Burnley solicitor who would also act for Manchester United, became a prominent member of the League's management committee and he felt that the League had produced 'arrangement, reliability, and competition, out of chaos, unreliability, and mere exhibition'.[86] That organisational structure also brought greater financial rewards to the clubs involved – something that Manchester-based journalists perceived as one of the main aims of the new organisation, the *Courier* recording that the League would be 'more successful financially to the promoters' than their usual footballing fixtures.[87]

It has been recorded in numerous publications, including many United official histories, that Newton Heath did not receive enough votes to join the League in 1888, but this is inaccurate because there was no voting process at the launch of the competition and Newton Heath were not present. Clubs were invited to the meeting by a small group of footballing figures from the Midlands and North West, with fifteen clubs attending the first true meeting of the League, held at Manchester's Royal Hotel on 17 April 1888: Aston Villa,

10 A Newton Heath football card produced by the J. Baines company, *c.*1886.

Preston North End, Bolton Wanderers, West Bromwich Albion, Stoke, Notts County, Derby County, Blackburn Rovers, Accrington, Burnley, Everton, Wolverhampton Wanderers, Halliwell, Sheffield Wednesday and Nottingham Forest. The last three effectively gate-crashed the discussions. They felt that they had a claim to become founder members, but the meeting determined that they could not be included at that stage because there would be some difficulties in arranging fixture dates. Instead it was agreed that the four lowest-ranked clubs each season would face a re-election vote and that others could then apply to join. It was also suggested that a second league including those three clubs and Derby Junction, Crewe Alexandra, Mitchell St George and others could be established later.[88] Newton Heath was not mentioned at all at this meeting. Had the club's status been higher it would inevitably have been considered, as it was based in a geographical region that would have complemented the new League well. Nevertheless, despite not forming part of the new Football League, in 1888 Newton Heath did take steps to formalise their fixtures for 1888–89. Working with several other ambitious clubs spread across the North and Midlands, they created an alternative competition called the Football Combination.

Created on 27 April 1888 with a membership of twenty clubs, the Combination took the Football League as its inspiration but was much less formal than the League and allowed each of its member clubs to arrange their own fixtures and play as many games as they wished. The only stipulation was that they had to take part in at least eight games. The prospect of organised, regular competition was an important step and Newton Heath published their own fixture list, feeling confident of a strong season of fixtures. Their first Combination game was a 4–3 victory over Darwen on 22 September 1888, and they played a total of eleven matches, winning seven, drawing two and losing two. They were the only Manchester representatives in the Combination, but they found the competition frustrating at times even though many of the clubs, including former FA Cup winners Blackburn Olympic, were of a significant standard. Some, including Olympic, struggled to fulfil all their fixtures and resigned from the competition. It became evident that the free and easy method of arranging fixtures was not an improvement, and this led to the mass resignation of eleven clubs, including the Heathens, in April 1889. The Combination effectively collapsed, but it was still an important period in the development of football, and in terms of long-term analysis the Combination can be viewed as an event which helped to focus minds during a transformational period. The experience, and a growing status developed through competition, helped the Heathens' ambitions to grow and they applied to join the Football League in 1889. As the League had determined, the bottom four clubs stood for re-election. Manchester played its part in the first re-election contest, held at the Douglas Hotel in Manchester. Nine clubs applied to join, while four sought re-election, with each existing League side voting for the four they wanted to see in the League. Those clubs seeking to join were allowed a maximum of five minutes to present their case, followed by the vote. It was not a successful day for Newton Heath, who received one vote out of the forty-eight cast and finished ninth. Despite their frustration, the Heathens worked with other rejected clubs and former members of the Combination to establish a new competition, the Football Alliance. Unlike the Combination this had a sound foundation and consisted of twelve northern and Midlands sides, although Darwen, Bootle and Newton Heath were the only Lancashire-area clubs. At the end of the first season the Heathens finished eighth, while Sheffield Wednesday were champions.

While the Heathens were pursuing a life in the Alliance other Manchester region clubs developed closer ties via another new competition. In March 1889 the Bury committee played a key role in the establishment of a Lancashire League with founder members including five clubs from the Manchester region (Bury, Heywood, Heywood Central, Hyde and West Manchester) and others from Blackpool, Earlstown (sic), Fleetwood Rangers, Higher Walton, Nelson, Oswaldtwistle Rovers, Blackburn Park Road, Rossendale and Southport Central. Although it was called the Lancashire League it must be recorded that Hyde was based in Cheshire but within the Manchester region, adding to the complex geographical nature of footballing communities in the North West. The Lancashire League commenced on 14 September 1889 and the first champions were Higher Walton, with runners-up Bury missing the title by a point. The following season Bury won the Lancashire League and the competition added significantly to the sporting make-up of the region, where the sport continued to develop, with Newton Heath, Bury and Ardwick all gaining some recognition by 1892. Newton Heath were recognised as the strongest team after their experience in the Alliance and their record in the Manchester Cup. By the start of the 1891–92 season they had made three bids to join the Football League, although each had failed. They had received no votes at all in 1891, when the League was increased to fourteen clubs, but that election did show how Manchester football was beginning to be viewed more positively than in previous years, as Ardwick also applied and received four votes – only two less than the re-elected West Bromwich Albion and Derby County. This was some achievement for a club making its first application and encouraged those from Ardwick to join the Alliance as a consolation prize. After a season participating in the Alliance, the opportunity came again for Ardwick and their neighbours, Newton Heath, to apply to join the Football League. This time an expansion of the League into two divisions provided the two clubs with a greater opportunity of success.[89]

Newton Heath and Ardwick were predominantly working-class clubs, as was Bury, and as the decades progressed it became recognised that professional clubs were managed and supported by the working class and lower-middle class. However, contemporary reports are less clear, and in 1894 an article claiming that rugby football was 'more popular amongst the working-classes' of the city than any other sport.[90] At first glance this seems to be at odds with the evidence of a growing soccer community, but it should be remembered that the split within rugby had yet to occur. Rugby at this time included the traditional clubs such as Manchester FC and the working-class clubs surrounding Manchester such as Salford (founded 1873), Rochdale Hornets (1871) and Oldham (1876). These pre-dated the working-class soccer clubs of Manchester by several years and were firmly established as representatives of their communities. Association football was still some way off becoming Manchester's leading sporting activity across the population, even though it had developed at pace between 1878 and 1892. It was rugby that remained the visible, popular sport across the conurbation regardless of class, thanks, in the main, to the vibrant working-class rugby clubs.

Notes

1 For example, 'En passant', *Athletic News*, 21 March 1883, 1.
2 *Bolton Football Field*, 11 October 1884, 10.
3 'Familiar faces', *Manchester Football Chronicle*, 7 October 1922, 3.
4 'Mr LM Sinclair', *Manchester Football Chronicle*, 28 January 1922, 3.
5 'Manchester and District Football Association', *Athletic News*, 17 September 1884, 2.
6 Ibid.
7 'Manchester and district v Hallamshire', *Athletic News*, 10 December 1884, 3.
8 Kidd, *Manchester*, 107
9 W. G. Pilkington, 'Manchester's merchants', in W. Brindley (ed.), *The soul of Manchester* (Manchester, 1929), 210–211.
10 'Man who made Hurst club famous', *Manchester Football Chronicle*, 21 October 1922, 3.
11 *The rules of the Manchester District Football Association* (Ashton-under-Lyne: William Brown and Son, 1887), 3; *The sportsman's year book for 1880* (London: Cassell, Petter, Galpin & Co.), 166.
12 'En passant', *Athletic News*, 22 October 1884, 1.
13 'Manchester and District Football Association', *Manchester Courier*, 18 June 1891, 3.
14 *Manchester County Football Association souvenir brochure 1884–1984*, 9–12.
15 Contemporary evidence of his attendance at the 1894 Manchester City meeting has not been identified and it appears that author Paul Toovey has mistakenly credited Nall with attendance when it was in fact Lachie Sinclair. P. Toovey, *Manchester City: the birth of the blues 1880–1894* (Stockport: Paul Toovey, 2009), 126; P. Toovey, *Manchester City: the early years 1880–1900* (Stockport: Paul Toovey, 2014), 132.
16 'Familiar faces', *Manchester Football Chronicle*, 7 October 1922, 3.
17 According to Herbert Dale, Newton Heath charged these figures for games during that opening cup season. 'Forty years of the football field: experience as a referee', *Manchester Football Chronicle*, 14 October 1922, 3.
18 'Outdoor sports', *Manchester Courier*, 10 October 1891, 17; letter to the FA from Manchester and District Football Association, 6 August 1896; Lancashire Archives,

DDX2708, Minutes of the Lancashire Football Association, 23 September 1896.

19 'Our football letter', *Manchester Times*, 3 October 1885, 7.

20 'Familiar faces', *Manchester Football Chronicle*, 14 October 1922, 3.

21 'Sporting intelligence', *Manchester Courier*, 12 November 1883, 3.

22 'Man who made Hurst club famous', *Manchester Football Chronicle*, 21 October 1922, 3.

23 Ibid.

24 'Association games', *Umpire News*, 26 April 1885, 3; 'Football notes and gossip', *Athletic News*, 28 April 1885, 4.

25 'Man who made Hurst club Famous', *Manchester Football Chronicle*, 21 October 1922, 3.

26 'Manchester and District Association', *Bell's Life in London and Sporting Chronicle*, 3 September 1885, 4.

27 West Manchester supporters displayed cards 'with the words "Play up West" worn in front of their hats'. *Bolton Cricket and Football Field*, 20 February 1886.

28 'Newton Heath v West Manchester', *Black and White*, 16 December 1887, n.p.

29 Several Newton Heath fixtures against prominent teams suggest crowds of this magnitude, such as 'Club notices', *Black and White*, 25 November 1887, n.p.; 'Newton Heath v Burnley', *Black and White*, 4 November 1887, n.p.

30 'Famous football players', *Black and White*, 13 December 1887, 495.

31 For example, the Ardwick Charity Cup competition. 'Ardwick v Hyde', *Gorton Reporter*, 18 February 1888, n.p.

32 'Football', *Bell's Life in London and Sporting Chronicle*, 21 April 1886, 4.

33 'Club notices', *Black and White*, 25 November 1887, n.p.; *Bolton Football Field*, 10 September 1887, 4.

34 L. Laine, 'Unfortunately she was the winner', in *Writing lives in sport* (Aarhus: Aarhus University Press, 2004), 116.

35 'Manchester and District Association', *Bell's Life in London and Sporting Chronicle*, 3 September 1885, 4; 'Manchester Football Association – draw for the senior and junior cups', *Manchester Courier*, 30 September 1887, 3.

36 'Football in London', *Manchester Courier*, 5 March 1891, 7.

37 Lancashire Archives, DDX2708, Minutes of the Lancashire Football Association, 28 July 1887.

38 Ibid., 29 June 1889.

39 Ibid., 28 June 1890–2 January 1897.

40 Ibid., 29 June 1889–15 April 1897.

41 'Outdoor sports', *Manchester Courier*, 10 October 1891, 17.

42 Lancashire Archives, DDX2708, Minutes of the Lancashire Football Association, 13 May 1896–23 September 1896.

43 C. Sutcliffe, J. A. Brierley and F. Howarth, *The story of the Football League* (Preston: The Football League, 1938), 67–70; Lancashire Archives, Letter to the FA from Manchester and District Football Association, 6 August 1896; Lancashire Archives, DDX2708, Minutes of the Lancashire Football Association, 23 September 1896.

44 Lancashire Archives, Letter to the FA from Manchester and District Football

Association, 6 August 1896; Minutes of the Lancashire Football Association, 13 May 1896–23 September 1896.

45 Lancashire Archives, DDX2708, Minutes of the Lancashire Football Association., 29 June 1889–15 April 1897; 'Manchester District Football Association', *Manchester Courier*, 18 June 1891, 3.

46 *Manchester County Football Association souvenir brochure 1884–1984*, 14.

47 'England v Ireland', *Athletic News*, 3 March 1885, 3.

48 'Football notes', *Manchester Courier*, 2 March 1885, 3; 'International match', *Belfast Newsletter*, 2 March 1885, 3.

49 'Football notes', *Manchester Courier*, 2 March 1885, 3.

50 'Manchester Association jottings', *Athletic News*, 19 October 1886, 5.

51 *Bell's Life in London and Sporting Chronicle*, 21 April 1886, 4; 'The Manchester Association club', *Manchester Courier*, 8 October 1883, 3.

52 'Grand association football club', *Manchester Courier*, 26 February 1885, 1; R. W. Lewis, 'The development of professional football in Lancashire, 1870–1914' (PhD dissertation, University of Lancaster, 1993), 44.

53 'Editor of the Football Field', *Manchester Courier*, 3 May 1909, 3.

54 'Important Meeting at Manchester', *Athletic News*, 5 November 1884, 3.

55 'En passant', *Athletic News*, 20 January 1885, 1.

56 'En passant', *Athletic News*, 27 January 1885, 1; 'Football', *Preston Herald*, 11 February 1885, 6.

57 'En passant', *Athletic News*, 17 March 1885, 1; 'Professionalism in football', *Kentish Independent*, 24 January 1885, 3.

58 'En passant', *Athletic News*, 1 September 1885, 1.

59 'En passant', *Athletic News*, 20 January 1885, 1; T. Mason, *Association football and English society, 1863–1915* (Brighton: The Harvester Press, 1980), 74–75.

60 'Professional bogie', *Sports Argus*, 20 April 1907, 4.

61 R. G. Barlow, *Forty seasons of first-class cricket: being the autobiography and reminiscences of Richard Gorton Barlow* (Manchester: John Heywood Ltd., 1908), 45–46.

62 Ibid., 46.

63 'The discoverer of Hyde Road', *Manchester Football Chronicle*, 23 March 1922, 3.

64 *Bolton Football Field*, 1 October 1887, 2.

65 'Football at the exhibition', *Bolton Football Field*, 1 October 1887, 2; *Bolton Football Field*, 22 October 1887, 3.

66 *Bolton Football Field*, 1 October 1887, 6.

67 *Bolton Football Field*, 22 October 1887, 3 and 6.

68 *Bolton Football Field*, 29 October 1887, 6.

69 'English Cup – first round', *Birmingham Daily Post*, 19 January 1891, 7; 'Notes on outdoor sports', *Derby Daily Telegraph*, 22 May 1895, 2.

70 He lived in the Liverpool suburbs of West Derby and Aintree. 'Lancashire Referees' Association', *Manchester Courier*, 19 September 1895, 3; Census returns, Fitzroy Norris 1901, https//:www.findmypast.co.uk (RG 13/3502); 'Killed in action', *Liverpool Echo*, 1 September 1915, 6.

71 'Killed in action', *Liverpool Echo*, 1 September 1915, 6.

72 Probate records, Thomas Valentine Fitzroy Norris, 1921.

73 'The discoverer of Hyde Road', *Manchester Football Chronicle*, 23 March 1922, 3.

74 'The man at the head of Manchester City', *Manchester Football Chronicle*, 23 September 1922, 3.

75 Ibid.

76 'The discoverer of Hyde Road', *Manchester Football Chronicle*, 23 March 1922, 3.

77 Ibid.

78 'The man at the head of Manchester City', *Manchester Football Chronicle*, 23 September 1922, 3.

79 Ibid. The date of his return to England is not known, although he is known to have been back in the Manchester region by the early 1880s.

80 'Club notices', *Black and White*, 25 November 1887, n.p.; 'Cancelling of lacrosse fixtures', *Black and White*, 25 November 1887, n.p.

81 'Forty years of the football field: experience as a referee', *Manchester Football Chronicle*, 14 October 1922, 3.

82 McGregor's letter quoted in Sutcliffe, Brierley and Howarth, *Story of the Football League*, 2.

83 Taylor, *The leaguers*, 4–5; 'Cup-tie v League football', *Coventry Evening Telegraph*, 27 October 1906, 2.

84 'Glossop and District Amateur League', *Athletic News*, 3 August 1903, 4.

85 'Cup-tie v League football', *Coventry Evening Telegraph*, 27 October 1906, 2.

86 'The League's coming of age', *Athletic News*, 11 January 1909, 4.

87 'Formation of a football league', *Manchester Courier*, 18 April 1888, 3.

88 'National Football Association league conference', *Shields Daily News*, 18 April 1888, 3.

89 The story of Ardwick and Newton Heath football clubs is told in the following chapter.

90 'Manchester', *Manchester Courier*, 16 June 1894, 14.

7

Football as a business

The Football League

The establishment of the Football League in 1888 and Newton Heath's participation in the Alliance, combined with success in the Manchester Cup, had provided the Manchester clubs with examples of what could be achieved. The Alliance, although not as successful as the Football League, did provide competition and Newton Heath were joined by Ardwick in 1891 after their first success in the Manchester Cup. By the end of the 1891–92 season both clubs wanted to establish themselves further; through their experience of participation in the Alliance League, they recognised the potential that well-structured competition could bring. By this time both clubs existed as businesses for the benefit of their shareholders. It is important to recognise that these businesses required the certainty of a regular income from gate receipts, and during 1892 an opportunity arose that gave both clubs the impetus they needed. The Football League's popularity led to the decision to add a second division for the 1892–93 season and to increase the existing division from fourteen clubs to sixteen.[1] Any club could apply to join either division, and it is probable that Ardwick and Newton Heath could have made bids for places in either division, especially as Ardwick had missed acceptance by only two votes the previous year. In fact, Ardwick were the highest placed side to miss out, three votes ahead of Nottingham Forest and Sunderland Albion. Newton Heath had not received any votes in 1891. They had a greater reputation than Ardwick for their football and had a genuine opportunity to win enough votes to be accepted into Division One, but there was a risk that if both clubs applied for the same division they would split the vote. Ultimately, whether for civic reasons or mindful of this potential, the two clubs did not face each other for the vote, unlike Merseyside's Liverpool and Liverpool Caledonians, neither of whom were elected.[2]

Newton Heath applied and were accepted into Division One, while Ardwick chose to apply to join the Second Division. By choosing this method Manchester was ensured two League sides rather than one, or even none. Surprisingly, considering their involvement in the development of the Lancashire League, Bury chose not to apply; nor did any of the other clubs in the Manchester region.

Bury did apply and were elected in 1894, while the next Mancunian team to apply were Lancashire League champions Fairfield Athletic, who tried unsuccessfully to join in 1895, 1896 and 1897. Fairfield folded shortly afterwards, as financial problems hit the club and its shareholders could not afford to bail the business out. The club had been established as a limited company in October 1892 and had distributed over 500 shares to shareholders, mainly from the Fairfield and Droylsden districts of east Manchester. As with most Manchester clubs, they comprised a mixture of local businessmen, artisans and general workers in a variety of trades and the club attracted a dedicated support during their brief life, recording crowds of 2,000 despite their ground being nothing more than a public house pitch. Their headquarters was the Gransmoor Hotel, a large, imposing public house. Financial problems never seemed to be far away. In 1895 the secretary was forced to write to Companies House to assure them that the club was still active. He blamed the club's lack of response to official requests over a significant period on his predecessor, who, it was claimed, had left the area and forgotten to pass on correspondence.[3]

Fairfield's development is typical of several football clubs across England which were established during this period as businesses with shareholders keen to establish a profitable football club to represent their town or district, leading to greater awareness of local products and businesses. It is widely known that the brewing trade became involved with football during these formative years of the League. There was regular national competition, as local brewers and public houses recognised the benefits of attracting a crowd of predominantly working-class men to a venue over which they had control. Fairfield's base at the Gransmoor fitted this pattern, and local publicans such as Tim Exley of the King's Head Hotel and other local civic and community leaders, such as factory owners and philanthropists, also backed the enterprise. At Fairfield the largest group of shareholders were publicans (10.4%), followed by chemists, surgeons, engineers and manufacturers (each between 5% and 6%). There were also three Fairfield shareholders who described themselves as 'gentlemen'.[4] Some of the clubs established across the country during the 1890s as pure business ventures, such as New Brighton Tower, managed to join the League and invested in their playing squads with the aim of becoming prominent. It is possible that Fairfield would have followed this path, but the team would have been in direct competition with Manchester City (the reformed Ardwick of 1894) and Newton Heath, both of whom were established in nearby districts of east Manchester.[5] New Brighton Tower found that attracting and employing players of the highest ability required a great outlay in terms of finance and time, whereas local players were easier to attract without finance. The employment of professional players across the board at Manchester's clubs caused financial struggles which could be resolved only by greater investment and increasing attendances, or by reducing investment in the squad. A poorer squad would impact on performances, as was demonstrated at Newton Heath, where in 1892 the new First Division club was unable to compete with long-established and more popular League clubs, causing Newton Heath to finish bottom of the First Division in their inaugural League season, only escaping relegation via the relegation-determining test match system. The *Manchester Evening News* was critical of the 'depressing conditions' experienced at First Division Newton Heath.[6]

The general view of Manchester's clubs at this time continued to be that Manchester was lagging still, even after the two sides had joined the League. Newton Heath's home was considered to be too far from central Manchester to attract good support, although this seemed illogical because the working-class districts had demonstrated great interest in the sport. The impression of Manchester's struggling status as a soccer city was compounded when the Heathens finished bottom of Division One in 1894 and were relegated. There had been controversy when the *Birmingham Daily Gazette* reported that the style of play employed by Newton Heath in their October 1893 4–1 victory over West Bromwich Albion was 'not football but simply brutality' and the Heathens had taken the newspaper to court.[7] The newspaper claimed that 'Perrins kicked Geddes in the spine of the back, raising a lump as big as a duck egg', and that another player was maliciously kicked on the ankle and yet another on the back of the head. The alleged libel concluded with the remark that the Heathens' style would perhaps create an extra run of business for undertakers. The court found that there had been libel, but that no substantial damage had been caused. The judge ordered the newspaper to pay one farthing damages, but both sides were ordered to pay their own legal costs, which were considerably more than a farthing. In effect, the Heathens were ridiculed for taking the matter to court.[8]

Manchester's other League club, Ardwick, enjoyed a good first season in Division Two, but the expense of travelling and other financial set-backs caused the committee to almost relinquish control during the following 1893–94 season. The resignation of secretary-manager Joshua Parlby and a move by shareholders to create a new club, Manchester City, forced Ardwick's committee into action, but it was too little too late, and Ardwick finished in the re-election zone, thirteenth out of fifteen clubs, in 1894. Another club struggling as the 1890s progressed was West Manchester, who had been in existence since 1884 and had experienced several developmental phases before becoming a limited company in 1892. Its shareholders were mostly based in the then middle-class Hulme/Moss Side districts and consisted of a variety of occupations, including the cricketer Richard Barlow, who held ten shares in the club at its formation in 1892. Of the occupations identified for West Manchester's shareholders in 1892 over 10% identified themselves as clerks, followed by 8% warehousemen (including one who described himself as a warehouse boy),

6% painters, 6% bookkeepers, and almost 5% recorded as brewers, cashiers and joiners.[9] The social mix was clear, with occupations of other shareholders recorded as artists, laundrymen, signwriters, athletic outfitters, engineers, tax inspectors, brass moulders and similar occupations. These details, and those for other clubs in the wider Manchester area such as Fairfield and Hyde, indicate that football club shareholders did not have to be from a particular class; they simply needed to have an interest in sport or their district. Subscription lists were open to all, and it is clear that clubs could attract shareholders across the classes, even if some could afford to buy only one share. That one share would buy the purchaser a place at the annual general meeting and the opportunity to speak openly about the performance and direction of the club, with as much right as any other shareholder, regardless of their status Despite this variety, West Manchester FC struggled to be profitable as the 1890s progressed and by 1897 mail addressed to the secretary was being returned and the club ceased to exist.

The Fallowfield final

While West Manchester and Manchester's League clubs were struggling the city did become the focus of national attention in 1893 when it staged the FA Cup final for the first time. This was the most important game played in Manchester during these formative years, but there were problems with crowd control and the game attracted the largest Cup final attendance recorded at that point. Most fans were neutral, which suggests that they were mainly living within travelling distance of the venue.[10] Much has been written about the 1893 Cup final. The most significant aspect, as far as the development of soccer in Manchester is concerned, was that the capacity of the venue was not enough, demonstrating the growing interest in the sport in the conurbation. The 1893 final, between Wolverhampton Wanderers and Everton, was the first FA Cup final, excluding replays, to be staged outside of London. It was held at the Manchester Athletic ground, a venue opened in May 1892 when the Manchester Athletic Club had relocated from the Old Trafford area, where it had existed with its only stand backing onto Talbot Road to the east of the present-day Lancashire CC ground. The Manchester Athletic Club had been established in 1887 by Tom Sutton, editor of *Athletic News*, demonstrating the significance of the newspaper to the development of sport in the region. Access to the new venue was limited, raising questions over its selection for the Cup final, although the choice may have had more to do with promoting the game in Manchester than with selecting a perfect venue. The North, and Lancashire specifically, was important in the development of the Football League and the rise of professionalism. The FA may have decided to stage the final there so as to remind enthusiasts of the significance of the FA and its cup competition; or

11 The scene at the Fallowfield FA Cup final of 1893.

maybe it wanted avoid accusations that the FA was a southern-based organisation reflecting southern values and not those of the northern clubs. This was an era when professionalism was being debated, and the FA was determined to represent both the amateur and professional games. Whatever the reason for the venue's selection, the Fallowfield final demonstrated that football was popular in the region and that Manchester would back high-profile and leading football events. The potential of football as a popular spectacle in the region came with this final which built on the successful staging of semi-finals in the 1880s.

A reported attendance of 45,000 with gate receipts of £2,559 should have guaranteed future finals at the arena, but crowd control and organisational difficulties were major problems. It was estimated that in fact over 60,000 attended the game, but even the 45,000 known to have been there were several thousand more than the ground should have coped with (Figure 11). The *Sporting Chronicle* highlighted a few key moments of the match, which ended 1–0 to Wolves, and then concluded its report with a final comment about crowd control: 'A large number of people were admitted without payment, and the police – 192 in number – were singularly inactive in the performance of what might be supposed were their duties.'[11] Others agreed, but felt that the police had resorted to heavy-handed tactics.[12] Since 1893 much has been made of the problems of the day and the game has been dubbed 'The Fallowfield Fiasco', but it was not the fault of the venue; rather, the organisers had failed to recognise the lure of the game in the North. As both Everton and Wolves had reached the final, and there was a growing interest in association football within Manchester, it was evident this would be an attractive fixture. Since 1893 those writing about the Fallowfield final have tended to overlook certain aspects, such as the fact that the FA's 45,000 estimated crowd size was about 13,000 greater than the next highest FA Cup final attendance (in 1892), and that the game had initially been moved from the Oval because it was agreed that the London venue could no longer cope with the size of crowd that football was attracting. The founder of the League, William MacGregor, suggested that the popularity of the game had not been appreciated: 'We were then at the beginning of the really big modern gates, and it is an admitted fact that the Association and the officials who were in immediate charge of the game woefully underestimated the interest that the match was destined to arouse.'[13] He highlighted that the pressure from the crowd forced wooden barriers to snap, leading to 'wild confusion', but the game was completed.[14]

The Fallowfield ground did not stage further FA Cup finals, but the following season it did hold an FA Cup semi-final, when Bolton defeated Sheffield Wednesday 2–1 and a more manageable 22,000 were in attendance. The venue's selection demonstrates that the FA did not consider the 1893 final as the catastrophe that later generations did. It may also be that the FA remained keen to demonstrate the attractiveness of their competition to a region where rugby was still viewed as the leading form of football. The FA staged another semi-final at Fallowfield in 1899, when crowd control was once again an issue. As Liverpool was leading Sheffield United 1–0 at half-time, the match was abandoned. The tie had commenced about thirty minutes late, around 4pm, and fans frequently encroached onto the pitch, halting the game on each occasion. One stoppage was reported by Sheffield officials as lasting fifty minutes. The first half came to an end at 5.45pm and the FA decided that the game should be abandoned. Fearful of what might happen, the FA insisted the that players should return to the field while they managed to get the match takings out of the ground and into a safe location. The replay took place at Derby County, and Fallowfield never again staged a major footballing fixture. Manchester's next FA Cup semi-final was played at City's Hyde Road ground in 1905.

In spite of these major incidents, Fallowfield remained a prominent sporting venue and staged many significant events. In rugby, it held the England–Scotland international of 1897 and the Northern Union Challenge Cup (Rugby League) finals of 1899 and 1900, while the Amateur Athletics Association championships were staged there in 1897 and 1907. The venue became known as a cycling arena and in 1934 it held the cycle races in the London Commonwealth Games. In 1955 the famous cyclist Reg Harris helped to purchase the venue from the Manchester Athletic Club with the aim of developing it further. It was later renamed the Reg Harris stadium, but struggled financially and in the early 1960s was sold to the University of Manchester. In 1994 the venue was demolished and student accommodation was erected on the site. In Wolverhampton a street was named Wanderers Avenue to commemorate Wolves' 1893 FA Cup success, and a stone replica of the Cup and the simple inscription 'Fallowfield 1893' was erected on one of the walls in the street (Figures 12a and b). That

(a)

(b)

12a and b Tributes in Wolverhampton to Wolverhampton Wanderers
and their 1893 FA Cup success at Fallowfield.

section of the street, often referred to as Fallowfield Terrace, was close to the Wolves' ground of that time, in the Blakenhall area, but has since been demolished.

By the spring of 1894 Manchester had been home to the FA Cup final and an international match and had staged the inaugural meetings of both the International Football Association Board and the Football League, but its two Football League clubs were struggling. Newton Heath were heading for relegation for the first time, while Ardwick was in disarray and its existence was being questioned. However, moves were afoot among business-minded members of both clubs to utilise the Manchester name to establish a stronger identity and presence in the conurbation.

Manchester City Football Club

On 14 April 1894 it was announced that 'On Monday evening Newton Heath played Ardwick "for the last time", as the posters pathetically put it. In the future the Manchester City club, which will shortly be affiliated with the Lancashire

Association, will occupy the old Ardwick venue, arrangements having been made with the MS and L Railway Company.'[15] The Newton Heath–Ardwick match was a friendly, ending 2–1 to the Heathens, but the transformation of Ardwick into City was the focus. While the Football League had offered Ardwick regular competition and therefore income, it had also increased expenses, with extensive travel costs, increased player-related expenditure and ground improvements. The club had developed rapidly during the early 1890s, but its leading officials were not experienced football administrators and were, in the case of Walter Chew and Lawrence Furniss, playing members of the 1880s church-based club. While the two had much to offer and both remained prominent in Manchester football into the 1940s, they were not known as football visionaries. Fortunately, in 1892 their community had seen the arrival of the former Stoke player and official Joshua Parlby.

Joshua Parlby was born in 1855 to a farming family at Hanley, Staffordshire and was separated from his parents during childhood when he was sent away to school.[16] The family's businesses were failing by the time Joshua was born and Parlby's father struggled to keep his family in the way he that had been accustomed. By 1864 Parlby senior had become a farming bailiff, earning £160 a year, which he considered insufficient to support his wife and family of four.[17] He suffered a breakdown and was admitted to a lunatic asylum, leaving Joshua's mother – a draper – and five children, including fourteen-year-old Joshua, to support themselves.[18] Joshua Parlby was admitted to Christ's Hospital School, a grammar school designed to teach destitute scholars a trade or skill, at the age of nine and he left at fourteen, following a request from his mother, presumably as a result of her husband's breakdown.[19] Parlby senior's employer, William Taylor Copeland, a Christ's Hospital School governor, had supported the original application to attend the school – an indication that social connections influenced the young Parlby's formative years, although the family's changed circumstances meant that none of his four siblings attended the school.[20] Parlby was educated in an environment similar to that of a public school and it was there that he gained his experience of football.

At school Parlby played 'rough football', a rugby-style game involving a spherical ball. On returning from London to his mother's home he joined Stoke, an association football club founded by old Carthusians, captained by a teacher and including a mix of lower- and upper-middle-class individuals.[21] Like Fitzroy Norris's experience at Nottingham Forest, Parlby found himself at a progressive club and part of a social group, comprised of men of varying backgrounds, helping the game prosper and grow. Stoke became one of the Football League's founding members, and although Parlby was not a particularly outstanding player he was a practical club member, being elected to the committee and representing Stoke at Football League meetings.[22] After moving to Manchester for family reasons, he sought to continue his involvement with football. As a member of the brewing trade and Stoke's League representative, the thirty-seven-year-old Parlby would have known people connected with Ardwick, while his involvement in the brewing trade would have brought other connections, such as with Chesters Brewery, a major shareholder in Ardwick. Many other shareholders were involved with the trade.[23] Parlby became Ardwick's first paid secretary in 1893 and received the opportunity to influence the city's sporting and cultural life and to establish a role for himself at a time when Manchester had a new urban aristocracy: a collection of businessmen who were seeking power in the city and nationwide. Perhaps indicative of the way that he operated, he changed the club's telegraphic address from 'Football, Manchester' to 'Parlby Football, Manchester' and the club's address to his home address, and within his first season in charge he planned to relaunch the club, breaking it away from its parochial position under Walter Chew, Lawrence Furniss and the Ardwick committee.[24] Parlby was not officially named as one of the protagonists behind the new Manchester City that rose out of Ardwick, but chroniclers of the sport accept that he was a prime mover, utilising his persuasive skills to bring the community together to establish City.[25] It is recognised that newer communities or societies are often more highly motivated to take risks than are older ones, and Parlby's arrival encouraged newer supporters and shareholders that the time was right to change the club, and that if it could not be changed then a new one should be established.[26] Once he became officially active his enthusiasm persuaded ordinary supporters that the time was right to lay Ardwick to rest and move forward with the more ambitious Manchester City Football Club.

Joshua Parlby saw how important Manchester itself was becoming and recognised the need to build a strong identity; possibly because of his own arrival in the city, he wanted to establish a Mancunian identity. According to Jack Prowse, a committee member at the birth of City, there wouldn't have been a club without Parlby's endeavours: 'That gentleman was wonderfully enthusiastic and active, and successful in raising money from all sorts of people.'[27] Parlby was a great orator and visionary, knowing how to promote the causes he believed in; but, significantly, he recognised that he had to persuade others to follow his own dream of establishing a strong and stable Mancunian club. There was resistance to the creation of City, and Parlby also had to persuade the Manchester FA and Lancashire FA that a new club was worthy of acceptance. All obstacles were overcome, and on Thursday 12 April 1894, at a rather crowded meeting of those supporting the establishment of City, it was formally announced that opposition to the new club had been abandoned and everyone was pulling behind the new 'City' club. As far as the committee was concerned, this meeting established City formally. Significantly, the enterprise was endorsed by Lachie Sinclair, the secretary of the Manchester FA, who felt that the new club would become one of the foremost in Britain.[28] It should be noted that Parlby was a strong supporter of the Manchester FA and was also a familiar presence at Lancashire FA meetings, where occasionally a situation would arise whereby he would be linked directly with the former Hulme Athenaeum secretary John Nall and Manchester Association's Fitzroy Norris. Norris would be minuted for his actions as a referee, while Parlby would defend his club after some misdemeanour or application, and Nall would be on a committee dealing with the complaints.[29]

Ardwick played their last competitive game, a 5–2 defeat away to Walsall Town Swifts, a few days after the Manchester FA's acceptance of City. The former club finished the Football League season thirteenth out of fifteen, and on Monday 16 April 1894 Manchester City Football Club Limited became an officially registered company, its registered address given as 31 Halsbury Street, Stockport Road, Manchester, which is assumed to be Parlby's home. Chesters Brewery agreed to provide finance to support the new club, which was some achievement as Stephen Chesters-Thompson was undergoing significant financial hardships at that time.[30]

There had been a question over Ardwick's debts, but by 12 May they had been cleared, although how this was achieved was not common knowledge at the time.[31] Long-standing committee member Lawrence Furniss was left to resolve the issue, and although he received some support from the club's bank he ended up paying £70 from his own savings to clear the debts. In 1922 his obituary highlighted that the payment of Ardwick's debts had left him struggling financially for some time, forcing him to put off his own wedding for three years.[32] Once Furniss had resolved this issue and Parlby had overcome the other domestic hurdles, Parlby sought to ensure that the club was accepted into the Football League. Significantly, a couple of coincidences aided his plans for the relaunch. First, the Football League had decided that the re-election meeting was to be held in Manchester, which provided him with a platform to explain the city's progression as well as that of his football club. Next, the Manchester Ship Canal was to be officially opened on the same day by Queen Victoria, allowing all Football League delegates and attendees to experience at first hand the significance of the city. The Ship Canal was a sign that the city's growth would continue for some time, as it offered Manchester development possibilities as an inland seaport, while Queen Victoria's presence demonstrated its national significance.[33] Within twelve years of the Ship Canal's opening, Manchester was ranked as the fourth major port in the country and remained so for the following sixty years. For an entrepreneurial visionary like Parlby, its opening provided him with an opportunity. The year 1894 was also significant because it marked the opening of the water pipeline from Thirlmere in the Lake District to Manchester, providing a dedicated supply of water to the city.[34] A fountain stands in Albert Square to commemorate this achievement, which added to the city's growing pride and significance.

At the League Annual General Meeting Parlby spoke convincingly of the ambition, finances and strength of the new club. It is vital to record that Parlby spoke of City as a completely new club, which is why the club has continued to record its foundation as 1894. Other clubs, most notably United, refer to their original formation as Newton Heath in 1878, some two years before they were known to play football and twenty-four years before they became Manchester United; but their history is similar to City's in that they re-formed as a new club in 1902. Parlby used his persuasive powers to impress the League committee:

> On May 21 1894, the day on which Queen Victoria opened the Ship Canal, Mr. Parlby applied for and gained admission to the Second Division. On that occasion, he was accused of being eloquent, and there was something of that quality in a fine well remembered peroration in which he told the assembled dignitaries of the League that it would be the endeavour of those associated with the club to whose name the club bore. A final hint that the League might add to the gaiety of the city was done. Without doubt it was largely a matter of personal influence.[35]

The link with the pride that the city felt in connection with the queen's visit and the opening of the Ship Canal was a key component of Parlby's presentation. At the meeting staged at the eighteenth-century Old Boar's Head Hotel, every attendee would have savoured Manchester's celebrations that day.[36] The opening of the Ship Canal was probably the largest commemoration the city had experienced. Manchester City Council set aside £10,000 to decorate and illuminate the city and the route that the Queen took from Manchester London Road station (Piccadilly) to the canal, and then back into Manchester to Exchange Station, close to the Football League's meeting (Figure 13). As well as street decorations, factory owners and ordinary people decorated their buildings throughout the city. Parlby, like many arrivals in the city during

13 Deansgate, Manchester dressed ready for Queen Victoria
to open the Ship Canal in 1894.

the 1890s, experienced a Manchester that was a major, significant, developing modern city and he wanted the football club to share in the ambition and progress of the city. Those involved with St Mark's and Gorton in the 1880s, such as Walter Chew and Lawrence Furniss, gave the club its community ethos, but Parlby was the visionary who created a club for Manchester. Parlby's new City gained enough votes to tie with Leicester Fosse in the election and were accepted into the Second Division. As Ardwick had finished in the bottom four, they would have had to apply for re-election; however it is extremely doubtful that Ardwick would have received the twenty votes that City did, even with Parlby's eloquence. Parlby's role in gaining acceptance for a club with no players and little finance was of great significance across Manchester. He also headed the poll for a place on the League Management Committee, maintaining both his sphere of football influence and his social connections.[37]

On the night of City's League election, and after the Queen had performed her duties and departed, there were banquets and fireworks as Manchester celebrated into the night. For Parlby, the celebrations took on an added significance and he hoped to benefit from the pride in Manchester that was exhibited during the Queen's visit and, via the new football club, to represent the dynamism of Manchester at its best.

Parlby's role as a publican, combined with his footballing knowledge, business acumen and persuasive oratory, helped to establish him within Manchester's sporting community. While social configurations undergo constant change based on the actions and interactions of interdependent individuals, Parlby, a structure-creating individual, was in a position to shape City much as he wanted to, once he had ensured the support of the directors.[38] It is likely that they recognised that his name, together with his entrepreneurial flair, would accelerate the club's development – reinforcing the view that societal connections influenced and aided the game's development, and that these crossed class boundaries. Parlby, nicknamed Falstaff due to his beard, size and rather loud manner, always appeared to understand how to manipulate situations in the club's or Manchester's best interests.[39] In later years City captain Billy Meredith described his persuasive skills: 'There are some men whose silver tongues are said to have the power of charming song-birds from the trees, and I believe Josh Parlby was one of them.'[40] Parlby was an opinion leader and change agent, reacting to circumstance by identifying opportunities and influencing others, and exhibited transformational leadership qualities.[41] Alongside his club achievements, he remained an active member of the League Management Committee until 1899.[42] City was not the only organisation to benefit from Parlby's attributes, as he also endeavoured to establish a stronger voice for the Manchester FA, whose members were predominantly amateur or semi-professional organisations.

The new Manchester club attracted investment and support. John Chapman, who was described as 'the most loveable of men and the friend of everyone', was the first chair of City. He had not been officially involved with Ardwick, although he did assist with fund raising for the struggling club and he had funded some of Ardwick's travel and supported Parlby's team in other ways.[43] Chapman's importance has hardly been recognised, partly because he was not a self-publicist and was often left in the shadow of others who claimed credit for the achievements and development of football in Manchester, but he worked tirelessly for City.[44] Manchester, thanks to Parlby and Chapman, now had its club, but it required players of quality if it was to fulfil Parlby's dreams of establishing a prominent club on the national stage (Figure 14).

Shortly after it was established City found its first star. An existing player, Pat Finnerhan, urged the club to approach his former colleague Billy Meredith to fill a gap on City's right-wing. Finnerhan's views led the club to seriously consider Meredith, whom Lawrence Furniss had originally spotted playing alongside Finnerhan for Northwich.[45] Furniss had previously refereed a game between Northwich Victoria and Middlesbrough Ironopolis, when he had spotted Meredith, and he knew what the player was capable of. He told City's chair and a long-convoluted process began which has been mythologised to some extent. Eventually Meredith signed amateur forms with City, after insisting that he should continue to live and work in Wales – perhaps suggesting that City was not perceived as a permanent member of the Football League at this point. His plan was to work in the mine all week and then travel to Manchester at weekends, with City arranging lodging for him in a house on Clowes Street.

Meredith's first game for City was a 5–4 defeat at Newcastle United on 27 October 1894. Seven days later he made his home debut in the game that all Mancunians had been looking forward to, the first League meeting between Manchester's clubs. Newton Heath had been relegated to Division Two at the end of the 1893–94 season via a defeat in the test matches to Second Division champions Liverpool. The first League derby ended in a 5–2 victory for Newton Heath. Meredith had scored for City, but the two opening defeats may well have caused him to wonder whether his move would be a successful one. He was not the only player uncertain whether football in Manchester could provide an appropriate living. Four City players – Wallace, Little, Ferguson and Calvey – were enticed by an American football agent who had spent considerable effort illegally persuading them that their lives would be much better if they moved to the United States to join the New York Soccer League in October 1894.

City finished ninth in Division Two at the end of their first season. The following campaign they finished second, entering the promotion-deciding test matches, where a loss of form and a rather amazing organisational own-goal caused City to lose their opportunity. Demonstrating that supporters were vital and were not there to be fleeced by clubs, supporters boycotted one of the test match games, as the club had raised admission prices, assuming that fans would

14 An early Manchester City football card produced by Baines & Co., *c*.1894.

pay extra for what was, in effect, the most important Football League game staged in Manchester to date. City fans demonstrated their dissatisfaction and the crowd and, crucially, the atmosphere, were less significant than expected. Prices returned to their regular level for the following game, but the damage had been done. In 1899 City did achieve promotion as Second Division champions at the end of the first season of automatic promotion and were joined by near neighbours Glossop North End, based twelve miles east of City's ground. Bury Football Club, ten miles north of City, had enjoyed promotion in 1895 and also had further success in 1900 and 1903,winning the FA Cup in both years.

Ground improvements in 1899 allowed City to accommodate approximately 28,000 fans, with 2,000 seated in a new main stand. The growth of crowds at Manchester's Blues coincided with the determination to turn the club into a force.[46] Their motives may have been based on profit, as City's football directors occasionally acted with their own interests uppermost in mind.[47] In 1903 the brewers on City's board voted against relocation plans because of the potential impact on their own takings, even though City's home was struggling to cope with the number of people who wanted to attend the games.[48] They did, however, make the venue available for charity events connected with the unemployed or the poor, such as a match between police forces to raise funds for a soup kitchen. This enabled Hyde Road to become recognised as a key venue within the city's community.[49] As Hill and Williams identified, football was 'more potent in creating a strong sense of geographical and cultural identity than individual sports'.[50] By the end of the century City and Bury were competing in Division One, Newton Heath in Division Two, while Stockport was seeking admittance to the League and Oldham's leading soccer club, Pine Villa, had been reformed as Oldham Athletic and were now members of the Manchester and District Alliance.

The rugby split

The sporting development that ultimately paved the way for soccer to eclipse rugby in Manchester was the rise of professionalism. The FA had successfully negotiated a path through the professionalism debates of the 1880s, ensuring it retained its authority by allowing the game to exist at both amateur and professional levels, and in doing so it saw off the threat of the British FA. In rugby this situation did not exist, and working-class clubs like Salford conflicted with middle-class and upper-middle-class clubs like Manchester FC. Manchester was a passionate rugby area, as was much of the North West, where rugby cup ties with crowds of 20,000 were not uncommon. England versus Scotland international matches were regularly played in either Leeds or Manchester to ensure large crowds, but the associated atmosphere was an 'anathema to those who ran the union', who saw in crowds nothing but a nuisance.[51] The passion and exuberance demonstrated in the North was typical of communities that saw sporting success as of major significance. A difference between rugby as experienced by working-class communities and by those who believed in the sport being an amateur one led to its split. This has been well documented, but prior to its occurring Manchester's soccer clubs became embroiled in rugby's debate.

In 1894, just as the soccer club Ardwick was re-established as Manchester City, the directors of Newton Heath had sought to relaunch their club as Manchester FC. City had promoted itself as a new football club for Manchester, and those at Newton Heath were concerned about their own future and status, hence their attempted name change. While Ardwick's relaunch as City may have been a threat to Newton Heath's position, the Heathens' potential name change was considered a challenge by the rugby authorities because, of course, Manchester FC was the region's leading rugby club. Discussions took place between the rugby union and the FA and a decision was made that Newton Heath would be prevented from changing their name.[52] The complaint did little to arrest the growth of soccer in Manchester, but it demonstrated the nervousness within rugby that their clubs were losing status at a time when professionalism was growing.

When the rugby split occurred in 1895 Manchester's rugby community experienced some confusion while the new order took shape, with clubs that had regularly competed against each other now in opposing camps. Those that continued as amateur outfits playing Rugby Union found life financially difficult. Manchester FC itself, the game's driving force in the North West, had been on the verge of disbanding, and with the sport split into two camps rugby's position of strength in Manchester was over.[53] Had Manchester FC, Broughton and Sale joined the exodus to professionalism, then the city might have remained a rugby city. Instead, the split impacted at every level of the sport; for example, referees had to choose which form of rugby they would officiate in.[54] Fred Kennedy, a former Free Wanderers and Broughton Rangers player who had established a reputation as a referee of quality following his retirement as a player in 1893, debated for some time which version of rugby to back. It was a tough decision for someone viewed as forward-looking. Ultimately, he chose to follow his former club, Broughton Rangers, into the professional Northern Union (Rugby League), but it was a difficult decision for him to make. For Kennedy, the move proved a wise one, as his status within the sport increased and he became a prominent advocate of the northern version of the game and helped oversee the transformation of the role of referee as participants took on professionalism in increasing numbers. He became Broughton Rangers' chairman in 1910–11 and was a member of the Rugby League Council and the League Management Committee. Kennedy was also responsible for the long-term development of The Cliff, Broughton's ground, which, in later years, became Manchester United's training facility.[55] His first club was Trafford Hornets, who played at the Old Mill Field before the land was purchased for the development of the Manchester Ship Canal, and then he was one of the founders of St Bartholomew's.

The split brought uncertainty and fracture to rugby and gave investors and entrepreneurs a simple choice – invest in a soccer club with potential to compete in national cup and league competitions, or in a rugby club that has local appeal but regional competition. While towns with a strong individual identity across Lancashire tended to back their local favourites, no matter what the sport, those in a conurbation like Manchester had the choice of three versions of football. The traditional club, Manchester FC, remained an outpost of the amateur rugby code and thereby limited its appeal. Others switched to the professional rugby league form of the game, but as there was not one club purporting to represent Manchester as a whole, and the wider Mancunian population focused on the more business- and national-minded soccer clubs. Pride and local identity ensured that rugby clubs such as Salford survived and kept a dedicated support, but as both prominent Football League clubs gained a foothold and sought to represent the whole of Manchester, as City had promised at their relaunch in 1894, the wider population backed their Mancunian representatives. As did local businesses, with two major breweries backing Manchester's prominent Football League sides by the early twentieth century, while Sir Edward Hulton, the proprietor of several newspapers, including the all-important promoter of soccer, the *Athletic News*, was the chairman by 1903 of City.

Rugby's split ended the dominance of the sport in Manchester, putting some clubs into financial difficulties and others into a period of stagnation. The entire rugby community was weakened at a time when soccer was succeeding both as a professional enterprise and as an attraction to ordinary Mancunians. Soccer was a simple sport to understand, and anyone could attend a game at Hyde Road or at Bank Street, as the numbers of boys and women demonstrated. During the mid-1890s soccer's leaders did not plot to bring down rugby or find themselves at loggerheads with the sport as they had during Fitzroy Norris's over-zealous promotion of Manchester Association two decades earlier; rather, they focused solely on promoting their own sport, making the split even more suicidal from the perspective of rugby in the region. Manchester had been one of the great strongholds of rugby prior to the divide, and without the split it might have developed as a national rival to soccer, particularly as the Football League remained predominantly northern and Midlands in its geographical coverage into the 1920s. But professionalism was such a strong issue that compromise was not achievable.

The rugby split was the fourth great act in a three-year period that transformed Manchester from a rugby city into a soccer city, and followed the extension of the Football League and the staging of the 1893 FA Cup final in the city and the establishment of a Football League club utilising the Manchester name. Manchester's soccer activities were still viewed nationally as of less prominence in the conurbation than those of rugby, but the handling code was no longer the force that it was while soccer was still growing. The relaunch of Ardwick as City and the club's subsequent Second Division title success in 1899 demonstrated that association football was in the ascendency, but there were still some issues with Newton Heath, the city's other prominent club, which was in a desperate state by the beginning of the twentieth century.

The collapse of Newton Heath

Following the aborted attempt to change their name to Manchester in 1894, Newton Heath existed as a Second Division club. They maintained several pro-motion challenges initially, but by 1900 they were a struggling Second Division team and had been in a desperate financial state for several years. They had suffered with poor purchases and investments, with players becoming injured shortly after signing.[56]

In 1902 Newton Heath finished fifteenth in the Second Division, one place above the re-election zone. This remained the club's worst placing until 1934, when they finished the season twentieth in the Second Division. During 1901 a bazaar was held at St James's Hall in the city centre, with the aim of raising £1,000 to solve the Heathens' financial worries, but it was not a major success, despite strong support from leading Manchester politicians and rivals City. It is known that several of the official patrons donating money were connected with City, including City chairman John Chapman, director John Allison and Edward Hulton and the famous kit manufacturer Alec Watson, who later sup-plied Cup final shirts to City. It is recorded that City themselves gave £10 and Chapman £1 1s, demonstrating that Manchester's soccer community recog-nised the importance of sustaining multiple Football League clubs. Manchester benefited from having two major sides in the city, and those associated with Manchester's Blues saw no conflict of interest. Saving Newton Heath and ensuring that the Football League had two Mancunian representatives was the right course to take, and City officials assumed that the Heathens would have done the same if roles had been reversed. Financially, Newton Heath remained in an appalling state and close to extinction, their secretary, Alf Albut, admit-ting that their gas supply had been withdrawn and meetings had to be staged by candlelight.[57] Albut was one of the most influential men in the development of United, for if he had not performed the desperate activities of 1901–2, the club would have died before it had had chance of salvation. Albut's actions at this time could be described as a series of interdependent events during a transitional period for the club.

On 11 January 1902 it was revealed that a winding-up order had been granted for the club at Ashton-Under-Lyne County Court.[58] Former direc-tor William Healey was owed £242 17s 10d. As with West Manchester and Fairfield, Newton Heath's difficulties brought into question how football clubs were structured and demonstrated how clubs that wanted to establish them-selves as national organisations required visionary leaders with entrepreneurial skills, such as Parlby at City. As with progressive clubs in twenty-first-century England, they also needed financial support. The Heathens' trial demonstrated that soccer still had some way to go to penetrate all areas of society. The judge failed to understand what a football club was and how it expected to generate a profit from playing sport. He granted Newton Heath's winding up and it was noted that there was no opposition at all. Two days later the *Athletic News* recorded further problems for the Heathens, as they were unable to fulfil their fixture with Middlesbrough, which was ultimately played in April, but this was another serious indication of the club's plight.[59] Attempts were made to keep the Heathens alive and the affair dragged on for some time, although the official receiver wanted to resolve the matter quickly and on 25 January it was reported that he wanted the court to grant William Walker, a cattle dealer from Salford, the Bank Street ground, which had been leased from Walker since 13 May 1898. The order was granted by Judge Reginald Brown and the receiver also announced that an offer had come in for £110 from someone wanting to purchase the stands and the fixtures and fittings. On 5 February a meeting of all creditors was held where it was agreed the Heathens' total liabilities stood at £2,670. By the end of February the FA had held a meeting with representatives of Newton Heath who claimed that they had formed a new club under a slight variation of the club's name and that the new organisation would be able to fulfil all the existing fixtures and satisfy the terms of the players' contracts. Whether this was an element of the receiver's strategy or a move by others is not clear, but it demonstrates that, as with Ardwick, there were people in the area who were keen to keep the Heathens operational.

On 1 March details of the Heathens' financial affairs were made public, showing that the club had 171 shareholders and that they had taken up 787 of the 2,000 shares created in 1892. A breakdown was provided of everything the club had received in terms of gate money and its expenditure during the period 1892 to 30 April 1901.

INCOME
Gate Receipts: £27,373
Tickets [presumably bought in advance]: £1,483
Donations: £335

EXPENDITURE
Salaries and Wages: £20,408
Gatemen: £530
Referees: £539
Training: £828
Football Utensils: £417
Legal: £271
Rents and Tax: £1,137

Hotels and Travel: £2,814
Printing and Stationery: £1,359
Police: £318
Total Assets = £127

Throughout March 1902 the receiver sought a way forward for the business, but was also aware of the non-footballing offers that had come his way for the land and stands. On 12 April 1902 matters were brought to a head when the club captain, Harry Stafford, wrote a letter to various newspapers outlining his dissatisfaction with the progress being made. The Newton Heath situation was concerning, and their supporters and officials hoped that Stafford could be the visionary, like City's Parlby, to not only save their club but help it to thrive.

Supporting businesses

By 1902 Manchester was home to a variety of businesses supporting the game of football, with the sporting press being the most obvious example. There were also kit manufacturers and suppliers, turnstile manufacturers, ticket printers and a full range of ancillary industries benefiting from the game, such as the brewery trade, cough sweet sellers, bookmakers and programme sellers. Russell has identified that Manchester had a 'flourishing sports service industry', with twenty sports outfitters active by 1912.[60] It was a complex range of inter-linked businesses relying on the local clubs and the sport itself to flourish.

The links between football and the brewery trade are well known, particularly in Manchester, where Ardwick was supported by Chesters Brewery and Newton Heath, following its re-formation as Manchester United in 1902, would owe its existence to Manchester Breweries, where it became, in effect, an appendage of the brewery.[61] The role of the brewers was to look after their own interests first, and there are examples of how both Manchester clubs were negatively impacted upon by such a close relationship as the twentieth century progressed.[62] While the brewing trade had some control over the region's prominent clubs it is important to challenge the wider shareholding of the clubs. How much any football club represented its local population can be assessed to some extent by Vamplew's analysis of club shareholdings, and he demonstrated that Manchester City's largest group of shareholders were skilled manual workers (36.8%). These figures provide an indication of the breadth of interest in football across the classes, and the analysis of English clubs that became limited companies between 1890 and 1912 is particularly interesting when comparing City, who possessed 212 shareholders, with other leading clubs of the era (Table 2).[63] The figures indicate a spread of interest at City, with the club having a larger combined percentage of shareholders in the semi-skilled manual and unskilled manual (20.2%) groups than any other club

Table 2 Manchester City shareholdings *c*.1900

Occupational group	Percentage of shareholders	Percentage of shareholdings
Aristocracy/gentry	0.0	0.0
Upper professional	0.5	1.0
Lower professional	4.2	5.3
Proprietors/employers within the drinks trade	9.0	32.0
Other proprietors/employers	13.2	11.8
Managers/higher administration	4.2	6.7
Clerical	10.4	5.7
Foremen/supervisors/inspectors	1.4	1.0
Skilled manual	36.8	23.2
Semi-skilled manual	12.7	9.4
Unskilled manual	7.5	3.7

Note: Comparative figures for Manchester United are not available.
Source: W. Vamplew, *Pay up and play the game* (Cambridge: Cambridge University Press, 1988), 291–299.

except West Ham United (31.2%) – although more shares were held by those shareholders at City (13.1%) than at West Ham (5.4%). Those groups also held a greater number of shares at City than at any other club apart from Reading (15.9%), and City's figures were significantly greater than those of all comparable clubs including Liverpool (0%), Everton (7.6%), Aston Villa (2.3%), Newcastle (2.7%), Tottenham (5.8%) and Arsenal (5.8%). While the shareholdings of football clubs may not be representative of those who attended, they do provide an indication of which sectors of society wanted football to succeed locally, whether for their own personal gain or simply for the enjoyment of seeing a successful club representing the district.

While shareholdings can paint a picture of those who invested and sought gains from the sport, and reviews of formal businesses – whether public houses close to the ground, turnstile manufacturers or prominent local companies – can point to a network of ancillary industries. There were some unsavoury industries associated with football. Gambling was of course one of these, but there was another practice that seemed to be extremely popular in Manchester which employed young boys to push their products onto match-attending football followers. This industry has received little attention over the years, yet Manchester was at the centre of the trade and any football regular during the 1880s and into the twentieth century would have been aware of it. This was the practice of selling funeral cards depicting specific results and, usually, the funeral or death of a team.

The sending of cards to mark a funeral began in the early 1800s and by the time of Queen Victoria's reign the practice had grown of sending cards after a funeral to people who had been unable to attend. High-quality mourning cards, printed on heavy card and comprising a formal, intricate design incorporating graves and other funeral-related imagery and including details such as the deceased's birth and death dates, would be sent. Inevitably, once an industry develops, entrepreneurs are often quick to establish ways to increase their market and potential money-making opportunities. This industry developed and cards were produced to mark significant high-profile deaths – such as of royalty, politicians, and other public figures. As football of all kinds grew in the 1880s the entrepreneurs saw a new market, and reports began to comment on the inevitable sight of funeral-card sellers.[64]

By 1885 the practice was established of issuing cards to defeated football teams, although it is worth explaining that there were multiple reasons for individuals to buy these cards commemorating sporting defeats. The first and most obvious reason was one-upmanship, the means of boasting of your victory over a team by reminding your opponents of their defeat. In this case, fans of the winning team would buy cards and keep them as a souvenir of a memorable victory, even though the main text focused on the opponents' defeat. The second reason was to remember your own team's defeat, not necessarily because you liked to dwell on the negatives but because you regarded the defeat as a plucky performance against a more established team. Many cards were produced for FA Cup games (Figure 15), and there are several examples of cards commemorating giant-killings. There are also examples of lesser-ranked teams being defeated by perceived giants, and in such cases, the supporter of the defeated minnow would keep the card as a memento of their plucky but unsuccessful challenge. A third reason to buy the cards was for victorious supporters to keep a collection of all the teams defeated during a Cup run, or of the games the supporter had attended.

There are several examples of football and rugby cards dating from the 1880s and it is known that sales took place at the Manchester Cup final of 1885. In addition to the legitimate business, there was also a criminal element who faked the cards. The printers were primarily ordinary local printers, and they would create two versions of a card, recording victories by each opponent. This guaranteed a sale, and each set would have such a mark-up that the production of two versions, one of which would be wasted, was still profitable. The sellers were typically boys or young men who would be paid a commission based on the number of cards they sold, and they would begin selling as early as possible, hoping that supporters would buy based on the winning position during a game – which could change – rather than wait until the final whistle. As soon as one team scored the boys would pull the appropriate cards out of their pockets and start selling the cards that marked the death of the losing team. Following the 1893 Cup final at Fallowfield it was reported that the sale of cards began twenty minutes before the end of the game at which Wolverhampton Wanderers won: 'an enterprising youth came across the pavilion shouting, "Everton funeral cards, one penny." The Everton supporters could not stand this, and the boy left amid hisses and groans.'[65]

Most sellers also became race-card sellers at horse-race meetings during the summer months and they saw this dual role as their occupation, never wanting to learn a trade or take up any other occupation. The impression is that they were willing entrepreneurs who knew how to make a profit by working the crowd and knew when the mood was right to sell their cards. It is difficult to prove how profitable the business was and, even with the methods employed to minimise risk, it was based entirely on the significance and result of games and the mood of the crowd. For major fixtures, such as the FA Cup final, more than 16,000 cards would be produced. At the 1908 final 8,000 unsold cards were discarded. Presumably these recorded the incorrect loser and a similar number of opposition cards would have been sold. That would equate to a possible total profit of over 5,300 pennies or £44 (pre-decimal money) for the youths selling the cards. Occasionally a printer or seller would be so convinced that one team would be victorious that they would produce only one set of cards for a match. During the 1890s a boy told a journalist that he had gone to the Derby–Newton Heath game with a stack of cards claiming that Derby had won, but Newton Heath managed a shock victory and not a single card was sold. Drawn games were the biggest disappointment to printers and sellers, but those involved still managed to reduce wastage by ensuring, where possible, that the cards were used again for replayed games. Knowledgeable printers avoided naming the venue and date for this reason. Some supporters would still buy cards marking a team's defeat after drawn games, such as when Sheffield United fans bought cards marking the death of Manchester City after a drawn FA Cup game in March 1914. The reason given in the local newspapers was confidence that the Yorkshire club would win the replay, but it was another drawn match. They did win the second replay, so potentially the cards from the original game became a more celebrated souvenir than normal.

Cup matches were the easiest and most popular games at which to sell the cards and the Manchester Cup seemed a particularly popular competition for them, presumably because the nature of a local contest increased the rivalry aspect. Evidence exists of cards produced for other regional competitions, such as the North Derbyshire League. Manchester-based sellers travelled to Bolton, Blackburn, Liverpool, Oldham and Bury throughout the season. Oldham was perceived as a tough place to sell, as 'Oldhamers were less demonstrative', according to one seller who related a tale of how sellers had to dodge spectators who became angry that the practice was continuing when they didn't want it to.[66] The industry remained active until the 1930s, and there are examples of cards produced on occasion after 1945, although by then it was not a vibrant industry. It seems reasonable to suggest that the Second World War changed perceptions, but it is more likely that the trade was coming to a natural end

In Loving Memory of

Manchester City,

WHO WERE BEATEN AT SWINDON IN THE ENGLISH CUP
ON SATURDAY, MARCH 5, 1910.

A Manchester Team came rushing along,
"Clear the way, mind your backs," was their cry.
The Swindon boys said "You'll find us too strong,"
So they did ! To the Cup say "Good-bye ! "

Result—Swindon 2 ; Manchester City 0.

15 A funeral card commemorating a Manchester City defeat in the FA Cup, 1910.

during the 1930s. The gap in meaningful, truly competitive fixtures during the war may also have caused those in the trade to cease operation, and it was certainly not a prominent aspect of Mancunian football by that time.

By the beginning of the twentieth century the city was still not recognised as a footballing power, but interest in the sport and the desire for success was growing and being noticed.[67] Football was gaining significance in Manchester year on year, as attendances demonstrate. Newton Heath attracted an average crowd of 7,000 in 1893, and City was the first club locally to reach 10,000, in 1896. By 1901 City's average was 18,300, the second highest in the League, although Newton Heath's crowds had dropped to around 5,400. The following decade would see soccer become Manchester's sport, but before that happened the death of Manchester's earliest soccer ambassador occurred. A year after acting as linesman in the 1896 Lancashire FA Cup semi-final, Nall died at the age of fifty-six while still in office at both the Manchester FA and the Lancashire FA, who sent a letter of condolence to his family.[68] The role that Nall played in the development of football in Manchester should never be under-estimated. He promoted participation, teams and competitions, remaining active within the community until his death, and helped to establish a League in Cheshire in 1893.[69] Nall had helped to establish Manchester's soccer community and was a key figure behind the sport's local development. At times soccer in the region deteriorated but, taking a long-range view, it is evident that the sport is one continuum stretching from the 1860s through to the present day.[70] Similarly, consider City's history in *longue durée* terms. The club became established in its present form in 1894 as a club to represent Manchester, and over several transformational periods it grew, found success, suffered hardships, moved twice and changed ownership, but it remains in essence the same football club performing its same role in Manchester society as it has always done.

Notes

1 Taylor, *The leaguers*, 4–6.
2 D. Twydell, *Denied FC: the Football League election struggles* (Harefield: Yore Publications, 2001), 6–11.
3 Records of Fairfield's correspondence with Companies House and its shareholder records and related material are held at The National Archives, Kew.
4 The Fairfield shareholding has a mix of occupations and social diversity, with coffee-tavern keepers rubbing shoulders with hairdressers, physicians, barmen, machinists, carters and bankers, among others. The share register contains details of a major, a retired publican and other leading figures within the Fairfield and Droylsden communities, some of whom were described as 'gentlemen', meaning that they were people of independent means.
5 New Brighton Tower was a club developed to attract visitors to the seaside resort on the Wirral coast, but the investment in players was not matched by support and the club resigned from the League during 1900–1 season.
6 'Monday September 4 1893', *Manchester Evening News*, 4 September 1893, 2.
7 'A football libel suit', *Sunderland Daily Echo,* 3 March 1894, 3.
8 *Gorton Reporter*, 10 March 1894.
9 *Clarion*, 2 April 1892, n.p.; documents relating to West Manchester Football Club are held in The National Archives.
10 *Pastime: A weekly record of lawn tennis, football, lacrosse, cycling & athletic sports*, 29 March 1893, 193–194.
11 Ibid.
12 *Sporting Chronicle*, 27 March 1893.
13 MacGregor in *The book of football*, 37–39.
14 Ibid.
15 *Gorton Reporter*, 14 April 1894.
16 'To be let', *Hereford Times*, 28 June 1851, 4; Census returns, Joshua Parlby 1861, https//:www.findmypast.co.uk (RG 9/1941).
17 An equivalent salary to a workhouse chaplain's. 'Wanted', *Manchester Courier*, 24 January 1863, 2; Parlby senior's petition to Christ's Hospital School, 1864, as detailed by Clifford Jones, Christ's Hospital School, 10 June 2014.
18 Correspondence with Geri Parlby on 12 November 2011. Parlby senior appears to have run into financial problems, and it is thought that he suffered a mental breakdown. *Perry's Bankrupt Weekly Gazette*, 5 November 1864, 12, reported his bankruptcy. Further correspondence held in The National Archives confirms his residency at an asylum.

19 Correspondence with Geri Parlby, 12 November 2011.

20 Information provided by Clifford Jones, Christ's Hospital School, 10 June 2014.

21 Correspondence with Mike Barford, curator of Christ Hospital School archives, 11 June 2014; MacGregor, *The book of football*, 87–88; Cooke and James, 'Myths, truths and pioneers', 5–23.

22 'The Football League', *Lancashire Evening Post*, 14 May 1892, 3.

23 Census returns, Joshua Parlby 1901, https://:www.findmypast.co.uk (RG 13/3696).

24 *Athletic News football annual* (Manchester: Athletic News, 1891–94).

25 *New football club for Manchester: the Manchester City Football Club* (Manchester: Manchester City Football Club, 1894); A. Ward, *The Manchester City story* (Derby: Breedon, 1984), 8.

26 C. Chase-Dunn, 'Through the obstacle(s) and on to global socialism', in I. Wallerstein (ed.), *The modern world system in the longue durée* (Abingdon: Routledge, 2016), 33.

27 'Well-known figure in City circles', *Manchester Football Chronicle*, 28 April 1923, 3.

28 'Promotion of a football company at Ardwick', *Manchester Courier*, 13 April 1894, 3. Some sources, most notably P. Toovey, *Manchester City: the early years*, state that John Nall was present and credit the Sinclair comments to him. Contemporary reports identified to date fail to corroborate this, although it is possible that the former Hulme Athenaeum founder did attend this meeting.

29 Lancashire Archives, DDX2708, Minutes of the Lancashire Football Association, 28 September 1892–2 January 1897.

30 Throughout June 1894 the *Gorton Reporter* carried detailed article on Chesters-Thompson's bankruptcy and financial issues.

31 *Gorton Reporter*, 12 May 1894, n.p.

32 'The man at the head of Manchester City', *Manchester Football Chronicle*, 23 September 1922, 3.

33 D. A. Farnie, *The Manchester Ship Canal and the rise of the port of Manchester 1894–1975* (Manchester: Manchester University Press, 1980), 167–169.

34 O'Reilly, 'Re-ordering the landscape', 35.

35 Unknown newspaper article dated April 1904 profiling Parlby, in the possession of Geri Parlby.

36 The Old Boar's Head stood on the corner of Withy Grove and Corporation Street and was replaced by Hulton's newspaper works in the 1920s. This was, by 2018, the Printworks entertainment centre.

37 '24,000 soldier spectators', *Manchester Courier*, 22 May 1915, 6.

38 P. Donnelly, 'Sport and social theory', in B. Houlihan (ed.) *Sport and society*, (Sage: London, 2008), 25; H. Bonde, 'Gymnastics and politics: Niels Bukh and the biographical genre', in J. Bale, M. K. Christensen and G. Pfister (eds), *Writing lives in sports: biographies, life-histories and methods* (Aarhus: Aarhus University Press, 2004), 53–54.

39 Ward, *Manchester City story*.

40 J. Harding, *Football wizard: the story of Billy Meredith* (Derby: Breedon, 1985), 28.

41 B. M. Bass and R. E. Riggio, *Transformational leadership* (New Jersey: Lawrence Erlbaum Associates, 2006).

42 Sutcliffe, Brierley and Howarth, *The story of the Football League*, 67–70.

43 'Features of football', *Manchester Football Chronicle*, 17 March 1917, 3.

44 Ibid.

45 'The man at the head of Manchester City', *Manchester Football Chronicle*, 23 September 1922, 3.

46 'The association game', *Manchester Courier*, 28 August 1899, 8.

47 D. Russell, *Football and the English* (Preston: Carnegie Publishing, 1997), 44.

48 Ibid.

49 'Police at play', *Daily Dispatch*, 3 March 1904, 6.

50 J. Hill and J. Williams, *Sport and identity in the north of England* (Keele: Keele University Press, 1996), 138.

51 P. Blackledge, 'Rationalist capitalist concerns: William Cail and the great rugby split of 1895', *International Journal of the History of Sport*, 18:2 (2001), 44; A. G. Guillemard, 'The foundation and progress of the Rugby Football Union from 1871 to 1880', in F. Marshall and L. Tosswell (eds) *The rugby game* (London: Cassell & Co, 1892), 71.

52 'Committee meeting held at the Craven Hotel, London', Minutes of the Rugby Football Union, 24 May 1894.

53 Collins, *Rugby's great split*, 189; *Yorkshire Post*, 13 May 1898, n.p.

54 It should be noted that the inaugural meeting of the new northern rugby union was held in Manchester on 3 September 1895 at the Spread Eagle Hotel.

55 'Familiar faces', *Manchester Football Chronicle*, 5 January 1924, 3.

56 'Familiar faces: Fred Palmer', *Manchester Football Chronicle*, 25 November 1922, 3.

57 J. A. H. Catton, *The story of association football: classic reprint* (Cleethorpes: Soccer Books Limited, 2005).

58 *Gorton Reporter*, 11 January 1902.

59 'En passant', *Athletic News*, 13 January 1902, 1.

60 Russell, 'Sporting Manchester', 2.

61 T. Collins, *Sport in capitalist society* (Abingdon: Routledge, 2013), 52.

62 Manchester City's potential ground move was frequently thwarted by Chesters, while United's move to Old Trafford came as a result of the brewery owning land there. That move caused the club to stagnate and struggle during the 1920s and 1930s.

63 Vamplew, *Pay up*, 291–9.

64 For example, 'The "Burnley News" in the United States', *Burnley News*, 29 July 1914, 2; 'By-Ways of Manchester Life', *Manchester Guardian*, 5 March 1898, 8.

65 *Pastime: A weekly record of lawn tennis, football, lacrosse, cycling & athletic sports*, 29 March 1893, 193–194.

66 'By-Ways of Manchester Life', *Manchester Guardian*, 5 March 1898, 8.

67 'Items', *Luton Times*, 27 January 1899, 6.

68 Lancashire Football Association cup record book, 1893–97; Lancashire Archives, DDX2708, Minutes of the Lancashire Football Association, 15 April 1897.

69 *Bolton Cricket and Football Field*, 19 August 1893, 6.

70 Braudel, *On history*, 75.

8

Identity

Major, a Saint Bernard

For all the efforts in the Victorian era when Manchester saw many well-meaning and important societies created, none of these established a global image of the city and its citizens, nor did they unite the population. If Manchester was discussed, it tended to be either because of its industry or for negative reasons concerning health, pollution and working conditions. Many organisations had been successful in improving the social life of the city and developing intellectual interests, while also improving conditions for poorer citizens, but these did not establish a Mancunian identity; rather, they developed societies and groups working for and with individual communities.[1] The fluidity of Manchester's population allowed 'new social groups, drawing themselves up by self-help and self-education', to develop their own social hierarchy, but none of these was in a position to unite the population.[2] By 1902 civic leaders were discussing a lack of unity and civic pride in Manchester.[3] The population of the wider Manchester region had reached 2,149,000 by 1901, although the city centre comprised only 30,000 residents at this time.[4] By then Manchester's population consisted of different occupations, classes, religions, nationalities and cultures and was more representative of Britain as a whole than were cities dominated by a particular industry or ethnic group.[5]

Football was beginning to give Manchester something positive to focus on collectively following City's relaunch in 1894 and subsequent Second Division title success in 1899, but the city housed two Football League teams by this time. If one was representing Manchester, then the attractiveness of any representing a district of the city, particularly if that one was struggling on the pitch, was likely to be less significant. In the major cities of Liverpool and Birmingham the names of prominent teams representing districts survived into the twenty-first century, with Everton and Aston Villa recognisable as significant entities throughout their existence. The difference between those two clubs and most other big-city clubs is that they achieved major success during the earliest years of League football, ensuring that they had established their names as two of England's greatest clubs by the beginning of the 1890s. Manchester's clubs reached maturity later, and not while they retained their district names. Now

that Manchester had its City team the impact on the district team was clear, and
Newton Heath struggled both on the pitch and financially, causing Heathens'
shareholders to question the direction of the club. If they wanted to achieve
anything nationally they needed to secure both their future and their identity.
The club's financial problems indicated it was about to collapse; however, the
intervention of club captain Harry Stafford was to dramatically alter the club's
fortunes. Stafford claimed that he and four other men, whom he did not name
initially, had offered to locate £1,000 to save Newton Heath, but that when he
had spoken with two of the directors they had wanted to be recompensed for
their shareholding first. Stafford felt that they were the men responsible for the
financial mess. Personal motivation seemed to be getting in the way and Stafford
urged supporters and businessmen to apply pressure on the directors to force
a change. A public meeting was held on 24 April 1902 at the New Islington
public hall in Ancoats, where a relaunch of the club seemed to be the only way
forward.[6] At that meeting James Bown raised the subject of the club's name:

> It had been mentioned to him that during the season one or two visiting clubs had
> been deluded by the name of the club in taking the wrong car through being mis-
> taken as to the situation of the ground. In consequence delay in commencement
> of the matches has been entailed. On this ground, and others of even a stranger
> character, he would suggest that the club's name should be changed, on approval
> of the League and the FA, to that of Manchester United. The question was asked
> would the new club be likely to be re-admitted to the Second Division under the
> name of Manchester United? In reply, Mr. West (the secretary) said they would
> have to apply but did not expect a difficulty. But he did say that as the bulk of
> supporters were from Newton Heath that he would like to find a way to retain
> that name.[7]

James Bown appears to have been the first person to raise question of the
club's name and it seems that he was the man who proposed the Manchester
United tag – which conflicts with the claims of club stalwart 'the redoubtable
Louis Rocca', who claimed that the name was his suggestion.[8] Contemporary
reports of the meeting make no such comment, stating that it was James Bown
who made the proposal, although there is a report of an earlier meeting during
which it was stated that an 'old member' had suggested the name.[9] Reports
imply that it was mentioned but was not debated at the earlier meeting and,
based on the description of the proposer and the attendees, it seems unlikely it
would have been the nineteen-year-old Rocca.[10] The development of Rocca's
version of the story demonstrates how sport history is dogged by myths and
there are many 'truths' which have been exaggerated as a result of 'a tendency
to misinterpret, oversimplify, misrepresent or even falsify the actual record'.[11]
Rocca's version may have been either an exaggeration of the facts or a delib-
erate attempt to gain credit for the club's identity, as can be demonstrated by
research into the formation of the Davis Cup.[12]

Another myth surrounding the name that gained momentum concerns the options discussed, and the often-repeated claim that three suffixes were debated – United, Celtic and Central. Contemporary reports make no such comment for either the March or April meeting, with the only discussion focusing on whether Newton Heath could remain in the title somehow. In actuality, the name Manchester Central could not have been proposed, as that name had already been utilised by another club, for which match reports appeared as early as 1892.[13] Also, another local club had been called Newton Heath Central – the former Ten Acres, which had played within a mile of the Heathens' Bank Street ground – and it is unlikely that the Heathens' committee would have selected a name that could bring comparisons with a neighbouring club. Manchester Celtic is another name that is difficult to accept as a proposal, although Rocca often connected Catholicism with United in later years. No proof of its discussion has been identified. The only names debated appear to have been Manchester United and West's suggestion of a continued name along the lines of Manchester Newton Heath. Regardless of the myths and discussions, the name Manchester United was chosen.

The *Manchester Evening News* was close to the club and had an office at the Bank Street ground, working to create publicity for the Heathens, and it explained the main reason for the change:

> The proposal to change the name of the Newton Heath club to Manchester United will not be received with favour in certain quarters, but there is no doubt that it is a step in the right direction. Visiting teams and their supporters have many times been led astray by the name of the club and have journeyed either by car or train to Newton Heath only to find that they were miles away from the home of the club.[14]

Although it is viewed as a name change, United was a new legal entity, as Newton Heath was heading for financial ruin and ceased to exist. United was established as a new club and stipulations were made at the creation of the new company that none of the former committee could 'interfere with the newly born child'.[15] It is understood that former Newton Heath chairman Fred Palmer had to pay to attend United games in subsequent years because it was considered to be a new club, and not one which he had been a director of. Palmer was deeply saddened when the bailiffs arrived to sell off all of Newton Heath's assets, including 'the stands, turnstiles, team and everything else' for £100, as he saw this as the end of the club.

The reasons for the new name and its selection are not entirely clear, although the name United was in vogue during this period. Often clubs are named after another successful club; for example, names such as North End proved popular following Preston's successes in the 1880s and led to clubs such as Glossop North End and Manchester North End. It is possible the use of United by other significant sides had a bearing on the choice. Sheffield United were FA Cup winners in 1902 and had been finalists in 1901, when the replay was staged at Bolton. In fact, the 1902 FA Cup final took place on 19 April, with a replay on 26 April, and so the Yorkshire side were in the headlines during the period when Manchester United was being established. The relaunch of Newton Heath followed a similar pattern to that of Ardwick, with members of the old clubs realising that serious change was required. Understandably, both United and City trace their origins back to Newton Heath and Ardwick, but legally and in the eyes of the authorities they were new clubs. During the twenty-first century the two clubs have taken a somewhat different view on whether to recognise and commemorate their formation dates as those of the original club or of the present-day organisation. In United's case, they record formation as 1878, when the Newton Heath L&YR set up its sports committee, although no evidence of footballing activity has been identified before November 1880 and United was established in 1902 as a new entity. The formation of the new club was important and was insisted upon by the FA, who consented to the new club on the following basis: 'consent was given to the formation of the Manchester United club, according to the usual conditions, in place of the late Newton Heath club, which was being wound up'.[16]

At City, the club's badge redesign in 2015 added a formation date of 1894, which is the appropriate date for their establishment as City, despite at least fourteen years of footballing participation before this date by their predecessor clubs. This transparency on the part of City adds to the question of footballing myths and what historians should do. If both Manchester clubs took the same stance, then United would appear to be a younger club not only than City but also than many of its other rivals. The earlier date is of great importance to United, as is evidenced by their claim to be 'the oldest team' competing in the Champions League.[17] There was one significant difference between the relaunches of the two clubs, and that was in their acceptance into the Football League. As Newton Heath had not finished in the re-election zone, the club did not face a vote for election as United. This was different to City's situation, where Ardwick was unlikely to be re-elected and so it was vital for the new club to stress that it was a separate entity from its predecessor. Those behind the new United club would benefit from informing the League that it was the same club, even if Palmer and the courts knew that it was not.[18] By the time that the League elections were being discussed and meetings held, United had convinced the Football League that they were simply changing the name of Newton Heath to Manchester United, something that had occurred at other clubs without any concern.[19] This was accepted without question and the club did not have to go through an election process that could have failed.

United were given every opportunity to succeed by the new leadership, who renovated the stands and decided to 'reserve the existing covered stand for donors and moderately high-priced season ticket holders' where there would be 'a number of plush seated chairs'.[20] One of the new investors was brewer John Henry Davies, a director of Walker and Homfrays and of the Manchester Brewery Company, and whose wife was the daughter of Henry Tate from the Tate and Lyle sugar company. Davies had played rugby in his early life and was not particularly known for his interest in association football.[21] The change is said to have come about when a dog used to raise money by Newton Heath captain, Harry Stafford, was found by the Davies family. The story goes that Stafford had taken his St Bernard dog, Major, to the 1901 St James's Hall bazaar to raise funds, and that Major had a collection box fastened around his neck. Major roamed around the stalls collecting money, but somehow he went missing. Eventually, it seems, the dog was found by Davies who, recognising that it was not a stray, set about trying to find the owner. Eventually Davies located Stafford and the brewer asked Newton Heath's captain about the collection tin. Stafford explained about the Heathens' financial worries and Davies became one of the wealthy backers in Stafford's plan to save the club in 1902. An alternative version of the story was told to the BBC by Davies's daughter, Elsie Partington, in 1973. She explained that her father's clerk had found Major on Oxford Road and that he had been lost after being shown at a dog show.

> It said on the collar: 'My name is Major of Railway Street, Crewe. I'm Harry Stafford's dog, whose dog are you?' We all thought that was a wonderful thing and that it must have belonged to someone with a keen sense of humour. My father sent for this Harry Stafford and he came to the house. I got so enamoured with the dog. I worshipped him nearly. My father tried to strike a bargain with him and asked would he sell him the dog. Harry Stafford said 'no, I wouldn't sell that dog for anything in the world. He saved my life at sea. There was a man drowning and I rushed in to save him. The man got very streperous and I had to knock him out and hold him with one arm and whistle my dog from the shore. Got hold of his collar and he brought us both in, otherwise I would have been drowned with the man. I think the world of that dog'.[22]

Elsie's birthday was approaching and Davies was determined to buy the dog for her. He investigated Stafford's background and discovered that he played for Newton Heath and that the club was in a desperate financial state. Davies challenged Stafford and asked, 'which means more, your club or your dog?'[23] Elsie continued:

> So Harry thought for a long long time and said 'well, I adore my dog, but I adore my team as well. What would you do Mr Davies?' and he said 'well, I would take it over completely and furnish you with a brand-new team. You would still be retained as captain and we'd make the ground decent. Everything would be made alright for you. Now, if I do that will you let me have the dog?' So, Harry Stafford said 'well, under those circumstances we'll make it a bargain.' And so,

the bargain was made in the morning room of Moseley Hall in Cheadle where
we lived and Harry Stafford went away very happy. On my twelfth birthday, he
came back with the dog.[24]

Major lived with Elsie until he died at the age of seventeen.[25] Elsie's version
is credible, as she was ten years old when Major was first brought home and
she explained how her father had investigated Stafford and his interests. Her
father's research would have highlighted the potential for the club and he
would have recognised the possibilities of linking his brewery company with
a popular venue for a predominantly working-class and male audience. It is
possible Davies already knew of the benefits Chesters Brewery had gained from
their close relationship with City, who used a public house owned by Chesters'
as their headquarters, while the brewery had exclusive rights to sell beer at the
ground. According to later reports: 'Davies thought about this old, poverty-
stricken, expiring football club [and] felt that a city like ours should not be left
with only one League team for the sporting public to interest themselves in.'[26]

Davies invested in the club, determined to make it a successful organisation,
and brought in John Bentley as an advisor, who also became chairman for a
period, and Ernest Mangnall as manager. He also invested in the club's Bank
Street ground, but it remained a relatively uninspiring venue and 'the playing piece was awful on wet days – there was a wicked story that one unhappy
groundsman fell six feet through the centre ring'.[27] The stands were of low
quality and attempts to spruce them up often resulted in humorous comments
in the press or among fans, such as when the directors' box was repainted and
carpeted with a plush red carpet: 'Wags called it the "royal box".'[28] During his
first few years as United's benefactor Davies understood little about the game
but, as with many of his business interests, he took every opportunity to learn
and to experience the club from as many angles as possible. Some match days
he would be spotted standing with ordinary supporters on the Bank Street
Popular Side, where he liked to hear the 'rough and ready comments of the
crowd', and he would report his experiences to the other members of the board.
On occasion he was known to leave the game early because his nerves could not
stand the tension any longer.

As Russell has commented, team sports are generally 'the most potent agents
of community identification if only because the participants invariably carry the
name of a particular town or region and because it is usually possible to find at
least one member who displays the characteristics demanded by local mythology'.[29] In United's case the name relaunch helped capture the imagination and
increased interest in the club, as evidenced by a club record attendance for the
first League game of the new season, while the stories of Stafford, Major and
Davies have provided the mythology that has become folklore within United
circles. These stories were fashioned, as Voigt suggests, to help present an

image of the club and its values and behaviour.[30] These and other stories have acquired their power and resilience because they provide a special social significance to the club, its individuals and its origins.[31]

United's first League season ended with the Reds fifth, behind Second Division champions Manchester City. It was a creditable performance for a new club and support had risen to almost 12,000 – still some way short of their Mancunian rivals, who attracted over 16,000, but almost three times the number Newton Heath had attracted twelve months earlier. The growth related to the club's new identity as a Manchester-wide club. Local identity, defined as an intense identification with a city, town or village where an individual has been born or has long residence or connection, has been the strongest of all the personal and collective territorial loyalties expressed by English sport.[32] Both Manchester clubs recognised this, casting off their district identities and adopting Manchester in their names, suggesting that civic pride or growing aspirations played their part. Manchester now had two popular progressive clubs, developing a football structure that would endure. Long-range thinking allows historians to recognise that, despite regular triumphs, failures and changes in the balance of power, this structure has a permanence that previously it had not been possible to achieve.[33]

The first successes

The Manchester FA's area of authority included several towns within the counties of Lancashire and Cheshire, and each developed their own football teams, with some gaining national prominence. One of these was Bury, approximately eight miles from central Manchester, where Bury Association Football Club became established at Gigg Lane. The club was formed by the merger of two church teams to establish an association football club in a town that was often perceived, like Manchester, as a rugby-dominant area. This has been disputed, but it is known that prior to the soccer club's existence a strong rugby community had existed.[34] As with so many clubs in the region, their formative years were difficult financially and Bury was in debt by £100 in 1887; nevertheless that year also saw Bury enter the FA Cup for the first time and their experience, together with the formation of the Football League in 1888, encouraged them and they became instigators behind the establishment of the Lancashire League in 1890. Bury's first success in that competition demonstrated the growing stature of the game and the political prestige attached to it, as the trophy was not displayed at Bury's Gigg Lane ground; instead, it was taken to London and displayed in the home of Sir Henry James, the Member of Parliament for Bury and the club's president. Successes in the Lancashire League continued, but support and club membership grew weary of the competition and in 1894 Bury applied to join the Football League and were accepted at the same meeting at which City replaced Ardwick. Appropriately, from a Manchester conurbation perspective, Bury and City met on the opening day of the League season. Bury won 4–2 and set the tone for what was to follow, winning the Second Division championship and gaining promotion via the end-of-season test matches.[35]

Bury's success continued for several years and in 1900 they became the first team from the wider Manchester region to win the FA Cup, defeating Southampton 4–0 in the final. Bury's Cup run ran alongside news from the Boer War and the two became inextricably linked in the minds of some Bury- and Manchester-based football enthusiasts. Journalist James Catton often commented on his own experiences at Bury's quarter-final tie with Sheffield United, which occurred on the day when news arrived of the relief of Ladysmith after a 118 days' siege which had included a significant number of men from Manchester and south-east Lancashire, including the Manchester Regiment. Catton talked of the large number of spectators and painted a general image of a town keen to recognise the exploits of its armed forces at a football match: 'When I was getting anxious a group of soldiers from Bury barracks marched up. The crowd ceased to jostle and began to cheer. As if by order they voluntarily opened out to let the men in khaki through to the ground. The platoon virtually marched in.'[36] The Ladysmith celebrations and Bury's FA Cup tie, which ended in victory, were linked in the minds of Bury residents and the mood of the town was positive, cementing this football tie as a key moment in the sport's development. This was added to as the team progressed, ultimately winning the FA Cup final 4–0 against Southampton of the Southern League. This great victory was followed in 1903 by an impressive 6–0 victory over Derby County in Bury's next FA Cup final, and they became the first side since Preston in 1889 to win the trophy without conceding a goal in the competition. Interest in the 1903 final was evident across Bury and seven special trains left the town, an estimated 2,000 travelling to London for the final. The London media made much of their arrival in the city and boasted about the amount of beer and whisky stored at each mainline London station awaiting the arrival of the Lancastrians. St Pancras alone had laid aside three rooms for Bury fans with forty barrels of beer, 200 cases of bottled beer and a plentiful supply of whisky.

The game was a rather one-sided affair and led to much criticism of Bury's opponents, Derby County, but it was still a remarkable achievement for a town of Bury's size to win the FA Cup twice in three seasons. The game and events surrounding it became embedded in every day society, helping to cement football as an activity which the people of Bury supported. If there were any lingering doubts as to the superiority of rugby over soccer, these would have disappeared when Bury returned home with the Cup the following Monday night. Bury historian Gordon Sorfleet has researched the significance to his town:

The two finals were the first proper successes the town had ever known. You must put it all into context. Bury only joined the League in 1894 and so promotion in the first season and two FA Cup wins within those first nine years is an achievement I can't think of any other team matching, and it can certainly never happen again. Sadly, I do think this was the turning point for football though. I believe that the money men started to take over – even then – and when you look at the sides who won the trophy in the years that followed they were mainly big city teams.[37]

It was not until 1912 that a 'town' won the trophy again, when Barnsley defeated West Bromwich Albion, and Sorfleet's views on the transformation of football from a sport in which a town could find success into one in which city clubs dominated do bear some reflection on the situation that occurred within the Manchester conurbation. While town teams have continued to find occasional success in national competition, such as Wigan's 2013 FA Cup win, the period after 1903 did see a growth in the business of football, leading to those clubs with greater support and financial backing finding success. From a Manchester perspective the transformation from relatively small-town success to big-city success is easily demonstrated by the developments of both Newton Heath and Ardwick, who had recognised the need to generate a Mancunian identity and strong business links by 1902. In the period after Bury's second success it was City who became the region's most popular club, and the one which first captured the imagination of the wider Manchester public. Bury's success had been inspiring locally, but there was little opportunity for growth beyond the town, and even then support could not be guaranteed: 'If gates can be taken as any criterion, interest in the doings of Bury seems to be on the wane. Recently the gate receipts at Gigg Lane have been remarkably low, and Saturday's engagement with the Wolves was no exception. There were only about 2,500 spectators and the receipts amounted to £35.'[38]

The following season demonstrated what could be achieved by a successful Manchester-named club, propelling the sport forward across the wider Manchester population. In 1903–4 Manchester City, under secretary-manager Tom Maley, mounted Manchester's first major challenge for the League title and progressed in the FA Cup. Maley, one of the founders of Celtic Football Club – who had also competed in athletic events at Ardwick FC – had given the club direction and focus, while former secretaries Joshua Parlby and Lawrence Furniss remained as directors to ensure continuity. Parlby acted as if City was his creation and the progress of 1904 was viewed by some in the media as Parlby's, not for specific action in 1904 but for creating the platform that had allowed the club to develop during the 1890s.[39] Parlby had demonstrated his willingness to use his footballing connections to aid the club's development, while others, including newspaper baron Sir Edward Hulton, owner of the *Athletic News*, had been brought into the club to help it progress. Hulton was the chairman in 1903–4 and under his overall direction the club's facilities had improved and City's popularity was on the increase, with the largest FA Cup attendance so far for either Manchester side watching City's FA Cup victory over Sunderland. This record was surpassed a few weeks later when City faced Middlesbrough in the quarter-final, with 30,022 – some sources claim 35,000 – bringing in £1,150. The popularity of these games caused a strain on the club's facilities and in the streets surrounding the Hyde Road ground with, for example, a barrier collapsing during one game, while some Mancunians stayed away because they feared injury.[40] City's directors knew that development was required and steps were taken to plan a move to a new, larger ground but these were thwarted by Chesters Brewery on numerous occasions, thereby limiting attendances.[41] Congestion and overcrowding led to City employing a variety of techniques to ensure that the stadium was full but safe. These included opening gates early to try to encourage fans into the ground in an orderly manner.[42]

City progressed through to the final after beating the reigning League champions Sheffield Wednesday in the semi-final, which saw a Goodison Park record crowd of 53,000 and receipts of £1,917.[43] It was described as the 'piece de resistance' and the highlight of the entire day's activities in the North, and it was also Manchester's greatest achievement to date, allowing Mancunians to feel proud of their city.[44] Significant attention followed, prompting Manchester United advisor John Bentley to comment on the eve of the Cup final: 'Since the City have become famous and especially as the Cup Finalists, it has been considered the proper thing to give every detail of their doings and I'm quite expecting to read that, while shaving, Meredith accidentally came across a little wart and the great international actually lost ten drops of his precious blood.'[45]

Over the weeks that followed the attention and football interest increased, with newspapers documenting minutiae on the game in the manner of a twenty-first-century tabloid, such as when a phrenologist was employed to determine whether City or their opponents Bolton would win, based on their intellect. These articles added to the growing status of football within the city and meant that Mancunian residents, regardless of class, location, gender or sporting affiliation, understood the significance of the game. The FA Cup run was covered extensively across the full range of media locally available and the invasion of London by supporters from the provinces became a focal point, as it had at most FA Cup finals between teams from outside the South East. For Manchester, this was a novel experience and travel agents stayed open late to accommodate all those wishing to buy tickets on the eve of the final.[46] Public houses in the city organised excursions, with many setting off early on the Friday morning, determined to make a holiday of it. Reporters from the North's leading newspapers journeyed with them, commenting on the spectacle of approximately 40,000 people travelling from Lancashire on over sixty railway specials to the final.[47] As well as direct travel to

London, Thomas Cook organised rail travel followed by breakfast in London, a tour around the capital and tickets for the final for what was described as a 'modest' 19s 6d.[48] The weekly rent of a five-roomed house with bathroom and a small garden in the Trafford area was 8s 6d in 1908, indicating that the excursion was not something the majority of Mancunians could afford.[49] Weekly wages for a stonemason, a well-paid occupation at this time, were typically around 40s. No match involving a Lancastrian side had ever aroused as much pre-match interest as the 1904 final and a record number of people travelled from the North.[50] The mix of social classes was evident, and reports discussed trains being filled with 'young men in the highest spirits' from Manchester joined by suburban-dwellers 'who drove to the stations in wagonettes'.[51] Much was made of the fact that music hall entertainer George Robey had sent the club good luck messages and provided other support before and after the final, demonstrating a link between two of the main entertainments of the working classes.[52] One newspaper article focused on the sight of flat caps everywhere in the capital and how Londoners were now aware that Manchester existed and that it was rightly a proud city.[53] St Pancras station was reported to have had more people packed onto its platforms that morning than on any previous occasion, while at least 16,000 people arrived at Euston during the night with nowhere else to go. City's officials travelled in a horse-drawn carriage with eleven or twelve on the roof and around six inside. Demonstrating that this was perceived as a prominent event in the wider Mancunian region, Stockport County secretary Sam Ormerod, who had also been a failed former City secretary, and John Bentley, the former Bolton secretary-manager and advisor to United, were known to be on board the City carriage. Reports of the scenes at the Cup final venue, the Crystal Palace grounds, described that there were many women present in the crowd and that most of these supported City, making as much noise as the men.

The actual attendance was a disappointing 61,374, with receipts totalling £3,000. The early morning rain had put off those within a morning's travel of the Palace, and many Lancastrians simply could not afford the expense of journeying to London and all that it entailed. Nevertheless, it did compare well with the attendance for the previous year's final and the finals pre-1901. Ultimately, any attendance of over 60,000 for an all-Lancashire final played in London before the days of comfortable wages and multiple transport systems was significant. The official guests demonstrated the significance of the FA Cup final in the national and sporting calendar and included music hall entertainers, sportsmen such as W. G. Grace, several prominent government officials and the prime minister, Arthur Balfour who was supporting City. He was the Member of Parliament for East Manchester and four years earlier had visited Hyde Road after being persuaded to become a patron of the club. City's Billy Meredith won the toss and elected to play towards the southern goal, where the Boys' Band of St Joseph's entertained the City followers. The band had followed

City to most of the key games that season, bringing a little extra atmosphere to the terraces. Music was embedded within Mancunian culture by this period and the inclusion of the band added to the spectacle of the final, but it was also a reminder of Mancunian culture and everyday life.[54] Both the Amalgamated Musicians Union (founded 1893) and the Incorporated Society of Musicians (1882) were established in Manchester and the city frequently led the way, while the connections between music and football became recognised and have remained through to the present day, with bands such as Oasis and the Stone Roses being part of the cultural mix of the city's footballing and musical performers and followers. Both football and music added to Manchester's identity and perceptions of the city around the world. From the earliest days at Hyde Road or Bank Street, bands played and supporters sang, so it was only natural that the same would occur at Manchester's first FA Cup final appearance.

The game ended in a 1–0 Manchester victory, with captain Meredith (Figure 16) scoring the only goal. Back in Manchester a crowd of over 8,000 attending a reserve game at Hyde Road paid between 3d and 6d, with news coming from Crystal Palace every fifteen minutes.[55] The 8,000 crowd was higher than the average crowds of three First Division clubs and all but three Second Division clubs. Elsewhere in Manchester news of the Cup victory soon spread and celebrations began. Newspaper publisher Edward Hulton & Co. had offered to wire half-time and full-time scores from Crystal Palace to any address for 1s per message, while special editions of Manchester's main newspapers were produced throughout the afternoon carrying the latest match reports and each edition sold out quickly.[56] Those waiting in Manchester demonstrated 'feverish interest' with almost every conversation in the city focusing on Manchester's success throughout the night.[57] The *Umpire* commented: 'scarcely, if ever, has the result of any event, sporting or otherwise, been awaited in Manchester with so much interest'.[58]

16 FA Cup-winning captain Billy Meredith, Manchester's first major star.

The following Monday an early evening League game at Everton resulted in City narrowly missing out on the League title. Already regarded by neutrals as the team of the season, a point stressed fifty years later, the team arrived back in Manchester later than expected, at approximately 9.30pm.[59] Understandably, most Mancunians were keen to see the conquering side bring home the Cup, but the civic leaders had been out of touch with the mood of the city. Rather surprisingly, when a civic reception was first proposed Manchester's leaders, including the chief constable, reacted negatively.[60] The people thought differently and by lunchtime that Monday the police chief and councillors had been forced to revise their plans and 150 policemen were hurriedly organised for the homecoming. The lord mayor announced that he had attempted to change his plans, but a prior engagement meant that he could not be present. This contrasted with Bury's – their nearest FA Cup-winning neighbours – celebrations in 1900 and 1903, where the mayor played a key role in welcoming the football team home.[61] Despite Manchester's initial civic reaction, the local population understood the significance, as did the media, who referred to some comments about football enthusiasts from the prime minister, who wore a blue rosette representing Manchester at the final and explained that it was not simply football fans, but all Mancunians who wanted to see their heroes.[62] Lord Stanley, the postmaster-general, told diners at a celebration banquet after the final that City's success would be celebrated and discussed by the prime minister at his next cabinet meeting.[63]

The city was full by 8pm, over ninety minutes before the team arrived back from Everton for the 1904 FA Cup homecoming and it was evident that the parade helped the game of football to attract interest from the wider population of Manchester, regardless of class or gender.[64] The social character of City's homecoming was commented on extensively, with the press highlighting the mix of people and the unifying aspect.[65] They commented on 'juveniles', 'corpulent old dames', 'young ladies standing at windows in the city's millinery shops', 'rough working men and larrikins', 'beshawled women', 'children in arms and hand', 'the middle-classes' and the 'proletariat' attending and celebrating.[66] The reporting added to perceptions of how collective identification 'makes people feel better and engenders a sense of place pride', and while it is possible to treat claims that City's 1904 success helped to establish a Mancunian identity as hyperbole, evidence exists of how similar successes have increased local pride.[67] The press focused on the density of the crowds on streets throughout the city and the sustained level of welcome throughout the two miles from the railway station to Ardwick, where City's home ground was.[68] Reports claimed that the entire population of Manchester had turned out, with Manchester's streets packed like never before. The FA Cup homecoming was different to previous city-wide celebrations, as it was the first time a major sporting organisation appealing to all areas of society from the city had achieved national acclaim. There were reports of lines of people twenty to thirty deep on both sides of all the streets on the route to Ardwick. Deliberately, City chose to tour some of the city's back streets, where they knew Mancunians often lived in squalid conditions. Visitors to Manchester were unaware that poorer members of the city's community were often hidden away in the city's back streets, the main roads and routes into the city being lined with shops, hiding some of the worst housing and factories. Approximately twenty-five years before City's homecoming Friedrich Engels had observed a systematic 'shutting out of the working-class from the thoroughfares, so tender a concealment of everything that might affront the eye and the nerves of the bourgeoisie'.[69] City knew that this was the case and the trophy parade journeyed down some of these streets.

Whether it was for their own development or a belief that this was a success which all the local population should share in is not clear, but this first sporting homecoming set the tone for all that followed and it demonstrated to all who doubted, that Mancunians enjoyed the success that the sport had brought to their city. Life was often grim in Manchester, but a major trophy success encouraged the wider population and proved extremely attractive to be associated with, even if it was simply as a spectator of the trophy parade.

The importance of civic rituals, – such as the staging of the Art Treasures Exhibition in 1857 and the Jubilee Exhibition of 1887 – for municipal pride has been recognised. They have been referred to as key elements in the development of tradition, and City's 1904 homecoming had a similar, if not greater, effect on Manchester's identity and Mancunian pride.[70] As early as the eighteenth century attempts had been made to foster Mancunian civic pride when a programme of building and other improvements occurred alongside the growth of charitable institutions and 'other forms of associated life helped to cement various social ties'.[71] All of these laid the groundwork for establishing a Mancunian identity, but it was the 1904 homecoming which established the strongest visible representation of a united, successful Manchester. Contemporary reports show that the 1904 FA Cup success captured the imagination of the general Manchester population in a way which no other celebration had managed. It could be argued that this was the point when the people of Manchester forged a footballing identity for the city; possibly even a true Mancunian identity, as via football all Mancunians, regardless of social status, religious background and length of residence felt that they had achieved something together as equals.[72] Tony Mason has argued that an honest, hardworking, meritocratic northern cultural identity came to be expressed through support for local football teams, and this is true for Manchester in 1904.[73] As time moved on Mancunians became more focused on their own preferred team, but in 1904 success on a national level had a unifying effect on all Mancunians and helped to create a winning mentality and identity. It was the determination of the club and the local population that allowed the spectacle to exist. The city's officials had been reluctant and reticent to spend any further time on the sport, but the people proved that this mattered to them, and it was not an orchestrated attempt by the council to make Manchester appear unified. It should be noted, however, that City, either wittingly or not, helped to establish themselves as a team for all Mancunians, as Joshua Parlby had wanted in 1894, by touring areas representing different communities and classes, thus setting the tone for the following decades. United enjoyed success in the years that followed but they did not manage to supplant City as the more popular Manchester club until after the Second World War.

It should be highlighted that only one of the City players who played in the FA Cup final was from Manchester, the majority coming from Scotland. Others came from Wales, the South East and the South West.[74] A. F. Hills was critical of the way the game had developed, causing clubs to 'hire a team of gladiators, and bid them fight our football battles for us', but what Hills had overlooked was that in Manchester the players were actually typical of those supporting the sport.[75] The inhabitants of the streets surrounding City's ground came from a variety of backgrounds and locations, many of them having moved into the city during the latter period of the nineteenth century.[76] If anything, the team on the pitch was more closely aligned with the residents of the city than with other areas of society. 'Manchester was proud of its City team, and expressed that pride in a manner enthusiastic beyond measure', highlighted the *Daily Dispatch* in a lengthy piece that commented on Mancunians climbing onto the roofs of music halls and other buildings to get a better view.[77] The fact that City had won the trophy was not the significant aspect; it was that the city of Manchester had won football's most coveted prize. This report comparing the homecoming to previous celebrations was typical:

> There were fully five times as many people along the route of the triumphal procession as were in the streets on the occasion of the visit of the Prince and Princess of Wales. Not even on the occasion of the rejoicings which followed the news of the relief of Mafeking was the enthusiasm greater than it was last night, and certainly the demonstration did the City infinitely more credit than did the wild saturnalia which was the outcome of General Baden Powell's successful resistance to the Boers.[78]

In Ardwick, at the end of City's homecoming, councillor Stewart made a speech which talked of how football had been a struggle in the city only nine years earlier but now Manchester was a leading force, while manager Tom Maley highlighted his delight at seeing Manchester associate itself so readily and enthusiastically with the FA Cup success.[79] Maley accurately summed up the importance of the moment when he told officials and the press that he was deeply moved by the reception and added: 'Perhaps love of sport had something to do with the bringing together of so great a gathering, but love of Manchester, had much more to do with it.' He also accurately stated that 'People looked upon the victory of the City club as adding to the reputation of the city.'[80] Giulianotti has stated that football shapes and cements national identities, and cites the game's international diffusion as coming at a time when most European and Latin American nations were formulating their cultural identities.[81] He talks of new cities being constructed and of populations existing with little to bind them, and suggests that football played its part in creating a community and folk heroes; and of the game helping develop an identity. While his argument was based on nation-states, the same philosophy could apply to developing towns and cities such as Manchester. It is apparent that the mood and interest of Manchester's citizens and politicians changed in a manner suggested by Huggins through the 1904 success: 'In Northern and Midlands towns, leading football sides, initially largely middle-class, became more socially mixed. As a team achieved success, businessmen and even aristocrats became involved; stadia expanded and civic pride improved. Local politicians began to show an interest, kicking off games, speaking at dinners, and welcoming victorious teams home.'[82]

By the end of the nineteenth century Manchester had become regarded as the northern capital and it led the way in the fields of economics, industry and politics, where it became 'the most nationally significant northern city'.[83] It also became a major centre for art, music, the theatre and publishing, with the *Manchester Guardian* leading the way in terms of national media representation within the city. The city's newspaper businesses also included several significant national sporting titles and yet, from a footballing perspective, the city had been left behind by its northern rivals, some of whom, including Liverpool, had initially lagged behind Manchester but had developed rapidly during the period from the late 1870s to late 1890s. The 1904 success began to change the impression of Manchester nationally, but more significantly it brought a realisation to the city itself that association football was important in building cross-community connections and a Mancunian identity. Football helped Mancunians to celebrate together and share in a communal environment. They gathered at the city's grounds and they made their identities known. There were multiple clubs in the conurbation, but they shared the recognition of what the sport could bring to the city, especially in the period after the 1904 FA Cup final.

Short-term impact of FA Cup success

Although homecomings and similar celebrations allowed a shared identity to be observed it could also be argued that the reporting of these moments tried to foster the idea of an all-encompassing community.[84] In certain contexts this type of activity can take on an extraordinary importance. The 1904 homecoming provided a means for all residents of Manchester to share in the glory and celebrate the city's success, but it did not allow them to meet and talk around the city as equals in normal, everyday life. FA Cup finals provide a mechanism for allowing a celebration of local attachment and place little-known towns on a national map, while the civic homecomings that follow such events allow the disparate parts and communities of a city to briefly appear to be made whole.[85] How briefly can be debated, but there are indications that Manchester's first homecoming became fixed in the minds of the city's residents. One reason for this was because Mancunians were able to relive the success repeatedly, as the final had been filmed and, along with film of the players with the trophy at Merseyside, shown in Manchester during the weeks following the final. This allowed those who hadn't attended the final to see the success for themselves. Already by this point moving pictures were beginning to attract large audiences and were a relatively cheap form of entertainment, especially for working-class youths.[86] Film of the final was shown in at least four venues in Manchester and Salford. Ticket prices ranged from 6d to 3s, and both the Regent Theatre in Salford and St James's Hall in Manchester showed the film at least twice a day.[87]

The film show at St James's Hall was reviewed and reports describe how Meredith could be seen scoring the goal, and all the most exciting moments from the match were alleged to have been captured and replayed to an appreciative audience.[88] Huggins has documented the significance of film in 'defining, depicting and propagating' identities, and its ability to help 'shape and support soccer's place in the wider society', and this 1904 footage provided a strong visual representation of Manchester's success for all those residents who had had no opportunity to experience the success first hand.[89] For any action to become significant in terms of helping to transform the sport, it has to transcend the short time span in which it is set, and the 1904 footage allowed this to occur. The moving images of the final supported an extensive volume of newsprint.[90] Manchester, as the most important centre of the newspaper industry outside of London and a major national centre for the sporting press, saw the success documented extensively.[91] Newspapers commented that St George's Day, the day of the final, had never seen such celebrations and directly linked this with the FA Cup final, and the density of media operations created a situation whereby this sporting success produced significant coverage, allowing the possibility that Mancunian success could generate more column inches than that of any other provincial city.[92] In addition to regional and national newspapers, several footballing handbooks were produced in Manchester, further supporting the view that newspapers had a significant impact on how FA Cup successes were perceived. Local newspapers helped to create legends about people and places and that their celebrations of Cup success and related homecomings established local feeling, reinforcing the experience in the minds of those participating and those who knew of the activity only via the media's coverage.[93] In 1904 national and regional newspapers from across Britain talked of the significance of Manchester's homecoming. The sport's popularity, and that of City itself, increased quickly, and ultimately this ended the possibility of rugby's ever regaining the upper hand. Soccer was here to stay and rugby, with its self-inflicted wounds still healing following the split of the previous decade, would never again be able to match soccer's status in the city, although some districts did remain leading rugby league centres.

As 1904 progressed footballing representation across the city increased. Shortly after, City announced a record profit of £2,200, with receipts equalling £12,000, and there were increasing signs of the game across the city.[94] The

Manchester Cup final, played a week after the FA Cup final, was watched by what was described as a 'very large' crowd of 18,000, while the 1903–4 season ended with City and United possessing the second- and third- highest average attendances in the League.[95] Significantly, United were a Second Division side while City were only a few hundred spectators less than Aston Villa, who had topped the chart for six successive seasons.[96] John Bentley in his weekly column for the *Umpire* described City as having 'a drawing capacity excelled by none'.[97] Well-wishing telegrams from Mancunians living around the country were received by City, while in January 1905 Mancunians ensured that the players were thanked for their boost to the region's image.[98] At a special commemorative dinner the players, trainer Jimmy Broad and secretary-manager Tom Maley were presented with commemorative gold watches paid for by collections taken among Mancunians. Mancunians were suffering great hardship at the time, both financially and healthwise, and recognising that ordinary residents performed collections and helped to raise funds to recognise City's achievement is significant. United's opening game of the 1904–5 season saw a large crowd of 16,000 watch a public practice match where, significantly, Manchester's lord mayor performed a ceremonial kick-off.[99] Football excursions, which had existed for over a decade, increased in frequency, and most away games saw rival railway companies trying to outdo each other with trips to the same Manchester away games.[100] Later in 1905 the press talked of Manchester as a footballing city, alongside its role as the fourth most significant port in Britain.[101] Manchester had also been proclaimed the second city of the empire by councillor Plummer.[102] Just as 1900 and 1903 had contributed to the solidification of association football within Bury society, the 1904 success brought the realisation that football could be a unifying celebration of Manchester, and by the time United won the same competition in 1909 the city council were ready for formal civic celebrations. The change in attitude in only five years demonstrates the point made by Hill and Williams, who stated that 'beneath the surface of these seemingly changeless celebrations of local achievement were concealed interesting developments in civic relationships. In short, the reception of the Cup Final team was gradually transformed from being a spontaneous celebration of club into a semi-official glorification of town. The reception was appropriated into civic ideology.'[103]

The 1904 success and homecoming, together with ground improvements at City and United, aided the growth of soccer, and it is this 'complex set of processes by which a culture is formed and a cultural system functions'.[104] The success of City during the early twentieth century added to the identity of Manchester and Mancunians, uniting citizens who had arrived in the city from a multitude of locations. The sport offered them the chance of a shared experience and camaraderie that was mainly positive, with an opportunity for glory that other areas of life could not bring. Football was an entertainment, but, unlike a visit to the music hall or theatre, it could help to shape a shared identity. While the journey to the final and subsequent celebratory homecoming were reported extensively and focused on the wide variety of Mancunians who took to the streets, the question of who watched football during this time is relevant to understanding whether football truly had bridged the classes and spread across Manchester. Russell says that many were excluded by the ticket prices.[105] It is therefore important to consider admission costs alongside weekly income and expenditure in order to gain an appreciation of the true cost of watching football.

In 1890 the Football League raised the minimum adult male ticket price to 6d, which may have been a move to limit attendance by the poorer, potentially rowdier, areas of society. Russell has compared this price to music hall and cinema, which he considers were lower, suggesting that many working-class supporters could follow their teams only in spirit rather than by attendance – although supporters at all Manchester's clubs would wait for three-quarter time, when the gates would be opened to allow some to start leaving, but also allow those waiting outside the opportunity to come in for the final few minutes. This practice continued into the late twentieth century. City's regular admission prices indicate a much greater spread of interest than is typically accepted and prices in 1904 were: Reserved seats in centre of stand – 5s; Entrance to enclosure – 1s; 'ends of stands' – 2s 6d extra (on top of enclosure price); 'seats inside rails' – 1s extra; Popular Side – 6d; Boys – 3d. However, City suspended the Boys' admission in a bid to satisfy overall demand for some of the FA Cup ties. Beaven claims that a charge of 6d was relatively cheap by the late 1800s and that a regularly employed semi-skilled worker could afford this.[106] By way of comparison, 1s would enable the purchase of one pound of good-quality rump steak, while a typical weekly rent for a 'two up and two down' terraced house in the Gorton area, close to City's ground, was 5s.[107] During this period an unskilled labourer working in the engineering trade in Manchester would take home a weekly wage of between 18s and 22s. Labourers in the Manchester building trade tended to take home between 22s and 30s at this time. According to Lewis, young workers were 'well paid, lads and boys averaged 9s 4d, and girls 6s 10d', while City's prices suggest that a broad range of social groups attended (Table 3).[108] Those willing to pay in advance were able to buy discounted season tickets. In 1904–5 22s 6d would buy a reserved seat in the Main Stand for seventeen League games.[109] It is not clear what category of seating this was, but even if it was the cheapest it represented a considerable saving of 11s 6d on the cheapest seats in the ground. It is known that as early as 1892 boys' season tickets were available in the uncovered Boys Stand and in that year one supporter holding a boys' season ticket was aged fifteen and the son of a draper.[110] Some Manchester boys and young adults attending League football were also the same people who were viewed as a menace when

Table 3 Manchester ticket prices, house rental and other expenses, 1904–8

	Price	
Item	*Shillings*	*Pence*
Boy standing ticket		3
Standing ticket		6
Covered standing ticket	1	-
Cheapest seat ticket MUFC (1902)	1	6
Cheapest seat ticket	2	-
Most expensive reserved seat ticket	5	-
Female unreserved seated season ticket (19 games, 1908)	7	6
Standing season ticket (19 games, 1908)	8	6
Covered standing season ticket (19 games, 1908)	12	-
Female reserved seated season ticket (19 games, 1908)	12	6
Unreserved seated season ticket (17 games)	15	-
Reserved seated season ticket (17 games)	18	-
Thomas Cook FA Cup final excursion	19	6
White granulated sugar		2
Scrag end (mutton neck)		5 to 6
Cheese		7
Back bacon		7 to 9
Pork chops		8 to 10
Beef rump steak	1	-
Tenement weekly rent	4 to 7	-
'Two-up two-down' terraced house in Gorton weekly rent	5	-
'Three-up three-down' in Hulme weekly rent	8	3
'Five roomed' house with bathroom and small garden in Trafford	8	6

Note: All match prices are for Manchester City unless otherwise stated and food prices are for one pound (454g) in weight.
Sources: Daily Dispatch, 15 January 1904, 6; *Manchester Evening News*, 23 December 1902, 1; *Manchester Guardian*, 14 July 1904, 3; United Kingdom Board of Trade, *Cost of Living*, 294–304; *Daily Dispatch*, 22 April 1904, 6.

they gathered at Smithfield Market on a Saturday night in large numbers, their main conversation being their own footballing prowess or 'the successes and disasters of "City" and "United"'.[111]

In 1905, when City's Hyde Road staged an inter-League game between Ireland and England and the FA Cup semi-final between Newcastle and Sheffield Wednesday, the ground possessed one significant grand stand, the large Popular Side terracing, a mixture of uncovered seats and terracing behind one goal, terracing behind the opposite end and a small 'Boys' Stand' in one corner. Ground descriptions show that at Hyde Road there were 6,000 seated in the main stand and around 3,000 seated behind a goal, while the rest of the venue comprised approximately 30,000-capacity terracing by this time.[112] Support increased for both Manchester clubs, and John Bentley boasted often of Manchester's interest in the game via his regular column in the *Umpire*. During 1904–5 he highlighted that United's home game with Bolton, with a crowd of 30,000, was a record for the Second Division and that it had beaten by a couple of thousand the division's previous best, which had been for a Manchester City home game. He commented that 'it shows what Manchester football is capable of when over 30,000 turn up at a Second Division match'.[113] However, City's attendances were hampered in 1904, as the ground was closed for several weeks as a punishment for financial irregularity in connection with the signing of a player. When it re-opened games had to be played on weekday afternoons to allow the club to fulfil its missing fixtures.[114] Supporters wrote to complain of the timing of these games, suggesting that work commitments would prevent their attendance, and these games did attract less than half of the attendance of corresponding fixtures.[115] One segment of the population which stood little chance of attending games no matter when they were played were the unemployed. The year 1904 was a peak year for unemployment in Manchester; rough sleeping became a significant problem and homeless refuges were oversubscribed in Ardwick, Salford and Manchester city centre.[116] In 1904 Manchester city council adopted a policy of hard labour for those in need of relief, and up to 200 men a day (903 individuals in total) were given the task of breaking up stone setts for use in road building at the council's Hyde Road depot, next door to Manchester City's football ground. The activity took place behind City's Stoneyard stand and the work was exceptionally tough. Quantities of less than 2.5 hundredweight received no payment at all and even the strongest men made little more than 1s for a 7.5-hour day. Despite this, the demand for work was so great in December 1904 that large numbers were turned away.

While admission prices provide an indication of social groups, the ethnic composition of the crowd is not clear. It is known that the Jewish community were keen to assimilate into Mancunian culture and business, and by 1897 the local press talked positively of their adoption of Mancunian life while remembering their own traditions.[117] One of the activities that the local Jewish population had adopted by 1901 was its support of Manchester football, and the *Dundee Courier* talked of 'the Jewish Colony' of Manchester actively supporting City.[118] By 1881 Manchester's Jewish population was estimated at 15,000 and by 1903 it was over 25,000, over three-quarters considered to be recent immigrants.[119] The majority of these had come from Russia, Austria and Romania, and numbers continued to increase up to the First World War. By 1914 Manchester's Jewish population had reached over 35,000, while the population of Italian, Lithuanian and Polish Catholics was small in comparison.[120]

In December 1904 John Bentley compared those who attended association football with those who attended the Varsity rugby match. He talked predominantly about the class of people who would bet, suggesting that those who attended association football were working-class. His column then went on to explain how attending football matches was a positive for the community: 'A workingman's family actually benefits by reason of his attending football, for instead of spending his time and his wages in a public house, he immediately goes home, and the "Missus" gets her wages.'[121] Women did attend games, particularly Cup ties, including the 1904 FA Cup final and the 1885 Manchester Cup final, but opportunities to attend on a regular basis would have been limited. Russell suggests that some women may have had no wish to attend, as they would have been grateful of the space that their menfolks' absence created for necessary domestic tasks or a brief period of time off.[122] City had been offering season tickets annually for female supporters throughout their Football League history, however, suggesting that there was enough interest to enable the specific tickets to be printed, marketed and sold each year (Table 4). It has been argued that football crowds before 1914 were mainly drawn from the skilled working and lower-middle classes, with increased semi-skilled working-class attendance after 1900, but Manchester's regular admission prices imply that there was a much greater spread of interest than has previously been thought and they provide an indication of the broad range of classes which the clubs aimed to attract. Comparing the figures for match expenditure with weekly wages shows that ticket prices, in the main, were a much lower percentage of income than they were in 2013, while the spread of admission prices suggests that a similar, if not greater, range of social groups attended Manchester's games in 1904. The variety of standing and seating options at City by the start of 1904–5 allowed choice, and ground descriptions indicate that there were almost 10,000 seated both behind one of the goals and in the main stand, where the central block of seating was upholstered. Standing provision totalled approximately 30,000, with about a fifth covered in 1904, but improvements meant that by 1910 the club could boast of covered accommodation for over 30,000. As such, a quarter of attendees for 40,000-capacity games paid up to 5s to sit, with around 24,000 paying 3d or 6d, depending on age, for uncovered terracing.

By the early twentieth century football in England had become a professional sport with a well-established national league of two divisions complementing the traditional FA Cup competition. Football has proved a potent vehicle for the generation of territorial loyalties, and, as towns and cities had developed to become too large to be knowable to their inhabitants, support of the local team provided 'symbolic citizenship'.[123] Success helped to establish civic pride and marked a turning point in the way the game was viewed by local civic leaders and, as a result, Manchester started the process of becoming established as a major centre for the game at all levels. Manchester became a footballing city.

Table 4 Comparison of weekly wage to match ticket prices

Occupation	Wage	Cheapest ticket price as % of wage	Highest ticket price as % of wage
Bricklayer	45/5	1.1	11.0
Engineering fitter	34/-	1.5	14.7
Building labourer	22/8	2.2	22.1
Engineering labourer	18/-	2.8	27.8
Cotton winder (female) piecework	11/- to 17/-	2.3 to 1.5	6.0 to 3.9
Construction/manufacturing industries (2013)	£529	4.9 (cheapest match ticket in 2013 £26)	11.0 (most expensive regular match ticket £58)
Service industry (2013)	£432	6.0	13.4
Retailing (2013)	£296	8.8	19.6
Minimum (thirty-five hour week) eighteen to twenty years (2013)	£176	14.8	33.0

Notes: Figures are calculated for a weekly wage in pence for 1904–8 and in pounds for 2013.
Lowest and highest female seated season ticket prices have been utilised to calculate an average ticket price for the cotton winder.
Percentage figures have been rounded to one decimal point.
Match ticket prices in 2013 were £26 (cheapest) and £58 (most expensive regular match ticket).
Pre-1971 values are in written in pre-decimal format, where 45/5 represents 45s 5d and 18/- represents 18s. Income figures for 2013 are based on a national average.
Sources: United Kingdom Board of Trade, *Cost of Living*, 806; 'Labour market statistics: EARN01: Average weekly earning', *Office for National Statistics*, November 2013.

Notes

1 Rose, 'Culture, philanthropy', 110–113.
2 Williams, 'The antisemitism of tolerance', 75.
3 'Manchester civic life', *Manchester Courier*, 24 February 1902, 8.
4 I. Douglas, R. Hodgson and N. Lawson, 'Industry, environment and health through 200 years in Manchester', *Ecological Economics*, 41 (2002), 239.
5 McHugh, 'A "mass" party frustrated?', 43.
6 *Manchester Evening Chronicle* was the first to report the story with its 25 April edition, while the *Manchester Evening News* followed on 26 April.
7 *Gorton Reporter*, 26 April 1902, n.p.
8 Green, *There's only one United*.
9 'Newton Heath club and its troubles', *Manchester Courier*, 19 March 1902, 3.
10 The report differentiates between older members, who had been interested in the club for several years, and younger men who were became interested in more recent times. This difference suggests that a reference to 'an old member' would have been to a person several years older than Rocca. Rocca is believed to have been a tea boy, working in the offices at times, and would probably have been named by journalists if he had been the 'old member' described.

11 J. Berryman, 'Introduction', in D. G. Kyle and G. D. Stark (eds), *Essays on sport history and sport mythology* (College Station, TX: Texas A & M Press, 1990), 3.

12 S. J. Eaves and R. J. Lake, 'Dwight Davis and the foundation of the Davis Cup in tennis: just another Doubleday myth?', *Journal of Sport History*, 45:1 (2018), 1–23.

13 In January 1892 Manchester Central faced east Manchester side Gorton Villa twice, including a game less than 2 miles from Newton Heath's home.

14 'Association', *Manchester Evening News*, 26 April 1902, 4.

15 'Familiar faces: Fred Palmer', *Manchester Football Chronicle*, 25 November 1922, 3.

16 'The FA and Manchester United', *Athletic News*, 4 April 1910, 6.

17 This claim appeared in the United match programme as part of a feature on the 2017–18 Champions League. That article claimed that City were the second-oldest, despite their earlier footballing activity. Evidence of the earliest known football game involving the predecessors of United shows that this occurred one week after the predecessors of City's earliest known game in November 1880, which means that the boast is questionable. *United review: official matchday programme*, 10 December 2017, 64.

18 'The FA and Manchester United', *Athletic News*, 4 April 1910, 6.

19 'Football', *Sunderland Daily Echo and Shipping Gazette*, 31 May 1902, 4.

20 'The Newton Heath Football Club', *Manchester Evening News*, 2 May 1902, 3.

21 'Man who made United', *Manchester Football Chronicle*, 20 January 1923, 3.

22 Elsie Partington, the daughter of John Henry Davies, interviewed on *Nationwide*, BBC, 18 December 1973.

23 Ibid.

24 Ibid.

25 Ibid.

26 'Man who made United', *Manchester Football Chronicle*, 20 January 1923, 3.

27 Ibid.

28 Ibid.

29 Russell, *Looking north*, 241.

30 D. Q. Voigt, 'Myths after baseball: notes on myths in sport', *Quest*, 30 (1978), 46–57.

31 T. Collins, 'The invention of sporting tradition: national myths, imperial pasts and the origins of Australian rules football', in S. Wagg (ed.), *Myths and milestones in the history of sport* (Hampshire: Palgrave Macmillan, 2011), 8–31.

32 Russell, *Looking north*, 245.

33 Braudel, *On history*, 75.

34 Interviews and correspondence with Gordon Sorfleet, Bury FC historian, 2006–8. James, *Manchester, a football history*, 77–79.

35 Catton, *The story of association football*.

36 Ibid.

37 Interview with Gordon Sorfleet, May 2007.

38 *Manchester Evening News*, 19 April 1902, n.p.

39 'Critical comments', *Umpire*, 24 April 1904, 9.

40 *Daily Dispatch*, 8 Match 1904, 7.

41 'A new ground for the City', *Daily Dispatch*, 20 April 1904, 6; Collins, *Sport in capitalist society*, 52.

42 'Advice to City spectators', *Daily Dispatch*, 4 February 1904, 6.

43 'Lancashire supreme', *Daily Dispatch*, 21 March 1904, 6.

44 'Today's programme', *Daily Dispatch*, 19 March 1904, 6.

45 James, *Manchester, the greatest city*, 53.

46 'Cook's railway booking offices', *Daily Dispatch*, 19 April 1904, 1; James, *Manchester, a football history*, 108–110.

47 'Manchester City team travel to London', *Daily Dispatch*, 22 April 1904, 6; 'Meredith's great goal', *Daily Illustrated Mirror*, 25 April 1904, 11; 'Advertisements', *Daily Dispatch*, 19 April 1904, 1; 'Reception of the news in Manchester', *Umpire*, 24 April 1904, 9.

48 'Manchester City team travel to London', *Daily Dispatch*, 22 April 1904, 6.

49 United Kingdom Board of Trade, *Cost of living of the working classes: report of an enquiry by the Board of Trade, 1908* [Cd. 3864], 294–304.

50 'Football blue riband', *Daily Dispatch*, 23 April 1904, 6.

51 'Excursion traffic', *Daily Dispatch*, 23 April 1904, 6.

52 'Scenes of jubilation in Manchester', *Daily Dispatch*, 26 April 1904, 5.

53 'Caps in the capital', *Daily Dispatch*, 25 April 1904, 4.

54 W. J. Galloway, *Musical England* (London: Christophers, 1910), 139.

55 'Advertisements', *Daily Dispatch*, 22 April 1904, 6.

56 Ibid.; 'Reception of the news in Manchester', *Umpire*, 24 April 1904, 9.

57 'Reception of the news in Manchester', *Umpire*, 24 April 1904, 9.

58 Ibid.

59 *The boy's book of soccer* (London: Evans Brothers, 1954); James, *Manchester, the City years*, 99–103.

60 James, *Manchester, the City years*, 99–103.

61 Hill and Williams, *Sport and identity*, 101.

62 'Mr Balfour at Saturday's football', *Daily Illustrated Mirror*, 25 April 1904, 7.

63 'Football at the cabinet meeting', *Daily Dispatch*, 25 April 1904, 5; 'Cabinet and football', *Daily Illustrated Mirror*, 25 April 1904, 10.

64 James, *Manchester, a football history*, 108–110.

65 '"City's" home-coming: enthusiastic reception of Meredith and his men', *Manchester Courier*, 26 April 1904, 6.

66 For example, 'Scenes of jubilation in Manchester', *Daily Dispatch*, 26 April 1904, 5; 'Manchester City welcomed home', *Edinburgh Evening News*, 26 April 1904, 4; 'The winners of the English cup', *Manchester Evening News*, 26 April 1904, 2.

67 J. Bale, *Sport, space and the city* (London: Routledge, 1993), 56–58.

68 'Scenes of jubilation in Manchester', *Daily Dispatch*, 26 April 1904, 5.

69 Engels, *The condition of the working class in England*

70 E. Hobsbawm, 'Introduction: inventing traditions', in E. Hobsbawm and T. Ranger (eds), *The invention of tradition* (Cambridge: Cambridge University Press, 1983), 9; O'Reilly, 'Re-ordering the landscape', 33.

71 Barker, 'Soul, purse and family', 15.

72 James, *Manchester, the City years*, 100–103.

73 Hill and Williams, *Sport and identity*, 85–112.
74 G. James, *Manchester City the complete record* (Derby: Breedon, 2006), 528–541.
75 Quoted in R. Holt, *Sport and the British* (Oxford: Oxford University Press, 1989), 144.
76 For example, Census returns, Higher Ardwick, 1891, https//:www.findmypast.co.uk (RG 12/3165); Census returns, Earl Street, Gorton, 1891, https//:www.findmypast.co.uk (RG 12/3174).
77 'Scenes of jubilation in Manchester', *Daily Dispatch*, 26 April 1904, 5.
78 'The winners of the English Cup: reception of the City team', *Manchester Evening News*, 26 April 1904, 2.
79 'Scenes of jubilation in Manchester', *Daily Dispatch*, 26 April 1904, 5.
80 'The winners of the English cup', *Manchester Evening News*, 26 April 1904, 2; 'Scenes of Jubilation in Manchester', *Daily Dispatch*, 26 April 1904, 5.
81 R. Giulianotti, *Football: a sociology of the global game* (Cambridge: Polity, 1999), 23.
82 M. Huggins, 'Oop for t' coop: sporting identity in Victorian Britain: as the climax of the football season approaches, Mike Huggins investigates the origins of Britain's morass of sporting rivalries', *History Today*, 55:5 (2005), 55–61.
83 Russell, *Looking north*, 20–21.
84 Russell, *Football and the English*, 65.
85 Russell, *Looking north*, 20–21.
86 B. Beaven, *Leisure, citizenship and working-class men in Britain, 1850–1945* (Manchester: Manchester University Press, 2005), 105.
87 'Advertisements', *Daily Dispatch*, 25 April 1904, 4.
88 'Advertisements', *Daily Dispatch*, 26 April 1904, 4; 'Fixtures at St James's Hall', *Manchester Courier*, 26 April 1904, 6.
89 M. Huggins, 'Projecting the visual: British newsreels, soccer and popular culture 1918–39', *The International Journal of the History of Sport*, 24:1 (2007): 80–82.
90 Braudel, *On history*, 67.
91 Russell, *Looking north*, 21.
92 'The day of the Rose', *Daily Dispatch*, 25 April 1904, 4.
93 Hill and Williams, *Sport and identity*, 86.
94 'Football', *Manchester Courier*, 14 June 1904, 11; 'The football field', *Manchester Guardian*, 29 August 1904, 9.
95 'Manchester Cup final', *Daily Dispatch*, 2 May 1904, 6.
96 B. Tabner, *Football through the turnstiles … again* (Harefield: Yore Publications, 2002).
97 'Manchester City meeting', *Umpire*, 23 October 1904, 11.
98 'Scenes of jubilation in Manchester', *Daily Dispatch*, 26 April 1904, 5.
99 'Manchester United', *Manchester Guardian*, 29 August 1904, 9.
100 'Football excursions', *Manchester Courier*, 10 March 1906, 9.
101 'Players from the nursery', *Manchester Guardian*, 20 November 1905, 3; Farnie, *The Manchester Ship Canal*, 167–169.
102 'London's competitor', *Daily Dispatch*, 27 April 1904, 3.
103 Hill and Williams, *Sport and identity*, 100.

104 A. J. Kidd and K. W. Roberts, 'Introduction', in A. J. Kidd and K. W. Roberts (eds) *City, class and culture* (Manchester: Manchester University Press, 1985), 3.

105 Russell, *Football and the English*, 56.

106 Beaven, *Leisure, citizenship*, 72.

107 United Kingdom Board of Trade, *Cost of living of the working classes*, 294–304.

108 Lewis, 'The development of professional football', 44.

109 'City ground and season ticket holders', *Umpire*, 6 November 1904, 11.

110 Census returns, John Bicket 1891, https//:www.findmypast.co.uk (RG 12/3165).

111 C. E. B. Russell, *Manchester boys: sketches of Manchester lads at work and play* (Manchester: Manchester University Press, 1905), 114.

112 'Manchester City ground', *Umpire*, 28 August 1904, 10.

113 'Leaves from my notebook', *Umpire*, 25 September 1904, 11.

114 'Manchester City's postponed fixtures', *Umpire*, 28 September 1904, 9.

115 'City ground and season ticket holders', *Umpire*, 6 November 1904, 11.

116 A. J. Kidd, 'Outcast Manchester', in A. J. Kidd and K. W. Roberts (eds), *City, class and culture* (Manchester: Manchester University Press, 1985), 63.

117 Williams, 'The antisemitism of tolerance', 91.

118 'Derby County are still Scraping Through', *The Dundee Courier*, 21 October 1901, 5.

119 Williams, 'The antisemitism of tolerance', 84.

120 B. Williams, *The making of Manchester Jewry* (Manchester: Manchester University Press, 1976), 327; Williams, 'The antisemitism of tolerance', 84.

121 'Football and betting', *Umpire*, 25 December 1904, 11.

122 Russell, *Football and the English*, 57.

123 D. Russell, 'Associating with football: social identity in England 1863–1998', in G. Armstrong and R. Giulianotti (eds), *Football cultures and identities* (Basingstoke: Macmillan Press, 1999), 19.

9

Scandal and rights

Scandal

The long-term impact of the 1904 FA Cup success was demonstrated by the increase in footballing activity in Manchester, with participation, competitions and the number of teams growing and attendances developing. Crowd figures fluctuated, but Manchester City became the best-supported club in the Football League in 1910–11 and 1914–15 and remained a major crowd puller into the present.[1] The successes gained in football and the subsequent homecoming in 1904 were reported as all-encompassing, with no differentiation in the levels of enthusiasm experienced across communities within the city.[2] This idealised Mancunian community may in itself have engendered a greater community spirit and, potentially, football helped to cement social stability. The 1904 success was considered to be Manchester's, and rivalry between the two major Manchester clubs was not an issue, many people supporting both at this point. This situation continued into the 1960s, with supporters tending to view success in terms of Manchester against the rest, and this was typical in many large cities. With United developing as a force in the Second Division and the Manchester FA affiliated directly to the FA, Manchester football appeared to be well organised, structured and progressive. It was perceived as part of Mancunian life, and when the winter of 1904/5 proved particularly harsh, with many locals dying of cold and malnutrition and unemployment high, football contributed to relief efforts. On 23 January City staged a charity game against music hall entertainer George Robey's 'Team of Internationals' at Hyde Road to raise money, and at that game and others at Hyde Road blankets were carried around the pitch for people to throw donations into.[3] These acts added to the acceptance of football in the city, and City also made their venue available for other charities and altruistic activities. This may have contributed to the allure of the club, which, through initiatives such as promoting schools' football and establishing a boys' stand free of parental involvement, gave the club a position of strength within the community. The special relationship between City and Mancunians could do nothing to prevent the devastating blow that was to follow, however.

Some FA officials considered City to be a nouveau riche club determined to ensure success and, in the days of a £4 maximum weekly player's wage, this usually meant making additional payments to players. As City was known to have several high-profile supporters, including the newspaper baron Edward Hulton, who had been chairman in 1903–4 and whose newspapers tended to promote the northern, professional clubs' views, it could be suggested that the FA was keen to limit the growth of professional, big-city northern clubs like City. The FA, perceived as a southern body dominated by amateurs, was unhappy with Manchester's success and its officials were keen to prevent football's amateur, sporting nature from being lost forever, although the battle had already been lost.[4] Nevertheless, the FA councillors liked to keep up the pretence and the FA decided to investigate City's 1904 success. Within two weeks of the FA Cup final the FA secretary, F. J. Wall, and a member of the FA General Council, John Lewis, arrived at Hyde Road demanding to see the club's books. Lewis was a somewhat controversial referee with fixed views on what was acceptable behaviour and what was not, and he was also a campaigner for the temperance movement.[5] Considering the relationship that Joshua Parlby and the club had with the brewing industry, Lewis's involvement was potentially an issue. Lewis and Wall spent the closed season examining City's accounts, scrutinising every document, determined to find proof of illegal wages and bonuses, but ended their investigations with nothing more than a couple of discrepancies in the transfers of Frank Norgrove and Irvine Thornley from Glossop. They uncovered receipts for unusual payments coinciding with the dates of the players' transfers and determined that these were signing-on fees paid to the players more than the £10 maximum then allowed. To preserve their amateur image, the FA had insisted on maximum signing-on fees in addition to the £4 maximum wage rule, but First Division clubs tended to break the rules, and some were adept at not bringing due attention to themselves. As Meredith said: 'Of course clubs are not punished for breaking laws. They are punished for being found out.'[6] Unlike the others, City was a club unable to keep its activities quiet.

In October 1904 City were fined £250 and Hyde Road was ordered to be closed for two games, while directors Joshua Parlby, John Chapman and Lawrence Furniss were banned for three years and the finance director, G. Madders, was suspended for life. This conflict with the public school-dominated FA brought the club support from the regional press and League officials, adding to the impression that Manchester's footballing culture was somewhat different to London's, a view certainly articulated by the Manchester-based sporting newspapers throughout the debate. The departure of Furniss, Chapman and Parlby was particularly distressing for those connected with the club, especially the loss of Parlby. His vision had established City as a major force and his long-term planning had raised the club from its status as a team representing a district to one that appealed across a major conurbation. Parlby remained interested in the affairs of the club, however, and four years later, at the age of fifty-four, he rejoined the board at a time when the club needed his direction once again. He remained active until 1915, when City made a presentation to mark his retirement and in acknowledgement of the part he had played in the club's relaunch.[7] Parlby was the first man to take Manchester football to a position of prominence in the national game. He died on 19 May 1916, aged sixty-one.[8]

With long-serving member Lawrence Furniss and chairman John Chapman also punished, the FA in effect banned City's three most influential figures. The player Irvine Thornley was suspended for the rest of the season, but the reasons why he received an illegal payment demonstrate more about the way the sport was developing than about the perceived profligacy of an ambitious club. In transferring to City, Thornley had been forced to relinquish a share in a lucrative butcher's business in Glossop for the uncertainties of professional football. Butchering provided a guaranteed income, or at least it was a more stable occupation than football. His decision to leave the business was a gamble, and so it is understandable that he would seek extra security and that the club would offer it. The payment was against FA rules, but was it morally wrong? The debates on player fees and income continued into the present, but the restrictions in place at the time seemed unreasonable. Thornley would undoubtedly have known of the deaths in 1902 of two of the City team, Di Jones and Jimmy Ross, and the financial problems that those tragedies caused for their families. Jones had cut his leg in the annual public practice match and within a week had died from blood poisoning and lock-jaw, while Ross had also died suddenly.[9] Neither player had had enough savings or investments to keep their families after their deaths; the precarious nature of a footballer's life would have been obvious to Thornley. Coincidentally, the FA had also been investigating Thornley's former club, Glossop, who, under the leadership of Samuel Hill-Wood, were also viewed as a progressive northern outfit keen to spend whatever it took to attract the best players. Hill-Wood would later turn his attentions to Arsenal, but at this time his club was Glossop and the FA uncovered suspicious information and discrepancies between their accounts and those of City, adding to the situation at Hyde Road. City and Glossop were not the only local clubs investigated at this time, as United were also rumoured to have made illegal payments to players and an investigation culminated in the presentation of a report to the FA Council which proved that illegal payments had been made and improper accounting procedures were in place. James West and Harry Stafford were held accountable and were suspended until May 1907.[10]

Despite the issues behind the scenes, the popularity of City meant that the club was able to continue its development both on the pitch and off, with over £2,000-worth of stadium improvements helping to increase capacity by around

10,000 by mid-November 1904. In addition, the club improved entrances and exits, and decorated the stadium, with almost every area of the ground painted blue and white, adding to the spectacle of match day when residents would walk through dark railway arches and smoky streets to reach the Hyde Road turnstiles. It was this spectacle that helped to ensure that Manchester's football fans were encouraged to be part of the experience. At Hyde Road supporters are known to have worn fancy dress, taken musical instruments and generally participated in the game's events. The Boys' Stand was home to a raucous and spirited gathering of boys and young men and they developed a close affinity with the club. Match day offered an escape from the reality of everyday life in a grim industrial city, and in the months following City's FA Cup win there appeared to be no greater place to experience the positives of Mancunian success. The nature of City's rapid development meant that the FA continued to keep a close watch on the club and, as the 1904–5 season neared its end, a controversial game led to the club receiving the largest punishment any League side had ever experienced.

By mid-April City, Newcastle and Everton were in contention for the League title, leading to a climactic final day whereby any of those teams might finish as champions. Everton's campaign was complete, and City and Newcastle were each a point behind; however, Newcastle had the better goal average. Manchester's team needed to beat FA Cup holders Aston Villa in their final match and hope that Newcastle would fail to win. The Villa–City game proved to be a physical contest with numerous off-the-ball incidents and dangerous tackles. It finished 3–2 to Villa, ending City's title hope, but there had been many flashpoints: 'Leake found [Turnbull] a real hard opponent and … gathered up a handful of dirt and hurled it at the City man. Turnbull was not hurt and responded with an acknowledgement favoured by the bourgeoisie – thrusting two fingers in a figurative manner at the Villa man.'[11] When Aston Villa's Leake realised that the referee was not looking he 'gave Turnbull a backhander', which led to further retaliation from City's Turnbull.[12] The controversy continued post-match, and as Turnbull walked down the tunnel he was pulled inside the Villa dressing room and the door was closed behind him. A few seconds later he was thrown out, yelling, with marks on his face and ribs where he had clearly been kicked. Police had to be called into the ground to protect the Manchester players and an angry mob attempted to stone the City party as they left.

The days that followed saw the controversy deepen, with some newspapers, most notably those from the Midlands, defending Villa's actions while others supported Turnbull.[13] As there had been physical play in City's crucial match with Everton eight days earlier, the FA set up a special committee to meet behind closed doors and consider the two games. Their investigations dragged on, and as the summer progressed the FA interviewed player after player in their quest for the full facts. This was considered suspicious, especially by the northern newspapers, who were now convinced that the committee were seeking a greater discovery than merely a disrepute charge against one or two players. With the FA meeting in secret, rumour spread, and most were northerners convinced that the southern FA would make City the scapegoats. On 4 August 1905 the committee announced the suspension of J. T. Howcroft and R. T. Johns, the referees of the games at Everton and Villa respectively, and that Tom Booth of Everton and City's Sandy Turnbull were to be suspended for one month; yet no mention was made of Villa's Leake. This seemed unjust, but then came the news that City's captain had 'offered a sum of money to a player of Aston Villa to let Manchester City F.C. win the match. W. Meredith, of Manchester City F.C. was suspended from taking any part in football or football management from August 4, 1905 until April 30, 1906.'[14] Initially Meredith claimed his innocence and suggested a reason for the findings, believing that Aston Villa had too much influence within the FA and that 'City is becoming too popular to suit some other clubs'.[15] He was appalled, and was further disgusted when he was banned from City, which, under FA guidance, was forced to distance itself from him. These actions prompted him to complain, causing the FA to set up a new commission as the whole affair began to unravel. The FA interviewed City players and management about the bribe and about potential illegal payments to players, and confusion engulfed Manchester's footballing community. Meredith changed his story, claiming that he had offered Leake a £10 bribe, but he told the commission that this had been at manager Tom Maley's suggestion and with full approval from the rest of the City team. The manager totally refuted the claim, but admitted that payments were made to players for more than the maximum wage, claiming that this was regular business practice in England. Meredith stated that if all First Division clubs were investigated, 'not four would come out scatheless'.[16] At least seven clubs were investigated between 1901 and 1911, including United. Many more were thought to have been guilty but escaped punishment.[17]

The commission reported on 31 May 1906 that in their opinion City had been overpaying for years and the players had gained control at the club, although none of this had been uncovered during the extensive and detailed investigation during the summer of 1904, raising questions about the validity of their opinion. It seemed incredible that Lewis and Wall, two of the game's most thorough administrators, had not uncovered such issues a year earlier, raising the question of whether the evidence existed at all. While the maximum wage was £4, it was estimated that Meredith had been earning £6 and another player had received £6 10s. Even the amateur Sam Ashworth was found to have received £50 on top of £25 expenses and was subsequently declared a professional by the commission. The punishment was harsh, with a total of seventeen current and former players being suspended until 1 January 1907.

Tom Maley and former chairman Waltham Forrest were to be suspended from English football *sine die*, while directors Allison and Davies were to be suspended for seven months. City were fined £250 and the suspended players had to pay a total of £900 in fines, but the entire process and bans were criticised. Three men appealed, as they had been reserve players during 1904–5 and, even after bonuses were included, had not received the maximum £208 in wages. Surprisingly, their appeal failed, as did a petition, signed by 4,128 Mancunians, against all the suspensions, demonstrating the significance of the sport to Manchester at the time and highlighting the injustice felt across the city. Billy Meredith was highly critical of the hypocrisy of those sitting in judgement: 'while their representatives were passing this pious resolution most of them had other representatives busy trying to persuade the "villains whose punishment had been so well deserved" to sign for them under conditions very much better in most cases than the ones we had been ruled by at Hyde Road'.[18] The punishment was the largest ever imposed, wiping out an entire team, its directors and one of the most charismatic managers of the period.[19]

For Meredith, City and Manchester the illegal payments scandal was to have major consequences. The player was forced out of the club that had made him a name, while City had to rebuild itself. The 1906–7 season was always going to be tough, but City's status as Manchester's leading club was also at risk, as United had been promoted the previous April and the two clubs would both be competing at the highest level for the first time. While City sought to redevelop their club, United opened the season with two victories and two draws. It was a promising start, but the most eagerly awaited fixture in the region was Manchester's first top-flight derby match. This was staged in December and was met with tremendous scenes, as the role football played in Mancunian life was visible to all that day. Newspapers reported on the preparations, including the news that a Glasgow architect, probably the renowned stadium designer Archibald Leitch, had overseen improvements to City's venue to accommodate a greater crowd.[20] City won the match 3–0, but the most significant aspect of the day in terms of Manchester football's *longue durée* came in the offices after the game, where the sale of several of the banned players occurred. Negotiations had been ongoing for some time, but it was derby day that brought the most significant transfers, although some footballing historians have mistakenly located the entire sale at the Queen's Hotel in the city centre. There were representatives from at least eight clubs at Hyde Road, but it took several days before the facts emerged of which clubs had been successful.[21] Ultimately, four of the club's most significant players, Herbert Burgess, Sandy Turnbull, Jimmy Bannister and Billy Meredith signed for United, with both City and their supporters delighted that these men were to remain local. The transfers occurred because United's manager, Ernest Mangnall, was able to find his way into the offices at City before his rival managers had the opportunity to do so. When he emerged the representative of another club, thought to be Everton, asked him: 'What have you been doing? I've been waiting to be called in. Who have you got?' Mangnall then reeled off the names which, in effect, were the most significant players involved.[22] City's decision to sell to United caused Everton to complain to the League, as they had been hopeful of signing Burgess and believed that his transfer had been performed in an underhand manner. Manchester's clubs wanted to ensure that these men remained in the region.

The Meredith transfer was the most significant, and it became complicated, demonstrating that football transfer dealings could still be somewhat suspicious, with mysterious payments being made that, considering the entire scandal had revolved around illegal payments, should have been investigated. City received nothing for the player; but worse, according to Meredith: 'I was given a free transfer and, as a result, I got £500 from a gentleman to sign for Manchester United and he also paid the £100 fine to the FA.'[23] Who that gentleman was remained a mystery, and while Mancunians were delighted that the player was staying in the region, the FA should have investigated, particularly as it had been Meredith's own testimony that had transformed the initial investigation from on-the-pitch disciplinary matters into an investigation of bribery and illegal payments.

While the immediate impact of the punishments and transfers was documented extensively at the time, little has been published on the long-term impact of the investigations into City, its players and officials. It damaged several careers and led to financial problems for some, including Sammy Frost, who committed suicide some twenty years later as a result of business failure.[24] The scandal in its entirety should be viewed as a transformational cycle during which multiple interrelated events led to the transformation of United's fortunes. In terms of Braudel's *longue durée* theory, this cycle demonstrates how a community or activity can adapt, progress and develop through events that, in isolation, are merely individual moments where people diverge from their normal activity. Sandy Turnbull's two-fingered reaction in the game with Aston Villa could easily have been forgotten, overlooked or punished at the time by the referee; however it led to a chain of activities which ensured that the game would be investigated further. Those investigations highlighted several other issues, seemingly minor in isolation, such as accounting errors, overpayment of players and unreliable evidence, which in turn caused a prominent football team to suffer a severe punishment and encourage its most important players to sign for its neighbours. Those neighbours were recognised as the less significant of the two clubs, and at the time of the transfers no one could have predicted what would happen, but the result was that those players helped to transform their new club into Manchester's next successful club. As with the appearance of a lost dog, the departure of Meredith and the others from City had been accidental, i.e. it had not been part of a grand plan established by either Manchester club, but its impact was significant. By this time City had been established as a successful club with vast support, and the bans did not lead to the club's failing, although they did end their trophy-winning potential for a while. United were some distance behind and appeared destined to always be the city's second team. The bans and transfers provided a platform and opportunity for United to establish their own success and to provide Manchester with two prominent and challenging clubs.

United's successes

The four former City players – Bannister, Burgess, Turnbull and Meredith – all made their United debuts on New Year's day 1907 against, ironically, Aston Villa, and it was with some satisfaction that Sandy Turnbull, the man who had been a central figure on the day of the infamous Villa–City match of 1905, netted the only goal of the match. Demonstrating the attraction of Meredith and the others, United's attendance that day was recorded by the club's management as 40,000, significantly higher than their average, which in 1905–6 was 13,950 as they were promoted from Division Two at the end of the 1905–6 season and in 1906–7 increased to 20,725. The immediate impact on the Reds was evident and, as well as a substantial increase in support, United found that the players helped to transform their fortunes. Prior to Meredith and the others arriving, United's record had not been great. They had struggled to establish themselves in the top division and were on eighteen points after winning six games, drawing six and losing nine. With the new players they achieved eleven victories, two draws and four defeats and, had the new players arrived earlier, United might well have challenged for the League that season. Instead they finished eighth.

The following campaign further proved the new players' significance as United won the League for the first time, becoming the first Manchester side to achieve that success. Meredith and the other former City men were key players in that achievement, with Sandy Turnbull the leading goal scorer with twenty-five goals from thirty games – a figure not bettered at United until Rowley netted twenty-six in thirty-seven games during the 1946–47 season. United had a phenomenal season, winning the title nine points clear of City, who finished third on equal points with second-placed Aston Villa. City's third-place finish was a remarkable achievement, considering the problems that had ripped the club apart, but United's success brought most pride and satisfaction to the region and one of the major talking points was the role of the former City men. It was evident that Meredith and the other former Blues made the difference between Manchester's two clubs, and their involvement first in City's glory in 1904 and then United's in 1908 was significant to this transformational period in Manchester's football history. The period continued to be successful for United, and in 1909 the Reds won the FA Cup for the first time. Approximately 10,000 supporters, a smaller number than in 1904, but still considerable, travelled from Manchester for United's first FA Cup final. Despite the fewer numbers it was remarked once again that 'a striking feature was the number of young women and girls making the journey'.[25] In Manchester similar scenes to those of 1904 followed, and the local media talked of 1904 and its impact. United asked City director Albert Alexander, who owned a carriage company, to lead United's homecoming as he had done in 1904, and the general impression was that this was a continuation of Manchester's success, not specifically that of one team. The council leaders even gave United a civic reception at the town hall – something for which the leaders had seen no reason for only five years earlier – and this allowed two main focal points for the homecoming, Central Railway Station and Albert Square, where crowds could gather. It is possible that the civic leaders recognised that 1904 had brought prestige to Manchester and that it had also allowed a means of encouraging patriotism in the city, especially at a time when unemployment, homelessness and food shortages were perhaps causing some to question whether Manchester had anything to offer them. The civic leaders may have realised that a suitably celebrated homecoming could have a cathartic effect locally – which supports Beaven's belief that the popular notion of citizenship can be defined by support for the local football club, rather than through municipal initiatives or civic architecture;[26] although Beaven goes on to argue that 'supporting the local football team cultivated a symbolic class-specific form of citizenship' rather than one supported by all classes.[27] Russell argues that football has undeniably been most effective in building local attachments.[28]

Ernest Mangnall managed United to another League title in 1911 and, appropriately, he was viewed by many as the major influence in each of those achievements, although another renowned footballing man, John Bentley, performed the role of chairman, director and advisor to the Reds at times during this period, earning on average £300 per year from 1903 and a total of £1,400 by 1909.[29] It is evident that Mangnall, with Bentley's advice and Davies' finances, had transformed United into a progressive, successful club where Davies was willing to make significant investments in order to establish a powerful club.

Union

While United became strengthened following the City bans, the players remained somewhat disgusted with their treatment by the footballing authorities. The investigation into their financial activities had begun in 1904, reopened in 1905 and led to bans until 1907. The length of the process and the bans impacted on their finances and careers. It is understandable that the entire experience would be remembered and considered whenever the affected players met, and in 1907 the illegal payments scandal was a catalyst for the establishment of a union. As far as Billy Meredith was concerned the illegal payments were fair – after all, they were illegal only in the eyes of the FA, not the fans, not the players and not the directors. Why should football clubs be limited in their ability to pay players a rate applicable to their value and to compensate them for loss of earnings, as in Thornley's case? Throughout industrial Manchester at this time there was much debate concerning working conditions and wages, and whereas some of the region's industries could guarantee a job for life, or at least gave that impression, footballers had few guarantees and a limited career span. Throughout his suspension Meredith considered the injustices which he and his team had suffered, and it is possible that he also thought back to the deaths of Di Jones and Jimmy Ross in 1902. City had staged a benefit match for the widow and children of the late Di Jones in September 1902 and held various collections, but other players' families were less well provided for.[30] Regardless of how well a club provided for its players, football's governing bodies gave them few rights and, as the illegal payments scandal had demonstrated, the FA would punish players when clubs were perceived to have been too profligate with their finances. Players required representation and, as the trade union movement grew, it was perhaps understandable that in a city viewed as a radical one attempts would be made to establish a footballers' union. One had been established in 1897 and Jimmy Ross is known to have been one of its founders. In February 1898 the union had drawn up its rules and made them public at a meeting held at the Spread Eagle Hotel in Manchester, where it was also revealed that 250 League players had signed up. Despite the support, the union had collapsed at the end of the 1900–1 season. In 1907 Meredith openly talked about resurrecting the union in some way.

On 2 December 1907 the first meeting of the new union was held at the Imperial Hotel, London Road, Manchester. In attendance were four members of City's 1904 Cup-winning side and Thornley, the player who had been punished in 1904 following financial discrepancies in his move from Glossop to City. Three of the City men were now with United, of course. Four other United men were present, including Charlie Roberts, and there were other players from several mainly northern clubs, although a Tottenham player also attended. John Davies, the wealthy brewer and United chairman became a vice-president, as did James Catton, the editor of *Athletic News*, while a City director acted as solicitor. These details are important, as they show that the clubs, certainly the larger clubs in the region, were keen to not only demonstrate their support but also participate in the union's development. United's chairman, Davies provided funds to help with transport for the union's benefit games, as he recognised that supporting the union would benefit his club initially, but as time progressed the management of both United and City began to distance themselves a little, especially when the union became more radical. In 1909 the union decided to take Reading to court on behalf of one of its players who was seeking compensation under the Workman's Compensation Act of 1906 in what was an important test for the union, which believed the club was deliberately prevaricating over settling the claim and that resolution could be achieved only through legal action. Union secretary Herbert Broomfield, a City player, carried out most of the union's action as the situation worsened, while the FA insisted that they alone decided disputes between football clubs and players, not a court of law. Broomfield countered this with strong argument, but it was not long before it became apparent that the issue would become a make-or-break moment for the union, especially as leading figures started to criticise it. The FA removed its official recognition from the union, which was a significant blow, and rumours of a potential players' strike circulated, with the newspapers full of comment and rumour. The union's chairman, Harry Mainman, had said in April 1909: 'We look upon the clubs as enemies of the players.'[31]

Inevitably, the union solicitor, City director Wilkinson, resigned, as he recognised a conflict of interests, and United's management became less supportive. The FA also announced that players must relinquish their union membership if 'they desire to continue their connection with the FA'.[32] This statement had a significant impact and the entire management committee of the union, except for secretary Broomfield and chairman Mainman, resigned. The summer of 1909 saw Broomfield working relentlessly on behalf of the union and his efforts helped to determine its strength in the following decades. As the 1909–10 season approached the situation came to a head at United, where players refused to resign from the union and were suspended by the club. United somehow avoided telling the players of their suspensions, and the first that Charlie Roberts knew of them was when the day's newspapers were delivered to his newsagent's shop. The following Friday Roberts and the other players arrived at United demanding their wages, but there was nothing for them and they were, in effect, banned from the ground, so Roberts and the others talked with Broomfield and he arranged for them to train at the Manchester Athletic Club ground in Fallowfield, the site of the 1893 FA Cup final.

A number of journalists and photographers were contacted and Roberts created a famous story when:

> After training a day or two a photographer came along to take a photo of us and we willingly obliged him. Whilst the boys were being arranged I obtained a piece of wood and wrote on it, "Outcasts Football Club 1909" and sat down with it in front of me to be photographed. The next day the photograph had a front page of a newspaper, much to our enjoyment, and the disgust of several of our enemies.[33]

On 11 August it was announced that Newcastle United's players would support United's men, and soon other significant clubs followed, including Oldham, Everton, Liverpool and Sunderland. Ultimately the growth in support made the threat of a players' strike likely, and inevitably this forced the parties to come together. After various meetings suspensions were lifted, wages were to be paid, the union recognised and the strike avoided, but there were plenty of complications along the way. Inevitably both the union and the FA claimed victory, but one of the key men, Billy Meredith, felt that Broomfield deserved the most praise, saying: 'Herbert Broomfield is the first player who has pointed out to the players that they can protect themselves by unity and that if their cause was right they had no reason to fear saying so', adding 'a grander, pluckier fight was never made than Broomfield has made!'[34]

Broomfield's name is often overlooked when the formation of the union and the 1909 Outcasts are discussed, but his involvement was significant during this transformational phase in players' rights and representation. The formation of the Professional Footballers' Association, as it became known, owes much to the men of the Manchester region who made a stand. The union needed and received support from beyond Manchester, but its creation came because of the desire by those punished as part of City's illegal payments scandal to improve conditions for their fellow professionals. Its success and continued growth came from the stand made by the Outcasts in 1909. Manchester gave birth to the union at a time when players were treated poorly by the football authorities. In the years that followed the City scandal and United's Outcasts, the importance of the union grew, but there were still serious financial hardships for players. Even the most successful of players found life outside of the game tough.

Old Trafford

While the players' union development demonstrated that Manchester's players were keen on strengthening their representation and power within the game, Manchester's clubs were seeking to build on the popularity of the sport by developing better facilities and capacities at their grounds. Ever since he had begun investing in United, club president John Davies recognised that United's Bank Street ground was inadequate, and this view intensified following the club's promotion in 1906, it began visiting League grounds of the quality of Villa Park and Goodison Park frequently. Davies had invested in facilities shortly after his arrival, but Bank Street could only ever be patched up and, as the Reds began winning trophies, he considered the options. He owned land at Old Trafford, to the west of Manchester, and had been hoping to develop a bottling plant there for his brewery. Its proximity to the Ship Canal and the huge Trafford Park industrial estate, developed at a rapid pace following the opening of the canal in 1894, made it a good location, but issues with the authorities prevented the bottling plant from being erected. The land was unprofitable unless Davies could identify an alternative use, and he realised that it could resolve the ground issue. As United's board was dominated by Davies and brewery officials, the idea was passed.[35] He decided to build the most modern stadium in the country and provided the £60,000 required for its construction, but Davies was not the altruistic figure often portrayed.[36] An FA inquiry in 1910 identified that he received rent payments from United for land that they did not use, the payments made to him between 1903 and 1909 totalling £5,743.[37] The FA concluded that 'Davies knew that the moneys he had been finding had been improperly expended, and special arrangements were then made to prevent his sustaining pecuniary loss, he continued from that time regularly and persistently to find further money for similar purposes, and to withhold the information from the auditor.'[38] Whether supporters recognised that their saviour was also profiting from the club at times is not apparent, but they did voice concern over the planned ground move, and they were not convinced that a move to Old Trafford would work for their club: 'the loyal old Clayton supporters did not like the idea at all. There were those who said such a huge place on the other side of the city would be a financial failure.'[39] The supporters' views were close to the truth, certainly during the three decades following United's 1910 move, and support dropped despite United winning the League title at Old Trafford in 1910–11. The ground was too far across the city for many of the club's traditional fans, and when the struggles of the 1920s and 1930s followed attendances plummeted, and the financial burden of the venue following Davies' death was too great. The selection of Old Trafford was somewhat odd. In 1909 the area as a whole was more salubrious than Clayton, but professional clubs like United and City relied on the patronage of the working classes to sustain them, and Old Trafford was no match for east Manchester when it came to density of working-class population.[40] Others saw Old Trafford's social character as a positive, suggesting that it could generate support: 'now that the United ground is in a more salubrious neighbourhood the people of Manchester will support them well'.[41] This may well have been part of the site's attraction, but United had become a successful club within a working-class district of the city, not a neighbouring middle-class borough, and it was 'the working-class parts of the city that provide a disproportionate contribution to football's fandom'.[42] The Old Trafford site was over five miles from the club's Newton Heath heartland, making it the furthest any club had ever moved. The previous furthest had been Sheffield Wednesday, who moved around three miles when they left Sheffield for Owlerton (Hillsborough) in 1899. Like Wednesday, United were moving outside of the city's boundaries. The Sheffield move has been described as 'daring and speculative' and the same was true for United's transfer to the relative peace and tranquillity of a middle-class borough on the opposite side of the city.[43] It was a major gamble and it financially crippled the club for more than two decades. Of course, there were trams and trains travelling to that part of the region, but a United supporter working on a Saturday morning in the Clayton area would have had to travel into Manchester city centre first, then out to Old Trafford in time for a 3pm or 3.30pm kick-off.[44] Regardless of supporters' feeling or potential issues Davies ploughed on with his stadium plans. Secretary-manager Ernest Mangnall was given control of the development, which was for a capacity of 100,000 with 12,000 seated and covered terracing for 24,000. These plans were scaled down somewhat, but what was delivered was significantly better than any earlier venue.[45] The dimensions were impressive, the entire area being sixteen acres, with the exterior circumference of the ground being approximately 2,000 feet. The ground was planned to be 630 feet long and 510 feet broad, with the width of the terracing 120 feet. The pitch was to be excavated to a depth of nine feet from ground level, resulting in the stadium being only about thirty feet high. The site did have one major flaw, and that was that it had to be constructed on an east–west axis rather than north–south. Typically, football grounds were designed with the main stand on the west side of the pitch and the goals at the northern and southern ends, for rather simple reasons. First, neither goalkeeper had to directly face the sun, and second, the directors and wealthier customers sitting in the club's main stand would not have their vision impaired by a glaring sun, assuming that games would be on Saturday afternoons. The geography of the site did not allow space for a 100,000-capacity venue to be constructed on a north–south axis, and even when the plans were scaled down the original layout remained, with hopes that additional developments would raise the capacity in subsequent years. In terms of admission charges these were priced at 6d, 1s, 1s 6d, and 2s, which were on a par with or, in some cases, cheaper than City's, although there was no mention of a reduced price for children or women.[46] The lowest adult price of 6d was relatively cheap. As a comparison, that amount could buy three pounds of white sugar or five eggs, demonstrating that a regularly employed worker could afford it.[47]

The £60,000 stadium opened with a visit by Liverpool, a club United were particularly close to at this time, but there were some difficulties. These included the inability to serve alcohol, as there had been a licensing issue and the stadium was incomplete.[48] The boundary walls were not finished and some windows had not been properly installed, allowing some to sneak in. The official attendance for Old Trafford's opening game was 45,000, an impressive figure, but only 5,000 more than Bank Street had held earlier that season, and at least 10,000 less than anticipated.[49] Davies had hoped that the move would immediately provide United with a greater volume of support, and logistically it ought to have done so as, unlike in east Manchester, there were few soccer clubs on this side of the city for supporters to choose between. There was one potential rival soccer attraction, the Manchester League side Salford United, who played at The Willows and had applied to join the Football League in 1907. Their application had failed, but they did win the Manchester League in 1910 and were performing well at the time when United became resident at Old Trafford in February of that season. Whether Salford United affected Manchester United's opening attendances is not clear, but the arrival of the League side did ultimately affect Salford. Manchester United were based on the border of Trafford and the city of Salford, and even the name United would have caused some confusion locally. The Salford club disbanded in the summer of 1910. Whether this was directly connected with United's arrival on their doorstep is not clear, especially as Salford was still one of the conurbation's strongest rugby areas. It may well be that the preference for rugby impacted on both clubs' ability to attract large crowds.

As far as the opening game at Old Trafford was concerned, United had been leading 2–0 at half-time, with Sandy Turnbull netting the historic first goal. Despite this great start United lost their way and were defeated 4–3. The 1909–10 season progressed with United winning all their remaining seven home games, increasing the attractiveness of the new venue, but attendances did not match the quality of what was on offer. Apart from a couple of 40,000-plus crowds, which caused one journalist to claim that 'There can be no question that United's new quarters have resurrected a new interest in the club', support appeared to be no better than at Bank Street and one match, against Everton, attracted only 5,500 spectators.[50] Match performance often played a part in supporter interest in Manchester at this time, and winning teams were expected to attract greater support than a struggling side, but this was not apparent at Old Trafford, where United won the League in their first full season at the 70,000-plus venue. That year their average crowd increased to 19,950 (from 16,950) but was over 6,000 less than seventeenth-placed City in their 35,000-capacity venue. Even United's average had been inflated somewhat by the first Manchester derby at the stadium, which had attracted a then record League crowd for either Manchester side of 60,000, adding almost 2,000 to the annual average. While Old Trafford would undoubtedly prove to be one of United's greatest assets in the long term, especially after 1950, the move in 1910 was not the success that anyone had expected. It did not boost crowds by the margin hoped, and it created financial problems for the club in later years once Davies was unable to bankroll the club. It was the best venue of the era and contrasted well with both Bank Street and Hyde Road, which were cramped venues surrounded by terraced streets and industry, but the identification of Mancunians, particularly those in east Manchester, with their teams meant that the venue was only part of the lure. Bank Street was part of its community, while Old Trafford was distant and difficult to engage with, despite its obvious quality. Studies in later decades have identified that fans 'display a proprietorial attachment to the football ground', and while little research has been published on ground moves of the early twentieth century it is apparent that they were not always welcomed.[51] Attachment to a place, no matter how ramshackle it may be, contributes to quality of life, and Bank Street had a character and popularity which ensured that it was missed by supporters who felt that they belonged to a strong community, with their own viewing spaces and stand preferences.[52]

Old Trafford, as the most modern stadium in the country, staged the 1911 FA Cup final replay and the 1915 final, dubbed the Khaki final because of the large volume of soldiers attending. These were watched by crowds of 58,000 and 49,557, respectively, while United's biggest home League crowd of the period, 60,000 for the Manchester derby in September 1910, was not bettered until 1920, when another meeting with City attracted 63,000. In the years in between only twelve League games and two FA Cup matches had attracted crowds above 40,000, the perceived capacity of Bank Street.[53] In terms of Braudel's *longue durée*, the move to Old Trafford should have been a key event in a transformational cycle, and in terms of quality of facilities and stadium construction it was a significant event, but in the full history of United it was an event which caused the club to stagnate somewhat. The convoluted financial arrangements established by John Davies restricted United's opportunities, and while he was openly perceived as the man who had funded the stadium, both his brewery and Davies personally benefited from the club's move. According to an FA commission investigating the finances of United, the club was paying unreasonable amounts for the stadium, including an annual rent of £1,229 for the ground itself, plus £740 for neighbouring land which it did not use, and had had to pay £18,000 to build the stands and offices.[54] Without Davies, United might well have remained at Bank Street, struggling along, but the relaunch of the club in 1902 could well have proved successful without Davies' investment and, as with City at Hyde Road, the familiarity of the ground and the passionate support of east Mancunians might well have generated new life for the relaunched club. Of course, Davies funded player acquisitions and made other improvements, bringing the club its first successes, and these continued at Old Trafford initially. United won the League in their first full season there, but that was their last success until the late 1940s and so, the move was a key event in the club's transformation from one that enjoyed a growing support at Bank Street and major success to one with dwindling support and limited success. It is rarely viewed in this manner, of course, as the United of the 1940s onwards and the remodelled stadium developed from the 1960s tend to provide a perception that United have always been a success and Old Trafford has always been packed, but it was not until 1949–50 that the stadium attracted an average crowd of more than half the stadium's perceived 75,000 capacity and, even then this followed several seasons at Maine Road which had lifted United's support to new levels.[55] Two events in the aftermath of United's move, connected with City, may well have impacted on the attractiveness of United: improvements to Hyde Road in 1910 and the appointment of Ernest Mangnall as the new City manager in 1912.

City's Hyde Road expenditure in 1910 was approximately £3,000, which was a fraction of the cost to erect Old Trafford, but they built three roofs and made improvements to the catering facilities and customer areas of the ground. To counteract the lure of Old Trafford, City boasted that the newly refurbished Hyde Road would hold over 35,000 under cover, whereas Old Trafford could manage only about a quarter of that. By providing cover on all four sides of the ground City enabled fans of all classes and types to watch games at Hyde Road in their preferred stands. The familiarity of City's home and its position within the working-class district of Ardwick, close to major tram routes, ensured its popularity and the 1910–11 season saw the Blues' average attendance increase by 8,000 and, apart from occasional seasons, they were the better-supported Manchester club until the Second World War, with an average attendance of more than double United's at times.[56]

Mangnall's move

The appointment of Ernest Mangnall as City manager was another key event for the clubs during this period. For City to convince him to leave United after their success and move to Old Trafford was some feat. Mangnall, like Parlby before him, was a footballing visionary and while he had control of affairs at United the club progressed; however, the Reds' first golden era ended abruptly at the start of the 1912–13 season with his sudden departure. Mangnall's last United game was the Manchester derby, when it was already known that he would become City's manager the following Monday and, indeed, he had already attended a City game at Nottingham and was thought to have participated in player selection.[57] City won the game 1–0, while his United side drew 0–0 at Arsenal in his absence. In addition, he attended the directors' selection meetings at both United and City prior to his last United match and made his feelings known about which players should be selected.[58] A film crew recorded the derby, and this is the oldest known surviving Manchester derby footage, which was shown in France under the title: 'Match De Football Manchester', although only nineteen seconds of it survive. The game was not a classic and City won 1–0, presumably giving Ernest Mangnall mixed feelings about the result, although one reporter aptly commented that 'United speeded their manager rejoicing with two points to his new club'.[59] At City Mangnall did not have the trophy success which he enjoyed at United but he did play a prominent role in the club's move to the working-class Moss Side area, where they built the 85,000-capacity Maine Road stadium in 1923, meaning that he had been responsible for managing both clubs' stadium moves. As a boy Mangnall had played football of both codes at Bolton Grammar School and won many prizes as a youth in cross-country running, and he had also cycled tremendous distances on an old penny-farthing bicycle in various competitions, even winning a race from Land's End to John O'Groats on one.[60]

Mangnall's impact stretched beyond the two Manchester clubs and he was one of the leading voices behind the establishment of a strong league for reserve football. In 1911 the reserve sides of the significant local League clubs competed in the Lancashire Combination; however, other clubs competing in that competition believed that the League clubs were blocking their own development and took steps to vote League club officials off committees. Mangnall felt that the situation needed to be resolved and he contacted all the prominent local clubs, receiving support from Bolton Wanderers, Bury, Crewe Alexandra, Glossop, City, United, Oldham Athletic, Preston North End, Stockport County and Southport Central. A meeting was organised in May 1911 with City director W. A. Wilkinson as chairman. Everton's Will Cuff was secretary and Mangnall outlined his plan for the Lancashire-based League sides to withdraw from the Combination and create a new competition. Further meetings followed in Manchester with every League club in Lancashire represented, plus Stockport County and Glossop. The name The Central League was adopted, and in June the founding thirteen members held an election meeting to select a further five clubs, one of whom was Rochdale. Rochdale had to withdraw due to an objection from the Combination which resulted in the FA blocking their membership and a financial loss on the season of £600, although the club did become a member twelve months later. As founder, Mangnall remained interested in the competition for the rest of his life. He was also credited with being one of the founders of the League Managers' Association and he had suggested establishing the National War Fund for football during the First World War.[61] Ernest Mangnall was a major influence on both United and City, although he tends to be remembered as United's first successful manager. He contributed significantly to both clubs, providing United with ambition and a stadium of quality and City with their own major stadium and the ability to strengthen their support.

Notes

1 Tabner, *Football through the turnstiles*.
2 Russell, 'Associating with football', 19.
3 'Items and incidents', *Manchester Courier*, 11 February 1905, 9.
4 Harding, *Football wizard*.
5 S. Inglis, *League football and the men who made it* (London: Willow Books, 1988), 108–109.
6 Harding, *Football wizard*.
7 'Football and war', *Manchester Courier*, 22 May 1915, 6.
8 Probate records, Joshua Parlby, 1916; Census returns, Joshua Parlby 1911, https//:www.findmypast.co.uk (RG 14/23845)
9 'Death of Di Jones', *Manchester Evening News*, 27 August 1902, 5.
10 'Payments to players', *Athletic News*, 4 April 1910, 6.

11 Reported in *Bolton Football Field* as quoted in Harding, *Football wizard*, 100–105.
12 Harding, *Football wizard*, 100–105.
13 *Birmingham Sports Argus* was particularly supportive of Aston Villa, while the Manchester-based papers supported City.
14 'Important FA meeting', *Athletic News*, 7 August 1905, 5.
15 'I am innocent', *Hull Daily Mail*, 7 August 1905, 4.
16 'A significant statement', *Northern Daily Telegraph*, 16 June 1906, 3.
17 'The FA and Manchester United', *Athletic News*, 4 April 1910, 6; S. Inglis, *Soccer in the dock* (London: Willow, 1985), 10–11.
18 Harding, *Football wizard*.
19 Inglis, *Soccer in the dock*, 18.
20 'City v United', *Manchester Courier*, 1 December 1906, 9.
21 *Daily Dispatch*, 6 December 1906, n.p.
22 'Recipient of Ching Morrison's present', *Manchester Football Chronicle*, 8 April 1922, 3.
23 Harding, *Football wizard*.
24 'Player's suicide', *Nottingham Journal*, 3 March 1926, 9.
25 Unidentified newspaper report quoted in R. Lewis, 'Our lady specialists at Pikes Lane: female spectators in early English professional football, 1880–1914', *The International Journal of the History of Sport*, 26:15 (2009), 2171.
26 Beaven, *Leisure, citizenship*, 77–79.
27 Ibid., 81.
28 Russell, *Looking north*, 245.
29 'The FA and Manchester United', *Athletic News*, 4 April 1910, 6.
30 'Football', *Dundee Evening Telegraph*, 30 August 1902, 5.
31 'The football squabble', *Yorkshire Evening Post*, 28 August 1909, 4.
32 'Drastic step by the FA', *Manchester Courier*, 4 May 1909, 3.
33 'The football dispute', *Exeter and Plymouth Gazette*, 1 September 1909, 6. www.m.thepfa.com/news/2015/10/28/pfa-purchases-charlie-roberts-1909-fa-cup-shirt.
34 Harding, *For the good of the game*, 82.
35 Collins, *Sport in capitalist society*, 52.
36 'Man who made United', *Manchester Football Chronicle*, 20 January 1923, 3.
37 Collins, *Sport in capitalist society*, 6.
38 'The FA and Manchester United', *Athletic News*, 4 April 1910, 6.
39 'Man who made United', *Manchester Football Chronicle*, 20 January 1923, 3.
40 *Athletic News*, 8 March 1909.
41 *Salford Chronicle*, 19 February 1910.
42 Bale, *Sport, space and the city*, 58–61.
43 S. Inglis, *The football grounds of Great Britain* (London: Willow Books, 1987), 95.
44 According to the *Time zone map*, 1914, produced by Manchester City Council Tramways Department, a journey from Bank Street, Clayton to Manchester city centre would take twenty to thirty minutes, with a similar length of time required for a journey from the city centre to Old Trafford.
45 'A fine ground', *Manchester Evening Chronicle*, 15 February 1910.

46 'Football gossip', *Daily Dispatch*, 15 January 1904, 6.

47 United Kingdom Board of Trade, *Cost of living of the working classes*, 294–304; Beaven, *Leisure, citizenship*, 72.

48 *Manchester Evening News*, 17 February 1910; *Salford Chronicle*, 19 February 1910.

49 I. Morrison and A. Shury, *Manchester United a complete record, 1878–1990* (Derby: Breedon Books, 1990), 210.

50 James, *Manchester, a football history*; Morrison and Shury, *Manchester United a complete record*, 210.

51 Bale, *Sport, space and the city*, 169. Interviews by Gary James with Manchester-based supporters in the 1990s identified that Manchester City's move from Hyde Road to Maine Road in 1923 was perceived by supporters as a move away from the club's roots and it was felt that Hyde Road's unique atmosphere could not be replicated at a concrete bowl of a stadium. It seems logical to suggest that those views would also apply to United's move from Bank Street.

52 J. Eyles, *Senses of place* (Warrington: Silverbrook, 1985); E. Relph, *Place and place-lessness* (London: Pion, 1976), 65.

53 Morrison and Shury, *Manchester United a complete record*. The two FA Cup attendances were 65,101 for the visit of Aston Villa in 1911, which was United's record crowd at the time, and 59,300 against Blackburn Rovers in 1912.

54 'The FA and Manchester United', *Athletic News*, 4 April 1910, 6.

55 James, *Manchester, a football history*, 211.

56 Seasonal attendance figures for City, United, Oldham, Bury, Stockport and Rochdale appear in James, *Manchester, a football history*. These show that United's average had dropped to 11,685 in the 1930–31 season, while City's was 26,849. The largest average enjoyed by either team prior to 1939 was 37,468 at Manchester City in 1927–28 when the Blues were a Second Division club and United were in Division One, attracting 25,555.

57 Some historians dispute that Mangnall was officially United's manager on the day of the derby, but leading newspapers of the period, most notably *Umpire* and the *Daily Dispatch*, are perfectly clear that he was officially in charge.

58 'Recipient of Ching Morrison's present', *Manchester Football Chronicle*, 8 April 1922, 3.

59 'City win with ten men', *Umpire*, 9 September 1912.

60 'Recipient of Ching Morrison's present', *Manchester Football Chronicle*, 8 April 1922, 3.

61 Ibid.

10

A strained relationship

Mangnall

Ernest Mangnall's time as manager of Manchester United had enabled the club to enjoy its first major successes, but it was to undergo several transformational cycles before it became a major force in the game. Its elevated status would come in the years following the Second World War but, utilising long-range thinking, Mangnall's time at United did provide some of the long residuals that aided that club's later transition, such as the Old Trafford stadium. Recognising the building blocks and the chain of interrelated events is important in understanding how a structure is established. The *longue durée* is the 'inexhaustible history of structures and groups of structures. For the historian, a structure is not just a thing built, put together; it also means permanence, sometimes for more than centuries.'[1] Mangnall's time at United established some of the club's structure, to which others, most notably Matt Busby and Alex Ferguson, would add. There the similarity ends, because after Mangnall had given improved structure to United he moved on to add a long residual to City.

The arrival of Ernest Mangnall at City demonstrated the inability of United to increase their support and status in the manner anticipated following the move to Old Trafford and their League title successes. City remained the leading club despite the success Mangnall had achieved at United, and the secretary-manager believed that a move to Hyde Road would provide him with the opportunity to create something special. At City Mangnall immediately consulted with the board, which included Joshua Parlby once more, on plans for a new stadium. City had been planning to move ever since achieving promotion for the first time in 1899, but a combination of Chesters Brewery's influence and the lack of a credible site had held them. Mangnall was expected to find a solution while also ensuring progress on the pitch. Facilities had improved considerably in 1910, and the ground was regarded as 'one of the finest football enclosures in the country', but the Hyde Road ground remained a restrictive venue with two railway lines, a boiler works and a terraced street hemming it in.[2] There was even a railway loop line that cut through the ground, in front of the Boys' Stand, which carried boilers in front of a stand from Galloways Boilerworks and on to the main line.

Mangnall appointed the renowned architect Archibald Leitch to design a new stadium. Leitch had worked with the club when Hyde Road was renovated and extended in the aftermath of the 1904 FA Cup success, and he had also worked with Mangnall before, when the two men played key roles in the design and building of Old Trafford. The City manager gave Leitch an office at the ground and they worked together on the aim of creating an 80,000-capacity stadium somewhere in east Manchester. Mangnall's diplomacy came to the fore at this time as he negotiated carefully with the directors, including Chesters Brewery, and the local council to find an appropriate site; but with Chesters having been adept at blocking moves in the past, he gave Leitch the task of investigating whether it would be possible to erect an appropriately sized modern stadium at Hyde Road itself. This seemed like an impossibility, but in June 1913 Mangnall and Leitch announced that an 80,000-capacity stadium would be constructed at the site of City's ground.[3] To achieve this, the entire site would be transformed, with the pitch being moved and turned by forty-five degrees, where it would be possible to establish a 115 yards x 70 yards pitch with two 22,000-capacity end terraces and two pitch-length stands capable of seating 4,000 each and a 9,000-capacity paddock in front. New entrances would be opened and a forecourt would be established on land neighbouring the ground, while every available space between the existing railway lines, boilerworks and houses would be utilised. It was a vast undertaking, expected to be completed by the start of the 1914–15 season, subject to approval.[4]

Despite the attractiveness of remaining at their traditional site, City became frustrated with the railway company and other landowners adjacent to the Hyde Road ground. They negotiated for over eighteen months, but were frustrated at every turn.[5] Blocking moves, stalling tactics and an inability to share the vision of what City was attempting to do meant that the option of staying at Hyde Road became increasingly unlikely. The match-day situation worsened at this time because overcrowding led to turnstiles being closed an hour before the start of many games to avoid crushing; fans were turned away, adding to the frustrations of both the club and Mancunians, especially when the calculation of final attendances revealed that the ground had not reached capacity. The situation needed to be rectified, either with a move or by all parties supporting the plans to build more turnstiles and improved entrances, and for related procedures to ensure that capacity could be reached, followed by extension of the stands. This was one of Leitch's greatest challenges, and City had only a four-year lease of the ground. Without an extended lease and the opportunity to incorporate the large triangle of land behind one of the goals which was owned by the railway company, the club were reluctant to spend the £21,000 which they had available in 1914.[6] Mangnall and Leitch were frustrated at every turn, and while they had developed ambitious plans the inability to persuade the local landowners of the value of leasing their land to the club prevented improvements that were desperately required. Similarly, Chesters Brewery's stranglehold over the club meant that a new site seemed unlikely, and it is no wonder that the club's chairman stressed the loyalty of City's support at key moments throughout the ground debates. The club's supporters were ordinary Mancunians who simply wanted to watch their team, but the ground issues often prevented them from gaining access, and mounted police were often called to move the crowds away because the authorities insisted that turnstiles had to be closed regardless of whether the ground was full. If the leaseholders would not allow additional developments, the situation had to be resolved by moving.

By May 1914 it was announced that City had identified another site, close to the Belle Vue Zoo and entertainment complex, although Mangnall tried to pacify the railway company and brewery by saying that it was premature to talk about the specific site.[7] The site, which ultimately became the Belle Vue Greyhound stadium, offered City more potential than a remodelled Hyde Road would have done and, most significantly, it would remove the club from the control of both the railway company and the brewery.[8] A month after playing down the possibility of moving to Belle Vue, the club announced that they had purchased the land and revealed that a 100,000-capacity stadium would be erected, under Leitch's guidance, in two phases, the first phase ending with an 80,000 initial capacity, after which the erection of double-deck stands would provide the additional 20,000.[9] It appeared that nothing could stop the development this time; but the outbreak of war placed the new stadium on hold, while City's existing Hyde Road ground was utilised for the stabling of horses (Figure 17).[10] The potential ground move rumbled on but remained on hold until the war was over. In 1920 a new plan for a 100,000-capacity stadium at Belle Vue seemed plausible, but further investigations demonstrated that the site was not suitable.[11] The lease was too short and the site was a little smaller than the club now wanted. Ultimately, under Mangnall's direction, the club would move to the 85,000-capacity Maine Road in 1923, some twenty-four years after City had begun looking for an alternative site. That site would strengthen City's position as Manchester's leading club by 1930.

Match-fixing

While City's stadium plans were halted by the war, football itself was not. Not initially, at any rate. Manchester's footballing debates during this period are typical of most English cities, with disapproval of the sport coming from authority figures while other sports that appealed to the upper-middle and upper-classes, such as horse racing, received little criticism.[12] The criticism of football's continuation came predominantly from the South and formed part of the protracted North–South professional–amateur debate, a 'conflict

FIVE YEARS AGO.

An Interesting Snapshot on our Ground during the Military occupation in 1914.

17 Horses stabled at City's Hyde Road ground.

over the game's soul that had erupted in 1884 and 1907'.[13] These debates and discussions have been well documented, but there was one, predominantly Mancunian, controversy that added to the feeling that football, or at least footballers, were out of touch with the situation of the country and the sacrifices many were making. This was the United fixed-game scandal of Easter 1915. To understand how this occurred it is important to consider the events following Mangnall's departure from United and how United's players were believed to have the upper hand in club affairs.

By the start of the 1914–15 season United were struggling and, with several players having been brought in during Mangnall's golden period, there were issues concerning the potential number of bonus payments due to squad members. From 1901 clubs could stage a benefit match after five years of continuous service, and again after ten or at the end of the player's career. Typically, United players would be allocated a League match for their benefit, often against rivals City, limiting their own profit from a high-profile game but guaranteeing the beneficiary a good income. The amount raised would vary, but United's solicitor and a prominent League official, Charles Sutcliffe, claimed that £200 was a typical figure – but he also admitted that £500 and even £1,000 was possible.[14] Sutcliffe was a well-regarded footballing figure who had been involved with the sport in Lancashire from an early age and became a Football League official responsible, among other things, for the creation of the fixture list each season. With a maximum wage of £4 in force, the benefit provided an opportunity for players to ensure that their post-football career was secure to some extent, and there were further opportunities to gain additional income, including, from 1910, talent money and bonuses for Cup-tie wins. This meant that teams occupying the top five places in both divisions of the League could distribute amounts to their players ranging from £55 in fifth place to £275 for the divisional champions. Similar amounts were available for those reaching the latter stages of the FA Cup. Sutcliffe was a major supporter of these bonus payments, stating that they were 'the reward for honest effort and enterprise on the part of the team to render the best possible service for the club'.[15] While other clubs, most notably United's rivals City, had been caught making payments to their players above the maximum allowed, United had until now managed to avoid an in-depth investigation. Presumably having two leading League officials in their ranks, Sutcliffe and Bentley, ensured that United remained within the laws of the game. However, as many of United's players had been involved in the establishment of the players' union, there was a feeling in the media they were keen to ensure that their demands were met, and that officials were intent on keeping them happy.

When war was declared against Germany on 4 August 1914, the Football League decided to continue with the new season. The competition had not been suspended for war at any other time, including during the Boer Wars, and Parliament and the public believed that the conflict would be over by Christmas. The First World War was not over by Christmas and focus on player activity increased. It was not too long before some of Manchester's biggest footballing names became embroiled in controversy. Sandy Turnbull, who had scored United's winning goal in the 1909 FA Cup final and was a star of City's earlier FA Cup success, was a prominent contributor throughout the pre-war City and United successes, but he became suspended in October 1914 for arguing with United's secretary-manager, John Bentley, in the dressing room.[16] The players threatened to strike if Turnbull's ban continued, and by the end of December 1914 Bentley had been replaced as United manager by John Robson. In 1912 Bentley had talked of clubs guaranteeing a minimum of £500 to players for benefit games, outlining how United had been paying Billy Meredith £200 per year for five years, plus a benefit of approximately £1,800. A total of £2,800 for five years' work, including three months' holiday per year, plus talent bonuses, was the final figure Bentley claimed they had paid to Meredith, although even at this point Meredith was in dispute with the Reds because he was adamant they had not paid him every amount they had promised him, including his own benefit money.[17] Bentley, during his time as United's manager, stressed: 'To put it straight, clubs cannot stand the strain, and if clubs "go under" then the player is bound to suffer. Isn't he?'[18] There were few men greater, in terms of footballing stature, than Bentley, and his removal demonstrated that a battle was underway for power within the club.

Player power appeared to be an issue, and this view intensified when an effort was made to help players at struggling clubs during the opening months of the 1914–15 season. The FA decided to collect a levy to provide a relief fund to support League clubs hit by falling attendances, determining that players on the maximum wage of £5 would be taxed 15%, while those on £2 would lose 5% of their pay.[19] While the playing staff of City and Oldham unanimously agreed to the scheme, United's players, many of whom were on the maximum wage, objected. The *Athletic News*, a newspaper where United manager Bentley had occupied the position of editor, was critical, and after several articles public opinion intensified. This led to the players accepting the situation, and they went on to pay the levy. Player power and the perceived insensitivity to the plight of their colleagues was damaging, but worse was to follow.

For much of the 1914–15 season United had struggled in the First Division and, with eight matches left, they were one point off the bottom, on twenty-five points from thirty-one games. Notts County were below them on twenty-five points from thirty-three games, followed by Chelsea on twenty-four points from thirty matches. If Chelsea were to win their game in hand, United would be in the relegation zone. Liverpool, United's next opponents, had played two games more than United and were on twenty-nine points in fourteenth place, and while it has often been suggested that Liverpool were safe and in mid-table, it is evident mathematically that Liverpool were some way off safety too. Apart from the 1914 FA Cup final, Liverpool had won the First Division title in 1901 – their first major trophy – but in the years that followed had hardly been viewed as a team that could challenge for honours. Potentially, the Liverpool players had reason to search for additional income, especially as the United men could demonstrate that in recent years theirs had proved to be the more profitable club for players to be with. The two clubs were extremely close, with several shared interests and causes, such as in 1906 when they jointly suggested to the Football League that only two colours of shirt should be worn by League clubs: red when playing at home and white when playing away.[20] It was obvious to all League sides that these were the two colours United and Liverpool shared and preferred, and the motion was defeated. Liverpool had also been the visitors when Old Trafford was opened and, while Manchester and Liverpool were rival cities at the time, the football clubs were supportive of each other and part of a Lancastrian elite that dominated the key positions within the Football League.

Before they played each other at Easter 1915, players from both clubs met at a Manchester public house and arranged to fix the score at 2–0 for United. The story of the fixed game has been documented extensively over the years, but it is important to highlight the key details here before outlining the significance of what followed. The United–Liverpool League game was played on Good Friday 1915 at Old Trafford and suspicions that it had been fixed appeared during the game itself, when supporters in the 18,000 crowd, United's highest of the season so far, began to whistle and voice their displeasure. Considering that United had a 2–0 lead at this stage and that they were playing at home, the criticism from the terraces was significant. Newspapers commented on Liverpool's laid-back approach, while fans and even the referee felt that they had witnessed a peculiar game, which included a missed penalty by United, taken by O'Connell instead of the team's regular penalty-taker (O'Connell is alleged to have insisted that he himself should take it). The ball was sent some distance wide of the post, which caused any doubters to question the motives of the player, while observers suggested that a specific score was important to the participants.[21] The second half was 'crammed with lifeless football' and Liverpool made no attempt at scoring.[22] The *Manchester Football Chronicle* suggested that some form of match-fixing has taken place: 'one famous old player said, "You don't need the War to stop the game, football of this sort will do it soon enough". Personally, I was surprised and disgusted at the spectacle the second half presented.'[23] Some reports focused on the errors more than on the positive aspects of the game: 'Play was scrappy, both sides shooting badly … there was not a dangerous forward on the field.'[24] This was a common theme: '[Liverpool's] shooting was wretched, as can be judged by the fact that Beale had not to handle for over half-an-hour. A more one-sided first half would be hard to witness.'[25]

The victory secured two points for United, which proved crucial in their

18 A photograph showing action in the Manchester United–Liverpool
fixed game of 2 April 1915.

fight for survival, and when the season ended they avoided relegation by one point.[26] In the immediate aftermath of the match the *Manchester Football Chronicle* had not been too positive about their future, believing that the players' demands were the problem: 'If the club does go down the present team would not be at all likely to regain the senior division. My own opinion is that of recent seasons there had been far too much talk about money at Old Trafford and too little about football.'[27] These were interesting comments when the motive behind the fixed game is considered. The consensus in studies during the late twentieth and early twenty-first centuries is that the game was fixed so as to enable a small band of players to gain income via betting wins on the outcome, as they were concerned that the war would affect their livelihoods. But if that was the case, then how did they persuade the others to participate in the scam? In any case, some of the United players had been promised wartime jobs working for a local Ford garage, which, they had been told, would provide them with protected occupations. Others expected to enlist in any case, and regardless of the uncertainty of war the players had experienced uncertainty throughout their careers. Even the leading players had never been guaranteed more than a couple of years at United. The close season was the period when offers would be made, such as in 1913 when it was reported that three of United's leading players had been signed up until the end of 1914–15 and others had not 'at present been re-engaged'.[28] Whatever the motives, the club was ultimately likely to gain more than the players, as those two points guaranteed a First Division future once the League programme was resumed.

Despite the concerns on match day itself, it was several days before newspapers began to highlight that the result seemed to be connected to a betting scandal and an investigation was set up.[29] Rumours had increased that there had been collusion over the result, and a £50 reward was offered by a betting organisation if someone could come forward to substantiate an allegation that the match had been fixed, following an unusual quantity of bets placed on a 2–0 result to United. The subsequent week's coupon 'bore a statement regarding the alleged plot. £50 reward being offered by [the bookmaker] for news that would trace the originator of the supposed scheme.'[30] The *Sporting Chronicle* published a notice from a bookmaker called 'The Football King' who was adamant that the game had been 'squared' and asked to 'receive reliable information bearing on the subject and we will willingly pay the substantial reward named above [£50] to anyone giving information which will lead to punishment of the offenders'.[31]

The Football League set up a commission to investigate the match consisting of Harry Keys (West Bromwich Albion), referee John Lewis, most often associated with Blackburn Rovers and one of the original investigators into City's illegal payments scandal, and, bizarrely, United's solicitor, Charles Sutcliffe. Sutcliffe had previously acted on behalf of Aston Villa when a player had taken legal proceedings against them, and had himself been embroiled in a match-fixing scandal in 1898.[32] In 1898 he was a director and former player of Burnley, who were promoted via the test matches after their game with Stoke had ended in a suspicious draw which ensured that both sides would play in the First Division but which, more significantly, was considered to have been fixed by the two clubs. Sutcliffe, acting as a League official rather than in his capacity as a Burnley director, proposed the extension of the First Division by two clubs to ensure that Blackburn and Newcastle, the two clubs adversely affected by the fixed match, could also compete at the highest level alongside his Burnley team. Despite his obvious conflict of interest, Sutcliffe was allowed to encourage others to support him and his proposal worked. He went on to introduce the automatic promotion system to ensure that a similar situation would not occur again and was acclaimed for doing so; but surely his team, Burnley, should have been punished – or at least forced to play Stoke again?

In 1905 Sutcliffe was chiefly responsible for another proposal to increase the size of the League, which, according to correspondence in the *Athletic News*, was another attempt at preserving a Lancastrian club and also involved United. The correspondent referred to the scheme as 'a Lancashire dodge to preserve Bury and elect Manchester United – the club in which the President of the League, Mr JJ Bentley, is so deeply concerned!'[33] The correspondent raised the 1898 scandal as evidence of Sutcliffe's willingness to change the rules to suit his preferred Lancastrian clubs. Clearly, Sutcliffe was adept at ensuring that football's questionable activities were investigated and resolved within the game, ensuring damage limitation by offering special treatment to those clubs that had lost out. As United's solicitor and a Football League committeeman, his skills of negotiation and pragmatism would be tested again in 1915, where there would be a conflict of interests, as the commission had to determine the reason for the fixed match. With United in a precarious position at the time, rigorous questioning of the club's management and board should have played a part; but this did not occur, if contemporary reports are to be believed.

With Sutcliffe on board, the commission began its work, but it seemed to be quite lethargic in its investigations, much to the disgust of the *Manchester Evening Chronicle*. On 30 October the newspaper was critical of the investigators when it revealed the surprising news that the commission had only just asked for the names of the players taking part in the game.[34] As United's solicitor Sutcliffe should have been capable of obtaining United's players' names at the start of his investigations and it is surprising that such a renowned and respected footballing administrator would not have taken steps at the start of his involvement to research the activities of those connected with his own club. Surprisingly, there was no mention of Sutcliffe's dual, in fact triple, role, but it is intriguing that the man with responsibility for defending United from a legal perspective and for 'moulding and fashioning the League' was part of an investigating body that was being criticised for its lack of interrogation of facts.[35] Indeed the media appeared to be supportive of Sutcliffe, often stressing that the game owed him a debt; and when his own role at United was questioned it was often stated that he had not been present at the game but had heard the rumours that it had been fixed.[36] Further media criticism followed of the time that the investigation was taking. The idea of player power is certainly one that's been discussed often in relation to the case, and yet men like Sutcliffe and Bentley were involved with United. Such important and well-regarded men seemed unlikely to yield to player demands, but the implication is that they did.[37]

Not only was Sutcliffe's position on the investigating body a curious one, but the influence of Liverpool chairman John McKenna must be considered. Liverpool had been investigated previously, with McKenna presiding over League meetings in 1913 following a controversial game between his team and Chelsea. Notts County had called for a full inquiry after indifferent play by Liverpool's players, while Bentley had written about that game earlier in the year.[38] According to Bentley, complaints had been made that some of the Liverpool men had not tried during the match on Easter Monday, and Bentley seemed to agree that the possibility of non-triers existed: 'possibly there is some justification for [these] very serious comments, for the fact remains that nearly one-half of the team which opposed Chelsea was dropped for the following Saturday against Manchester United'.[39] Bentley talked of other instances where players had been 'bought', but tried to play down the suggestion as far as he could. He did refer to the fixed test match between Stoke and Burnley which led to both Blackburn and Newcastle being promoted in 1898 which was 'unquestionably arranged', but the respected footballing administrator claimed that the fixed match had brought a benefit in that it 'enlarged the League to admit Blackburn Rovers and Newcastle, and disposed of the promotion and relegation deciding Test [40]Matches'.

Bentley was on United's payroll for much of the early twentieth century and was always a prominent League official, and yet his belief in resolving a match-fixing scandal by increasing the size of the League rather than punishing the clubs demonstrated how football's League officials acted in a manner which tried to appease those who had suffered rather than punish those who had acted corruptly. Surely, punishment for the men who performed the crime and, at the least, a replayed game for the clubs, ought to have been the minimum sanctions imposed by the League. While match-fixing is wrong, the punishments rarely fitted the crime. Individuals would suffer, but rarely did the clubs receive any punishment, suggesting that League officials were quite happy to label players as cheats but would not punish those clubs that benefited. There was no incentive or deterrent for the clubs and, with club officials in positions of power at the Football League or on the investigating committees, it was apparent they could avoid investigation of their clubs. It has been highlighted that the League Management Committeemen gained financially from their involvement with the sport: 'It is not clear how much Sutcliffe earned from his football-related work, although no doubt it could be profitable. Indeed, he was paid at least £50 for a few months assisting the floatation of Oldham Athletic in 1906.'[41] He was also 'known variously as "the brains of football" or the "football dictator"'.[42]

The governance of League football at this time was primarily in the hands of Liverpool chairman John McKenna, United solicitor Charles Sutcliffe and Blackburn Rovers' John Lewis, and while each man was well respected within the game it is somewhat perplexing that men so closely associated with the two clubs accused of match-fixing could elect investigators to question the players but refrain from investigating the clubs' roles in the game. Surely, the investigation should have sought to answer the questions about payments made by the clubs to their players and the future guarantees that it was occasionally suggested had been made. Sutcliffe, as a member of the investigating committee, did not go far enough, and yet his 'analytical mind' was recognised as being important in uncovering the 'hard facts of a case'.[43] Known as the 'power behind the throne' during McKenna's presidency of the League, Sutcliffe was able to lead and direct the Football League's developments and investigations how he saw fit, and typically this would include a special place for the teams from Lancashire. It seems ludicrous that officials from the clubs involved could play such important parts in the investigation, which took considerably longer than anticipated and led to some frustration in the media.[44] On Merseyside the *Liverpool Echo* was persistent in its drive to uncover what had occurred and it pressured the commission for a verdict. The *Echo* was adamant that a verdict of 'not proven' would have been pronounced, had it not been for their persistence, and there was some logic behind this.[45] The newspaper was clear: 'Why Manchester United wanted to win the match was plain: By success they would escape the meshes of the relegation problem.'[46] But it was the specific scoreline that then led to the view that there were also betting implications.

On 23 December 1915 the commission gave its verdict and the findings were that several players had hatched a plot to fix the result and scoreline of the match for financial gain. This resulted in eight players being permanently suspended from taking part in football or football management and banned from entering any football ground in the future. They included four players from Liverpool and Turnbull, Whalley and West from United. Another player, Lol Cook (ex-Stockport County) from Chester, was also banned but no one quite understood his involvement, while City's Fred Howard was also suspended for twelve months when football was resumed after the war. The report also suggested that other members of United had been involved, although the commission admitted that it could punish only those whom it could prove guilty. As December neared its end more information and stories emerged and the implications were felt immediately. The morale-boosting 1915 Christmas Day derby match between City and United at Hyde Road was affected, as both Enoch West (United) and Fred Howard (City) were dropped. Similarly, Turnbull and Whalley were stopped from playing for the Footballers' Battalion against Birmingham.

The match-fixing was discussed at length. Some suggested that United's potential relegation had been the reason, and it is accurate to state that if United had been enjoying a good season the prospect for a 'fix' would have reduced (odds of 7–1 would not have been offered, had United been mid-table), but the game had been several weeks from the end of the season. An early attempt could have been made to avoid relegation in this manner, of course, and it is possible that other games may have been fixed to enable this situation. However it is considered, the result caused Chelsea rather than United to end the season in a relegation position. The *Athletic News*, despite its Manchester leanings, was not impressed: 'Manchester United have been extremely fortunate in escaping from the consequences of the acts of men for whom they are technically responsible … Manchester United enjoy a place they have not honestly won and Chelsea are called upon to suffer an indignity they do not honestly deserve.'[47] The generally held view is that the motivation for the fixed game was money, although *Athletic News* was quick to point out exactly how much United's first team had earned:

> The wages of the players in 1913–14 were £5,573 15s and in 1914–15 £5,810 1s 11d. There does not appear such a reduction here as should tempt any man to scheme for money in an illegitimate manner … The players had bonuses of £60, and the travelling expenses cost £909. The receipts of the first team matches declined from £13,397 to £6,081, and the total revenue fell from £16,022 to £11,708. The debit balance is not surprising when the players take £5,810 out of £6,081 taken at the more important matches.[48]

Once again United's financial position was highlighted, suggesting that some took the view that there had been other motives, or that the players held too much power. In the 1980s Simon Inglis expressed the opinion that the players were simply on the make.[49]

When the verdict was given the commission commented on the competing clubs: 'There has never been the slightest allegation against the clubs or their officials. It is therefore, unnecessary to exonerate them from blame or complicity.'[50] By this time the composition of the commission had changed somewhat, with FA representatives also on board, although Sutcliffe remained as one of the investigators. Regardless of who was on the committee, even the most supportive of individuals must have considered that a game that was fixed and discussed in the dressing rooms of both clubs must have been known to the coaching staff and management of those clubs and yet, unlike the Meredith bribery allegation of 1905, an investigation of the clubs themselves did not occur. The *Sheffield Daily Telegraph* commented that 'a club is responsible for the action of its players, and Manchester United could not have set up any sound argument against such a course had the League reinstated Chelsea'.[51]

United officials did speak at subsequent hearings as players appealed against their punishments – including director Harold Hardman, who said that the 'second half of the game was a weird exhibition. West repeatedly kicked the ball out of play'; and yet, when questioned, Hardman did not think the match had been fixed.[52] He claimed that he 'had a better idea of the honesty of the players', and went on to play West in subsequent games, admitting that United did not question West or the others on their approach in the fixed match: 'We thought it better not to say anything to our players, but to leave them to be dealt with by the FA Commission.' As United did play some of these men in subsequent games, that should have brought investigation from the League. Selecting men whom the club's own directors had seen kicking the ball out of play raises several questions. Even if no official connected with United was aware of the scandal, or even aware of the rumours, then surely they should have been concerned by a player's apparent inability to keep the ball in play. The Football League should have questioned United's decision to continue to play men who were not acting in the interests of the club, but it was not only their selection that demonstrated that the club still backed those players, as United visibly gave positive support to the men involved. George Anderson, despite his involvement in the scandal, was made the club's match programme cover star in January 1917.[53] United still perceived him as a hero and treated him well, despite the disgrace and scandal that he had allegedly helped to bring on the club, of which they were not supposed to approve.[54]

Long-term implications

In 1916 it was recognised that the fixed game had had a significant impact on the League, with United being safe from relegation while Chelsea had been relegated 'because the match was faked'.[55] Once the First World War had ended Chelsea rightly made their formal appeal against relegation and the League Management Committee agreed that their relegation 'would be unjust'.[56] It also determined that United could not now be relegated and so came up with a plan to increase both divisions of the League by two clubs, allowing United and Chelsea to remain in an enlarged Division One.[57] This move was agreed at a special League meeting, and it has been suggested that the purpose of the increase was to prevent a breakaway of southern clubs by ensuring that London clubs remained in the top flight.[58] The special meeting of the League was merely one event within the much longer debate stretching back to the fixed game of April 1915. The debate had rumbled on throughout the war, but it was not until the League meeting in 1919 that a resolution could be found. By that time the League had issued pardons to some of the players on account of their war service.

When the Football League met to determine how the 1919–20 season should develop Liverpool's McKenna presided and asked Sutcliffe to propose the resolution which was to increase the League from forty clubs to forty-four. Sutcliffe did so, and talked openly of his desire to see Chelsea accepted into the enlarged First Division, claiming that it would be an act of justice and encouraging all to support them.[59] There were dissenting voices, and the Everton chair suggested that United should be relegated, and not Chelsea, adding that the idea of increasing the League every time a club was judged to have been unfairly treated was wrong.[60] He made it abundantly clear that he felt United should be relegated, and this resulted in an extraordinarily angry response from Sutcliffe – who, it should be remembered, had acted as United's solicitor and a member of the investigating commission. Sutcliffe was said to have taken the position that Liverpool were 'the most guilty', and added that if Everton were to pursue this line then perhaps the solution would be to relegate Everton's neighbours and United.[61] It seems that this came across more as a threat than a reasoned opinion, and the Everton chair backed down, stating that he was against the League's increase but would accept it if the vote was in favour. The possibility of Everton's neighbours being relegated appears to have been the deciding factor in his accepting the views of Sutcliffe, who has been described as 'quiet and yet with an incisive way of piling up convincing arguments in debate' and 'known for his ability to use logic and sarcasm to demolish his opponents'.[62]

The increase in the League is often discussed from the perspective of Arsenal's promotion and Tottenham's relegation, but, had the Liverpool–United match-fixing scandal never occurred, the implications for London's clubs might never have been significant. The mood of the League meetings was that Chelsea had been hard done by, with little said about Tottenham's plight – but this often gets overlooked today as we consider the apparent injustice of Tottenham's relegation, from a division that was about to be increased, for Arsenal. According to Simon Inglis, McKenna was a friend of Arsenal's Norris and gave a passionate speech urging League officials to give Arsenal the additional place, stating that the 'President, the Committee and the clubs had succumbed to a rich and powerful politician and property dealer'.[63] He goes on to say that 'never had the League been so manipulated as it was in 1919. One can only ask, what were puritanical men like Sutcliffe and Lewis doing throughout this unseemly business.' The comments about Sutcliffe seem at odds with contemporary knowledge about him, while Inglis' views on Arsenal's promotion suggest that McKenna was another person who put his club and connections above what was morally correct. There was never any suggestion that McKenna had been aware of the match-fixing plot in 1915, and, indeed, Inglis thought he was 'cruelly torn by the commission's findings'. Inglis quotes McKenna as being somewhat disappointed with Liverpool's players: 'had we known their connection with this affair … We would have had no dealings with them in any shape.'[64] But Inglis implies that McKenna used his position to promote the club of his friend. Regardless of the Arsenal–Tottenham situation, it was Chelsea's position that was the key to preserving the League from a possible breakaway by London clubs. Chelsea was innocent, yet Sutcliffe's focus was on preserving United and Liverpool's status, not on Chelsea's survival. If this was the case, then why did he not do more to ensure that Chelsea survived and United and Liverpool had points deducted? The crux of the matter is that those responsible for the Football League tended to act in the interests of their clubs and appeared to preserve their relationships and avoid conflict while attempting to bring others into their circle. League increases often came about either to protect a club which members did not want to lose or to bring into membership a club that offered geographical expansion or had recognisable connections to the existing structure. These changes can be viewed as part of a *longue durée* process during which the professional game became national, but they also ensured that power remained with officials who would make judgements based on their own connections and interests.

The wider public had often perceived the FA as being out of touch and representing a clique; indeed the judge in the Knocker West trial was critical: 'football ought to be pure, and the witness is now saying that even the Association itself is not pure'.[65] The same was true for the Football League. When the fixed match scandal occurred Sutcliffe and Bentley were powerful and respected League officials, but they were also closely connected with United. It was inevitable that they would want to blame the players, while finding ways to protect the clubs involved and the League structure. Sutcliffe was known as being 'loyal and generous to his close friends' and he has been portrayed as a dedicated but ruthless man who exerted great power within the game.[66] In terms of Manchester's history, the verdict preserved United's status in Division One but damaged perceptions of the players. The 1904 scandal had seen Mancunians support their players, but by 1919 attitudes had changed. Society had changed as a result of the war, and attempts by footballers to earn additional cash by fixing games would not be tolerated.

Player issues were not confined to United and Liverpool. Another scandal had occurred on 3 April 1915 when the Oldham players had behaved petulantly throughout their match with Middlesbrough, culminating in the stubborn refusal of Oldham's right-back, William Cook, to leave the field when he was sent off for a foul. After attempts had been made to make the player see sense, the referee had abandoned the match. This was viewed as the most controversial moment in the professional game's history and resulted in a lengthy ban for

Cook and a fine for Oldham. At this point Oldham were second in the table, two points behind leaders Manchester City, and their behaviour reinforced the opinion that footballers really ought to consider the sacrifices being made elsewhere. The wider public's views of footballers during these years changed. Pre-war, they had appeared to be fighting the same battles as ordinary working-class people, with campaigns for union representation; but by the end of the war the media and the Football League had created an image of the footballer as someone who was somewhat selfish and looking to make additional income however he could. It was the player scandals and match-fixing that did most to damage the game in the Lancashire region at this time, not specifically the sport's war-time continuation. These actions on the part of players 'provided valuable ammunition for those middle-class critics who regarded [football] as essentially corrupt and guided by money'.[67] In the case of Manchester's clubs, bribery, match-fixing and illegal payments dogged the period from 1904 through to 1919, both City and United gaining headlines for problems with their players. While City appeared to have cleaned up their act following their punishments of 1904–6, United seemed unable to move forward, and their own illegal payments scandal of 1904 was followed by the match-fixing scandal, investigations into the club's ownership and an ongoing battle with Billy Meredith over benefit money which he claimed he was never paid.[68]

The significance of these match-fixing scandals and player-related issues is that a simple episode such as the increase in membership of the Football League is merely one event within a sequence of events in a transformational cycle; and that, in this case, analysis of each League meeting and an interrogation of the evidence reveals a broader series of episodes that transformed the structure of the League.

Notes

1 Braudel, *On history*, 75.
2 'Directors decide to purchase Gorton site', *Manchester Courier*, 10 June 1914, 3.
3 'Manchester City's enterprise', *Athletic News*, 9 June 1913, 1.
4 Ibid.
5 'Extension badly needed', *Manchester Courier*, 9 March 1914, 8.
6 Ibid.
7 *Sheffield Star Green 'Un*, 16 May 1914, 1.
8 'Manchester City's new ground', *Manchester Evening News*, 23 May 1914, 4.
9 'Directors decide to purchase Gorton site', *Manchester Courier*, 10 June 1914, 3.
10 *Sheffield Star Green 'Un*, 8 August 1914, 1.
11 'Manchester City's new ground', *Sheffield Daily Telegraph*, 19 August 1920, 9.
12 'A few days ago', *Sphere*, 20 March 1915, 312; 'Will the war change England?' *War Illustrated*, 27 February 1915, 26; 'Mr. Chapman's reply to kill-sports', *Manchester Courier*, 22 May 1915, 6.

13 Russell, *Football and the English*, 75.

14 'Points for players', *Athletic News*, 22 March 1909, 4; 'Football benefits: a serious problem', *Athletic News*, 11 September 1911, 4.

15 Discussions on the bonus system appeared frequently in the *Athletic News* during the aftermath of Manchester City's illegal payment scandal of 1905. See issues for 8, 15 and 29 January 1906. For a review of the development of bonus payments see Taylor, *The leaguers*, 106–118.

16 'Manchester United player suspended', *Manchester Courier*, 9 October 1914, 2.

17 'Players' benefits', *Derby Telegraph*, 12 October 1912, 2.

18 Ibid.

19 Inglis, *League football*, 94.

20 'Footballiana', *Athletic News*, 4 June 1906, 5.

21 For example, 'An Old Trafford win,' *Manchester Courier*, 3 April 1915, 2; Manchester United do well', *Sheffield Daily Telegraph*, 3 April 1915, 5; *Daily Dispatch*, 3 April 1915; 'Football', *Liverpool Daily Post*, 3 April 1915, 8; *Athletic News*, 31 May 1915.

22 'Good Friday's football', *Daily Dispatch*, 3 April 1915, 2.

23 *Manchester Football Chronicle*, 3 April 1915, 1.

24 'Manchester U 2 Liverpool 0', *Sheffield Daily Independent*, 3 April 1915, 8.

25 'Two-nothing defeat', *Liverpool Daily Post*, 3 April 1915, 8.

26 Ibid.

27 *Manchester Football Chronicle*, 3 April 1915, 1.

28 'Manchester United', *Athletic News*, 9 June 1913, 1. Meredith, Roberts and Wall had been signed until the end of the 1914–15 season; West had an agreement until summer 1916; while Bell and Duckworth had not yet been re-engaged, suggesting a level of uncertainty each year for some players.

29 'Important inquiry in Manchester', *Manchester Evening News*, 20 April 1915, 5; 'A football inquiry', *Liverpool Echo*, 21 April 1915, 8.

30 'Football betting', *Liverpool Daily Post*, 22 April 1915, 8.

31 'Big football sensation', *Leeds Mercury*, 24 April 1915, 3.

32 ' A football inquiry', *Liverpool Echo*, 21 April 1915, 8.

33 'Footballiana', *Athletic News*, 15 May 1905, 4.

34 *Manchester Evening Chronicle*, 30 October 1915.

35 *Sheffield Star Green 'Un*, 9 September 1916, 6.

36 'A sports causerie', *Lancashire Evening Post*, 14 July 1917, 5; 'Football loses action', *Globe*, 17 January 1919, 5.

37 'The League and Football Association', *Athletic News*, 25 April 1910, 1.

38 'Liverpool—Chelsea match: the report withheld', *Yorkshire Post*, 5 April 1913, 16; 'Non-trying teams', *Derby Daily Telegraph*, 5 April 1913, 4.

39 'Non-trying teams', *Derby Daily Telegraph*, 5 April 1913, 4.

40 'Non-trying teams', *Derby Daily Telegraph*, 5 April 1913, 4.

41 Taylor, *The leaguers*, 60.

42 Inglis, *League football*, 110.

43 'Charles Sutcliffe: An appreciation', in C. Sutcliffe, J. A. Brierley and F. Howarth, *The story of the Football League* (Preston: The Football League, 1938), 166.

44 'A football mystery', *Sunday Pictorial*, 19 December 1915, 22.

45 'Worst blow football has had', *Liverpool Echo*, 23 December 1915, 6.
46 Ibid.
47 'Chelsea's sportsmanlike spirit', *Athletic News*, 10 January 1916, 1.
48 'Manchester United's affairs', *Athletic News*, 27 December 1915, 1.
49 For Inglis' account of the scandal see his *Soccer in the dock*, 31–55.
50 'Football scandal', *Liverpool Daily Post*, 24 December 1915, 3.
51 'What it means to Chelsea', *Sheffield Daily Telegraph*, 12 January 1916, 5.
52 'A weird exhibition', *Manchester Evening News*, 6 July 1917, 5.
53 Every member of both the United and Liverpool teams that met on Good Friday 1915 continued to play in Football League games that season for their club.
54 A portrait photograph of Anderson wearing a jacket and tie was the only photograph on the cover of their match programme for the visit of Blackpool, 13 January 1917.
55 'The football fakers', *Sheffield Star Green 'Un*, 1 January 1916, 2.
56 'Echo of a squared match', *Sheffield Daily Telegraph*, 25 February 1919, 6.
57 'Four new clubs elected', *Yorkshire Post*, 11 March 1919, 12.
58 Taylor, *The leaguers*, 15–17.
59 'League ready for next season', unknown newspaper cutting dated 11 March 1919.
60 Ibid.; 'Four new clubs elected', *Yorkshire Post*, 11 March 1919, 12.
61 'League ready for next season', unknown newspaper cutting, dated 11 March 1919.
62 Inglis, *League football*, 110.
63 Ibid.
64 Ibid.
65 'Football trial', *Globe*, 16 January 1919, 5.
66 Inglis, *League football*, 109.
67 M. Taylor, *The association game* (Harlow: Pearson, 2008), 122.
68 'The FA and Manchester United: what the commission discovered', *Athletic News*, 4 April 1910, 6.

11

School, work and leisure

By 1919 the Manchester region housed multiple leagues and competitions for all ages and there were tournaments for women, developed during the war, with several factory teams such as those representing female railway workers, iron-founders and area munitions works.[1] There was a Manchester Ladies Football League which also played representative games and had sought affiliation to the FA. Women's football was popular even though the footballing authorities were not supportive, and teams such as Dick Kerr's Ladies from Preston, frequently played in the region. Local clubs continued the sport into the post-war period, until the FA decided to sanction clubs which allowed women to play on their grounds. The official line was that the physical nature of the sport was not suitable for the female frame, but it was widely felt that the leaders of the men's game were simply concerned with the growing popularity of the sport among women and its possible effects on the male version of football. This was a national issue, not merely a Mancunian one, but in later decades the Manchester Corinthians re-established a community of female participants as the game entered the late 1940s, continuing into the 1970s. Some of their later players continued their playing activities into the 1980s, a couple having appeared for Manchester City Ladies during that club's formative years.[2] Further analysis of the community of female players and the involvement of women in football is required.

Schools

Manchester's widespread footballing community was visible by 1919 and there was a thriving football scene across the conurbation. At schoolboy level the sport had never been more popular, mainly because of the efforts of several prominent footballing enthusiasts whose actions followed the process outlined by Bonde, who has stated: 'Society is made up of the (often unconscious) structure-creating actions of the individuals in it' without which 'the individuals would lose their bearings'.[3] The Manchester Schools Football Association (MSFA), representing schools in Manchester, Stretford and Salford, was established by individuals and created a structure that developed and promoted the game extensively. Its origins can be traced to September 1889, when a new school was opened in Waterloo Road under the headship of George Sharples, a former Bolton Wanderers player. This came three years after James Burn Russell had suggested that Manchester ought to have 'a hundred acres or so of free greenfield' to allow its residents space to breathe and play, stating that a lack of opportunities was turning children into 'a breed of "loafers" and "muffs"' whose 'poor pence cannot afford the lease of a field for cricket or football'.[4] Sharples recognised the value organised school football could have for his pupils and he persuaded other teachers to support him in establishing regular competition.

Initially, occasional games were played; then, in 1890 the first organised fixture list was established, together with a shield, purchased via fundraising collections. The shield became a prize possession among Manchester's schools and was still being competed for into the 1970s, when it was stolen during a break-in at a school. By the start of the 1892–93 season the competition had grown to such an extent that there was a programme of home and away fixtures for three leagues of six clubs each and other related activities. A few years later the committee introduced Captain Ball, which was primarily intended for female participants.[5] Neither the football tournaments nor the Captain Ball games had specific clothing requirements, and children were known to play in clogs, which may even have been the regular choice at this time.[6] Clogs were a frequent cause of problems, as injuries could result when children kicked at each other for the ball. In 1902 a strongly worded letter advised schools that clogs should no longer be worn. Images of teams suggest that the quality of clothing varied somewhat. The Ducie Avenue football team, which won the Shield in 1893, sported white buttoned-up cricket shirts with sleeves rolled down and fastened, some boys wearing neck-ties, an assortment of caps and knee breeches, with socks, ankle-length boots and shin guards (Figure 19). These boys were under the age of thirteen. A second competition was added in 1894 to accommodate schools where boys were slightly older, up to the age fourteen at the start of each school year.

At this period the organising body was officially known as the Manchester and District Schools Athletic Association (although it was ostensibly a foot-balling body) and regional games were developed. The first Manchester Boys fixture occurred during 1893–94 against Bolton Boys, who were also partic-ipating in their first regional game. This became an annual fixture, usually played on Shrove Tuesday at City's Hyde Road ground, and was supplemented with a fixture against Sheffield in 1894–95 (Figure 20). Subsequently, Oldham, Halifax and Leeds were added to the list of opponents, demonstrating that at a school level these towns had enough association football interest to compete, despite their general acceptance as rugby towns. Selection games were also held. In 1896 a Probables v Possibles was staged at Hyde Road to pick the

19 Ducie Avenue School football team, 1893.

20 Action in a Manchester Boys game at Hyde Road before 1910.

Manchester Boys side, while other district games such as North Manchester v South Manchester were also held on occasion at Hyde Road, as were local trophy finals. The significant level of interest in association football within the area was demonstrated when a game was staged between boys from the Elementary and Board Schools of Manchester and Sheffield ninety minutes prior to the 1893 FA Cup final at Fallowfield. The match, played on the full-size pitch and consisting of thirty minutes each way, was recognised as the first occasion when a crowd in excess of 20,000 had witnessed an association game between 'small boys'.[7] By 1901 the growth in MSFA membership led to the instigation of a complicated selection process for players to represent Manchester, with selected players from each league within the association playing those from another, followed by a Probables v Possibles game to narrow down the selection.

Most boys were delighted to participate and to be selected to represent the city, but officials recognised that a stronger identity and collective celebration were needed, and each game became significant for its social as well as its footballing activities. Games at Hyde Road would often be followed by a meal at a city-centre establishment or a nearby school, and medals bearing the Manchester coat of arms were purchased, to be presented to participants alongside badges for their caps. The association was often poorly supported by teachers within the region when it came to organisational matters, relying perhaps too much on Sharples and other committeemen, but there was active support for cross-school games and related activities. In 1898 the association purchased two sets of jerseys and a kit bag for the Manchester Boys; prior to this, they had looked on Waterloo Road school to provide their jerseys on loan. The association's new kit was not well maintained, nor was it of good quality, and three further purchases were made between 1900 and 1911. Whether it was to keep costs down or to show a connection to Manchester City FC is not clear, but the kit consisted of pale blue jerseys, buttoned up to the neck, white shorts and navy blue stockings with two white rings on the tops – in effect, the City kit of the period. The colours were changed to tricolour hoops of claret, amber and blue in 1931.[8]

By 1899 twenty-one schools had been admitted into the association, although league space could not be provided for five of them as there were still only two divisions of eight clubs each; however the committee had vowed that clubs excluded in one year would be added the next, if they could meet appropriate criteria. By 1900 membership of the MSFA leagues had grown to nineteen, and it increased further to twenty-four by 1901, twenty-six the year after and thirty-four for the 1902–3 season.[9] A logistical change at this time was the introduction of printed player-registration forms to ensure total clarity of legitimate players and to help enforce disciplinary procedures. Discipline was often an issue, and disputes arose concerning the legality of players based on age or school transfer. One age-related dispute saw the committee insisting that a school must hand back the shield it had won, while another dispute lasted for over a year as two schools argued about the ages of three boys who had no evidence of their age. Records do not show why this confusion arose. Possibly the boys were recent arrivals in the area or they had no parents and the school was attempting to provide some stability in the lives of its charges. Domestic matters within both the school and the association helped to develop a framework and encourage the boys to follow rules and to bring organisation to their activities. For that alone, the association was vital in nineteenth-century Manchester, but as time progressed its leaders were determined to help their pupils to participate in sport outside the school environment.

Football and other sports were often restricted in Manchester, particularly at some of the city's few green spaces, and the MSFA felt that children would benefit by using these spaces both within and outside school time. Meetings were held with Manchester councillors and the Manchester Parks superintendent, Mr Lamb, which resulted in an agreement that football could be played on appropriate green spaces within the city so long as a teacher was present. This was an important development, but it still meant that in some densely populated areas the limited amount of green space could not be utilised for children's own games outside of the school environment. Many working-class districts of Manchester lacked public parks or even relatively small spaces for children to enjoy and play in, and Ancoats, Gorton and Hulme had mounted unsuccessful campaigns to create parks from the 1840s.[10] Charles Russell of the Manchester and Salford Playing Fields society, established in 1907, voiced his concern that the available grounds were so far away that many city boys would not arrive at the vast Heaton Park, six miles north of West Gorton, until the start of the second half.[11] Even if there was a large park nearby, children often found that they were unwelcome and there were frequent complaints about their behaviour.[12]

Football was growing within the school environment and this led to some internal wrangling and disagreements about the region to be covered. As with the debates about whether Manchester itself should be considered as merely the area contained within the city boundary or the area that considered itself to be part of a greater Manchester region, the dispute forms an important part of the geographical picture of the region at the time. Some of the leading voices within the MSFA saw the growth of football in the school environment positively; but they also perceived logistical problems, and for this reason it was often discussed how best to restructure competition and areas of authority. The suggestion was frequently aired that schools within the city of Salford should break away and have their own association. Few schools in Salford joined the association in its early years, and as late as 1903 the association decided to write to the secretary of the Salford branch of the National Union of Teachers to highlight that no team from the city had entered that season's competitions and stating that the association would drop the Salford name from its title. After significant debate it was decided the name would remain and that attempts would be made to encourage wider participation. Whether the lack of association football-playing member schools in Salford was simply an organisational matter or was connected with the city's general preference for rugby at this time is unclear, but it should be remembered that both Manchester and Salford had been viewed as rugby cities into the 1890s. Manchester's move towards association football gained pace during the latter years of the nineteenth century and the difference between schools in the neighbouring cities may have been part of this general shift. Salford remained part of the association until 1913, when it had enough interested schools to be able to establish its own association.

During its formative years the MSFA took a benevolent view, raising funds via its membership, competitions and match attendances and believing that the organisation had a duty to improve the well-being of children. As well as annual sports events at Belle Vue, which had been a key feature since the association's formation, the committee donated funds to local school- or children-related charities and to the Free Meal Fund, which aimed to provide a daily meal at school for all children . In 1901 over £10 was allocated to the Free Meal Fund and a further £100 was given to other charitable causes. In terms of competition the committee frequently restructured their Cup and Shield competitions to ensure that as school-leaving age was increased over the following decades the two competitions would retain their equivalent differential, i.e. the Shield would be for the oldest age group.

Those responsible for the MSFA appear to have been visionaries to some extent, and on 8 April 1902 the association's Executive Meeting proposed the formation of a national Inter-City Schools Association. This received some support across the country, but not enough for the idea to become established. Nevertheless, the association persevered and continued to build connections and stage games with a growing band of similar associations which by 1902 included opponents from Lancaster and Nottingham in addition to those from neighbouring towns in Lancashire and Yorkshire. Fixtures with Derby followed, but an offer to face London Boys had to be turned down, as City's Hyde Road ground was unavailable and United had failed to respond to the MSFA's letters. A London schools party did play in Manchester in 1904, and Manchester teachers hosted South London's Boys in their homes for a few days. The arrival of a group of schoolboys from London was considered such a remarkable event that the two teams paraded through the streets of Ardwick to the Hyde Road ground, dressed in their playing kit and led by the St Joseph's Band, City's regular pre-match entertainers.[13] As the London visit demonstrated, the association was growing its football connections. It also ensured that its annual sports day at Belle Vue developed and prospered, and by 1901 the date had become fixed in the calendars of all schools within the city of Manchester and was granted special status as the Manchester Schools' Sports Day by the Manchester School Board, which allowed it to be a 'Sports Holiday', meaning that all schools and their teachers would be free from normal school activities and expected to attend this annual event. It was viewed as the culmination of the sporting year; prizes were awarded and the MSFA, as the founders, viewed it as their day for many years. In 1902 there were 1,100 competitors for the various prizes. All teachers were expected to attend, and if they did not action would be taken both by the Schools Football Association and the Schools Board.

Connecting structure

The Manchester Schools' Sports Day was supported by the Jennison family, who owned the Belle Vue complex, and each year a fee was agreed for the hire of the venue. Each year the Manchester officials would meet with Belle Vue's management after the games to pay the agreed amount, which was subsequently returned in a gesture of altruism. This, together with annual school subscriptions of 2s and 6d per school, ensured that the association could carry out its activities. At times it received unexpected amounts of income, as in 1915 when Manchester City paid a dividend of £1 to its shareholders. The receipt of the dividend suggests that either MSFA had invested in the club or had been given shares by City.[14] The connection with City was important, and supports the impression that the early twentieth century was a period when City's success inspired many. In 1905, less than a year after City's FA Cup success, an analysis of the leisure activities of Manchester's young males highlighted the importance of football in the lives of the youngsters: 'If a stranger in Manchester should happen on a winter's Saturday afternoon to spend an hour or two in watching one of the great football matches on the Manchester City ground in Hyde Road, he would be most surprised by the very large number of young lads gathered together to watch the game.'[15] Those young lads, thanks to the efforts of the MFSA, had the opportunity to play too. This was important in the growth of the sport, and City's own support increased and included a recognisable youth element during this period. The FA Cup success, the encouragement at school and the fact that many school games were played at City's Hyde Road were connecting elements which produced a welcoming and natural environment to the boys.

The link between the MSFA and City may well have come via teacher Jack Prowse, who was on the City committee and was also a referee.[16] At each school where he was employed he established football teams and competitions, and he spent much of his life promoting football at a junior level. In later life he was credited with having been largely instrumental in the establishment of the

MSFA.[17] Manchester Boys were often known as the City Boys, emphasising the strong connection between the professional football club and the city itself. From the environment created by the MSFA and the junior leagues, talented youngsters emerged, supplementing the players brought to Manchester by Newton Heath/United and City. The growing interest in football after 1904 had led to significant improvements in football provision across the city and the growth of football during this period was a factor in the creation in 1907 of the Manchester and Salford Playing Fields Society, which began a process of developing sports pitches across the two cities.[18] FA Cup success in 1904 had increased interest, but it was initiatives within schools and workplaces that allowed the game to flourish.

The Playing Fields movement in Manchester developed out of the Lads' Clubs movement, whose officials had found it increasingly difficult to find fields for sporting activities; even when fields were located there was 'no security of tenure, as with the advent of the speculative builder, it was necessary to move further and further out of the City'.[19] As early as the 1860s Hulme Athenaeum had been forced out of their Pooley's Park ground as building developments encroached on their pitch. The Lads' Clubs believed that through their competitions they were providing boys with public school-style training which 'it is almost impossible for the Elementary Schools to provide'.[20] Sport played an important part in the clubs, and members of the different clubs met each other at football, cricket, fives, harriers, swimming, gymnastics, chess, draughts and other activities. The Lads' Clubs and Playing Fields Society were complementary organisations, improving the lives of boys and young men.

The main objectives of the Playing Fields Society included increasing the amount of public and private playing fields and other open spaces and to 'endeavour to influence public and private bodies, with a view to the provision of sufficient playing fields to meet the requirements of the various districts'.[21] At the society's grounds the committee established dressing tents for the players and rented out pitches to working lads' teams. It was estimated in 1915 that every Saturday afternoon there were 2,000 boys and young men present on the five fields held by the society at that time. Many of the participating teams were not connected to Lads' Clubs 'or any recognised institution', making it 'doubly difficult to find playing accommodation but for the provision made by the Society'.[22] The society was a major influence on the sporting direction of Manchester City Council; through its influence the Manchester Parks Committee was encouraged to establish a system of play centres for children and the Education Committee adopted a scheme of organised games for school children in the city's public parks. The society helped to establish similar organisations in the neighbouring towns of Bolton, Stockport and Rochdale.

Footballing participation was growing across Manchester, and in the first years following the 1904 FA Cup success the impact was clear. Figures revealed

by the headmaster of Manchester Grammar School showed that playing football was the most popular activity among his pupils, with watching football
coming a close second, while the lord mayor claimed that 1904 had made him
more 'proud than ever of Manchester'.[23] While football was not specifically
mentioned in his comments, it is true that football had allowed Mancunians to
celebrate together and, as a result, to engender a form of civic pride and citizenship, reflecting comments made by Beaven in his study of Coventry.[24]

In 1904 steps were taken to establish a national network of football-playing
schools, led at times by William McGregor, the founder of the Football League.
The MSFA was invited to participate, but did not do so, although it did provide three referees who officiated at seven of the nineteen games, including the
London v Sheffield Final. The following year Manchester did compete, and
reached the final, losing to Sheffield at Goodison Park. James Leigh, headmaster of Bank Meadow School, became Manchester's representative on the
national committee in 1906 and utilised his position there and his status within
Manchester's educational system to campaign for better sports facilities for
schoolchildren. His aim was to ensure that all schools had an equal chance
of participating in football and he suggested providing financial assistance to
poorer schools. This sadly, was challenged by other committeemen, but it was
approved eventually and occasional games were staged simply to raise funds for
desperate schools. School was typically the place where most boys first encountered organised football in which they could participate, but the availability of
the sport depended on dedicated teachers, like Leigh and Prowse, who believed
in the value of physical activity. These teachers committed many hours each
week to the sport, and a review of school team photographs from the early
twentieth century reveals the pride which schools and teachers placed on their
teams, particularly when they achieved success. Often a school team would
paint their school's name and the year on a team ball and place it in a central
position in the annual team photograph, alongside any trophy or medal.[25] The
quantity of surviving team photographs from the pre-1919 period and the
increasing number of participants in the MSFA competitions demonstrate that
Manchester's transformation from rugby city to soccer city was also played out
at school level. The attractiveness of professional soccer and the availability
of the sport at school level firmly fixed association football as Manchester's
leading team sport by the early twentieth century, although rugby did remain
prominent in some areas of the Manchester conurbation, such as Salford and,
to some extent, Oldham.

Despite the establishment of the Manchester and Salford Playing Fields
Society in 1907, the biggest issue affecting the MSFA prior to the First World
War was the availability of pitches, despite numerous attempts to work in
partnership with Manchester's parks. In 1908 the association's James Leigh
believed that the city council's Manchester Playing Fields Committee had done

nothing to help the schools, and he challenged them year after year to provide support, until a landmark moment at the end of the 1909–10 season when the Parks Committee agreed to install goal posts at Platt Fields park for the use of schools. Platt Fields set aside forty of its eighty acres for cricket and football, as well as tennis and bowling greens.[26] This was followed by a more significant agreement in September 1910 between council officials, James Leigh and Tom Fox, the secretary of the Lancashire and Cheshire Federation of Trades and Councils. Fox wrote to Leigh: 'I have given instructions to the Superintendent of Parks that he is to put up some goal posts on [Donkey] Common and that you are to be permitted to play organised games on the terms as laid down in your letter of yesterday's date. I hope these arrangements will be completed for next week. Go ahead and play to your heart's content.'[27]

Three days after receiving this letter Leigh received another, stating that space had been allocated and goal posts were to be erected for fifteen pitches at eight locations.[28] This was a remarkable increase and demonstrated once again that the growth of football depended on a few dedicated individuals such as Leigh, who fought to obtain facilities and promoted the game however he could. Leigh's achievements improved the situation significantly, while the Manchester and Salford Playing Fields Society also brought a considerable number of pitches into use and by 1929 had set up seven major playing fields covering 115 acres and helped to establish 182 football-specific grounds within public parks, although even that was still not considered satisfactory.[29] By way of comparison, analysis in 2011 showed that there were a total of thirty-nine grass pitches available for junior/youth teams and 164 for senior teams, with a total of forty-six synthetic pitches also available within the city of Manchester.[30] It was often suggested that boys needed greater opportunities to play and that their presence as spectators at professional games was because of limited opportunities to play themselves, and this issue of lads attending football matches continued into the inter-war period.[31] Although football received a great deal of criticism from authoritative figures for its inability to provide appropriate recreation for these boys, some, particularly those involved with the MSFA and with Lads' Clubs, challenged this view, claiming that participation as a spectator was 'healthy'.[32] Charles Russell, a pioneer in the setting up of Lads' Clubs in Manchester, stated his view as to why young people attended professional football games at Hyde Road and Bank Street instead of playing on a Saturday afternoon, and believed that it was because there were not enough playing fields to accommodate all those juvenile spectators who wished to play the game. He also suggested that attendance at football matches allowed boys to observe the experts and learn the subtleties of the game. He also compared football with cricket, making the assumption that cricket was less attractive to 'Manchester lads' because they had less opportunity to observe the sport and that when they did play they were often at a disadvantage unless they were already skilled in bowling or batting, whereas football gave everyone an equal opportunity.

While James Leigh was involved with the MSFA it seemed that the organisation would continue to grow and exert its influence on the city council and other bodies to provide better facilities and opportunities for football at a school level; but, sadly, Leigh was forced to resign from his post in 1911 for family reasons. This was a significant blow, and followed the death of James Bradley, one of the association's longest-serving members. It caused the association to lose direction a little, but a restructuring of its competitions in 1912 led to the development of a top division based on the strength of its teams instead of simply on geography, as before. This was an important move, particularly as notice was given the following year that Salford would be establishing its own association and therefore its schools would be resigning at the end of the 1913–14 season. The loss of these schools and the departure of some teachers following the outbreak of war in 1914 limited the work of the MSFA, and the number of schools able to field teams declined. Reduced staff availability and interest also limited the opportunities for children to play football.[33] Post-war, the organisation was further restructured, particularly when it took on responsibility for promoting cricket in schools and established a cricketing section. The Manchester and District Schools Athletic Association as it was known by this time was to be divided into sub-groups, each with responsibility for its own sport, and the organisation's £86 of funds in hand were split between football, which received £50, and the rest. This difference between the sports illustrated that the main aim of the organisation had always been to promote football first.

Outside of the schools' system and the Lads' Clubs, association football was developed to some extent by the boys themselves. By 1905 the leading outdoor game for Manchester youths was association football, and it was played throughout the year, regardless of sporting season. Teams consisting of 'quite small boys' were in the habit of training regularly to develop their skills and stamina. They also smoked, attended the music hall and carried on other unhealthy pursuits.[34] Many children used small balls or tightly rolled-up newspapers. Within a year of City's 1904 FA Cup success, Charles Russell described how in August each year youths of 'almost any street in the poorer quarters of the town' gathered together to create their own club. He wrote of boys from the age of ten upwards creating clubs and gave a detailed example of the steps they would take to find equipment such as balls and goalposts. This included calling from door to door in their neighbourhood asking for pennies to create a team that would perform in a business-like manner. Russell suggested that this process would continue if the boys decided that they wanted a particular football shirt to create an identity for the team. Older boys would form football teams in connection with 'practically every Sunday School, Mission Hall, and Lads' Club within and around' Manchester.[35] Often these organisations would

have multiple teams and run their own leagues. Boys would play in any location until they were evicted, and games would be played on back streets, quiet
corners, every little croft and every available field near the city. In the winter of
1904 an attempt was made to remedy the enormous shortfall in playing fields
when lists of teams needing grounds were compiled and teams were connected
to those landowners who had suitable fields. Sixty teams representing approximately 1,000 boys were given an opportunity to play via this system. Many
came from the working-class districts of Ancoats and east Manchester and they
were predominantly groups of lads not affiliated to a parent organisation, such
as a church or Lads' Club.

With football at a junior level growing both within and outside the school
environment, it can be assumed that those boys would attempt to continue
playing into adulthood. The number of football leagues under the jurisdiction
of the Manchester FA grew from eight in 1903–4 to eighteen by the start of the
1908–9 season.[36] Not only was there a sharp increase in the number of leagues,
but the majority of them had several divisions; for example, the Manchester
and District Football League (established in 1905) had four divisions by 1914,
while the North-West Manchester League had three divisions.[37] The Gorton
and District & Manchester Central League had seven divisions as early as the
1904–5 season, with a total of forty-eight teams in the top four sections representing church sides, boys' clubs and street teams.[38] The Manchester, Salford,
and District Association Football League consisted of five divisions with joining
fees ranging from 5s to 10s per team. Some of these divisions were age based, the
youngest being aimed at teams with an average age of fifteen. The Manchester
and District Alliance had seven divisions based on age, the youngest aimed at
fourteen-year-olds and the oldest open to twenty-year-olds and upwards.[39] The
North Manchester and District Amateur Football League had four divisions,
and for most of the region's leagues each division would typically consist of at
least twelve clubs, although some clubs had sides playing in multiple leagues or
divisions. This shows a remarkable increase in football participation. It is also
worth noting that numerous informal competitions and leagues would have
been set up without the approval of the Manchester FA. Within the organised
leagues were a variety of teams with names such as Manchester Welsh, Denton
Tramways, Manchester Dairymen and Didsbury Wednesday, showing that
there was a strong mix of company-based teams as well as community clubs.[40]
By this time football was prevalent across Manchester's communities.

Perhaps the first major tangible sign of the significance of the game to
Manchester came in March 1920 when King George V attended City's League
meeting with Liverpool at the Hyde Road ground, a venue often criticised
for its facilities and location. Although he had first attended the FA Cup final
in 1914, the king was not known to be a football fan, but his attendance did
allow a crowd of 40,000 predominantly working-class members of the city to

see him. Russell wrote of the king's attendance at the 1914 FA Cup final that the 'monarchial embrace of popular culture, no matter how light, had much to recommend it as the crown sought to build its repertoire of "democratic" practice. His visit would have been impossible unless football's place in society was secure.'[41] Those sentiments apply equally to Manchester football.

Notes

1 For example, see 'Football field', *Manchester Evening News*, 1 September 1917, 2; 'Ladies football match', *Rochdale Observer*, 23 January 1918, 1.

2 In 2017–18 a project by Gary James to interview former players of Manchester City Women/Manchester City Ladies players identified Lesley Wright and Gail Duncan as former Manchester Corinthian players.

3 H. Bonde, 'Gymnastics and politics: Niels Bukh and the biographical genre', in *Writing lives in port* (Aarhus: Aarhus University Press, 2004), 53–54.

4 J. B. Russell, *The children of the city: What can we do for them?* (Edinburgh: MacNiven and Wallace, 1886).

5 Captain Ball is viewed as a low-impact alternative to other ball sports. The ball is passed among players, with the aim of scoring a goal. Players are not allowed to run when they have the ball and must maintain a distance of two to three feet from other players. The version played in Manchester at this time appears to have utilised a football and may have been more football-like than the present-day game of Captain Ball.

6 F. W. N. Hill, *The story of the Manchester Schools Football Association* (Manchester: Manchester Schools FA), 4.

7 'Manchester School Boys v Bury School Boys', *Manchester Courier*, 22 February 1900, 3.

8 Hill, *The story of the Manchester Schools*, 11.

9 Hill, *The story of the Manchester schools*, 4–7.

10 O'Reilly, 'From "the people"', 143.

11 'City playgrounds', *Manchester Evening News*, 8 July 1907, 5.

12 Manchester Archives and Local Studies, Manchester Central Library, M9/68, Parks and cemeteries Minutes (28), 134 and (36), 8.

13 Ibid., 8.

14 Ibid., 12.

15 C. E. B. Russell, *Manchester boys: Sketches of Manchester lads at work and play* (Manchester: Manchester University Press, 1905), 67.

16 'Well-known figure in City circles', *Manchester Football Chronicle*, 28 April 1923, 3.

17 'Man who made United', *Manchester Football Chronicle*, 20 January 1923, 3.

18 W. H. Brindley, *The soul of Manchester* (Manchester: Manchester University Press, 1929), 249; W. Melland, 'Playing fields movement', in *The book of Manchester and Salford* (Manchester: George Falkner & Sons, 1929), 213.

19 McKechnie, *Manchester in 1915*, 110–111.

20 Ibid., 107–109.

21 Ibid., 110–111.
22 Ibid.
23 'The schoolboy's holiday', *Manchester Guardian*, 6 May 1905, 6; 'St. Mary's, Deansgate', *Manchester Courier*, 10 October 1906, 8.
24 Beaven, *Leisure, citizenship*, 45.
25 The photographic collection of the Manchester Schools Football Association, now held at Manchester Central Library, includes many such photographs from a variety of schools and years. Some teachers can be seen in the annual team photograph for several successive years, demonstrating the longevity of their involvement.
26 J. J. Sullivan, *Illustrated handbook of the Manchester City parks and recreation grounds* (Manchester: Manchester City Council 1915), 79.
27 Letter from Tom Fox to James Leigh, Bank Meadow School, 2 September 1910.
28 Pitches were installed at: Ten Acre Lane (four); Hulme Hall Lane (three); Gibbin Street, Beswick; Abbey Hey Recreation ground (two); Gorton Park (two); Grey Street; and Donkey Common (two).
29 Melland, 'Playing fields movement', 213; Brindley, *The soul of Manchester*, 249.
30 *Analysis of the value of football to Greater Manchester*, 27–29.
31 Brindley, *The soul of Manchester*, 251.
32 Russell, *Manchester boys*, 64.
33 Hill, *The story of the Manchester Schools*, 12.
34 Russell, *Manchester boys*, 56–61.
35 Ibid., 61–63.
36 'Manchester and District Association', meeting minutes of the Football Association, 1908–9, 21.
37 'Manchester and District Football League', *Manchester Evening News*, 19 August 1914, 4.
38 'Association', *Umpire*, 24 July 1904, 11; 'Gorton and district and Manchester Central League', *Umpire*, 25 September 1904, 9.
39 'Association', *Umpire*, 24 July 1904, 11.
40 'Manchester and District Wednesday League', *Umpire*, 25 September 1904, 9.
41 Russell, *Football and the English*, 74.

Conclusion

By 1919 Manchester was regarded as a footballing city with two prominent, popular and successful Football League clubs bearing its name and other professional teams established within its conurbation. It had its own football association and a multitude of leagues and competitions at every level. Major finals, international and representative games had been held there and football was in evidence, being an important component of the region's identity and culture. The sport had crossed class divides, although by 1919 it was most commonly associated with the working classes. There had been some public school influence and it is possible that connections between Hulme Athenaeum and the Birley family in the early 1860s had planted the initial soccer seed in the region. However, the main influences and participants in the 1870s and beyond came from experienced enthusiasts from Manchester, Stoke, Nottingham and Scotland. Some of these were public school boys, such as Stuart Smith; but others, such as Fitzroy Norris, John Nall, Jim Ingram and Arthur Andrews, were not. Manchester's story was not simply about public school boys or, for that matter, the story of the lower-middle classes.[1] In actuality, it was individuals from the lower-middle class, with a multitude of influences, who were most significant in the diffusion of the game in Manchester, suggesting that each region may possess its own set of circumstances. Individuals are the skeleton on which society's body takes form, and without the actions of Nall, Norris and others Manchester's footballing skeleton might never have developed into a fully functioning body.[2] These individuals adapted, redeveloping their positions and competencies to enable continual progress within soccer as it developed into a professional business.[3] Their roles altered as society changed, but by maintaining their interest and enthusiasm they provided continuity and direction, allowing Manchester's footballing community to develop. Their involvement allowed them to gain a deep understanding of the issues of an evolving sport, and through their efforts Manchester had become recognised as a footballing city by the early twentieth century. A complicated series of processes forms a culture, and this includes football, whose development in Manchester was not about a few individuals or two professional clubs, but was a conglomeration of all relevant individuals and clubs and their multiple external influences.

Manchester's footballing history is multifaceted, as is the case for every region, and the city was undoubtedly recognised as a rugby-playing one through to the early 1900s, even though a soccer community had existed during the 1860s. With few opponents west of the Pennines, it was difficult for this soccer community to grow, most clubs preferring a rugby version of the sport. The city did stage several of soccer's landmark moments, such as Stuart Smith calling for one set of rules; the establishment of the International Football Association Board; meetings to form a breakaway British FA; the Football League's first meeting; the first FA Cup final outside of London; the establishment of the Professional Footballers' Association and so on. A picture could be painted suggesting Manchester was at the forefront of soccer development from the 1860s, but that would place too much significance on individual events. Historians must identify events but, as this book has demonstrated, they must also search to understand wider themes enabling the full picture of how soccer developed town by town, region by region, nation by nation to be painted.[4] For any professional sport to prosper it needs motivation, interest, entrepreneurs, a willing public and financial security. In Manchester, prior to the establishment of the Manchester FA, soccer struggled to gain the foothold it needed in order to replace pedestrianism and rugby, while fighting off the newly introduced sport of lacrosse. Rugby's demise as Manchester's leading team sport came as a result of self-inflicted wounds and a proactive soccer community, with two clubs keen to represent the whole of Manchester being supported by entrepreneurs who could see how to make their businesses successful. After the rugby split Manchester was left without a rugby union side capable of generating widespread interest across the conurbation, and its northern union sides represented districts or towns rather than the city. In contrast, Manchester's soccer clubs not only saw an advantage in taking the city's name but also managed to encourage wider interest through their ability to compete on a national stage. Once soccer clubs began to find trophy success the opportunity for rugby of either code to displace it as Manchester's leading team sport was lost. Events like rugby's split and City's 1904 FA Cup success are usually viewed in isolation, but these were more than mere individual moments; they linked ideas, experience and good practice to aid football's local development. These chains are transformational cycles in the sport's development, and eight transformational cycles have been identified for Manchester's soccer development up to 1919.

Phase one: Traditional mob football was played, which resulted in a ban in 1608.[5]

Phase two: Informal football was played on the streets and fields.

Phase three: The city's first rugby clubs were formed and the Hulme Athenaeum developed.

Phase four: Experienced Manchester-based footballers created a club which
    established regular fixtures, and another association football team was
    formed by a well-established rugby club.
Phase five: Several clubs were formed across the city, the Manchester FA
    was created in 1884 and cup competitions were established.
Phase six: Manchester had its first national success in 1904 and a footballing
    identity developed.
Phase seven: From 1904 football reached maturity across Manchester.
Phase eight: The rights of professional footballers were brought to the fore,
    while club support became strong.

The rules, structure, ambition and community that Mancunians recognise
in their football today were initially defined and developed during these eight
transformational cycles. There was some overlap, but the cycles demonstrate
how the sport evolved and came to prominence, providing an example, which
could apply elsewhere, of how football became embedded within a culture.
However, it would be an error to assume that association football across the
world developed in exactly the same manner, as analysis of specific cities and
regions would undoubtedly uncover locality-specific differences and factors.[6]
The growth of Manchester's owed most to a series of overlapping subcul-
tures, including individuals who helped to propagate the sport, where for those
developing the game the desire to play was more important than class background. Each individual was specific to their time, place and conditions, and by
understanding these individuals and their societal connections we can begin to
uncover how football's diffusion and development was not so straightforward
as traditionalists might think.

This research into Manchester's footballing culture has utilised a full-time
framework, based on the work of Braudel, and has demonstrated that more
regional studies utilising this approach are needed to map football's growth.
Understanding the origins of football within regions is 'an arduous task', but
it can be effective if we focus on making sense of the sport's full-time history
and transformational phases, rather than focusing on Eureka moments.[7] It is
an embracing theory, and now that we have the tools and the means to overcome many of the traditional objections to considering long-term history this
approach will produce a more critical, intensive and valuable synthesis of evidence, allowing each regional study to add to the whole, rather than appear as
a rival position.[8] Any aspect of sport can be researched within this framework
by considering the individual moments and understanding how they connect
with each transformational cycle. Causal explanations can be complex and are
often not easily identified, but it should be apparent that for any sport to
develop there need to be a series of factors that come about perfectly to create
a Goldilocks 'just right' opportunity. Manchester's Goldilocks opportunity for

soccer came through the events, the links between them and the transformational cycles that have been identified in this study. The building blocks were formed, and the long residuals of City, United, the regional governing body, the players' union and so many other aspects of footballing life were created and rose to prominence.

Manchester is an important region for the study of football's development because its conurbation consists of several towns and two cities each with its own identity, but all combining via connections, interests, ideas and attitudes. The rapid growth of the city, with workers arriving from across the United Kingdom and mainland Europe, ensured a regular influx of cultures, ideas and skills, including sporting interests, and this helped football to become woven into the cultural fabric of Manchester. Every city and region will have its own specific influences, and historians need to adopt a similar analytical approach, searching for events, their influences, links and related transformational cycles, if we are ever to truly map the origins and development of football on a global scale. Manchester provides an example that can be utilised in any city region of the world and it would be intriguing to compare Manchester's development with full-time analyses of Madrid, Buenos Aires, Milan, Munich and others.

Finally, football, like the life of a city, goes in cycles. Today United are the most successful English club domestically, but a hundred years ago they hardly registered as a force, and maybe in another hundred years they will have been overtaken by other teams. This is how sport ebbs and flows. Long-range thinking allows us to see patterns and cycles, ensuring that events and individual moments are considered for their connections and not for how brightly they shine at one moment in time. This book has shown why, in a city so well known for football, it remains vital to focus on both the detail and the patterns to ensure that we recognise the truth of a region's history.

Notes

1 G. Pfister, 'We love them and we hate them', in J. Bale, M. K. Christensen and G. Pfister (eds), *Writing lives in sports: Biographies, life-histories and methods* (Aarhus: Aarhus University Press, 2004), 151.
2 Bonde, 'Gymnastics and politics', 49.
3 Ibid., 51; Bass and Riggio, *Transformational leadership*.
4 McNeill, 'Fernand Braudel, historian', 133.
5 'Old Manchester', *Manchester Guardian*, 6 November 1847, 4.
6 P. Bailey, 'The politics and poetics of modern British leisure', *Rethinking History*, 3:2 (1999), 151.
7 Torrebadella-Flix et al., 'The origins of football in Spain', 472.
8 D. Armitage, 'What's the big idea? Intellectual history and the longue durée', *History of European Ideas*, 38:4 (2012), 493–507.

Index

Lightning Source UK Ltd.
Milton Keynes UK
UKHW010923120622
404255UK00006B/793